MW00616071

DIPLOMATIC GIFTS

PAUL BRUMMELL

DIPLOMATIC GIFTS

A HISTORY IN FIFTY PRESENTS

HURST & COMPANY, LONDON

First published in the United Kingdom in 2022 by
C. Hurst & Co. (Publishers) Ltd.,
New Wing, Somerset House, Strand, London, WC2R 1LA

Printed in Great Britain by Bell and Bain Ltd, Glasgow

The right of Paul Brummell to be identified as the author of
this publication is asserted by him in accordance with the
Copyright, Designs and Patents Act, 1988.

A Cataloguing-in-Publication data record for this book
is available from the British Library.

ISBN: 9781787386457

This book is printed using paper from registered sustainable
and managed sources.

www.hurstpublishers.com

To June and Bob, my mother and father.

CONTENTS

CONTENTS

CONTENTS

CONTENTS

CONTENTS

ACKNOWLEDGEMENTS

I would like to thank Michael Dwyer, Publisher and Managing Director at Hurst, for the unstinting encouragement he gave me to write this book, and the faith he has shown in it. The great team at Hurst, including Daisy Leitch, Kathleen May and Lara Weisweiller-Wu. Tim Page, for his editing skills. Alexander Evans, Strategy Director at the Cabinet Office, whose introduction to Michael set me on this road. Jan Melissen, Jorg Kustermans and all fellow participants in a *Hague Journal of Diplomacy* forum that provided a fine opportunity to hear from others exploring the fascinating world of diplomatic gifts. Mark McWilliams, Cathy Kaufman and all those involved in organising the inspiring Oxford Food Symposium, for the opportunity to prepare and present some thoughts on the use of food and drink as a diplomatic gift. Emmanuel Magro Conti, Senior Curator, Maritime and Military Collections at Heritage Malta, for introducing me to the story behind the Maltese portrait of Catherine the Great. Above all, my thanks to Adriana, for her support, enthusiasm and understanding, and to George, source of the most lovely distraction. And while I have no intention of thanking the COVID-19 pandemic for anything, its actions in closing off alternative sources of entertainment did encourage me to focus more squarely on the researching and writing of this book.

FIGURES

1. The Amarna Letter known as EA161, from Aziru, Canaanite ruler of Amurru in modern-day Lebanon, to the pharaoh, now in the British Museum, London. (Wikimedia Commons) https://commons.wikimedia.org/wiki/File:Amarna_Akkadian_letter.png

2. The Trojan Horse imagined at the Troy archaeological site. (Wikimedia Commons) https://commons.wikimedia.org/wiki/File:Kon_trojanski_RB.jpg

3. The *Alexander Mosaic* from the House of the Faun in Pompeii, depicting the Battle of Issus between Darius III and Alexander the Great, now in the Naples National Archaeological Museum. (Wikimedia; Berthold Werner, 2013) https://commons.wikimedia.org/wiki/File:Battle_of_Issus_mosaic_-_Museo_Archeologico_Nazionale_-_Naples_2013-05-16_16-25-06_BW.jpg

4. Three wise men bearing gifts. A mosaic in the Basilica of Sant'Apollinare Nuovo, Ravenna. (Wikimedia Commons; Ввласенко) https://commons.wikimedia.org/wiki/File:Three_Wise_Men_from_the_East._Part_of_the_mosaic_on_the_left_wall_of_the_Basilica_of_Sant%27Apollinare-Nuovo._Ravenna,_Italy.jpg

5. Hydraulic organ depicted on a Roman second-century CE mosaic found at Zliten in modern-day Libya. (Wikimedia Commons) https://commons.wikimedia.org/wiki/File:Mosaique_Zliten.jpg

6. Twelfth-century fresco of an elephant carrying a castle, from the Hermitage of San Baudelio de Berlanga, now in the Museo del Prado, Madrid. (Metropolitan Museum of Art – Public Domain, The Cloisters Collection, 1957) https://www.metmuseum.org/art/collection/search/471830

7. Byzantine Emperor Nikephoros II Phokas, described by Liudprand of Cremona as 'a monstrosity of a man, a dwarf, fat-headed and with tiny

mole's eyes'. (Wikimedia Commons) https://commons.wikimedia.org/wiki/File:Nikiphoros_Phokas.jpg

8. King Louis IX carrying the Crown of Thorns. A thirteenth-century stained glass now at the Metropolitan Museum of Art. (Metropolitan Museum of Art – Public Domain, The Cloisters Collection, 1937) https://www.metmuseum.org/art/collection/search/471218

9. The Pallium of St Lawrence, a gift from Michael VIII Palaiologos to the Republic of Genoa. (Musei de Genova) https://www.museidigenova.it/en/textile-manufacture-court-empire-nicaea-pallium-san-lorenzo

10. *Mamalucke*, an early sixteenth-century etching by Daniel Hopfer, now in the British Museum. (Wikimedia Commons) https://commons.wikimedia.org/wiki/File:Three_Mamelukes_with_lances_on_horseback.jpg

11. The beaver, depicted in the twelfth-century *Aberdeen Bestiary*. (Wikimedia Commons) https://commons.wikimedia.org/wiki/File:Beaver_(Aberdeen_Bestiary).jpg

12. *Reception of a Venetian Delegation in Damascus in 1511,* attributed to the circle of Giovanni Bellini, now at the Musée du Louvre. (Wikimedia Commons) https://commons.wikimedia.org/wiki/File:Venetian_embassy_to_the_Mamluks_in_Damascus_in_1511_workshop_of_Giovanni_Bellini.jpg

13. *Four Studies of an Elephant* by Giulio Romano, depicting the animal gifted to Pope Leo X. Now at the Ashmolean Museum, Oxford. (Heritage Image Partnership Ltd / Alamy Stock Photo)

14. Dürer's *Rhinoceros*, a woodcut based on a sketch of the creature later gifted by King Manuel I of Portugal to Pope Leo X. (Rosenwald Collection) https://www.nga.gov/collection/art-object-page.47903.html

15. *The Field of the Cloth of Gold*, a 1545 work of the British school. A venue for competitive gift-giving between King François I of France and King Henry VIII of England. (GL Archive / Alamy Stock Photo)

16. The horned helmet given by Holy Roman Emperor Maximilian I to King Henry VIII. (Marco Secchi / Alamy Stock Photo)

17. The Ghaznavid ruler Mahmud of Ghazni receiving a robe of honour from Abbasid Caliph al-Qadir in 1000. Miniature from Rashid al-Din Hamadani's *Jami'al-Tawarikh*, Edinburgh University Library. (Wikimedia

FIGURES

3%9Fmeisterpalast_(Grandmaster%27s_Palace)_an_der_Republic_
Street,_Valletta_-_panoramio.jpg

26. *The Reception*, a caricature by James Gillray, depicting the Qianlong emperor as indifferent to the gifts presented by Lord Macartney during his embassy of 1793. (Wikimedia Commons) https://commons.wikimedia. org/wiki/File:The_Reception.JPG

27. The Duke of Wellington hosting a banquet in the Waterloo Gallery, Apsley House, the paintings of the Spanish Royal Collection lining the walls. A representation in a nearby underpass. (Photo: Paul Brummell)

28. Nicolas Hüet le Jeune, study of the giraffe given to Charles X by the viceroy of Egypt, 1827. (The Morgan Library & Museum) https://artsand-culture.google.com/asset/VwGQL5IshPaI8g

29. The *Shah Diamond*, depicted on a Soviet stamp of 1971. A diplomatic gift offered as an apology, following the murder of the Russian minister in Persia, Alexander Griboedov. (Wikimedia Commons) https://commons. wikimedia.org/wiki/File:The_Soviet_Union_1971_CPA_4069_stamp_ (Shah_Diamond,_16th_Century)_large_resolution.jpg

30. Cleopatra's Needle in London, a gift from the governor of Egypt that took the recipients decades to collect. (Photo: Paul Brummell)

31. The Thomas Jefferson peace medal of 1801, featuring clasped hands, a crossed tomahawk and peace pipe, and the words 'peace and friendship'. (Brooklyn Museum) https://www.brooklynmuseum.org/opencollection/ objects/62740

32. Palm Cottage, Gillingham, home from 1855 to 1861 of Sarah Forbes Bonetta, the former slave gifted by King Ghezo of Dahomey to a British naval commander. (Photo: Paul Brummell)

33. Caroline and Kerry Kennedy peering from the *Resolute* desk in the Oval Office, a diplomatic gift that maintains a prime location at the heart of US power. (Wikimedia Commons) https://commons.wikimedia.org/wiki/ File:Caroline_Kennedy_Kerry_Kennedy_Resolute_Desk_a.jpg

34. The Statue of Liberty, a gift from the people of France to the people of the United States of America. (Wikimedia Commons; Dominique James) https://commons.wikimedia.org/wiki/File:Statue_of_Lib-erty_-_4621961395.jpg

35. Washington, DC cherry blossom: a flowering reminder of a 1912 gift from Tokyo to the US capital. (Wikimedia Commons) https://commons.wikimedia.org/wiki/File:Washington_C_D.C._Tidal_Basin_cherry_trees.jpg

36. A Maybach DS-8 Zeppelin Cabriolet. A state limousine variant of this car was presented by Adolf Hitler to the maharaja of Patiala. (DaimlerChrysler AG; licensed under the Creative Commons Attribution-Share Alike 3.0 Unported license; https://commons.wikimedia.org/wiki/Commons:GNU_Free_Documentation_License,_version_1.2) https://commons.wikimedia.org/wiki/File:Maybach_Zeppelin_DS_8_Cabriolet_1.jpg

37. Presentation of the Sword of Stalingrad, a gift from King George VI of the United Kingdom to the citizens of Stalingrad, at the Soviet embassy in Tehran, 1943. (Wikimedia Commons) https://commons.wikimedia.org/wiki/File:Presentation_of_the_Sword_of_Stalingrad,_Soviet_Embassy,_Tehran,_Iran,_1943_(24377436736).jpg

38. The Trafalgar Square Christmas Tree, gifted annually by the city of Oslo to London, in 2019. (Photo: Paul Brummell)

39. A boxcar of the Merci Train, a gift from France to the United States in thanks for US post-war food aid. (National Archives and Records Administration – Wikimedia Commons) https://commons.wikimedia.org/wiki/File:Photograph_of_boxcar_from_French_%22Merci_train,%22_a_gift_from_France_to_the_United_States_in_grateful_recognition_of..._-_NARA_-_200078.jpg

40. The Volgograd Planetarium, a seventieth birthday gift from the people of the German Democratic Republic to Joseph Stalin, inaugurated only after the recipient's death. (WikiCommons; A.Savin) https://commons.wikimedia.org/wiki/File:May2015_Volgograd_img17_Planetarium.jpg

41. US President George W. Bush presented with a bowl of shamrocks by Taoiseach Bertie Ahern in 2006. (Wikimedia Commons) https://commons.wikimedia.org/wiki/File:White_House_shamrock_ceremony_2006.jpg

42. A mute swan. (Wikimedia Commons) https://commons.wikimedia.org/wiki/File:Mute_swan_Vrhnika.jpg

43. John F. Kennedy Memorial, Runnymede, standing on the acre of English ground gifted by the United Kingdom to the United States of America. (Photo: Paul Brummell)

INTRODUCTION

Well, that was embarrassing. It had all gone so well. French President François Hollande, accompanied by his ministers of defence and foreign affairs, was given a hero's welcome on his arrival on 2 February 2013 in the Malian city of Timbuktu, newly liberated from fundamentalist rebels with the support of French troops. The authorities presented the president with a cute baby camel. The anguished screeching of the animal should perhaps have served as a portent of what was to come. Since a baby camel could not easily be accommodated on the presidential plane, it was left with a family in Timbuktu while transportation arrangements were sorted out.

Two months later, the world's press gleefully alighted on a report by the Reuters news agency relating that French soldiers in Mali had discovered that the family entrusted with the camel's safekeeping had been inadequately briefed on their guardianship role. Sad to relate, the camel had provided the central ingredient of a particularly tasty *tajine*. The mortified local authorities quickly promised to provide the president with a larger and better-looking camel.[1]

While it is widely known that the giving and receiving of gifts are a common element of diplomatic encounters between heads of state and government, they tend today to engage the interest of the press and public only in three contexts: when they pose particular challenges, often arising in the case of gifts involving animals; when there is a whiff of corruption around them; or when they highlight cultural differences between giver and receiver. The latter are conveniently showcased in press articles with titles starting 'The most bizarre diplomatic gifts …' or suchlike.[2] Here you will read that His Royal Highness the Duke of Edinburgh was once gifted a straw penis sheath by the Kastom people of the Pacific island of Tanna in Vanuatu,[3] or that Argentinean President Néstor Kirchner gave his US counterpart 300 pounds of lamb in 2003.[4]

This treatment as a comedic footnote to international relations underplays the significance of diplomatic gifts as a practice that dates to prehis-

1

tory, a feature of diplomatic engagement across all eras and continents. At their finest, diplomatic gifts have constituted a symbol of lasting friendship between two powers. The Statue of Liberty was a diplomatic gift. So were the cherry trees that herald springtime in Washington. Gifts have sealed treaties, and marriage deals. Yet misjudged gifts have also sunk them. A gift from the wrong source can end a promising career. The Trojans were slaughtered because they failed to look their gift horse in the mouth. Cross-cultural gifting is fraught with risks of misinterpretation. Gifts have often held different meanings for giver and receiver. They have created both understandings and misunderstandings. In doing so, they have helped to shape our world.

Part of the challenge around an appreciation of the importance of diplomatic gifts is that word 'gift'. It implies something pleasant and can lead to the consideration of diplomatic gifts as nothing more than a courtesy, worthy of a smile and a handshake, but simply a preamble to the real business of the engagement. This is indeed how most modern leaders and diplomats think of diplomatic gifts most of the time, though this was not true of their predecessors, as we shall see. Some discover to their cost that gifts are tricky.

Oliver Franks appeared to define the description of an 'establishment figure'. He was a permanent secretary at the Ministry of Supply, where his wartime role had been outstanding; ambassador to the United States; chairman of the Organisation for European Economic Cooperation, a forerunner of the OECD; and chairman of Lloyds Bank. He gave the BBC's Reith Lecture in 1954, on the theme of *Britain and the Tide of World Affairs*; and in 1960 he was narrowly defeated by Harold Macmillan in the election for the chancellor of Oxford University. He was tall, intellectual, offering gravitas and moral authority. He was also somewhat austere and puritanical.

Yet when his name is recalled today, it is as likely to be for an anecdote about a Christmas gift as for any of his fine career achievements. It is a tale found in the after-dinner speeches of many a British diplomat and, as is customary for tales of this nature, the details change with the telling. Sometimes the name Oliver Franks disappears from the story completely; and the setting is moved to various parts of the world to suit the occasion. In its standard version, the tale runs roughly as follows. It was the run up to Christmas in 1948. Sir Oliver Franks, the British ambassador to Washington, was interrupted by his secretary, who informed him that the local radio station had called to ask what he would like for Christmas.

Franks, a man of frugal tastes, thought long and hard before replying. That Christmas Eve, the radio station put out a special holiday broadcast of the Christmas gifts requested by ambassadors accredited to the United States. The French ambassador had asked for world peace. The Soviet ambassador had requested freedom for those enslaved by imperialism. The British ambassador had asked for a small box of crystallised fruit.[5]

We will look at fifty diplomatic gifts, from the earliest times to the present day. Some rank among the most famous gifts in human history, inspiring literature and art. Others are much less well known but illuminate a facet of the diplomatic gift-giving process. Before embarking on our historical journey, it is necessary to say something about gifts and something about diplomacy.

Gifts

A French sociologist named Marcel Mauss stalks the study of gifts like a proprietary ghost. A nephew of Émile Durkheim, his discipline-founding 1925 study, *Essai sur le Don*,[6] looks at the way that gift exchange builds order in certain societies. Mauss examined the anthropological research of Bronisław Malinowski in the Trobriand Islands, east of New Guinea. In his seminal account of 1922, *Argonauts of the Western Pacific*,[7] Malinowski had set out the results of his close observation of and indeed participation in the lives of the islanders, a method of field research that was to prove influential for the discipline of anthropology.

Malinowski had described a remarkable system of inter-tribal exchange, which he termed the *Kula* Ring, involving the inhabitants of a large ring of islands of western Melanesia. Just two goods were exchanged, a red shell necklace and a white shell arm bracelet. They were exchanged in elaborate public ceremonies and would be held for only a short period of time before being passed on in another ceremony. Malinowski found that the necklaces were moving clockwise around the ring through these exchanges, while the arm bracelets moved anti-clockwise.[8]

Mauss alighted on some important features of the *kula*. It was a complex system of gift exchange, characterised by groups, not individuals, although conducted by chiefs as representatives of the group. The donors at one ceremonial exchange would be the recipients at the next. The donors would pretend modesty when giving away the gift, which would typically be thrown on the ground before being accepted. The objects themselves were highly valued: possession comforted and soothed.[9] Yet the items were not retained for long: they would be gifted onwards around the ring. Crucially, receipt of a gift obliged the recipient to make a future return gift. The *kula* system of gift exchange was reserved exclusively for these valuable products, and was aristocratic in character. It existed alongside more familiar exchange systems, such as *gimwali*, which involved an exchange of useful goods through bargaining, a vulgar procedure that would never be seen in the ceremonies of the *kula*.[10]

Mauss argued that there were parallels between the *kula* exchange of the Trobriand Islanders and the potlatch, the gift-focused feasts of indigenous peoples of the north-west coast of America. These feasts struck outside observers as wasteful: goods carefully accumulated over the year would be recklessly consumed, handed out as excessively large gifts, or even deliberately destroyed.[11] Mauss contended that in the system of gift exchange practised by these peoples such apparent excess was in fact entirely logical. Prestige and thus power was earnt by conspicuous generosity. It was a highly competitive process, with leaders seeking to outdo each other in the magnitude of their gifts and feasts.

In the potlatch system, gifts had to be returned, with interest. He argued that the concept of interest here was not intended, as in market economies, to recompense the original donor for losses incurred through the passage of time, but rather as a means of humiliating them.[12] Those who could not return a potlatch risked losing their rank; even their freedom.[13] The potlatch was an example of what Mauss called a 'total prestation': it combined religious, economic, social and legal elements.

In a study of ancient Roman, Hindu and Germanic systems, Mauss contended that the systems of gift exchange in the Trobriand Islands and the north-west coast of America were not simply characteristic of certain indigenous communities in the Pacific but part of a wider human history. He argued that contemporary market economies had lost important elements of social solidarity deriving from the 'total prestations' of these gift economies. Echoes of them were however to be found, for example in social welfare systems.

Three main features of the system of gift exchange, as described by Mauss and then pored over by numerous later commentators, require specific discussion in order to understand the role of gifts in diplomacy. First, the objective behind the gift. Second, why the character of the gifted object changes by virtue of its being a gift, and how it can be understood differently by giver and receiver. Third, the importance of reciprocating the gift.

INTRODUCTION

The objective behind the gift

For Mauss, the gift economy had a social function. Gifts created and maintained social relationships.[14] He drew a distinction between two types of exchange. In gift exchange, a social relationship is established by the act of gifting, binding giver and receiver together. In commodity exchange, there is no enduring link created by the transaction.[15] The act of purchasing an item completes the relationship between buyer and seller. Diplomacy, as we shall see, is all about the conduct of business between geographically distinct groups. Such business is facilitated by the existence of a continuing social relationship between these groups. Hence the importance of diplomatic gifts as a means of establishing and then maintaining these relationships.

Of course, not all social relationships are alike. Scholarship in this field has demonstrated a tension between those who view gift exchange as predominantly a practice of solidarity and those who see it as predominantly about the exercise of authority.[16] In attempting to understand the varied objectives behind the offer and choice of a gift, the categorisation of human relationships set out by US anthropologist Alan Fiske in his book *Structures of Social Life* provides a helpful model.

Fiske argues that there are four basic types of relationship.[17] The first he calls Communal Sharing. Exchanges are based on connectedness or identification to others. Gifts given as a mark of love, friendship or gratitude fall into this category. So too do gifts that stem from the insecurity of the giver about the strength of the relationship, where the gift is a means of attempting to fortify it.[18]

He terms the second relationship Authority Ranking. The objective here is to underline personal status or power. The relationship here is typically uneven, with one of the parties giving lavishly, the other awed by or dependent on their benevolence. Gifts in this category can sometimes be characterised by contempt on the part of the giver.

Fiske's third category is termed Equality Matching. The exchange here is a balanced one. The giver offers a gift in the full expectation that it will be reciprocated with an equivalent gift.

The fourth category is termed by Fiske Market Pricing. Here the objective is to secure a material benefit from the gift. It will be given in the expectation of generating a greater return from the recipient.[19]

The diplomatic gifts in our stories depend on different forms of relationship between giver and receiver. Thus, the lavish gifts of the Chinese

Qianlong emperor to tributary states fall into the category of Authority Ranking, while gifts offered as attempted bribes may be characterised as Market Pricing. The notion of reciprocation forming the central theme of Fiske's third category, Equality Matching, is particularly important in an understanding of diplomatic gifts, and we will look at this in more detail.

Giver and receiver may understand the objective behind the gift differently. We have already noted that there are many different motivations for making a gift, some of which are actively harmful to the recipient. It follows that gifting often includes an element of obfuscation of motive. Consider, in the realm of diplomatic gifts, two states each considering themselves the superior of the other. A gift interpreted by the giving state as a show of its technological or cultural superiority may be interpreted by the receiving one as a form of tribute.

Swiss historian Christian Windler has explored the relationship between Christian France and the Islamic beys of Tunis in the eighteenth century, showing how what were viewed by the former as voluntary gifts were depicted as tribute by the latter. Windler argues that the ability of each side to cast the transaction in their own way actually facilitated productive exchange.[20] Cultures with very different assumptions were able to adapt to each other.[21]

It is worth underlining that gifts meet the objectives of the giver. This is an obvious point sometimes obscured by associations of gift selection with painstaking consideration of what it is that the recipient would like. Gifts appear to be about the recipient. Yet attempting to ensure that the chosen gift lifts the heart of its recipient is not necessarily simply an altruistic endeavour.

The gifted object

The gifted object is different from other ostensibly identical objects by virtue of its being a gift. In a system of commodity exchange, the purchased object is alienated: it maintains no continuing relationship with the seller. It is fungible, capable of being replaced by an identical item. There is nothing unique about it. In a system of gift exchange, the gifted object is in contrast inalienable. It retains a link to the giver, providing it with both an individuality and a history. It is unique.[22] Mauss argued that a gift incorporates the spiritual essence of the donor. He used the example of gift-giving in Maori societies, in which gifts were imbued with a spiritual power, or *hau*, through which the giver maintained a hold over the recipient.[23]

An example serves to illustrate the different characters of a gifted and a purchased object. The summit of G8 countries held in Genoa in July 2001 is mostly remembered for the anti-globalisation protests that surrounded it. US President George W. Bush followed the summit with a visit to Rome, and bilateral talks with the Italian prime minister, Silvio Berlusconi. Among the gifts received by the president from Berlusconi were three navy blue silk twill ties, made by the renowned luxury menswear brand of Battistoni.[24]

Under the US rules governing the president's acceptance of gifts, set out in the 1966 Foreign Gifts and Decorations Act and subsequent amendments, the president would not have been permitted to keep the gifts received from Berlusconi as personal gifts, assuming that their cost exceeded the statutorily defined 'minimal value'.[25] Rather, he would have accepted them on behalf of the United States, typically to be deposited with the National Archives and Records Administration.

A tie is normally considered to be a thin piece of material worn under the collar of a shirt and knotted to allow the material to hang down the shirtfront. Based on this definition, the ties gifted by the Italian prime minister have the form of ties, but not the function of them. They are destined not to be worn, but retained, functioning not as a necktie but as a gifted reminder of US–Italian friendship. An object that is gifted retains a personality, an individuality, arising from the fact of its having been gifted, which an identical object purchased as a commodity does not possess.

This is at the heart of the idea set out by anthropologist Arjun Appadurai in his introduction to the edited volume *The Social Life of Things,* arising from a conference at the University of Pennsylvania, that social lives are not the sole preserve of people: objects have them too.[26] The social life possessed by an object is not, however, a constant. If the circumstances under which an object is gifted are forgotten, it loses its specific identity and becomes a commodity. This commodity might in turn become obsolete, becoming an item of junk. Through the further passage of time, the item of junk might become an antique.[27] We know that many Byzantine silks were sent to western Europe as diplomatic gifts. With few exceptions, however, we have no idea which of the Byzantine silks surviving in the churches and royal collections of western Europe were gifted. They remain valuable works of art, but they have lost the personality that arose through their status as gifts.

Some gifted objects are easier to alienate than others. Our neckties are, as we have noted, distinguished from other identical ties by virtue of being a gift, and thus carry with them the memory of that gifting relationship. As objects otherwise identical to neckties purchased as commodities, the process of converting such gifts to alienated commodities is however more straightforward than would be the case for a gifted portrait of the person making the gift. In the case of the latter, it is more difficult to erase, by accident or design, the memory of the gifting relationship, because the object itself bears the marks of that relationship.

American anthropologist Annette Weiner, setting out what she described as 'the paradox of keeping-while-giving',[28] argued that some objects, which she characterised as inalienable possessions, held the power to define the status of the owner, serving as a vehicle for bringing the past to the present, and invoking the histories of ancestors.[29] She argued that the owner of such objects would endeavour not to give them as gifts, but rather to keep them, and bequeath them to their descendants, given the vital role of these objects in preserving the owner's hierarchical position. She gave the example of the sacred *churinga* boards of Central Australian Aboriginal peoples such as the Aranda, which were required to stay hidden, and not to leave the clan house.[30]

Weiner argued that gift exchanges would be characterised by an attempt to avoid relinquishing these highly valued status-defining inalienable possessions, typically by gifting more alienable items.[31] Such a strategy will not be successful in all situations. Thus, in Maori funeral practices, the most precious valuables, or *taonga*, are given as gifts, including nephrite or 'greenstone' ornaments, feather cloaks and fine flax mats. In these cases, while the gifts may be held for years, they will eventually be returned to the original donors or their descendants on an equivalent occasion. The items are considered to be held in trust by the recipients.[32]

A gifted item such as a portrait will rarely fall into this category of the most highly valued inalienable possessions of the owner, holding the power to determine their status. Monarchs in eighteenth-century Europe for example often maintained something of a production line of their likenesses for use as diplomatic gifts. Such particularly hard-to-alienate gifts offered the giver the advantage that it was more difficult for the recipient to erase the memory of the gift from the object. Such objects also tended to be more difficult, or at least risky, for the recipient to monetise. For this reason, gifts intended as bribes would more likely use easily alienable objects, like cash.

The importance of reciprocation

Mauss identified three obligations as central to gift exchange. They were the obligation to give presents, the obligation to receive them, and the obligation to repay gifts received.[33] Denying these obligations was to deny the social relationship with the other party.[34] Reciprocation, then, was vital to the system's stability.

Mauss argued that the incorporation within a gift of the spiritual essence of the donor further strengthened the requirement for reciprocation. He observed that, in Maori societies, if a gifted item was passed on, any present received in return should be gifted to the original donor, as it would retain the *hau* of the original gift.[35]

This emphasis on the spiritual power of the gift has been a strongly contested element of Mauss's work. Claude Lévi-Strauss acknowledged a debt to Mauss's contribution to the ideas that led him to develop the discipline of structural anthropology.[36] However, he found Mauss's reliance on the *hau* as unnecessary, a rather magical notion that was required only because Mauss had viewed the gift as instituting a system of reciprocity rather than as a component placed into such a system.[37]

Mauss used the Hindu texts of the *danadharma*, the law of religious gifts, to support his arguments on the spiritual power of the gift. The example of a donor of cattle, who prior to making the gift would sleep on the ground with the beasts and eat their food, served vividly to demonstrate a gift embodying the giver.[38] The gift in the *danadharma* embodies more specifically the giver's sins: a burden that is transferred to the recipient.[39] Gifts then can be dangerous, even poisonous. While the German word *Gift* once retained a meaning close to that of the English word, as seen in compounds such as *Mitgift*, meaning 'dowry', its meaning today is 'poison'.

Anthropologist Jonathan Parry, delivering the 1985 Malinowski Memorial Lecture at the London School of Economics, argued however that the *danadharma* example did not support Mauss's contention that there was an obligation to repay gifts received. Since the gift here bore the sins of the giver, there was no sense in which the donor would want it back. Thus while Mauss had invoked the 'spirit of the gift' to explain the necessity of its return to a donor with which it was irrevocably linked, in this example, it must never return to the donor, or so would the sin.[40]

Parry argued that such 'pure gifts', with no expectation of reciprocity, were more characteristic of economies with a sizeable market sector, allowing the gift to be separated from the economic significance it had in societies such as those of Melanesia and the north-west American coast. They were also often associated with a specific type of belief system offering the prospect of reward, not in this world, but in the next one, with different outcomes depending on present conduct. The non-reciprocated gift becomes in this context a means of atonement for sins and a means to salvation.[41]

From the perspective of the recipient, reciprocation is though the safest strategy. In the Trobriand Island or north-west coast of America contexts, failure to reciprocate means humiliation. In other contexts, it can suggest subordination or dependency. Some of the warmest diplomatic gifts in the stories that follow are gifts of thanks, such as the Christmas tree given each year by the city of Oslo to London, and the Merci Train sent in 1949 by France to the United States. These too are reciprocations: gifts sent to acknowledge, respectively, support received during the Second World War and the post-war reconstruction support provided through the Marshall Plan. The gifts may be seen as helping to avoid a status of indebtedness and dependency, and maintaining instead an ongoing positive social relationship.

The non-reciprocation of a diplomatic gift may suggest that the transaction, while offering the outward pretence of a gift, is better understood as a tribute payment, for example, or a bribe. The dividing lines between these forms of transaction can become blurred,[42] and, as we shall see, they may be perceived in different ways by the giver and receiver.

Time is an important consideration here. If a gift places the receiver in a position of debt in respect of the giver, then risks are minimised by offering a return gift as quickly as possible. Modern diplomatic meetings frequently involve the simultaneous exchange of gifts, which is the safest strategy of all. French sociologist Pierre Bourdieu argued, however, that such immediate reciprocation destroys the function of gift exchange by denying the ability of the giver to exercise power over the recipient by generating a sense of obligation in the latter.[43] For Bourdieu, immediate reciprocation suggests a rejection of the original gift and implies ingratitude. Equally, delaying too long before reciprocating the original gift is suggestive of indifference.[44] A time lag between gifts helps to maintain the continuing social relationship that is the essence of gift exchange, and therefore to sustain diplomatic engagement,[45] though it should not be so long as to appear to deny the desire for a continuing relationship.

Diplomacy

Diplomacy is required when two groups live separately but have some need to conduct business. Exchange relations must be established. Some form of immunity for those conducting the communications between the groups is necessary to allow them to carry out their work. To understand the evolution of the practice of diplomatic gifts over time, we need to understand the evolution of the wider practices of diplomacy. While the term 'diplomacy' began to be used in its modern sense only in the late eighteenth century,[46] its practice is older than recorded history.

The birth and development of diplomatic practice

The former diplomat Harold Nicolson, writing on the eve of the Second World War, noted that while the first diplomats would once have been considered to be the angels, as messengers between heaven and earth, to more grounded modern societies the origins of diplomacy lie instead in Cro-Magnon or Neanderthal peoples. Different social groups would have realised the need to grant an emissary the ability to deliver unmolested a message between them.[47] Writing more than seventy years later, another British diplomat-turned-author, Tom Fletcher, made the same point, though he also gave the first diplomat a name: Ug.[48] He was guessing.

Another literary diplomat, Ragnar Numelin, Finland's minister in Brussels in the late 1940s, combed anthropological sources to demonstrate that many tribal societies had established systems under which messengers between the tribes were able to discuss trade and make peace in a protected environment, fed and sheltered by their hosts.[49] There are historical records of the exchange of envoys dating to third-millennium BCE Mesopotamia.[50] The subject matter of the first of our stories, the Amarna Letters of the fourteenth century BCE, reveals a well-developed system of relations between the great powers of the day, conducted through diplomatic messengers, with Akkadian serving as a diplomatic lingua franca.

The Bible contains much diplomatic exchange. Consider the plight of Hezekiah, the reformist and godly king of Judah, who had seen the Northern Kingdom of Israel centred on Samaria fall to the Assyrians. That same power was now menacing Judah itself. The Assyrian king,

Sennacherib, had taken the fortress city of Lachish, just 30 miles from Jerusalem. Hezekiah tried everything to keep his throne, including attempting to pay off Sennacherib with gold and silver stripped from the house of the Lord,[51] and an alliance with Egypt. Sennacherib despatched envoys to Jerusalem, accompanied by force, and these took up position just outside the city, where three envoys from Hezekiah came out to meet them. The head of the Assyrian delegation, identified by his title as the *Rabshakeh*, urged Hezekiah to break off his alliance with Egypt, a 'bruised reed',[52] and pledge instead to Sennacherib.

Hezekiah's envoys asked the *Rabshakeh* to speak in Aramaic, clearly the diplomatic lingua franca of its day, rather than Hebrew, so that the citizens on the walls of Jerusalem above them should not be able to hear the conversation. The *Rabshakeh* entirely ignored this injunction and, speaking directly to the people in Hebrew, called on them to surrender and each would enjoy their own fig tree, vine and well, albeit after being exiled to another land, rather than remain under siege and forced to 'eat their own dung, and drink their own piss'.[53] The citizens however remained loyal to Hezekiah. Jerusalem held firm.

Ancient Greece provided fertile ground for the development of diplomatic practice. Nicolson highlighted, from the Homeric period, the office of herald (*kerykes*), accorded diplomatic privileges in order to convey messages to rival powers, as well as carrying out a range of other duties, from serving the royal household to maintaining order at assemblies. The heralds were protected by the god Hermes, the messenger of the gods, a deity associated with charm but also cunning, and indeed trickery.[54] Many would argue that these attributes fit the modern diplomat well.

In the Greece of the classical age, the presence of many small city-states, each believing themselves the equal of the others and sharing a common language, provided the ideal soil for nurturing diplomatic practice. Nicolson noted that the city-states chose as their diplomatic envoys their finest orators, whose task was to make a magnificent and persuasive speech before the popular assembly of the recipient city.[55] Pericles and Demosthenes were among those assigned diplomatic missions.[56]

The sophistication of the diplomacy of classical Greece is illustrated by the historian Thucydides' description of the conference of the Peloponnesian League convened by Sparta in 432 BCE to hear the grievances of those members of the league, such as Corinth, who argued that Athens had violated its treaty obligations and should be punished through war. Athens had a diplomatic delegation in the city and was allowed to participate in the debate. Unsurprisingly, the Athenian delegates were not in favour of a declaration of war against Athens. Their arguments failed to win the day, and war was duly declared, but even then, the Athenian delegation was allowed to finish its business in Sparta unmolested.[57]

In both China and India during the first millennium BCE, there were also complex patterns of diplomatic exchange in a context of many independent political entities of roughly similar size, underpinned by linguistic and cultural similarities, though these systems tended to look back to an idealised empire.[58] The Indian treatise on statesmanship of the fourth century BCE, the *Arthaśāstra*, traditionally credited to Kautilya, adviser to the first Maurya emperor, offers much advice on diplomatic conduct, couched in a language of hard-nosed realism, with intelligence gathering placed at the heart of diplomatic work.

Unlike classical Greece, ancient Rome provided an unpropitious environment for the development of diplomatic practice. The Roman Empire was built on the military expansion of a power that had no equal.[59] There was little perceived need for the development of sophisticated diplomatic skills. The latter only came into their own with the decay of Rome.

The Byzantine Empire was a master of diplomatic practice, sorely needing it to offset its declining military might.[60] Byzantine diplomacy employed ceremonial self-promotion, flattery, intelligence gathering and bribery. Its techniques were passed westwards, for example through its close association with Venice.[61] Lavish ceremony, as a means of impressing foreign envoys with a display of greatness, was one of the planks of Byzantine diplomacy: in the tenth century, the scholarly Emperor Constantine VII Porphyrogenitus penned, or at least commissioned, a *Book of Ceremonies*, setting out the protocol rules surrounding court ceremonies as a manual for his successors to follow. The focus on intelligence gathering and extensive use of misinformation characteristic of Byzantine diplomacy helped to fuel a lingering reputation of ambassadors as spies.[62]

The pattern continued in later centuries of diplomatic practice developing in contexts involving an interdependent network of competing states of roughly equivalent size, or under powers that claimed dominance but were politically or militarily weak. Where there was one dominant power that did not recognise the existence of any equals, diplomacy was relatively less important. China forms another example of the latter for much of the imperial period.[63]

The establishment of permanent ambassadors

Diplomacy thus far had been a matter of temporary missions: envoys sent by a ruler to another kingdom or state for a specific purpose, whether to establish trading relations, negotiate a marriage or sue for peace. Diplomatic gifts were an important component of almost all such missions, and indeed in a sense the mission itself was a gift. The embassy was mobile. Its arrival would be the occasion for pageant. Depending on the importance of the visiting polity, the arrival of a foreign diplomatic mission might be a source of prestige, and pride.

A crucial development that would change the relationship between diplomacy and location and mark the emergence of diplomacy as a profession took place in Renaissance Italy. It was the establishment of permanent ambassadors. That this development should take place in Italy was no accident. Here again, the regional context was propitious for major developments in diplomatic practice: a large number of city-states, none dominant, each dependent on alliances with others for their well-being, meant that each state needed constantly to nurture its relationship with the others, and required as much accurate information as it could gather about their strengths and plans.

The question of the identity of the first permanent ambassador has been the subject of much academic debate and is impossible to answer. When is a lengthy temporary mission considered permanent? One Bartolino di Codelupi was, for example, sent to the court of Bernabò Visconti in Milan in 1375 to represent Lodovico Gonzaga of Mantua in the arrangement of a marriage contract between the two families. He remained at the court to further cooperation between Mantua and Milan more broadly, and was still there in 1379.[64]

In 1446, Nicodemo Tranchedini da Pontremoli was sent to Florence by an Italian *condottiero* named Francesco Sforza, tasked with maintaining close contact with Sforza's ally, Cosimo de' Medici, banker and effective ruler of the city, who would help Sforza secure the position of duke of Milan in 1450. Nicodemo was confirmed in his post in Florence and remained there for another seventeen years.[65]

In 1454, the Peace of Lodi brought to an end the longstanding conflict between Milan and Venice, recognising Sforza as the ruler of Milan and restoring to Venice certain northern Italian territories. An alliance for the preservation of peace named the Lega Italica was established, with most Italian states joining it. The Peace of Lodi established an unstable equilibrium between Italian states, in which the work of resident ambassadors found its calling, both in information gathering about the intentions of the host state and the ability to intervene quickly. The exchange of resident ambassadors also became a natural way to welcome new entrants to the league.[66] Rome in the late fifteenth century became a particularly important incubator of diplomatic practice, where the Italian city-states would send their most able ambassadors, and where the papal practice of addressing them collectively led to the forerunner of the diplomatic corps.[67] From Italy, the practice spread to other parts of Europe.

The Peace of Westphalia

Another peace settlement in Europe, more than two centuries later, is often identified as the source of the guiding principles of the modern international order: that all states are equal, that states hold sovereignty over their territory and domestic affairs, and that states shall not interfere in the domestic affairs of other states. Enshrined in the Charter of the United Nations, these principles are often referred to in international relations theory as the 'Westphalian system' in honour of that peace settlement of 1648. The problem is that there is little clear reference to any of these concepts in the texts of the treaties that made up the Peace of Westphalia.

The treaties ended the Thirty Years' War, which had grown out of a conflict between Protestant and Catholic states within the Holy Roman Empire, embracing many of the major powers of Europe. There was no grand pan-continental peace treaty. Rather, two separate, essentially bilateral, treaties were signed in October 1648: the Treaty of Münster, between the Holy Roman Empire and France, and the Treaty of Osnabrück, between the Holy Roman Empire and Sweden.[68] The peace settlement did not stop all of the ongoing conflict in Europe: the war between France and Spain continued until 1659. The treaties contain nothing on the issue of sovereignty or the balance of power, being concerned with rather more practical considerations.[69]

The Peace of Westphalia did however reflect an important change, which would be highly significant in the development of an international order based on state sovereignty. This was the move away from a conception of supreme authority held by the pope or the Holy Roman Emperor as the vessel for the expression of God's will on earth. This helps explain the condemnation of the Westphalia peace settlement by Pope Innocent X in his bull *Zelo Domus Dei*. In accepting the peace, the Holy Roman Emperor was signing up to an unfavourable settlement with his notional inferiors.[70] However, this loss of power over other states was not brought about overnight by the Peace of Westphalia. The authority of pope and emperor had been in relative decline for centuries. Nor was the change completed in 1648: the Holy Roman Empire was to last until 1806.

One of the pieces of evidence often given in support of the origin of the principle of territorial sovereignty within the Peace of Westphalia lies in its endorsement of the principle of *cuius regio, eius religio*: that the ruler should have the right to determine the religion of their subjects.[71] But this principle dated from the earlier Peace of Augsburg of 1555, and the Peace of Westphalia tempered its provisions in important respects, including by giving all citizens the right to emigrate and guaranteeing freedom of conscience. It thus served to limit rather than enhance state sovereignty in this area.[72]

The principles we now know as the 'Westphalian system' instead emerged gradually and were in no sense completed in 1648, the peace marking a step towards the replacement of a universalistic concept of a Christian unity with a particularistic one based on state sovereignty.[73] The tension between these principles was one of the sources of wrangling over matters of precedence to infect European diplomacy at this time. Pope Julius II had laid out a table of precedence, binding only in the Papal States, in 1504, which had placed France above Spain. The matter of their relative standing was the source of much animosity between French and Spanish representatives across Europe. In 1661, at a procession of diplomatic coaches to mark the arrival of a new Swedish ambassador in London, the jockeying for position between French and Spanish coaches resulted in several deaths and almost occasioned a war.[74]

The professionalisation of diplomacy

A profession of diplomacy was emerging, characterised by secret negotiations and elaborate ceremonial,[75] its practitioners aristocratic. Manuals were available to guide their work, such as *El embajador*, written in 1620 by Don Juan Antonio de Vera y Zúñiga and translated into French as *Le parfait ambassadeur*. The many ties across the European nobilities gave the profession a somewhat fraternal character.[76] The process of professionalising diplomacy was though a gentle one: the first British secretary of state for foreign affairs was not appointed until 1782.

The term 'diplomacy' has its origins in the ancient Greek verb *diploun*, to fold double,[77] and the associated noun *diploma*, referring to folded official documents that gave the bearer a set of privileges.[78] The term 'diplomatica' was in use by the beginning of the eighteenth century to refer to the study of letters of privilege to establish their legitimacy. *Corps diplomatique*, a term initially referring to an archive of such texts, came gradually to mean all the envoys accredited to a specific court.[79] With the French Revolution, and the establishment of a *comité diplomatique* by the Constituent Assembly, the term, and the committee's remit, broadened from a narrow focus on the study of treaties to broader matters concerned with foreign affairs. The modern term 'diplomatic' was born.

However, its initial use was in a negative sense, reflecting a perception of diplomacy as privileged, aristocratic and secretive. For revolutionary France, diplomacy was a practice of the Old Regime.[80] A 'new diplomacy' was called for, with a stronger trade focus, and more openness.[81] The 'new diplomacy' would however have to wait.

The Congress of Vienna of 1814–15, which aimed to establish a peaceful foundation for Europe following the removal of Napoléon, was in some respects the high-water mark of the old diplomacy, with no time for republican or revolutionary currents. The congress, and a later gathering at Aix-la-Chapelle in 1818, dealt with the thorny question of precedence by establishing four classes of heads of mission, with precedence within each class determined not by the importance of the state or its ruler but by the date of presentation of the ambassador's credentials. The framework established at Vienna would underpin a relatively peaceful century across Europe, but its dramatic collapse in the First World War was accompanied by renewed appeals to a 'new diplomacy' based on openness, not secret treaties: the 'open covenants of peace, openly arrived at' that formed the first of US President Woodrow Wilson's 'Fourteen Points' of January 1918.

A new diplomacy

This focus on openness was a conscious reaction to the secrecy that had defined the diplomacy of Byzantium and Renaissance Europe and characterised it ever since. Resident ambassadors had always used secret codes to convey their frank despatches. While this aspect of diplomatic activity remains to this day, it has been accompanied by a stronger focus on 'public diplomacy', with diplomats becoming shapers of open debate.[82] This emphasis on connections outside the narrow confines of the royal court or foreign ministry reflects the emergence of the democratic age, the development of mass communications and the proliferation of actors, outside as well as within governments, involved in shaping foreign policy. Historically though it is not as new as is often portrayed: in some senses, it harks back to the diplomatic communications of classical Greece, which also had a public character, its envoys serving as political advocates in public assemblies.

This broadening of diplomacy, involving many more actors and open debates, has had a considerable impact on diplomatic gifts, as we shall see, from stronger public scrutiny over gifted items to public inputs into the choice of particularly significant gifts.

There were other changes afoot. One of these concerned the basis for the privileges and immunities enjoyed by envoys. The emphasis had long been on personal representation, in which the diplomat represented the person of the sovereign who had sent them and demanded therefore to be treated with the deference due to the sovereign. This coloured their role and behaviour, encouraging a preoccupation with the lavishness of their clothing, entertainment and gifts and hindering information gathering as diplomatic envoys became reluctant to be seen outside the exalted royal circles appropriate for their own sovereign.[83] With the decline of absolute monarchies and the emergence of democratic states came a return to the original basis for immunities, dating from prehistoric times: functional necessity. Privileges and immunities are needed because a diplomat cannot perform their functions without them. This is the principle that underpins the Vienna Convention on Diplomatic Relations of 1961.

There are echoes here of a change in the practice of diplomatic gifts that we will explore in our stories. Rather than the personal gifts of an individual, the sovereign, these increasingly became more like regulated gifts from one state to another, surrounded by ever more rigorous rules aimed at avoiding accusations of corruption.

Technology has been an important agent of change in diplomatic practice. Diplomacy is all about communication between polities, and innovations in transportation and communication technologies have repeatedly transformed the way it has been conducted. At the dawn of the nineteenth century, US President Thomas Jefferson is said to have complained to his secretary of state: 'We have not heard from our ambassador in Spain for three years. If we do not hear from him this year, let us write him a letter.'[84] The technological advances of that century, from railways and steamships to telegrams, were to change all that. On the one hand, this led to a stronger direction of ambassadorial activity from headquarters, reducing the scope and requirement for heads of mission to take important policy decisions without consultation. It is in this sense that British Foreign Minister Lord Palmerston is said to have greeted the arrival of the first telegram on his desk in the 1840s with the comment that 'this is the end of diplomacy'.[85] On the other hand, rapid communications increase the ability of ambassadors abroad to contribute to policy debates at home.

Further innovations in transport and communications, from aircraft to telephones to Twitter, have promoted direct contacts between political leaders without the requirement for the intercession of a diplomatic envoy. Direct meetings between rulers have taken place for many centuries, particularly to conclude important negotiations. Thus in 921, Henry the Fowler, king of East Francia, and Charles the Simple, king of West Francia, signed a treaty of friendship and mutual recognition, the Treaty of Bonn, on a ship in the middle of the Rhine. The river marked the border between the two kingdoms and was considered neutral territory. Such meetings were however long exceptional, arranged with difficulty and often danger. Technological change has made these meetings routine. With the development of summit diplomacy following the Second World War, groups of influential leaders are often able to meet together to discuss the key challenges facing our planet. Leaders are able to offer diplomatic gifts direct to their counterparts, without needing an envoy as intermediary.

A global diplomacy

The conventional account suggests that the system and practice of diplomacy refined in European courts was belatedly exported to the rest of the world through European imperialism.[86] The new sovereign states emerging as a result of decolonisation following the Second World War embraced this system, and indeed saw overseas diplomatic representation as a badge of a hard-won independence.[87] Thus the diplomacy of the United Nations, of the post-Second World War order, is based on principles and practices forged through European centuries. That diplomacy has as its central organising principle the sovereignty of territorial states, albeit a principle challenged by the proliferation of non-state actors in this globalised world, from civil society organisations to multi-national corporations, as well as organisations with a supranational character, such as the European Union. The United States was long suspicious of a European-dominated diplomatic system and slow to engage with it. The first official overseas trip made by a US president while in office did not come, and here's a good pub quiz question, until 1906, when Theodore Roosevelt inspected the Panama Canal construction site.[88] When the US did engage fully, however, it too embraced the system.

From around the eleventh century, the territories of the Latin-speaking Christian world tended to adopt an exclusive diplomatic outlook, considering themselves a club of which non-Christian polities were not members.[89] When European explorers reached America, they encountered societies who were not Christian but who were also, unlike the Islamic societies with which they were long accustomed to dealing, not even aware of Christianity. Under the exclusive model they had developed, European polities simply failed to acknowledge the Amerindian societies as suitable subjects for diplomatic intercourse.[90]

But the polities with which European societies were engaging around the world had their own systems and practices of diplomacy, and these have played a more significant role than the conventional account holds in shaping the modern-day diplomatic order.[91] Thus Ottoman diplomatic practice, for example, drew from Islamic principles, making a separation between the abode of Islam (*Dâr al-Islam*) and the abode of the infidels (*Dâr al-Harb*),[92] allowing relations with the latter through the abode of treaty *(Dâr al-Sulh)*, involving the payment of tribute by the non-Muslim powers.[93]

Our stories include several examples of gifting between polities using different systems and practices of diplomacy. The risk, as we shall see from an example of the interactions of western European powers with China at the end of the eighteenth century, was of a mutual failure of recognition,[94] with neither party treating the other as a proper counterpart. Diplomatic gifts between political entities characterised by wildly different levels of development, forms of government and types of diplomatic practice involve some of the highest risks, with major potential for misunderstandings. They also involve some of the greatest scope for the transfer of technology and ideas previously unknown to the recipient. They can change the world.

*c.*1353 BCE

TWO GOLD-PLATED WOODEN STATUES

A GIFT FROM AKHENATEN, PHARAOH OF EGYPT, TO
TUSHRATTA, KING OF MITANNI

The Amarna Letter known as EA161.

In 1887, a local woman was digging in an area of ruins close to the village of el-Till in Egypt. She was extracting *sebakh*, the phosphate-rich material derived from the decomposed mud bricks of archaeological sites, used as fertiliser, but was also on the lookout for antiquities. She struck something. One of a large collection of small clay tablets. She sold them on for a few piastres.

Thus, at least according to a second-hand account of the story, was discovered a set of diplomatic correspondence of the fourteenth century BCE known as the Amarna Letters. Some 382 tablets have now been identified. The ruins in which the tablets were found were those of the city now known as el-Amarna, the ancient city of Akhetaten, the purpose-built capital of Pharaoh Akhenaten. The tablets had been stored in a building identified by archaeologists as the 'house of correspondence of the pharaoh', the foreign ministry of its day.[1] They cover a time span of up to thirty years. The oldest letters date from the rule of Amenophis III, Akhenaten's father,

21

and thus must have been brought to Akhetaten from an archive in the former capital, presumably because they contained information that might need to be checked or referenced. The archive concludes at the time of the abandonment of Akhetaten under Pharaoh Tutankhamun, son of Akhenaten.

A few of the tablets are fragments of what appear to be practice efforts in learning the cuneiform writing in which they are inscribed, including copies of extracts from mythological texts.[2] The large majority of the tablets however fall into one of two broad categories. The first category, the most numerous, is that of vassal letters, written by the rulers of cities in the Levant controlled by Egypt and who were vassals of the pharaoh. Deferential in tone, they cover issues like the payment of tribute and supply of labour, their obligations to support and reinforce Egyptian troops crossing their territory, and frequently details of their feuds with rival local rulers. Some sixty letters come from Rib-Adda, king of Byblos, whose correspondence takes the form of desperate pleas for help from the pharaoh in his dispute with the rulers of neighbouring Amurru. The pharaoh seems to have been unmoved, and Rib-Adda receives a rebuke for writing too frequently.

We will focus on the second category of letters, those between the pharaoh and rulers of powerful independent states. The correspondence embraces five great powers of the day; the Hittite Empire in Anatolia; the Kingdom of Mitanni, which fell between the Hittite lands and the Egyptian territories of the Levant; Assyria and Babylonia, lying farther to the south and east of the Mitanni kingdom; and Egypt itself. Egypt's empire remained mighty, thanks to the conquests of Thutmose III in the preceding century, but the new pharaoh Akhenaten was plunging the country into uncertainty through his radical reforms. He abandoned polytheism in favour of a religion focused on the sun disk Aten, moving the capital to Akhetaten to be free of contamination from the old gods. While, in favouring a more naturalistic style of artistic expression, his regime was perhaps closer to modern Western tastes, his reforms broke up the existing structures of effective administration, and his rule gradually descended into religious and economic strife.[3] The ancient Egyptians certainly seem to have regarded his rule as an aberration: his son Tutankhamun renounced Aten, restored the polytheistic religion, and moved the capital. Akhetaten was abandoned, together with the philosophy underpinning it.

This category of 'great king' correspondence reveals a developed system of international relations. The tablets are mostly written in Akkadian cuneiform, the writing system of ancient Mesopotamia, and not in

Egyptian hieroglyphics. The messengers conveying the tablets were important diplomatic agents and seem generally to have been individuals closely connected with the royal palace.[4] They were duly treated as important personages. Thus King Tushratta of Mitanni reported back to Pharaoh Amenophis III that he had given his messenger and interpreter 'many presents, and ... made them very glad because their mission was pleasant'.[5] The work of a diplomatic messenger was not though without its challenges, and several kings complained to the pharaoh about the lengthy detention of their messengers, in one case for six years. Foreign leaders in turn resorted to detaining Egyptian messengers as bargaining chips, the king of Alashiya (in present-day Cyprus) keeping some for three years.[6]

Diplomatic gifts are at the heart of the system of international relations revealed by the Amarna Letters. The rulers of the time had no hesitation in spelling out exactly what they wanted, sometimes specifying the desired quantity too. It is clear from the correspondence that reciprocity was expected. Thus a Kassite king of Babylon, Burna-Buriaš II, in a letter to Akhenaten, complains that Egyptian messengers had arrived three times without once giving him a beautiful greeting-gift: as a result, he had not sent any beautiful gifts to the pharaoh.[7] A wide range of gifts is mentioned in the Amarna Letters. There are references to ivory statues, furniture, chariots, jewellery, oil, horses and oxen. It transpires that the gift Burna-Buriaš was particularly hoping for was one of the lifelike stuffed animals the Egyptians were noted for. He further specified that he was quite relaxed as to whether a land or aquatic creature was selected.

Above all other gifts, however, what the other kings wanted from Egypt was gold. Lots of it. The letters drip with their desire for the precious metal. They hold the view that gold is as plentiful in Egypt as it is scarce in their lands; 'plentiful like dirt' as Tushratta puts it in one complaining missive to the pharaoh.[8] A tablet, sent by one Zita, believed to be the brother of the Hittite King Suppiluliuma I, addresses the pharaoh respectfully as 'father', reflecting the fact that the sender of the letter was not a king. Zita records that he is sending the pharaoh 'as your greeting gift a present of sixteen men'.[9] What he wants back is gold. He implores the pharaoh to send him some, and to let him know whatever else he would like in return for it.[10]

When the kings received gold from Egypt, they frequently complained about the size and quality of the gift. Burna-Buriaš laments that one gift of gold was not even a quarter of the promised quantity. The loudest and most persistent complaint arose in respect of King Tushratta of Mitanni's two gold statues.

The sad tale unfolds through a series of letters, for Tushratta was a frequent correspondent on a matter that clearly wounded him grievously. Tushratta, it seems, had been promised two solid gold statues from Amenophis III, one depicting Tushratta himself and the other his daughter, Tadu-Hepa. The statues seem to have been a gift promised in return for the despatching of Tadu-Hepa as a bride for Amenophis III. The pharaoh had sadly since died, but Tushratta expected his successor Akhenaten to honour the gift. Two gold statues were sent to Mitanni. Tushratta was however dismayed to find that, instead of the promised solid gold, he had been sent two wooden statues covered with gold plate. The other goods sent by Akhenaten also failed to conform to the promised quality.[11]

Tushratta claimed that he was well aware that Amenophis III had prepared the promised solid gold statues, as his messengers had seen the finished articles while in Egypt,[12] a reference that seems to confirm that intelligence gathering was a core function of a king's messengers. He clearly believed that Akhenaten had switched the statues for inferior ones. Tushratta even attempted to enlist the support of Akhenaten's mother, Tiye, in the affair of the statues, writing to ask her to confirm to Akhenaten the contents of the gift promised to Mitanni by Amenophis III.[13] All this agonising over the statues was perhaps a reflection of Tushratta's deeper worries about his kingdom. The marriage of his daughter to Amenophis III had been part of an attempt to forge an alliance with Egypt at a time when Mitanni was under threat from the growing power of the Hittites to the west and Assyrians to the east. The apparent willingness of Akhenaten to fob him off with cheap goods would have been a huge source of worry, not just because he didn't get the solid gold statues but also because this suggested that Egypt no longer regarded Mitanni as a serious power to be respected.[14] Indeed, events did not go well for either Tushratta, assassinated by one of his sons, or Mitanni, which was to become a puppet state of the Hittites before being swallowed up by Assyria.

What of Tadu-Hepa? She seems to have become a wife of Akhenaten after the death of Amenophis III. She would almost certainly have taken an Egyptian name following her marriage, so it is difficult to be sure of her fate. It is possible that she may be the wife named Kiya, who at one point enjoyed great favour. Not, however, for long. Kiya's name was erased from monuments and she disappeared from the record, perhaps a victim of the worsening relations between Egypt and Mitanni.[15] There is no evidence that Tushratta ever did get his solid gold statues.

*c.*1250 BCE

A WOODEN HORSE

A GIFT FROM THE GREEKS TO THE TROJANS

The Trojan Horse imagined at the Troy archaeological site.

One of the most famous of all diplomatic gifts, the Trojan Horse, provides an extreme example of a central rule underpinning such gifts. They are chosen to serve the interests of the giver.[1] These interests are admittedly usually more about flattering the recipient in the hope of securing future commercial or political advantage than about securing the immediate capture of their capital. Virgil's celebrated description of the unheeded warning of the Trojan priest Laocoön, '*timeō Danaōs et dōna ferentēs*', 'I fear the Greeks, even when bearing gifts', offers a sensible perspective of caution when confronting a diplomatic gift more broadly.

The Trojan Horse is part of our popular culture, used to describe an ostensible gift that is designed to harm. A 1978 hit record of that title by Dutch girl group Luv' offers the story of a would-be lover seeking to insinuate himself in our heroine's heart through subterfuge. The object of his attention has, we are told, not yet opened the gates. We are left to speculate on the denouement of the tale. British band Manfred Mann stuck more closely to the classical account in their 1964 record '5-4-3-2-1', except that it was not the Greeks who descended from the wooden horse. It was the Manfreds. In computing, a Trojan horse is malware that dupes users by misleading as to its true purpose. The horse has become part of our language. When British Foreign Secretary Ernest Bevin was asked in 1949 about the prospect of supranational European institutions, he is alleged to have responded: 'If you open that Pandora's box, you never know what Trojan 'orses will fly out.'[2]

The story of the Trojan War was placed at the centre of ancient Greek literature and has been an inspiration for artists, writers and musicians ever since, through the epic poems of Homer, the *Iliad* and the *Odyssey*. Yet the Trojan Horse is surprisingly peripheral to these works. The *Iliad*, set in a brief period of the tenth year of the long siege of Troy,[3] makes no explicit mention of the wooden horse at all. There are but three brief hints of the subterfuge to come. One is a speech by the Trojan king, Priam, preparing the funeral pyre of his son Hector, in which he urges the Trojans to bring timber into the city without fearing any sneaky ambush by the Greeks. The very last words of the *Iliad* refer to the dead Hector as 'breaker of horses'.[4] The implication here is that the poem's audience is already familiar with the tale of the Trojan Horse and able to interpret these oblique references as portents of the carnage to come.

The horse does appear in the text of the *Odyssey*, the tale of the ten-year long home journey of Odysseus following his decisive role in the war, the relevant references serving to highlight the cunning of Odysseus as the architect of the plan.[5] A more detailed account of the story of the Trojan Horse appears in the *Aeneid* of Roman author Virgil,[6] the story of how Trojan hero Aeneas becomes the ancestor of the Romans. For Virgil, this example of Greek subterfuge suited his Trojan-oriented narrative well, so it is no surprise that he made the most of it.

What is particularly striking is the distance in time of the writings of Homer and especially Virgil from the events they purport to describe. Little is known about Homer, including whether he actually existed at all, or whether his name was used as a label to encompass a poetic tradition. The *Iliad* and the *Odyssey* appear to have been composed between around 800 and 600 BCE, several centuries after the events they chronicle. Virgil's *Aeneid* was written between 29 and 19 BCE, more than a millennium after the fall of Troy. The tales would have come down to Homer through an oral tradition. Homer, as a poet, would have selected from them in a way that suited his story, and in the *Odyssey* he was writing a story about

Odysseus. In some other retellings of the tale of the Trojan Horse, in the works of other writers and through images on vases and other artworks, Odysseus frequently gets a much smaller role, and is on occasion absent altogether. Epeios, the builder of the horse, and the goddess Athena take centre-stage.[7]

The story of the Trojan Horse to have come down to us is largely a composite of the accounts of Homer and Virgil. It runs as follows. The Trojan War was precipitated by the capricious games of the gods, as Paris, son of King Priam of Troy, tasked with judging which of three goddesses was the fairest, chose Aphrodite. In return, Aphrodite made Helen, the beautiful wife of Menelaus, king of Sparta, fall in love with him. He took her to Troy, and the Greeks followed with a fleet of 1,000 ships. Through ten years of war, the many deeds, both heroic and cruel, committed by great warriors such as Achilles, were unable to resolve the stalemate.

The war was finally ended, not by great military feats on the battlefield, but by trickery. Odysseus had a plan. He instructed Epeios to build a wooden horse, big enough to hold an elite force of Greek soldiers. Epeios accomplished this with the help of the goddess Athena. The Greeks then feigned departure. A Greek soldier named Sinon volunteered to be left behind with the wooden horse, which, according to one classical account, even had a plaque on it, reading: 'For their return home, the Greeks dedicate this thank-offering to Athena.'[8] A touch that resonates across diplomatic gifts through the ages to the modern-day compliments card.

Sinon convinced the Trojans that the horse was an offering to atone for their earlier theft of the palladium, the wooden image of Athena that protected the city, as well as to ensure a safe journey home, and the Trojans brought the horse into the city. Laocoön guessed the plot, but he and his sons were quickly despatched by sea serpents sent by Poseidon, like Athena one of the gods favourable to the Greek side in the war, before his warning could be heeded. Another Trojan to suspect trickery was Cassandra, daughter of King Priam, but her curse was to utter true prophecies that would never be believed, and she was ignored. The Trojans instead celebrated the departure of the Greeks. At night, the soldiers emerged from the horse, opened the gate to the rest of the Greek forces, and the Trojans were massacred with great brutality.

Although the war ended in Greek victory, the gods were angered at the brutal manner of that victory, including the despoiling of temples, and punished the Greeks by delivering a fierce storm as their fleet returned. Some were shipwrecked. Odysseus managed to get back home only after an epic ten-year adventure-filled journey. While the gift of the wooden horse was a brilliant ruse to secure the city, the underhand and brutal nature of that victory meant that, in the end, there were no winners.

Did these events actually take place? By the early modern period, many questioned whether a city called Troy had ever existed. Archaeology would provide the answer. In the nineteenth century, an English expatriate named Frank Calvert, whose family owned part of the mound at Hisarlik in Anatolia, close to the Dardanelles, became convinced that this was the site of the ancient city. Calvert persuaded a wealthy German archaeologist named Heinrich Schliemann, who was single-mindedly trying to find the archaeological evidence of Homer's city, to lead an excavation there. They had indeed found Troy, though Schliemann had found the wrong Troy. He assumed that the city described by Homer lay at one of the lowest archaeological levels and dug a great trench through the site. The city he excavated belonged to the early Bronze Age, a millennium too early to be associated with the Trojan War.[9] Hisarlik is a complex site, with nine principal occupation levels and various sub-levels. Later research at the site has shown that the two leading candidates for the Troy destroyed by the Greeks are the settlements known as Troy VIh and Troy VIIa, whose interpretation was complicated by Schliemann's incautious excavation.

Historical evidence supplements the archaeological record. A Swiss scholar named Emil Forrer argued that the place name 'Taruisa' mentioned in Hittite texts corresponded to the Greek Troia, and 'Wilusa' referred to its alternate rendering as Ilios, there being metrical evidence from the *Iliad* and *Odyssey* that Ilios was originally rendered as Wilios.[10] If the 'Ahhiyawa' referred to in Hittite texts is a reference, as most scholars believe, to the Greeks, or Achaeans as Homer often calls them, a fragmentary story emerges from the texts in which Troy, or Wilusa, was a subject state of the Hittite Empire. The Greeks were problematic, including in providing support for a renegade named Piyamaradu, who attacked Wilusa. There is indeed one reference to the Hittite and Ahhiyawan kings having gone to war over Wilusa.[11]

Mycenaean pottery found at Troy is further evidence of contact between Trojans and Greeks.[12] A picture dimly emerges of conflict between two empires: the Hittites and the Mycenaean Greeks, which could have provided the setting for the Trojan War. While the archaeological evidence is disputed, the settlements of both Troy VI and Troy VIIa seem to have ended abruptly, the former through an earthquake, the latter possibly through fiery devastation. Both the Hittite and Mycenaean Empires would decline shortly thereafter.

But if Troy was a real place, and even if, more speculatively, there was indeed a Trojan War resulting in the sacking of the city by Greeks, surely the Trojan Horse itself was a work of fiction? The tale of troops hiding undetected in a wooden horse as the Trojans brought it into the city just feels too fanciful.

It is not however the first such story involving soldiers penetrating a besieged city through the ruse of a diplomatic gift. Several hundred years earlier than the fall of Troy, a papyrus describes a ploy by a general of Pharaoh Thutmose III, taking the city of Joppa by sending in a large gift of tribute in which 200 soldiers were concealed in baskets.[13]

Looked at from the perspective of a diplomatic gift, there is a certain logic to the choice of a horse as the creature through which the subterfuge was committed. Horses were clearly important to the Trojans. The *Iliad* is full of references to the Trojans as horse traders, and the prefix 'hippo-' appears in relation to many Trojan names.[14] Hittite royal archives include tablets referring to the training of horses.[15] A horse-related gift would therefore be judged by the Greeks to be likely to please the Trojans. A horse-shaped object was credible too as an offering to Athena, a goddess associated with the taming of horses.[16]

Writers in both classical and modern times have attempted to rationalise the story of the wooden horse by interpreting this fantastical creation as a reference to something more prosaic. The chief candidate is a battering ram. Pausanias, a Greek geographer of the second century CE, describes the creation of Epeios as a device aiming to breach the Trojan walls.[17] Reliefs suggest that Assyrian siege engines could look distinctly horse-like, particularly when covered with dampened animal hides for protection against attack with fire.

Alternatively, could the Trojan Horse have been a ship? The candidate here involves a type of Phoenician ship decorated with a horse's head and referred to by the Greeks as a *hippos*. Homer even refers to ships as 'sea-horses' at one point. The Trojan Horse, it is argued, might have been the tribute of a ship of this kind, with the Greek soldiers hidden in the hull.

A third theory is that the Trojan Horse is a metaphor for an earthquake. These are common in the region, and the archaeological evidence sup-ports the suggestion that an earthquake may have been responsible for the destruction of the settlement of Troy VI. Poseidon, one of the gods most ardently supporting the Greek side during the war, is best known as the god of the sea but was also god of both horses and earthquakes. If Athena represented the taming of horses, Poseidon embodied their wild nature.[18] So the gift of a horse might be a literary device to represent a destructive earthquake wrought by Poseidon to bring down the walls of the city and let in the Greeks.

A problem with such rationalising explanations is that they jar with the consequences of the wooden horse. The Trojan Horse is a brilliantly successful ruse: resulting in the immediate defeat of the Trojans and ending the long war. But it is not heroic. The gods turn against the Greeks for the brutal manner of their victory. When, in the *Odyssey*, Demodocus sings of the Trojan Horse and the defeat of Troy, the reaction of Odysseus is not satisfaction in recollection of his cunning, but to weep uncontrollably. A sense of shame hangs over the Trojan Horse. There would have been no such shame in the use of a battering ram,[19] or in the destruction of the city by an earthquake. We will never know if the Trojan Horse actually existed. But it does exist in the poetry of Homer and Virgil, from where it continues to inspire.

Lest it be thought that diplomatic gifts that contain a nasty surprise within are confined to the realms of mythology and ancient history, consider the case of a delightfully carved wooden plaque of the Great Seal of the United States, presented to the US ambassador in Moscow, W. Averell Harriman, by a delegation of Soviet Young Pioneers in August 1945, as a symbol of the friendship between the two wartime allies.[20] The Great Seal plaque was proudly hung in the ambassador's study, where it remained for several years.

It was eventually discovered to contain a covert listening device. With no battery or electrical circuitry, this proved to be a passive cavity resonator, activated by an external radio signal, at which point sound waves generated by conversations in the study would be bounced back as an audio signal to those listening in. It was only discovered when in 1951 a British technician was surprised to overhear American conversations on a Soviet radio channel. The listening device was the work of Léon Theremin, better known as the inventor of the electronic musical instrument that takes his surname.[21] Dubbed 'The Thing', it was a Trojan Horse for the twentieth century.

332 BCE

A WHIP, A BALL AND A CHEST OF GOLD

GIFTS FROM DARIUS III, KING OF THE ACHAEMENID EMPIRE, TO ALEXANDER THE GREAT, KING OF MACEDON

The *Alexander Mosaic* from the House of the Faun in Pompeii, depicting the Battle of Issus between Darius III and Alexander the Great.

This is the story of a diplomatic gift used, unsuccessfully, as a taunt. The gift plays out in a very specific way. The specific pattern is repeated by a different gift made more than 1,700 years later. An established and powerful leader is subject to military threats from an ambitious young ruler of neighbouring lands. The leader sends this young ruler a gift mocking his youth and inexperience, and advises him to abandon his plans of conquest. The young ruler reinterprets the gifted objects in a way that suggests they represent good omens for his success in defeating the powerful leader. The ambitious young ruler is victorious.

The story appears in a fantastical account of the deeds of Alexander the Great, known as the *Alexander Romance*. This was sometimes wrongly attributed to Callisthenes, a Greek historian and companion of Alexander the Great, who however predeceased Alexander, and in fact seems to date

31

from the third century CE, its unknown author generally, if rather unkindly, referred to as Pseudo-Callisthenes. The Greek-language original version has been lost, but the exploits of Alexander were a source of fascination during the Middle Ages, and the biography appeared in a mushrooming number of versions: some eighty, in twenty-four languages, by the seventeenth century.[1] The *Romance* presents the tallest of tales, becoming more far-fetched with every retelling.[2]

The gift from the ruler of Achaemenid Persia Darius III to Alexander is described in different ways in the various versions of the *Romance*: a fifth-century Armenian translation is believed to provide one of the closest approximations to the lost original.[3] The tale of the gift runs as follows. During his long campaigning against the large but unstable empire of Darius III, Alexander had sacked the city of Tyre (a historical event, which dates our tale to 332 BCE). Alexander then received a group of messengers bearing gifts from the Achaemenid ruler. These consisted of a whip, a ball and a chest of gold. The gifts were accompanied by a letter, in which Darius hurled a range of insults at Alexander, whom he advised to withdraw his troops and return to the lap of his mother, since at his age he still needed breast-feeding. Ouch. The gift of the whip was to demonstrate that Alexander still required discipline, the ball would give him something to play with children his own age, and the gold would allow Alexander to pay his 'thieves' to return home. If Alexander failed to heed the message of the gifts, he would be captured and crucified.[4]

Alexander read the letter out to his troops, who were alarmed at Darius's threats. Alexander however interpreted these tough words from the Persian leader as a sign of physical weakness: Darius lacked the strength to act, so he made a show of it in his writing. Alexander penned a return letter to Darius, in which he reinterpreted the meaning of Darius's gifts in his own favour. Alexander took the whip to mean that he would thrash Darius's forces and then make them slaves. He interpreted the ball as a sign that he would master the world: a sphere. The gold suggested that Darius had already indicated his obedience to Alexander, and was paying tribute.[5] This exchange presaged the defeat of Darius by Alexander's army.

One curiosity about the three gifts presented by Darius is that they are very different in nature. The whip and the ball are allegorical in intent, aiming to mock Alexander's youth and inexperience. The gold, in contrast, is an entirely functional gift: to provide Alexander with the funds to get his troops back to Macedonia and out of Darius's lands.[6]

In the retelling of the *Alexander Romance* across time and place, there were sometimes alterations to the gifts from Darius. Thus, a Syriac-language version adds a further gift to the whip, ball and gold: 10 measures of sesame seeds. Darius writes that if Alexander can count the seeds he will know how many troops he possesses. This engenders the response from Alexander of putting some of the seeds in his mouth, concluding that, while they are indeed numerous, they are tasteless. Alexander sends Darius some mustard seeds in return. On tasting some of those, the worried Persian leader comments that, while few in number, they are sharp.[7] The seeds reappear in some other versions of the tale, though not always from the same plant. Thus, one German version involves Darius despatching poppy seeds and getting peppercorns in return from Alexander.[8]

There seems to be no historical evidence of Darius making any such gift to Alexander. Nor have any hints of the story been found in sources independent of the *Alexander Romance*.[9] So it does not seem to be drawn from any wider legend about Alexander and, like much else in the *Alexander Romance*, appears to have been made up by its author.

The story does though have an antecedent in the tale, recounted among others by Herodotus, of gifts sent by the Scythians to Darius I in the course of his campaign, almost 200 years earlier, into the Scythian lands. The story runs that the Scythian chiefs sent Darius, without further explanation, a bird, mouse, frog and five arrows. (Which sounds rather like the kind of diplomatic gift you would expect from a cat.) Darius interpreted the gifts as representing Scythian submission to his power. A Persian nobleman named Gobryas offered an alternative explanation: that this was a threat, and the Persians would have to turn themselves into birds, mice or frogs to hide from the Scythian arrows. Since the Scythian campaign was altogether frustrating for Darius, who found it hard to engage with a nomadic people who lacked cities to protect, Gobryas's explanation was perhaps the more accurate.[10]

This earlier tale is structurally simpler than that of Darius III's gift to Alexander, with no trumping retort, but it similarly constitutes an allegorical approach to diplomatic gift-giving. A much later tale from a different part of the world is though almost identical in structure to that of Darius III's gift. It is found in the pages of Shakespeare, in the first Act of *Henry V*.

During a lull in the Hundred Years' War, the dauphin of France sends some emissaries to King Henry in England. The first ambassador offers a message from the French dauphin every bit as undiplomatic as that of

Darius's letter to Alexander. It similarly focuses on Henry's youth and inexperience. The dauphin:

> Says that you savour too much of your youth,
> And bids you be advised there's nought in France
> That can be with a nimble galliard won.[11]

The ambassador explains that the dauphin has therefore sent a gift suited to the king's character, and urges that he give up his claim to territories in France. The gift: tennis balls. The implication being that Henry is better suited to passing his time in frivolous youthful pastimes than waging war against the French.

Just as with Darius's gift to Alexander, this enrages its recipient and has the effect of summoning a trumping retort that subverts the meaning of the gifted objects. The tennis balls are transformed into cannon balls:

> And tell the pleasant prince this mock of his
> Hath turn'd his balls to gun-stones; and his soul
> Shall stand sore charged for the wasteful vengeance
> That shall fly with them: for many a thousand widows
> Shall this his mock mock out of their dear husbands;
> Mock mothers from their sons, mock castles down.[12]

It is tempting to venture that Shakespeare was drawing on the story of Darius's gift from the *Alexander Romance* in order to draw a parallel between Henry V and Alexander the Great as two youthful, dynamic and militarily successful rulers. However, unlike Darius's gift, that of the tennis balls presented to Henry is to be found in historical accounts. The tale features in Raphael Holinshed's *Chronicles of England, Scotland and Ireland*, whose second edition of 1587 was a key source for Shakespeare's history plays. Holinshed in turn seems to have drawn on earlier accounts, notably the *Chronicle* of Thomas of Otterbourne and the *Liber metricus* of Thomas Elmham, both of whom locate the event at Kenilworth, a castle favoured by Henry V.[13]

Surely though the tale cannot be true? Such a mocking gift makes for fine literature, but terrible diplomacy. The effect of the dauphin's gift is to so infuriate Henry that it strengthens his inclination to attack the French, setting in motion a chain of events that lead to Agincourt. While this passage in *Henry V* serves to underline the dauphin's ill-fittedness to rule, surely no one, however poor their diplomatic skills, could reason that sending a provoking taunt of a gift might advance their objectives of dissuading the English king from launching a campaign against them?

A more detailed account suggesting the possible historical origin of the tale is found in the writing of another contemporary chronicler, John Strecche, a canon of Kenilworth Priory, whose accounts focus on Henry's visits to Kenilworth Castle.[14] Strecche reports that Henry sent ambassadors to the dauphin in France to broker marriage with Catherine, the French king's daughter. The negotiations were fractious and unsuccessful, and Strecche records that the French in their frustration hurled insults at the English ambassadors, suggesting – in reference to Henry's youth – that they would send him little balls to play with as well as soft pillows to sleep on. On return to England, the emissaries reported these comments back to Henry, who was furious, threatening that he would play games with his cannon balls in the French streets. Soft pillows would be no use to the French, as he would hammer on their houses at dawn.[15] Hot tempers generated by tough and unsuccessful negotiations are a somewhat familiar feature of diplomatic life, and this account of the origin of the story feels more plausible than one based on the physical despatch of actual tennis balls. We shall never know, and the story does not seem to find any reference in French chronicles.[16]

Not all rulers wish to be diplomatic all the time, and there are documented historical examples of the use of gifts as a means of taunting or insulting the recipient. Thus in the 1430s, the leader of the Turkmen tribal federation of Aq Qoyunlu, Uthman Beg, sent a gift to the Mamluk ruler Sultan Barsbay comprising a mirror, sheep and robe of honour. The recipient was not pleased. The mirror suggested femininity, the sheep submission and, as we will see in a later story, a robe of honour was a gift offered by a superior to an inferior.[17] Barsbay does not however appear to have provided a trumping retort in response.

c.4 BCE

GOLD, FRANKINCENSE AND MYRRH

A GIFT FROM THE WISE MEN FROM THE EAST TO JESUS CHRIST

Three wise men bearing gifts. A mosaic in the Basilica of
Sant'Apollinare Nuovo, Ravenna.

Perhaps the most famous present in human history, the gift of gold, frankincense and myrrh by the wise men from the east to the infant Jesus, has inspired not only countless nativity plays, but also the very theme of the giving of presents at Christmas. Whether this can be viewed as a diplomatic gift depends on the answer to two questions. Who were these wise men? And who did they perceive the infant Jesus to be?

Given the prominence of the three kings from the Orient in contemporary retellings of the birth of Jesus Christ, there is surprisingly little detail given to the story in the Gospels. The nativity story itself appears in St Luke's Gospel, in which Mary and Joseph travel to Bethlehem in accordance with the taxation requirement of Caesar Augustus. There being no room at the inn, the newborn Christ is laid in a manger. Shepherds, watching their flock by night, are given the good news by the angel of the Lord.

The wise men from the east play no part, however, in this story. Their sole appearance comes in St Matthew's Gospel. Their visit to Bethlehem does not appear to coincide with Christ's birth: he is described as already a 'young child'.[1] The traditional placing of the wise men at the nativity is thus not borne out by the scriptures.

St Matthew's Gospel tells us that the 'wise men from the east'[2] arrive in Jerusalem, asking for the whereabouts of 'he that is born King of the Jews'.[3] They had seen his star in the east and had come to worship him. This request disconcerted the local ruler, Herod, who considered that the title 'king of the Jews' belonged to him. Having sought advice from the local chief priests and scribes, Herod is told that the prophecies foretell that the future ruler will be born in Bethlehem and directs the wise men to that town. The star reappears and leads the wise men to the young child. They fall down and worship him, and present him gifts of gold, frankincense and myrrh.

Herod attempted to use the wise men for his nefarious plan, by asking them to let him know when they had found the child, so that he might come and worship him too. Herod's designs were of course rather different, as his subsequent order to slay all the little children of Bethlehem of two years and under was to prove. Fortunately, God had warned the wise men in a dream not to return to Herod, so they simply headed off home, avoiding Jerusalem. With that, they disappear from the biblical narrative. The wise men were then looking for one that is born 'king of the Jews', a formulation that suggests they sought a child they believed was destined to take the role of a future political leader. This was not of course to be the destiny of Jesus Christ,[4] who was never to exercise political rule over anybody. It does though suggest that the wise men interpreted their journey as one of homage to a royal leader, and supports the suggestion that the gifts had a diplomatic character.

Who were the 'wise men from the east'? Matthew is silent on two features that have become central tenets of the way the wise men are presented to us today. Nowhere does he state that they were kings, and nowhere does he state that there were three of them. There is though an important clue to their identity in the Greek word used in Matthew's Gospel to describe the visitors, *mágoi*, whose precise meaning is not properly conveyed by the usual English translation of 'wise men'.

The *mágoi*, better known in their Latin plural, *magi*, were identified by Herodotus as one of six tribes of the Median people in the north-west of modern-day Iran. They were a learned tribe, the source of priests both for other Median tribes and the Persians.[5] The term magi came to be used more broadly to refer to priests of Zoroastrian and other Iranian religions. Greco-Roman writers identified these priests with the practices of magic and divination, including through the interpretation of dreams and astrology.[6] Indeed, the origin of the word 'magic' lies in the Greek *mágos*.

While astrology tended to be viewed negatively in Christian traditions because of its fatalistic determinism,[7] the magi are not referred to pejoratively in Matthew's Gospel, even though their status as astrologers is underlined by the comment that they came to worship the king of the Jews through the evidence of 'his star in the east'.[8] There are parallels between the story of the wise men and that of Balaam in the Old Testament Book of Numbers. Like the magi, Balaam is a foreign figure who arrives into the biblical narrative 'out of the mountains of the east'.[9] Both are the subject of attempted manipulation by a malevolent figure: Herod in the case of the magi; Balak, king of Moab, in that of Balaam. In neither case is that manipulation successful. Balaam, urged to curse Israel, delivers only positive prophecies, including the arrival of a 'Star out of Jacob'[10] that appears to foreshadow the journey of the magi.

A connection was made by early Christian authors not just between the star predicted by Balaam and that followed by the wise men,[11] but also between the individuals themselves. According to the third-century scholar Origen of Alexandria, it was reported that, descended from Balaam, 'a race and institution of magicians flourished in parts of the East'.[12] Therefore, on the birth of Christ, the magi were able to recognise the star and its significance in a way that the people of Israel did not. The story of the wise men as presented in Matthew can suggest the universality of the Christian message, in bringing non-Jews from other lands to worship the child. It can also suggest that the magi worshipped the infant as the future king of the Jews, an appropriate recipient for grand diplomatic gifts, rather than as the son of God. In this reading of the scriptures, the magi have correctly interpreted the significance of the star but have misread its message.[13]

The identification of the wise men with Zoroastrianism is made explicitly in an apocryphal text known as the *Arabic Infancy Gospel*, which probably derives from a Syriac original, believed to have been composed in the fifth or sixth centuries. This document follows the main lines of the story of the wise men as set out in Matthew, but with two significant embellishments. It claims that the wise men, in their journey to Jerusalem, were following 'the prophecy of Zoradascht', that is, Zoroaster.[14] And the magi receive a return gift: they are given one of the child's swaddling bands by Mary. On returning home, they cast this swaddling band into their holy fire. It is unharmed by the flames. They venerate the cloth among their treasures. In a longer recension of the text, Zoroaster is identified with Balaam.[15]

The story of the wise men was developed and embellished in all manner of early Christian writings, taking the tale in various directions. Among the most elaborate is a document known as the *Revelation of the Magi*, preserved in a later Syriac manuscript of the eighth century known as the *Chronicle of Zuqnin*, from the Turkish monastery where it was produced.[16] The tale is written from the perspective of the magi themselves, who are twelve in number. They live in the land of Shir, which seems to be located roughly on the territory of present-day China. They are wise men and kings, known as magi because of their practice of silent prayer.[17] They are descended from Seth, son of Adam, who wrote down revelations from his father in the world's first books. They have placed these in a Cave of Treasures of Hidden Mysteries within the Mountain of Victories, the scene of a monthly ritual of prayer. They have been waiting for generations for the appearance of a star above the Mountain of Victories, which will herald the arrival of God in human form.

The great day arrives, the star comes down to the Mountain of Victories and transforms itself into a human being. This being asks the magi to bring the unspecified gifts they have deposited in the cave exactly for this purpose, and take them to the place where it is being born in human form. Transforming itself back into a star, it guides the magi miraculously to Jerusalem, whose inhabitants are unable to see the star. In this version of the story, the star itself tells the magi not to obey Herod's request to tell him where the Messiah is to be found. In Bethlehem, the magi find the child in a cave, place their crowns under his feet and offer him their treasures. The star guides them back home, where the apostle Judas Thomas later arrives and baptises the magi, who then preach the Gospel across the world.[18]

The prevailing picture of the magi however gradually emerged as one depicting them as three kings. Their identification as kings serves to fulfil prophecies of the Old Testament in relation to the Messiah, such as that of Psalm 72 that 'all kings shall fall down before him'.[19] The view that they were three in number was helped along by the number of gifts they brought, with one gift associated with each king.

The first identified document giving the kings the names by which they are now most commonly known is the *Excerpta Latina Barbari*, the Latin translation of a lost Greek chronicle. The translation was made in

Merovingian Gaul in the sixth or seventh centuries, by someone with an imperfect knowledge of the two languages: hence 'bad Latin'. The original Greek text probably hails from fifth-century Alexandria.[20] The translation names the magi as Bithisarea, Melichior and Gathaspa, now more frequently rendered as Balthasar, Melchior and Caspar. An eighth-century text known as *Collectanea et flores*, falsely attributed to the Venerable Bede, ascribes a different age to each of the magi:[21] an elderly, white-bearded Melchior, a middle-aged, black-bearded Balthasar and a youthful, clean-shaven Caspar.

The magi were given not just different ages but different geographical provenances, with Balthasar frequently depicted in Renaissance art as black.[22] While the magi had largely been portrayed identically in their earliest depictions in Christian art, wearing the Phrygian cap that identified them as hailing from Persia,[23] their differentiation helped to emphasise the universal appeal of the Christian message.

Marco Polo, travelling along the Silk Road in the second half of the thirteenth century, recounted in decidedly matter-of-fact terms in his *Travels* seeing the 'large and beautiful monuments' that were the tombs of the three magi in the Persian city of Saba.[24] The bodies of the magi, who were called Jaspar, Melchior and Balthazar, were visible, with their hair and beards remaining.

He was able to find out no more about the men in Saba, but three days' travel away, in a village named Cala Ataperistan, 'the castle of the fire-worshippers', he was told that three kings of that region had travelled to worship a newborn prophet, bearing gifts of gold, frankincense and myrrh. The child had given them a small box in return, and they had departed. On their return journey, they had opened the box to find that it contained only a stone. The meaning of this gift was that the faith that they were developing should become as firm as a rock, but, failing to grasp the gift's significance, they had chucked it in disappointment down the nearest well. At that moment, a heavenly fire descended into the well. The magi immediately realised their mistake and the holy power of that gift, and took some of that fire, carefully carrying it back to their home country, where they placed it in a beautiful church. From that day, they kept the fire burning. The people of the area thereby became fire-worshippers.[25]

In the 1990s, writer Paul William Roberts travelled to the Iranian city of Saveh and identified an old mosque with Christian and Zoroastrian precursors, which he felt might have been the site of the tombs seen by Marco Polo, although, confusingly, there were just two sarcophagi in the building.

He tracked down a ruined castle nearby with the help of a Saveh dentist cum budding historian, concluding that he had reached Cala Ataperistan.[26]

The best-known reputed location of the bodies of the three kings is neither in Iran nor anywhere else to the east of Bethlehem, but Cologne Cathedral. The Shrine of the Three Kings is a glittering triple sarcophagus, the twelfth-century work of Nikolaus von Verdun and his assistants. The present Cologne Cathedral, the largest Gothic church in northern Europe, was purpose-built to house it. It is said that the relics of the magi were discovered by Saint Helena and taken to Constantinople. From there, they headed to Milan in 344, when they were entrusted by the emperor to Eustorgio I, bishop of Milan, who had journeyed to Constantinople for the confirmation of his election as bishop. He reputedly brought them to the city in a marble sarcophagus pulled by oxen. On arrival into Milan, according to different tellings of the tale, the oxen collapsed or the cart became irretrievably stuck in the mud, and Eustorgio took this as a sign to build a church at that spot to house the relics. They remained there until Friedrich I Barbarossa's raid on Milan in 1162, when they were looted and gifted to the archbishop of Cologne. Cologne Cathedral is today the most visited landmark in Germany, attesting to the continuing draw of the magi.

What of the gifts presented by the wise men? They seem to have been entirely credible as diplomatic gifts of the time: all were expensive and desired commodities, typical of gifts to prominent personages in the pre-modern era.[27] The Old Testament Book of Isaiah, in its vision of the glorious future of Jerusalem, offers a foretaste of gifts of gold and incense.[28] The three gifts are frequently ascribed a symbolic significance. Thus, the *Collectanea et flores* suggests that the gold presented by Melchior is a symbol of Christ's kingship, the frankincense offered by Caspar represents his divinity and the myrrh given by Balthasar symbolises his mortality, myrrh being associated with the embalming of bodies. This is also the symbolism suggested by the popular Christmas carol, 'We Three Kings of Orient Are', composed in 1857 by John Henry Hopkins Jr. The story offered to Marco Polo has it that the different gifts are an attempt by the magi to ascertain whether the child is an earthly king, a god or a physician. If the infant took the gold, he was a king, if he took the frankincense, a god, if the myrrh, a physician. Since he accepted all three gifts, they concluded that he was at once king, and god, and physician.[29]

The wise men described by Matthew thus evolved in Christian writing and representation from depictions as Zoroastrian priests to three kings, of different ages and different geographical backgrounds. Matthew suggests that they regarded the infant as one who was born king of the Jews, and it seems entirely credible to view their gifts as diplomatic ones. In such an interpretation though, there is a sense that the wise men, while venerating the infant Jesus, were doing so as a king rather than as the son of God. As so often with diplomatic gifts, the encounter was interpreted differently by the giver and the receiver.

757

AN ORGAN

A GIFT FROM CONSTANTINE V, EMPEROR OF THE BYZANTINE EMPIRE, TO PÉPIN III, KING OF THE FRANKS

Hydraulic organ depicted on a Roman second-century CE mosaic found at Zliten in modern-day Libya.

Diplomatic gifts frequently contain an element of boastfulness. Offering a gift comprising a technology unknown in the receiving state has a dual advantage for the giver. First, the gift is likely to be appreciated, as something entirely new. Second, it serves to send an implicit message about the technological superiority of the gifting state. It can provoke awe. It can open up new markets for this advanced product, though this is not a relevant consideration in all contexts. In some situations, the gifting state will however be mindful of the risk that the gift might enable their technological advance to be studied, and copied, and comparative advantage lost. In this process of studying, and copying, a diplomatic gift may provide a conduit for the transfer of ideas and technologies between different cultures.

The gift of an organ from the Byzantine emperor to the Frankish King Pépin III in 757 has been identified by some historians as a seminal one, the occasion for the reintroduction of the organ into western Europe,[1] an event that would pave the way for the intimate association between that instrument and church music. It has even been suggested that the emperor's gift may have been a double organ, played simultaneously by two organists, allowing for the performance of two-part music, and the source of the whole tradition of Western polyphony, a style that would then transfer from the organ into the vocal field.[2]

Such arguments however load a great deal on to a single gift about which little is actually known. The exploits of the Frankish kings are recorded in the *Royal Frankish Annals,* which, although propagandist in tone, are a vital source in understanding the politics of the time. The arrival of the organ from Constantine V, the Byzantine emperor, was clearly a major event, garnering some twenty references in the annals,[3] but the amount of detail offered by these references is thin. The date was 757. The organ was a gift, arriving with other gifts. Pépin, the Frankish king, was at Compiègne. The organ was previously unknown in the country. The gift was part of the Byzantine emperor's efforts to enter into peaceful relations with the Franks.[4] There is nothing here about what type of organ this was, or what Pépin gave in return. There is also a possible reference to this organ from a source on the gifting side, in the form of a twelfth-century copy of an earlier work in Arabic by an engineer named Muristos, who talks of the construction of a hydraulic siren organ for an unnamed Frankish king.[5] If this is a reference to the organ sent to Pépin, this suggests it may have been more a loud noisemaking device than a musical instrument.

Before considering the question of whether the organ gifted by the Byzantine emperor really was the mechanism for the reintroduction of the instrument to western Europe, another question arises: what was the motivation of the emperor in making such a fine gift to the Frankish king? Pépin III, also known as Pépin le Bref (the Short), was the son of Frankish Prince Charles Martel and father of Charlemagne, and thus had the genealogical misfortune to be sandwiched between two more celebrated historical figures. This has had the effect of rather overshadowing his own achievements, which were in themselves considerable, including as the first Carolingian to become king of the Franks, securing the support of the pope to dispose of the figurehead Merovingian ruler Childeric III in 751, who was conveniently placed in a monastery.

If Pépin's nickname seems a little harsh, it was as nothing when set against that accorded to the Byzantine Emperor Constantine V, who was popularly known as Constantine Copronymus, or Constantine the Dung-Named, a name linked to a tale that as a baby he defecated in the baptismal font just as the priest was calling his name out. The harshness of the nickname was down to the opposition generated by his championing of iconoclasm, a movement condemning the devotional use of images and veneration of relics. Constantine was also an able administrator and military leader who strengthened Byzantium's eastern frontier and control of the Balkans.

With Constantine focused on Byzantium's immediate neighbours, the empire's territories in Italy were relatively neglected. The Exarchate of Ravenna fell to the Germanic Lombards, who were in turn defeated by Pépin, acting in support of the papacy, to whom he would donate the conquered lands, marking the creation of the Papal States. This alliance between the papacy and the Carolingian kings would reach its apotheosis in the crowning of Charlemagne as 'emperor of the Romans' by Pope Leo III on Christmas Day 800. This all gives the impression of an increasing distance between western and eastern Europe: the separate worlds of Byzantium, the Greek-speaking Christian east, on the one hand, and on the other the alliance between the papacy in Rome and the Carolingian kings, the Latin-speaking Christian west.[6]

The extent of the separation between these two Christian worlds should however not be overstated. There remained a good deal of trade and diplomatic exchange between them.[7] Constantine V wanted the restoration of his territories in central Italy and seems to have alighted on a strategy to achieve this through wooing the Frankish king and thereby breaking the Frankish alliance with the pope. This was the context in which Constantine sent his fine diplomatic gift of an organ to Pépin III. The numerous references to the gift in the annals suggest that it indeed landed well, though it would in any case have been in Pépin's interests to highlight the gift as evidence of the international acceptance of his rule, his ouster of the Merovingians being a relatively recent memory.

Constantine's courtship of the Frankish king extended to an offer, albeit unrealised, for the marriage of his son Leo, the future Leo IV, with Pépin's daughter Gisela. There is some evidence that these overtures had an effect, with Frankish support for the popes becoming notably less substantial towards the end of Pépin's reign, though Pépin's death in 768 put a halt to this dalliance.[8]

The Byzantine emperors continued to make diplomatic overtures to Pépin's son Charlemagne. The empress-regent, Irene, commenced negotiations, again destined not to bear fruit, for the marriage of her son Constantine to Rotrude, daughter of Charlemagne. Rotrude eventually became a nun, following her aunt Gisela to Chelles Abbey. Constantine met a worse fate: he was blinded by supporters of his mother, Irene, clearing her path to rule alone.

By the late 780s, Charlemagne and Irene were pitted against each other in southern Italy and all thought of alliance was gone. Late in Charlemagne's rule, in 812, organ diplomacy reared its head again: emissaries of the Byzantine Emperor Michael I Rangabe reportedly brought one to Charlemagne's court at Aix-la-Chapelle.[9] It is not clear whether the organ was a diplomatic gift. A suggestion that it was surreptitiously studied by Charlemagne's craftsmen rather suggests that it was to be taken away again by the emissaries at the conclusion of their mission. Some historians question whether this organ ever existed, since the account is found not in contemporary sources but the late ninth-century work of Notker Balbulus (the Stammerer — this was quite the historical period for pejorative nicknames), and it is possible that the story may have been confounded with Pépin's organ or another gift.[10]

So was the gift of an organ to Pépin III the key link in the reintroduction of the instrument to western Europe and its introduction to church music? The construction of the first hydraulic organ is usually credited to Ctesibius, a Greek inventor based in Alexandria in the third century BCE, a city that was then a scientific powerhouse.[11] The use of the hydraulic organ spread across the Roman Empire. One was unearthed in excavations in 1931 at the Roman site of Aquincum in present-day Budapest: an inscription revealed it to be the gift of a magistrate named Victorinus to a guild of which he was president.[12] Several Roman emperors had a passion for the hydraulic organ, including Nero.[13] It accompanied weddings, gladiatorial contests and circus performances, though it was not linked to the early Christian church.[14]

When, in the fourth century, Roman Emperor Theodosius I had an Egyptian obelisk of Thutmose III re-erected in Constantinople, a relief sculpted on the pediment depicted two organs in a scene at the hippodrome.[15] In the Byzantine Empire, the organ seems to have continued to be associated with secular contexts, including large public spectacles, not religious ones. The technology of the pneumatic organ, using bellows, was also developed. In western Europe, however, the technology of organ construction appears to have been lost during the barbarian migrations.[16] Thus, by the eighth century, Byzantium was in possession of a technology lost to the Franks.

The historical record is however simply too weak to be able to tell us with any clarity the importance of the gift to Pépin III in the process through which organs came to be associated with the churches of western Europe. While the organ gifted by Constantine V was clearly special, there are few clues as to what type of organ it was, and as we have seen, at least one of these hints that it may have been more akin to a siren than a musical instrument.[17] The interpretation of early texts for evidence of the diffusion of the organ in western Europe is challenging, not least because the Latin word *organum* was used in ambiguous ways: as likely to refer to 'organised music' in general as to a specific musical instrument.[18]

In 826, Charlemagne's son Louis I (the Pious) brought a Venetian church minister named Georgius to Aachen, where he constructed a hydraulic organ in the Byzantine style.[19] The ninth-century Utrecht Psalter contains an illustration of a double hydraulic organ, with the two players each depicted urging their two pumping assistants towards greater exertions.[20] Ambitious size seems to have been a trend in the early organs: one built at Winchester Cathedral in the tenth century had 400 pipes, two players and required seventy men to work it.

While it is impossible to say with certainty how important a role was played by the organ gifted to Pépin III in the reintroduction of the organ to western Europe, it was clearly a gift that was both remarkable to and appreciated by its recipients. Two generations later, the organ was sufficiently desired as a musical instrument that his grandson brought an expert craftsman from Venice to construct one, thereby demonstrating that the technology of Byzantium had been mastered in the Frankish kingdom too.

AN ELEPHANT

A GIFT FROM HARUN AL-RASHID, CALIPH OF THE ABBASID CALIPHATE, TO CHARLEMAGNE, EMPEROR OF THE CAROLINGIAN EMPIRE

Twelfth-century fresco of an elephant carrying a castle, from the
Hermitage of San Baudelio de Berlanga.

Our stories include a veritable menagerie of wild beasts, including two elephants, for a good reason. Exotic animals were gifts guaranteed to impress. In earlier times, unfamiliar animals could seem magical. The first sight of a rhinoceros or giraffe before the era of mass communications was a thing of wonder. The gifting of a mighty and unfamiliar beast such as an elephant would suggest power on the part of the giver. For the recipient, the possession of such a creature would in turn be a mark of their importance, to be paraded for the wonderment of their subjects.

The possession of exotic animals was in many times and places an occupation reserved for a ruling elite, with beasts gathered in menageries in royal palaces. The impracticality of the gift of a wild beast ensured its exclusivity and added to its prestige. Transporting the gift was frequently a major and sometimes dangerous undertaking. Exotic animals had a habit

51

of dying when moved to strange climes and fed unfamiliar diets. Their upkeep could be hugely expensive. The term 'white elephant' derives from the receipt of sacred beasts from monarchs in south-east Asia: it was both a great honour to receive such a creature and a major financial outlay. There are many examples of the regifting by monarchs of exotic animals received as presents, perhaps after the initial wonderment generated by the creature had started to pale, and the expense had started to bite.

The gift at the dawn of the ninth century of an elephant named Abu'l Abbas involves two of the great rulers of the age, Harun al-Rashid and Charlemagne. Harun al-Rashid was the fifth Abbasid caliph, who presided over a golden era of the caliphate, with Baghdad one of the most opulent cities of the world. Charlemagne, crowned by the pope in St Peter's Basilica in the year 800 as 'emperor of the Romans', was no longer simply the Frankish king, but the first emperor of western Europe since the fall of the Western Roman Empire.

While Harun's capital of Baghdad and Charlemagne's of Aachen were distant from each other, there were good reasons why the two leaders would be interested in working together. Both were concerned about the ambitions of two other powers: the Byzantine Empire in the east, and the Umayyads in Spain. The latter had posed a major challenge to the Franks in the previous century through an invasion of Gaul halted by their defeat by Charlemagne's grandfather, Charles Martel, at the Battle of Tours in 732. The Umayyads had been overthrown in the east by the Abbasids in 750 but remained entrenched in southern Spain under Abd al-Rahman I, a continued thorn in the side of both Franks and Abbasids.

Good relations with Harun al-Rashid were important to Charlemagne for reasons of religion as well as geostrategy. Jerusalem fell within the Abbasid territories, and Charlemagne showed a strong interest in the well-being of the Christians of Palestine.[1] This interest was fuelled by the diplomatic activities of the patriarch of Jerusalem, who in 799 sent a monk to Charlemagne's court at Aachen, bearing relics and a benediction as gifts.[2] The patriarch's motives in sending such a mission were less likely to do with any grand political design, for he would not have dared to cut across the role of the caliph, Harun al-Rashid, on this score, and more about exploring the potential generosity of Charlemagne as a supporter of his church.

If this was indeed the patriarch's goal, it seems he was successful, for Charlemagne sent his own envoy, a priest named Zachariah, back to Jerusalem with the monk, laden with gifts for the holy places.[3] While

Charlemagne was in Rome for his coronation in December 800, Zachariah arrived back, accompanied this time by two monks sent by the patriarch, bringing with them as diplomatic gifts the keys of the Holy Sepulchre and Calvary, and a banner.[4] The later account of a Breton monk named Bernard the Wise, visiting Palestine in the 860s, offers a description of Charlemagne's largesse in Jerusalem, mentioning that he had funded a hostel for Western pilgrims and a library at the Church of St Mary, and hinting that the church itself and some further property may also have benefitted from his generosity.[5]

There had already been exchanges between the Franks and Abbasids. Pépin III, Charlemagne's father, sent a diplomatic mission to the then Abbasid caliph, Al-Mansur, in 765. The mission returned three years later, accompanied by emissaries of the caliph bearing diplomatic gifts.[6] Pépin personally escorted the emissaries as far as Marseille on the way back.[7]

Charlemagne sent a delegation to Harun al-Rashid in 797. According to the *Royal Frankish Annals*, it comprised three emissaries: Lantfrid, Sigimund and a third man, a merchant named Isaac the Jew.[8] Four years later, in 801, two envoys arrived in Italy, where Charlemagne was then travelling, one sent by Harun al-Rashid, the other probably by his governor in North Africa, Ibrahim ibn al-Aghlab. They brought the sad news that both Lantfrid and Sigimund had died during the mission, but the rather happier tidings that Isaac was on his return journey from Baghdad, bearing many gifts from the caliph, including an elephant.[9]

Charlemagne tasked his notary Ercanbald with organising a ship to bring Isaac, elephant and other assorted gifts from North Africa, and they duly arrived in Liguria in the autumn of 801.[10] Given the onset of winter, they delayed marching over the Alps until the following year. Isaac arrived in Aachen in the summer of 802, having successfully delivered the elephant, whose name, we learn from the *Annals*, was Abu'l Abbas.

Since no elephant had been seen in western Europe for generations, Abu'l Abbas presumably inspired wonderment, but the *Annals* are frustratingly silent on the matter. The creature gets just one further mention, in 810, when Charlemagne learned of an incursion by the Danish King Gudfred. On his way to battle, Charlemagne stopped at a place called Lippeham, possibly at the confluence of the Rivers Lippe and Rhine. Here, we are told, the elephant died.[11] The reference to the animal in the context of Charlemagne's battle preparations might imply that the Carolingian emperor used him as a war elephant, but the *Annals* offer no information on this score.

According to Einhard, dedicated courtier of Charlemagne and author of his master's biography, *Vita Karoli Magni*, Charlemagne had specifically asked Harun al-Rashid for an elephant.[12] While this assertion might suggest both that this was a solicited diplomatic gift and that securing an elephant might have been part of the motivation for the despatch of Charlemagne's mission of 797, Einhard is a highly unreliable source, dedicated to rearranging the facts to present the Carolingian emperor in the most favourable light possible. Einhard also claimed that the elephant was the only one possessed by the caliph.[13] Einhard's assertions here essentially seek to change the meaning of the gift. From a present that would presumably have been intended by Harun al-Rashid as a demonstration of the wonders of the caliphate, Einhard's reworking of the story has the effect of highlighting not Harun's power but Charlemagne's: a ruler so mighty that the Abbasid caliph is prepared to give him his sole elephant at Charlemagne's request.[14]

There were further diplomatic missions between Aachen and Baghdad. Charlemagne sent a second delegation in 802, which returned some four years later. One of the envoys, Rodbertus, died during or shortly after his return, continuing the alarmingly poor survival rate of Charlemagne's ambassadors to the Abbasid court. Einhard suggests that this delegation first visited Jerusalem, with gifts for the Holy Sepulchre, before heading to Baghdad where, he claims, the caliph offered Charlemagne jurisdiction over holy sites in Jerusalem, offering him 'that sacred and salutary place'.[15] In 807, an envoy of Harun al-Rashid named Abdulla arrived at Aachen. Two representatives of the new patriarch of Jerusalem, monks named George and Felix, were also there, though it is not wholly clear from the *Annals* whether this was a joint mission of both caliph and patriarch.[16] Abdulla brought more lavish gifts, and while there were no elephants this time, the chronicler of the *Royal Frankish Annals* was particularly taken by a remarkable water clock that, among various intricate features, marked the hours by means of brass balls that dropped on to a cymbal.[17]

Thus, there were a succession of cordial diplomatic missions, involving some remarkable gifts. What though did they achieve? There has been much debate around Einhard's reference to the ceding by Haroun to Charlemagne of jurisdiction over holy sites in Jerusalem.[18] There is no mention of such an award in the more measured and reliable *Royal Frankish Annals*. It is likely that Einhard, in his efforts to rearrange the facts to place Charlemagne in the best possible light, refashioned something minor into an impressive-sounding concession. This might be a considerable over-egging of the gifts by the patriarch of the keys of the Holy Sepulchre and Calvary, which would have been purely symbolic in nature.[19] Other scholars have suggested that Haroun might have made a small concession to Charlemagne, such as the Church of St Mary the Latin in Jerusalem, whose library the Carolingian emperor endowed.[20]

If Einhard greatly overstated the importance of what, if anything, was granted to Charlemagne in Jerusalem, the work of Notker Balbulus, 'the Stammerer', towards the end of the ninth century, embellished matters even further. In its pages, Harun al-Rashid hands over the Holy Lands to Charlemagne, though, since the domains of the Carolingian emperor are so distant, Harun offers to take on the role of steward of the lands on his behalf.[21] As the myth of Charlemagne grew with the passage of time from the emperor's life, the stories became ever more fantastical: the tenth-century account of a monk named Benedict has Charlemagne himself travelling to Jerusalem, his exploits in the east being little less than the peaceful subjugation of the local rulers.[22] These works seek, in increasingly fanciful ways, to demonstrate the domination of Charlemagne's influence across the known world, as a true successor to the emperors of ancient Rome. Yet while Western accounts embellished with increasing fervour the achievements of Charlemagne's diplomacy with Baghdad, the Abbasid records made no reference to it.

In truth, the results of these exchanges between Aachen and Baghdad seem to have been decidedly modest. The memory of Abu'l Abbas the elephant has however survived. In 2018, a medieval studies student at the University of Notre Dame in Indiana named Karen Neis published an illustrated children's book about the elephant's journey from Baghdad to Aachen.[23] It highlighted the way that a Christian, Muslim and Jew worked together to transport the elephant thousands of miles, in a text that aimed to reassure children who might be worried about having to move home. Elephants, it seems, are never forgotten.

950

A SILK CLOAK AND A BAG OF GOLD COINS

A GIFT FROM CONSTANTINE VII PORPHYROGENITUS, EMPEROR OF THE BYZANTINE EMPIRE, TO LIUDPRAND, ENVOY OF BERENGAR, MARGRAVE OF IVREA

Byzantine Emperor Nikephoros II Phokas, described by Liudprand of Cremona as 'a monstrosity of a man, a dwarf, fat-headed and with tiny mole's eyes'.

The association of individual powers with signature diplomatic gifts has been a feature of many historical periods, from the gold of ancient Egypt to the cigars of modern-day Cuba. Such signature gifts should be desired products, not widely available outside the gifting state, or at least not to the quality it can produce, and closely associated with it, and thereby able to serve as a form of calling-card.

One of the most notable signature products in the history of diplomatic gift-giving, in a practice spanning hundreds of years, was the gifting of silks by the Byzantine Empire. Between the fourth and twelfth centuries, silk served as an integral part of the ceremonies of the Byzantine court.[1] Silk was prominent in the curtains and coverings of palace life. The elaborate silk costumes of the emperor inspired a sense of awe among his subjects.[2] The use of different costumes for each type of official at court served as a mark of a clear hierarchy.[3]

Silks were costly. The cost was in part a function of the technical complexity of the product and the high raw material costs involved. The weaving of intricate patterns required specialised machinery, skilled labour and much time. The dyes used to make the most valued silks were expensive to produce, particularly in respect of the most coveted colour of all, the imperial purple, extracted from the glands of sea snails of the 'murex' family.[4] The cost and rarity of the silks was further enhanced by the policies of the Byzantine Empire in regulating their production, including through an imperial monopoly in respect of the murex purple silks, and through tight restrictions on exchange.[5]

Silk was not produced in Christian western Europe before the tenth century. This region was reliant on silks from Byzantium and from Islamic powers in the east and, from the eighth century, Spain.[6] Silk was a desired product in western European courts. It was used, as in Byzantium and the Islamic east, for ceremonial attire and curtains and wall hangings. The desire of Western courts to replicate the grand ceremonial of the Byzantine Empire was also perhaps part of the appeal here. In the Christian west of Europe, silk had two further functions that seem less clearly displayed in its use in the Christian east. Both of these appear in a religious context: as a shroud for dead rulers or the relics of saints, and to line or protect the pages of religious books.[7]

Silk was therefore a product not readily available to the rulers of Western Europe, but highly desired by them. It embodied the authority and opulence of the Byzantine Empire, giving it the quality of a signature product. It was high value but compact, and thus easily transportable. It was, in short, the perfect diplomatic gift.

As is so often the case with diplomatic gifts, the meaning of the gift was however rather different when viewed from the perspectives of giver and receiver. For Byzantium, the emperor was God's regent on earth. The presence of Christian kingdoms outside its borders could be reconciled with this model by investing their rulers with the attributes of imperial courtiers.[8] Gifts of silks from Byzantine emperors were intended to place the recipient in a form of symbolic subservience. External rulers were accorded different ranks in the Byzantine hierarchy according to their perceived importance. Of the many Byzantine patterned silks to have survived in western Europe, most of those bearing imperial motifs such as portraits of Byzantine emperors or depictions of lions or eagles are found within the territories of the medieval kingdom of France and the Holy Roman Empire. This appears to reflect the Byzantine view that only these two rulers could properly be considered kings. Other Western rulers were assigned a lower status, and less prestigious silken gifts.[9]

It is possible that the use of silks by Western Christian rulers in sacral as well as secular contexts marks an attempt to change the meaning of the gift,[10] removing its association with subservience to the Byzantine emperor. A fabric probably gifted to the Holy Roman Emperor Henry II, patterned with many embroideries depicting an enthroned emperor, provides one example of this process. The embroidered portraits bear an inscription that appears to be the name 'Henry', which has led to an assumption that the portraits are those of Henry II himself. Yet they appear stylistically to depict a Byzantine emperor. US scholar Warren Woodfin has argued that this is exactly what they were. He suggests that the awkwardness of a gift bearing the portrait of the Byzantine emperor, and thus symbolising the imagined subservience of the Holy Roman Empire to Byzantium, was neatly circumvented by the addition of the word 'Henry' next to the portraits, thereby converting them to images of Henry II himself. After Henry's death, the silk was placed on his tomb, though it later underwent a further transformation from a silk hanging to a cope, linked to Henry's spouse Cunegunda, possibly in connection with her canonisation in 1200.[11]

A good illustration of the attractiveness of Byzantine silks as diplomatic gifts is provided by the entertaining writings of Liudprand of Cremona, a tenth-century counsellor, priest and diplomat who described two contrasting missions to the Byzantine capital of Constantinople on behalf of two different rulers.

Liudprand was born into a wealthy family of Pavia in northern Italy around 920. His father had led a diplomatic mission to Constantinople in 927 on behalf of Hugh of Arles, the king of Italy. Diplomatic gifts had both impeded and assured the success of that mission. Two dogs, one of Hugh's presents to the emperor, Romanos I Lekapenos, had very nearly bitten their intended recipient. Fortunately, he had added a highly valued gift of his own: two Slavonic tribal chiefs, then in revolt against the emperor, captured when they had attempted to attack his convoy on its way to Constantinople.[12] Liudprand's father sadly died shortly after his return. His mother married again and, establishing a pattern, his stepfather led a further mission to Constantinople on behalf of Hugh in 942. Liudprand meanwhile had himself joined the royal household, initially as a singing page.

Hugh of Arles died in 948, and power in Italy fell into the hands of Berengar, the margrave of Ivrea, though the title of king was formally held by Hugh's son Lothair until the latter's death in 950, possibly poisoned by Berengar. Liudprand became a private secretary to Berengar, who decided to despatch a mission to Constantinople in 949, after receiving a letter from the emperor, Constantine VII Porphyrogenitus, inviting him to send an envoy.[13] Liudprand, whose writings show a distinct hostility to his master, records that Berengar's main motive in his choice of envoy was to find someone who would undertake the journey at no cost to himself. He persuaded Liudprand's stepfather to underwrite the expense of sending his stepson as his envoy on the grounds that it would provide the young man with a good opportunity to learn Greek.[14]

Liudprand is awestruck at his first meeting with the emperor, writing of the roars emerging from bronze lions, and of an emperor raised to the ceiling. Making conversation difficult. Liudprand finds himself embarrassed by the fact that the parsimonious Berengar has not provided him with any fine diplomatic gifts for the emperor. He has been furnished with nothing more than a letter and is forced to pretend that the gifts he had purchased himself, which he had intended to present on his own account, came from his master. These include various items of weaponry and, a gift particularly esteemed by the emperor, four young eunuchs. Traders of Verdun were apparently at the heart of the European eunuch business at the time.[15]

The eunuchs seem to have done the trick, as Liudprand receives a dinner invitation from the emperor three days later. Again, he finds this an impressive affair, writing of fruit brought in on golden bowls that are so heavy they are swung on to the dining table by means of ropes hanging through openings in the ceiling. Liudprand receives a 'handsome present' at the end of the dinner, though he does not reveal what.[16]

His stay in Constantinople seems to have been an extended one, as he is still there for the Feast of Palms, where he witnesses a lengthy ceremony in which the emperor hands out presents to the office-holders of his court. These are carefully calibrated to match the rank of the recipient and take the form of bags of gold coins and silk cloaks. The first to be summoned, the marshal of the palace, carries off an evidently considerable weight of gold coin on his shoulders, together with four cloaks. The emperor sends his chancellor to enquire how Liudprand is enjoying the ceremony, at which the envoy, fishing outrageously for a gift for himself, responds that 'it would please me ... if it did me any good'.[17] While not the most subtle of approaches, it evidently achieved its aim, as Liudprand is presented with a large cloak and a pound of gold coins: '[A] gift which he willingly made and I even more willingly accepted.'[18]

Liudprand became increasingly disillusioned with Berengar and headed to Germany, where he managed to join the court of Otto the Great. Liudprand flourished, undertaking diplomatic missions on Otto's behalf, evidently making himself useful in supporting Otto's Italian ambitions and securing the title of bishop of Cremona. In 968, Liudprand undertook a further mission to Constantinople, a role that formed the subject matter of his book *Relatio de legatione Constantinopolitana*. His impressions could hardly have contrasted more strongly with those of his mission in 949, for the decidedly undiplomatic Liudprand seems to have detested everything from start to finish.

The purpose of Liudprand's mission was to conclude a treaty of marriage between his master's son Otto, the future Otto II, and the daughter of the former Byzantine emperor. It was probably doomed from the start, as the Byzantine emperor, the military strategist Nikephoros II Phokas, was concerned about Otto's activities in Italy, and it would be completely undermined by the arrival while he was in Constantinople of a delegation from Pope John XIII. The latter had attempted to intervene in support of the marriage, but his letter to the Byzantine emperor served only to offend the Byzantines by appearing to equate Nikephoros as 'emperor of the Greeks' and Otto as 'emperor of the Romans'.[19] The papal envoys ended up in a Byzantine jail.[20]

Liudprand moans about every aspect of his treatment and stay in Constantinople, from the quality of his accommodation to the demeaning table position he is accorded at official dinners. He describes Nikephoros as 'a monstrosity of a man, a dwarf, fat-headed and with tiny mole's eyes'.[21] And much more in that vein. According to Liudprand's account, most of the exchanges between envoy and emperor involved little more than insults and point scoring. Liudprand becomes progressively more agitated that, as the months drag on and with all prospect of a marriage contract clearly off the table, the Byzantines still do not give him permission to leave their city.

When finally allowed to depart, Liudprand's last argument with his Byzantine hosts concerns silks, providing clear evidence of their attractiveness in western Europe. His hosts accuse him of attempting to smuggle silks out of Constantinople in his baggage and demand that he produce all those he has acquired during his stay, allowing him to keep only the lower quality items. They take away all the prestigious items of purple silk.

Addressing Otto and his son, Liudprand rails at the unfairness that 'these soft, effeminate creatures, with their long sleeves and hoods and bonnets, idle liars of neither gender, should go about in purple, while heroes like yourselves, men of courage, skilled in war, full of faith and love, submissive to God, full of virtues, may not!'[22] The response of his hosts to Liudprand's complaints is essentially to argue that the superiority of the Byzantine Empire in wealth and wisdom should be matched by superiority in dress.

Liudprand continues his arguments against the confiscation of his silks, claiming that back home prostitutes and conjurors wore Byzantine silks, procured from traders from Venice and Amalfi. His hosts are outraged and promise that such smugglers will in future be given a beating, 'and have their hair clipped close'.[23] Liudprand's final gambit is to point out that during his earlier mission in the time of Constantine Porphyrogenitus he had purchased a far larger quantity of silk and faced no such problems on departure. His hosts suggest that this is a reflection of the esteem in which Nikephoros holds Otto. Thus insulted, Liudprand is able to leave, minus his purple silks. He leaves some parting thoughts about his stay in the form of a poem scribbled on the wall of his detested lodgings, evidently an early equivalent of a scathing Tripadvisor review.

By restricting access to their finest silks, the Byzantine emperors could ensure that these remained among the most desired of diplomatic gifts.

*c.*1028

A FRAGMENT OF THE TRUE CROSS

A GIFT FROM THE EMPEROR OF THE BYZANTINE EMPIRE TO MANEGOLD, COUNT OF DONAUWÖRTH

King Louis IX carrying the Crown of Thorns.

Religious relics form a distinctive category of diplomatic gifts. The distinctiveness arises for two principal reasons. First, because they are gifts highly desired by recipients who are co-religionists, but of much less interest to recipients who are not. Second, because their value is not easy to quantify, unlike a gift of, say, gold. This means that for the recipient of such a gift, it is difficult to determine an appropriate level of reciprocal gift. We will explore the consequences of this inherent imbalance.

The veneration of relics characterises some religions, but not all. For example, in the Christian religion, it became from early times an important component of the cults of saints and martyrs.[1] From the belief that saints can intercede on behalf of the faithful flowed a veneration of the physical remains and personal effects of saints. They were credited with the power to heal, to win battles, to transform lives. The tombs of saints became the destination for pilgrimages. For Christian rulers, the possession of relics was both an affirmation of their authority and a symbol of power. The Seventh Canon of the Second Council of Nicaea in 787, reversing the iconoclasm of the Byzantine emperors earlier in the eighth century, stipulated that no church should be consecrated without relics. This all fuelled an insatiable demand for these objects of veneration.

A long-term outcome of this desire for relics across the Christian world was captured by Mark Twain in *The Innocents Abroad*, reporting on his package tour through Europe and the Holy Land in 1867. At the Cathedral of San Lorenzo in Genoa, where he was taken to view the chest containing the ashes of St John the Baptist, he railed at the proliferation of relics in the churches he had visited across the continent. 'As for bones of St Denis, I feel certain we have seen enough of them to duplicate him, if necessary.'[2]

The Byzantine Empire played a crucial role from at least the seventh century until the fall of Constantinople to the Ottomans in 1453 in safeguarding the most precious relics of the Christian world.[3] The range and significance of relics amassed in Constantinople made the city an important centre of Christian pilgrimage. Arriving as a pilgrim in 1200, Dobrinia Iadreikovich, the future archbishop of Novgorod, dutifully recorded his visits to seventy-six shrines in the city and another twenty-one in the suburbs, listing forty-six sacred relics in the Great Church of St Sophia alone.[4] The most venerated relics of all were those connected with Christ's Passion, among them the True Cross, the Crown of Thorns, the Holy Lance and the sandals of Christ. The possession of these relics gave the Byzantine emperor spiritual and thereby political authority.

The Byzantine Empire was also an essential source of relics for Christian western Europe. As the fortunes of that empire waxed and waned, the principal means by which the rulers of the Christian West obtained those relics also changed: from diplomatic gifts, to looting, to sale.

While the Byzantine Empire was at its height, relics were used as highly prized diplomatic gifts. We have examined Byzantium's use of embroidered silks as a gift able to project the emperor's wealth and superiority. The gifting of relics similarly served to project wealth, in this case spiritual, but also superiority. Relics were particularly suited to the latter function precisely because they were so hard to reciprocate. However splendid a return gift was offered, it could not match the spiritual significance and power of the relic. Thus the emperor was able to assert his dominant position.

Among gifts of relics of the True Cross made by Byzantine emperors was a fragment sent in the late sixth century by Emperor Justin II to Radegund, the widow of Chlothar I, Merovingian king of the Franks. Radegund, now revered as St Radegund, commissioned the Italian nobleman, poet and

future bishop of Poitiers Venantius Fortunatus to produce works to celebrate the processional arrival of the relic[5] into the monastery she had
established on her estate near Poitiers, renamed the Abbey of the Holy
Cross in honour of the new acquisition. His composition, 'Vexilla regis
prodeunt' ('The royal banners forward go'), is still a revered hymn today.

Our story begins in 1027 when Conrad II was crowned Holy Roman
Emperor in Rome. Conrad quickly despatched an embassy to the
Byzantine court, both to establish relations and more specifically with the
aim of securing a bride from the Byzantine imperial family for his son, the
future Henry III. The seriousness of the mission was demonstrated by the
eminence of the figure chosen to head it, Bishop Werner I of Strasbourg,
a close confidant of Conrad, who had accompanied him on his first Italian
expedition.[6] The senior secular member of the embassy was Manegold,
count of Donauwörth in Swabia. They set out for Constantinople in the
autumn of 1027, though their journey to the Byzantine capital was made
more challenging by the refusal of King Stephen I of Hungary, who would
have felt threatened by the prospect of closer relations between the two
emperors, to allow the mission to cross his lands, forcing them to take a
riskier maritime route.[7]

It was not clear who was intended to be Henry's bride. The Byzantine
emperor, Constantine VIII Porphyrogenitus, had three daughters, but all
were middle-aged and not an obvious match for Henry, who was ten. Two
rather serious problems then arose. First, Bishop Werner died in October
1028. Second, Constantine VIII followed him just a fortnight later.
Constantine had, just before expiring, managed to appoint his daughter
Zoë empress and arrange her swift marriage to her cousin, Romanos III
Argyros, who was persuaded to repudiate his existing wife under threat of
blinding if he did not.[8] Manegold returned home without having secured
a bride for Henry.

The mission was not, however, a failure. Romanos III had acknowledged
Conrad's imperial status and sent an embassy with a letter confirming this
fact, accompanied by various relics, including a fragment of the True Cross.
The embassy was also a success for Manegold personally, not least because
he himself received another relic of the True Cross while in Constantinople.
On his return to Donauwörth, Manegold founded the Abbey and Convent
of the Holy Cross to safeguard the precious relic. The convent was
refounded as a monastery by Manegold III in the early twelfth century.[9]

The story of how Manegold acquired the relic is told in a twelfth-century
account of the visit to Constantinople of a monk named Berthold, sent by

the abbot of Donauwörth to gather details of the object at the heart of the monastery. Berthold's account, which understandably casts Manegold in a favourable light, records that Manegold was able to build up a friendship with Constantine VIII, who in a weak moment offered to make him a gift of whatever he wished. Manegold seized his opportunity and asked for a relic of the True Cross he had seen earlier. Constantine was unwilling to part with the relic, which was used in the coronation ritual. However, bound by his word, he did so. Following Constantine's death, the reliquary was found to be missing during the preparations for Romanos's coronation. Manegold was suspected of theft, and his accommodation searched. Nothing was found, Manegold having taken the precaution of sending the reliquary on ahead to Donauwörth. Declaring his mission over, he returned home.[10]

This is of course an unreliable account. A papal bull issued by Leo IX in 1049, on the occasion of the consecration by the pope of the Abbey and Convent of the Holy Cross in Donauwörth, identifies the donor as Romanos, not Constantine, and the relic may therefore more straightforwardly have been a parting gift from Romanos III on Manegold's departure from Constantinople.[11]

The sack of Constantinople in 1204 at the chaotic culmination of the Fourth Crusade and the installation of the Latin Empire of Baldwin I was to change dramatically the means by which relics reached Christian western Europe. The era of the careful diplomatic gifting by Byzantine emperors of mostly small-scale relics, in a way that underlined the superior status of the giver, was replaced by a mix of much less controlled giving, focused on the friends of the leaders of the Fourth Crusade, and outright looting.[12]

The Latin Empire faced an increasingly precarious existence, both militarily and economically. Following the death of Emperor John of Brienne in 1237, relics were increasingly treated as items to be monetised in a desperate attempt to prop up a crumbling regime. The most famous example concerns one of the most precious relics of all, the Crown of Thorns, placed on the head of Jesus before his crucifixion. The heir to the throne of the Latin Empire, Baldwin II, had been sent in 1236 on a mission west to the pope and to the pious King Louis IX of France, a relative, its aim to secure Western Christian support for the beleaguered empire. John of Brienne had died in his absence, and the barons of Constantinople had arranged a loan with the Podestà, the official in charge of Venetian possessions in the Latin Empire, and other Venetian and Genoese merchants, using the Crown of Thorns as security.[13] By 1238, with the money already gone, a Venetian banker named Nicolò Quirino agreed a further, more stringent loan, with the Crown of Thorns again providing the security.

Baldwin II, in Paris, and desperate for French support, had enticed Louis IX with the prospect of the Crown of Thorns for his own growing collection of relics. This could he suggested be a gift.[14] In essence, a commercial transaction was recast as a diplomatic gift to make it seem less materialistic. Louis sent two Dominican monks to Constantinople to complete the deal, but they arrived to find that the pawned crown was about to be shipped off to Venice. They were allowed to accompany it, and one stayed on in Venice to watch over it at the treasury of St Mark's Basilica while the other returned to France. On learning of the relic's whereabouts, King Louis immediately despatched ambassadors to Venice to pay off the loan and secure the crown.[15] Louis IX built the Sainte Chapelle in Paris to house the precious relic, the centrepiece of his efforts to make Paris a centre for medieval Christendom.[16] The impoverished Baldwin II, sadly, was required to take ever more extreme measures to secure funds, resorting to mortgaging his son and heir, Philip de Courtenay, to Venetian merchants as security for a loan.[17]

Following the Byzantine recapture of Constantinople in 1261, and particularly in the last century of the Byzantine Empire before the fall of the city to the Ottomans in 1453, economic necessity frequently required either the sale of relics, often disguised as 'donations', or their use as diplomatic gifts. The context of the latter was however entirely unlike the gifts of the empire in its heyday. Instead of serving as symbols of the superiority of the Byzantine emperor, these were gifts of desperation. With Constantinople under siege from the Ottomans, the long journey to western Europe of Emperor Manuel II Palaiologos was an attempt to secure assistance from its courts. The ambassadors Manuel sent out across the continent were often accompanied by gifts of relics. Thus he sent King Martin I of Aragon a fragment of the tunic of Christ that had healed the bleeding woman, and a piece of the sponge of Christ's Passion. King Charles III of Navarre received a fragment of the True Cross and another piece of the same tunic.[18]

While such relics were still highly esteemed as gifts, in the changed circumstances they must have lost some of their aura. With the loss of Constantinople's power and many of its treasures, so the mystique around the relics was diminished. For Byzantium, the need to commodify its most prized relics in an attempt to ensure its survival in the end undermined its role as the sacred guardian of this religious heritage.[19]

1261

AN EMBROIDERED SILK

A GIFT FROM MICHAEL VIII PALAIOLOGOS, CO-EMPEROR OF NICAEA, TO THE REPUBLIC OF GENOA

The Pallium of St Lawrence.

We have examined the special place of silk as a favoured diplomatic gift of the Byzantine Empire over several centuries. Yet while many Byzantine silks have survived in Christian western Europe, often in ecclesiastical contexts such as the provision of shrouds for the relics of saints, it is rarely possible to link these to specific diplomatic gifts or otherwise trace how they arrived in the west.[1]

One important exception comes from the city of Genoa in northern Italy. It is a large silk, known as the Pallium of St Lawrence, measuring some 1.28 by 3.76 metres, beautifully embroidered, and coloured with the sought-after purple dye.[2] It depicts the future Byzantine Emperor Michael VIII Palaiologos, accompanied by St Michael, being shown into the Cathedral of Genoa by St Lawrence. It also includes a sequence of scenes illustrating the life and martyrdom of St Lawrence and associated martyrs St Sixtus and St Hippolytus. An encomium to Palaiologos delivered by the orator Manuel Holobolos indicates that this silk was a diplomatic gift from Palaiologos to Genoa, linked to the signing of the Treaty of Nymphaion in 1261. The surviving material evidence, the diplomatic gift itself, offers insight into the context.

The thirteenth century was a challenging time for Byzantium. Constantinople had been sacked in 1204 during the Fourth Crusade and was ruled by the Latin Empire of Constantinople. The Byzantine refugees from the city had regrouped into three rival successor states, Nicaea on the western coast of Asia Minor, Epirus in Greece and Trebizond on the Black Sea.[3] Each claimed to represent Byzantium in both an imperial and ecumenical sense. The recovery of Constantinople was the practical step that would decide between these claims. Michael VIII Palaiologos in Nicaea also had a more personal need to demonstrate his legitimacy, having reached his current position as co-emperor with the young John IV Doukas Laskaris through a coup against John's previous guardian.

Genoa too was experiencing a difficult time. The Latin Empire in Constantinople favoured their arch-rivals, Venice, and tensions between the two maritime republics had led to the naval Battle of Acre in 1258 and a comprehensive Venetian victory. Genoa was looking for a means of regaining its position in the eastern Mediterranean.

The solution to the tribulations of Nicaea and Genoa was an alliance. Nicaea wanted military support to secure Constantinople; Genoa was looking for commercial advantage in the eastern Mediterranean. In reaching out to an Italian state for military support, Michael VIII Palaiologos was following an established Byzantine pattern. In 1155, then Emperor Manuel I Komnenos entered into an alliance with Genoa involving a Genoese commitment to defend Constantinople in return for trading privileges and the receipt of an annual payment of gold coin and two silks, plus more gold and another silk for the archbishop.[4] The alliance was never honoured, but its structure formed the model for the arrangement reached by Michael VIII Palaiologos and Genoa more than a century later.

The Treaty of Nymphaion was signed in March 1261 at the favourite winter residence of the Nicaean emperors, the present-day Kemalpaşa in the Turkish province of Izmir. Its terms, highly favourable to Genoa, are an indication of the desperation with which Michael wanted their military support to take Constantinople. Genoa undertook to provide fifty ships at the expense of the emperor. There were provisions for the export to Nicaea of Genoese arms and horses, and of the entry of its citizens into Nicaean military service. In return, Genoa would receive considerable trading concessions, including a merchant quarter in Constantinople and other major cities. The treaty also, in an echo of that of 1155, stipulated the payment by Nicaea of gold coin and two silks annually to the commune of Genoa, with further gold and another silk to the archbishop.[5] The alliance with Nicaea had its downsides for Genoa, not least that in pitting itself against the Latin Empire it risked papal excommunication, but the favourable terms of the treaty served as ample persuasion.

Somewhat ironically, with the ink barely dry on the treaty, Michael secured Constantinople without needing Genoese support. His general, Alexios Strategopoulos, and what a wonderful name for a military commander that is, learnt that the garrison and Venetian fleet were absent from Constantinople conducting a raid and took the city with his small force. The Latin Emperor Baldwin II fled the city, and Michael was able to enter it in triumph on 15 August 1261 and have himself crowned as emperor.

The encomium of Manuel Holobolos, probably delivered at Christmas 1265,[6] describes the circumstances of the signing of the Treaty of Nymphaion, though of course in terms entirely favourable to Michael VIII Palaiologos. Holobolos describes a meeting between the Genoese envoys and the emperor, in which Michael addresses them with erudition and grace, and they respond with great deference, describing him as their father. They convey the Genoese wish to become Byzantine subjects, with Michael as their leader, and ask for a decorated silk bearing the emperor's image, which would be a source of great pride for the city. Holobolos records that the emperor presented the envoys with two fine silks. His description of the second of these, which he clearly regards as the more important, closely corresponds to the silk that has survived in Genoa; including in referring to the presence of scenes from the life and martyrdom of St Lawrence and his companions.[7]

In gifting a fine embroidered silk to Genoa, Michael was following a longstanding Byzantine diplomatic tradition, but the gift was clearly a particularly important one, in that it had been made for this specific occasion. The inscriptions were written in Latin, a language familiar to the recipient audience rather than the expected language of Byzantine embroideries. The depiction of Michael entering Genoa's Cathedral of San Lorenzo is of course a reference to the alliance between the two powers, and the choice of the life and martyrdom of the same saint for the hagiographic part of the design of the silk is a further nod to Genoa.

While the silk projects images of the alliance between Nicaea and Genoa, the embroidery is also intended to praise Michael. The imperial scene of Michael being ushered into the cathedral by St Lawrence is placed within the hagiographic story of the saint's life and martyrdom. The telling of that story through the embroidered silk highlights Lawrence selling the vessels of the church and distributing the proceeds to the poor. In focusing the tale on a message of giving and generosity, the silk is intended to highlight Michael's own generosity. This was to prove somewhat ironic, given that later Byzantine opinion was critical of Michael for offering excessively generous terms to the Genoese, causing Byzantium considerable commercial pain.[8]

Michael would repeat the gifting strategy of a prestigious silk embroidered to commemorate a specific event. In 1274, he gifted an embroidered silk to Pope Gregory X to mark the Second Council of Lyon and Michael's agreement to the reunification of the eastern and western churches. While this silk has not survived, it is described in a Vatican inventory of 1295 in terms that suggest that it bore many structural similarities to the Genoa silk. It is said to have been an embroidered purple silk, containing inscriptions in both Greek and Latin, and incorporating a depiction of Pope Gregory X presenting Michael VIII Palaiologos to St Peter, as well as scenes from the lives of the apostles.[9]

Not all Michael's silken gifts were successes. The contemporary Byzantine historian George Pachymeres reported that Mongol ruler Nogai Khan was decidedly unimpressed by gifted silks, complaining that they had no practical value and offered no protection from the elements.[10] Silks, long the favoured diplomatic gift of Byzantium, remained however central to Michael VIII Palaiologos's arsenal of gifts. As a ruler dedicated to the recovery of the Byzantine capital of Constantinople, and then to the reconstruction and renewal of the city as well as to the consolidation of his own personal legitimacy, no more the usurper in Nicaea but the acknowledged emperor, a desire to restore the past glories of silken diplomacy is unsurprising. With Michael's passing, the prominence of Byzantine silks as prestigious diplomatic gifts would however soon pass too. The loss of the silk production centre of Nicaea to the Ottoman Turks and the development of silk production in the west damaged supply and demand, respectively. Icons and, as we have seen, holy relics, became more characteristic diplomatic gifts of the last years of the Byzantine Empire.[11]

In Genoa, we know from an inventory that Michael's embroidered silk was to be found in the cathedral treasury in 1386. It seems to have been moved from the cathedral in the seventeenth century. A stone plaque dated 1663 suggests that the reason for its move, into the city's seat of civic rather than ecclesiastical power, was to give it greater prominence.[12] It has served as a testament of Genoa's glorious history; an object of municipal pride. A favoured diplomatic gift for several centuries, Byzantine silks had a good run.

1353

SIXTY SLAVES

A GIFT FROM AL-MUJAHID 'ALI, SULTAN OF YEMEN, TO AL-SALIH SALIH, SULTAN OF EGYPT

Mamalucke, an early sixteenth-century etching by Daniel Hopfer.

The Mamluks, meaning 'owned', were slave soldiers, a prominent part of the military apparatus in Syria and Egypt from the ninth century, achieving particular importance under the Ayyubid dynasty in the twelfth and thir-teenth centuries. Following the death of the Ayyubid sultan during fighting to repel the Frankish crusader assault on the Egyptian port of Damietta in 1249, the Mamluks murdered his heir and took control of Egypt. They established a sultanate that would last until its overthrow by the Ottomans in 1517. Centred on Cairo, it covered for most of its history Egypt, Syria and territory stretching into Anatolia, Mesopotamia and the Hejaz region of the western part of the Arabian Peninsula.

The Mamluks achieved military success, and the gratitude of the Islamic world, in both expelling the Crusaders from the Levant and defeating the Mongols, who had destroyed the Abbasid caliphate in Baghdad. Through their control of the holy places of both Christianity and Islam, in Jerusalem, Medina and Mecca, their sultanate was an important place of pilgrimage for the peoples of many lands. Egypt under Mamluk rule became the hub of the spice trade route from India to the Mediterranean. They installed a shadow Abbasid caliphate in their capital Cairo, which became the major city of the Islamic world.[1] The historian Ibn Khaldun, who lived in the city in the late fourteenth century, wrote that Mamluk Cairo 'surpasses anything one can imagine'.[2]

The Mamluks were not native to the lands they controlled. They were mainly Turkic steppe peoples from Central Asia, and after 1382 Circassians from the Caucasus region. Title and property were, in theory at least, not inherited, and the Mamluk regiments were constantly replenished with new captured recruits. Succession was often settled violently, and few sultans died of natural causes, but the sultanate itself, enriched by the profits of the spice trade, became for centuries a major power, known for the opulence of its architecture and the quality of its metalware and glassware.

Doris Behrens-Abouseif, Professor Emerita at the University of London School of Oriental and African Studies and an expert on Islamic art and architecture, has studied the gifts given and received by the Mamluk sultanate, providing a valuable analysis of the attitudes towards diplomatic gifts in the medieval Islamic world.[3] Diplomatic ceremonial was an important part of Mamluk engagement with foreign powers. Visiting envoys were offered elaborate hospitality, ensuring that they would return home with stories of the wealth and opulence of the Mamluk court. The giving and receiving of gifts were central elements of these diplomatic engagements. The presentation of the gifts was part of the ceremonial of the diplomatic mission, with gifts customarily displayed for the sultan and courtiers to view. Diplomatic gifts to the Mamluks were not treated as personal gifts for the sultan, but as state property, and would typically be shared out with the sultan's emirs, for whom the gifts were regarded as part of their remuneration.[4]

The diplomatic gifts favoured by the Mamluks ranged widely, including textiles, horses and other animals, slaves, spices, gold and jewellery. Behrens-Abouseif notes however that the Mamluks rarely selected as diplomatic gifts the typical export items for which their sultanate was most famous: for example, carpets, enamelled glass or silver inlaid metal objects.[5] Rather, a central priority in the choice of gift seemed to lie in the concept of *tuhaf*, or 'marvels',[6] the ability of the gift to generate a sense of wonder or excitement.

Items that had been imported from distant lands, including recycled gifts, were not at all frowned upon, but actively favoured, as more likely to be able to inspire marvel through their exoticism. The use of such imported objects as gifts had ancillary benefits in serving to emphasise the international links and cosmopolitanism of the giver. The gifting by Mamluk sultans of Chinese porcelain and spices underlined their control of the trading routes to the east. Exotic animals were a good example of imported gifts rich in *tuhaf*, such as the giraffe gifted by Sultan Qaytbay to the Florentine leader Lorenzo de' Medici in 1487,[7] which we will encounter in a later story.

The focus on the ability of the gift to generate wonder meant that second-hand gifts were also frequently favoured, their back-stories lending the gifts a sense of pedigree.[8] This recalls Mauss's emphasis on the spirit of the gift.[9] Objects linked personally to the sultan, including items of clothing they had used, were regarded as a particular sign of appreciation. This was to find an echo in the favouring of portraits of themselves as diplomatic gifts by European monarchs in a later era, as we shall see.

The Mamluk sultans also favoured gifts that reflected the identity of their regime, centred on a military elite.[10] Arms and armour were prominent among Mamluk diplomatic gifts, as were horses, gifted together with elaborate trappings, including bejewelled saddles. Ceremonial textiles from the royal manufacture in Alexandria were a frequent gift. In the case of robes of honour, which we will explore further in a later story, these implied a subordinate relationship on the part of the recipient and would typically be given to a visiting envoy or to a vassal. A gift of a robe of honour to a Mamluk sultan would be taken as an insult. When such a garment was sent by Shah Rukh, ruler of the Timurid Empire, to the Mamluk Sultan Barsbay, the latter was so incensed that he ordered the waterboarding of the unfortunate Timurid envoy.[11]

The content of Mamluk gift exchanges also depended on the specific political context. Slaves and weapons were for example common Mamluk gifts to fellow Muslim rulers, but not to Christian recipients.[12] The pattern of gift exchange with the Rasulid sultanate, which ruled Yemen from 1229 to 1454, illustrates how the nature of the relationship between the two powers shaped the pattern of gifts exchanged.

The assumption of power by the Rasulids in Yemen has some parallels with the birth of the Mamluk sultanate. An officer of Turkmen origin attached to the Ayyubid army that had taken Yemen in the twelfth century was able in turn to take control when the departing Ayyubid governor left him in charge.[13] Under the Rasulids, Yemen became a significant regional player, principally because of its strategic location along the spice trade routes, at the meeting point between the Indian Ocean and the Red Sea. Transit trade through Aden was the principal source of Rasulid wealth.[14]

The relationship between the Mamluks and Rasulids was complex. The two sultanates were in competition in respect of both control of the Red Sea and of the Islamic holy places of the Hejaz. At the same time, they depended on each other in respect of the lucrative spice trade, in which the Rasulids had established themselves in an indispensable intermediary position, and they were allies in the face of external threats from Crusaders and Mongols.[15] Diplomatic gifts were an important part of the maintenance of a broadly stable relationship between the two sultanates, but with the Mamluks by far the stronger of the two, these took the form of an unequal exchange. The Mamluks considered the Rasulids as a vassal state, and Rasulid gifts to the Mamluk sultan were a form of tribute, apportioning to the Mamluks a share of the Rasulid benefits from the Red Sea trade.[16] The gifts were considered to represent a Rasulid contribution to Mamluk military action in the cause of Islam as a whole.[17] Gifts from the Rasulid sultan were accordingly expected to be lavish, and were eagerly awaited in Cairo.

The Rasulid diplomatic missions that brought them were large affairs, settling for extended periods in Cairo, and imposing a considerable hospitality commitment on the Mamluks. The Rasulid envoys coming to Cairo would have had a range of tasks to accomplish beyond the presentation of the sultan's diplomatic gift package. These would have included purchasing items for their sultan and recruiting artisans and soldiers, to whom they promised generous remuneration in Yemen.[18] Rasulid sultans chafed at the burden of the elaborate gifts and from time to time withheld them, but threats and reprimands from the Mamluk sultan generally had the effect of re-establishing the exchange.

A gift in 1353 from then Rasulid Sultan al-Mujahid 'Ali to his Mamluk counterpart al-Salih Salih offers a good example of the content of these large Yemeni gift packages. According to the Mamluk-era historian Al-Maqrizi, this included, inter alia, sixty slaves, 4,000 pieces of porcelain, 150 bags of musk, a civet horn, garments, pepper, ginger, spices and an elephant. These items mirror in many ways the diplomatic gift choices of the Mamluks, including an emphasis on gifts able to provoke wonder, like the elephant and porcelain from distant lands. Exotic gifts like these were often recycled by the Mamluks as their gifts to foreign courts.[19]

Al-Maqrizi specifies that the sixty slaves offered as part of this gift were those to have survived the journey to Egypt out of an original 300. A brutal statistic, but deaths of slaves en route would have been anticipated, serving to enhance the value of those surviving the journey. Human beings also feature among the return gift from the Mamluk sultan, sent with the Yemeni mission on its return journey four months later. They included some of the magicians and acrobats for which Mamluk Egypt was renowned.[20] In some circumstances, human beings offered a particular advantage as diplomatic gifts, specifically where they had the prospect of achieving a prominent or trusted position in the recipient society, since they could in a sense perform an ambassadorial role in representing the gifting country in a way that inanimate gifts could not. Of the diplomatic gifts prominent in Mamluk exchanges, this would have been true of gifts of mamluks themselves, the young men recruited for military roles who might eventually attain senior, even ruling, positions. It could also have been true of gifts of skilled artisans and performers, slave girls who might be destined for a place in a royal harem, and eunuchs.

The uneven nature of the relationship between the two powers is also expressed in the nature of gifts specifically requested by the Rasulid sultans. Thus in both 1267 and 1281 the Rasulid sultan asked his Mamluk counterpart for one of his used shirts as a symbol of *aman*, representing peace and protection. The response of Sultan al-Zahir Baybars in 1267 was to add one of his suits of armour, a reminder of his military prowess.[21] The composition of gift exchanges can thus say much about the power relationship between two rulers.

1489

SEVEN BEAVERS

A GIFT FROM THE TOWN COUNCIL OF REVAL TO HANS, KING OF DENMARK AND NORWAY

The beaver, depicted in the twelfth-century *Aberdeen Bestiary*.

The dawn of the thirteenth century saw the Livonian Crusade, a campaign of conquest and Christianisation of the pagan peoples of present-day Estonia and Latvia. Pope Innocent III declared this region as *Terra Mariana*, the Land of St Mary. The territories of Livonia were divided between the victorious crusading parties: Catholic bishoprics, the Danes and the Livonian Brothers of the Sword, a Germanic order of warrior monks who later evolved into the Livonian Order of the Teutonic Knights. In the aftermath of an uprising in the mid-fourteenth century, the Danes sold their colony in Estonia to the Teutonic Knights, who passed this on to the Livonian Order. In 1419, a Livonian Diet was established to regulate disputes between the Livonian Order and the various bishoprics, which together formed the rather loosely structured Livonian Confederation of Catholic Germanic states, increasingly watchful around the risks of Russian expansion.

Another key player in the political economy of the region was the Hanseatic League, the Germanic commercial and defensive confederation of market towns around the Baltic Sea. The town of Reval, present-day Tallinn, on the Gulf of Finland on the northern shore of Estonia, had been granted a charter modelled on Lübeck Law during its period under Danish control.[1] This provided for a governing town council, with representatives drawn from the most successful merchants. The social structure of Reval involved a German ruling class and an Estonian peasantry.

Reval became a prosperous port, thriving on its position on the key transit route to the Russian market towns within the Hanseatic network, especially Novgorod.[2] As the fifteenth century approached its end, the Hanseatic League was however facing increasing pressure from the growing ambition and strength of the territorial states.

In 1481, Johannes, known as Hans, became king of Denmark on the death of his father, Christian I. He wanted to restore the Kalmar Union, which had joined under a single monarch the kingdoms of Denmark, Norway and Sweden, a grouping whose roots lay in an attempt to counter Germanic and Hanseatic influence in the region. Hans was confirmed as king of Norway in 1483 but was kept from the throne of Sweden by separatist regents for all but four years of his reign.

Hans wanted to cut the Hanseatic League down to size, encouraging competing English and Dutch traders, negotiating with Russia to trim the league's influence and insisting on annual renewal of the Hanseatic privileges. It was in the context of one such set of renewal discussions that the council of Reval decided in August 1489 on a diplomatic gift to Hans that they hoped would make him more favourable to their case. Their choice was seven beavers.[3]

We have seen the important role played by exotic animals as diplomatic gifts, combining attributes of curiosity and rarity. The beavers presented to King Hans would not though have been destined to be admired as living creatures beyond perhaps the moment of their presentation. The use of the beaver as a diplomatic gift was less about the charm of the creature than about what could be used from it, its attractiveness heightened by the fact that beavers had been extinct in Denmark for five centuries, so they held a rarity value from the perspective of the recipient.[4]

In fifteenth-century Europe, the beaver was valued for its fur and its meat. The attractiveness of the latter was enhanced by the curious exemption of the beaver's tail from the bar on eating meat during Lent. In this respect, it joined the ranks of marine mammals such as whale, dolphin and porpoise, considered as fish.[5] Also allowed were the barnacle goose, believed by some to be hatched from barnacles,[6] and the puffin, also said to have fish-like qualities, though sadly reputedly also tasting lousy.[7] The exemption of the beaver's tail seems to have been secured through a mix of its somewhat scaly, fish-like appearance and a belief in some quarters that the tail never left the water.[8] Thus in 1525, at a banquet held in Reval during Lent to celebrate the visit of the master of the Livonian Order, three beaver tails formed the highlight of the meal, the small number consumed suggesting that this was considered a luxury food indeed.[9]

That the gift of beavers to the king of Denmark in 1489 was made in August suggests, however, that the Lenten appeal of the meat from its tail was not a central consideration. The beaver offered another highly prized resource: castoreum. The castor sac located between the genitals and anus of the creatures produces this oily secretion, used by beavers to water-proof their fur and mark out their territory. It is used even today in the perfume industry and food production, thanks to its allegedly vanilla-like aroma. Beavers no longer have to die to extract the substance, though the alternative requires the anaesthetisation of the animal and the milking of its castoreum gland, which appears to be enough to discourage wide-scale continued use. It does though make an appearance in a Swedish schnapps named BVR HJT, pronounced 'Bäverhojt' or 'Beaver Shout'.

In medieval Europe, castoreum was prized for its medicinal qualities, which appear to stem from the presence of salicylic acid, an important component of aspirin. The twelfth-century Benedictine abbess Hildegard von Bingen wrote that beaver testicles could be drunk in warm wine to reduce fever.[10] In identifying the source of the castoreum as the beaver's testicles, Hildegard was following a misconception that had persisted since ancient times: mistaking external bumps connecting to the castor sacs for testes.

This misconception is at the root of the tale of the hunted beaver, one of the stories credited to Aesop, the slave and fabulist of ancient Greece. When hunted, so the story goes, the beaver, which has a keen appreciation of the reason for the hunter's interest in it, will bite off its own testicles and throw them towards the hunter. The latter will give up the hunt and take the prized castoreum. If the same beaver is hunted a second time, it will rear up and display its lack of sexual organs to the hunter, who abandons the chase. Perhaps unsurprisingly, the tale is rather rarely included these days in col-lections of *Aesop's Fables*, not least because the accompanying illustration is likely to prove alarming to young readers, but it does appear in various medieval bestiaries, including the twelfth-century illuminated manuscript known as the *Aberdeen Bestiary*. This adds a Christian moral to the tale: those wishing to heed the word of God and live chastely should cast off their vices and throw them into the face of the devil. The latter retires in defeat, seeing that the human has retained nothing belonging to him.[11]

This widely diffused tale adds a further consideration as to why beavers were particularly appropriate diplomatic gifts in the Christian Europe of the late fifteenth century. The beaver's chastity and bravery in the face of the devil presents the creature as symbolic of a good Christian.[12] As we have seen, diplomatic gifts are frequently also selected to highlight the culture of the gifting country. Beavers were still widespread in medieval Livonia, while extinct in Denmark. Yet records suggest that three of the beavers forming that diplomatic gift to King Hans were not brought from Reval at all but purchased in Lübeck. The reason for this is unclear. Perhaps they replaced beavers that died on the sea voyage along the Baltic. Perhaps the gifters had a late panic that their present was insufficiently grand. The price paid for each beaver was roughly equivalent to that of a good horse,[13] showing the keenness of the council to impress the king.

For a more recent example of the beaver as a diplomatic gift, we may head across the Atlantic. The Eurasian beaver was hunted to near extinction for its fur and castoreum, but as European supplies dwindled, the New World stepped in. By the seventeenth century, 'beaver' largely meant the North American, not European, animal.[14] This was the source used to meet an emerging fashion for beaver hats.

In 1670, King Charles II of England granted a Royal Charter to the 'Governor and Company of Adventurers of England, trading into Hudson's Bay', giving Prince Rupert of the Rhine and his associates a trading monopoly across all lands whose rivers drained into Hudson's Bay, amounting to about 40 per cent of the territory of modern-day Canada. Thus was born the Hudson's Bay Company, which from its initial focus on the trapping of beavers would diversify in many directions, eventually arriving at its present status as a major retail group.

That Royal Charter of 1670 did though come with a condition. It required the company to pay a rent of two black beavers and two elk whenever a British monarch visited the territory covered by the charter, known as Rupert's Land. This was a pretty good deal for the company, as the rent has only been paid four times. The first came in 1927, when the future King Edward VIII accepted two mounted elk heads and two black beaver pelts on behalf of his father.[15] The fourth and final time the rental ceremony has been performed came in 1970 and is notable because the beaver part of the rent was paid in live animals rather than pelts. It came during a royal tour of Canada and formed part of the company's 300th anniversary celebrations. The same year, the company became a Canadian corporation and moved its headquarters from London to Toronto, at which point the rent obligation was removed. Queen Elizabeth II was presented with the beavers in a tank. The beavers reportedly misbehaved throughout the ceremony.

1512

FIFTY BLOCKS OF CHEESE

A GIFT FROM THE REPUBLIC OF VENICE TO QANSUH AL-GHAWRI, SULTAN OF EGYPT

Reception of a Venetian Delegation in Damascus in 1511,
attributed to the circle of Giovanni Bellini.

Food and drink have a distinctive place in the story of diplomatic gifts. This arises because of their indispensability to the practice of diplomacy. Visiting envoys must be fed and watered. Meals and receptions provide an opportunity for discussions in more informal settings than audience halls or across negotiating tables, with friendship emphasised by the act of breaking bread together.[1] The polity hosting a diplomatic mission is thus usually required to provide gifts of food and drink, in the form of meals and entertainments or simply to sustain the visiting mission.

In addition to this essentially compulsory character of food and drink as a diplomatic gift, these items also enjoy some specific advantages when set against other gift items. Luxurious and unfamiliar food and drink products fall into the category of *tuhaf*, or 'marvels', which as we saw in an earlier story was central to the diplomatic gift strategies of the Mamluk sultans. They can inspire wonder. They also provide an excellent means of showcasing the culinary culture and agricultural products of the gifting state. This is seen today in the focus by many countries on gastrodiplomacy, using cuisine as a form of soft power.[2] Because of the human need to eat and drink, and because meals are associated with family, friendship and conviviality, gifts of food and drink can be used to suggest warmth in the diplomatic relationship.

There is a challenge here too: as objects that are designed to be consumed, accepting a gift of food and drink requires a degree of trust. This risk is not always taken. The federal registers reporting modern-day diplomatic gifts to US presidents record that gifts of food and drink items are 'handled pursuant to US Secret Service policy',[3] or in other words are not destined to be consumed by the intended recipient.

The gifting strategies of the Republic of Venice in the sixteenth century show how food and drink was used as a diplomatic gift in both contexts: to provide hospitality and sustenance for visiting diplomatic delegations, and as luxury gifts to foreign rulers. We will look specifically at the example of cheese.

In common with many other powers, the Venetian government of the sixteenth century perceived it as their duty to provide hospitality to visiting diplomatic delegations. This often included the provision of accommodation. It also included a good deal of food and drink. This was in part offered in the form of elegant banquets, in which the sophistication and richness of the food and the elaborate accompanying spectacle were intended to give the visitors an impression of Venetian wealth and power. The setting of the banquet served similar objectives. Thus, a Muscovite embassy visited Venice for twenty-three days in the summer of 1582 en route to Rome. The banquet organised in honour of the delegation was set up in the Arsenal, the building in which weapons were stored and ships built, and thus a symbol of Venetian maritime power.[4]

Food and drink was also offered to the visiting envoy in the form of a gift package provided on arrival, known as *refrescamenti*, or 'refreshments'. These gift packages comprised items of a predominantly luxury character, including Venetian specialities. They would typically include sugar, a range of nuts, herbs and spices, fresh fruit, high-quality fish or meat, and a barrel of Moscato wine. They also featured various sweet confections such as the sugar-coated nuts or fruits known as *confetti*.[5] For the Muscovite embassy of 1582, the Venetians offered food provisions for the entire duration of their stay, including the services of the doge's own chef to prepare it. This was no small undertaking: the thirty-strong diplomatic delegation managed to get through 500 melons during their stay.[6] Venetian records note four cheeses among the items provided to the Muscovite embassy: mozzarella; *marzolino*, a sheep's cheese made from spring milk; the soft *giuncata*; and *piacentino*.[7]

Gifts of cheese from the Venetian Republic were not just made to sustain or impress visiting envoys. They were also used as prestigious gifts to foreign rulers. The spice trade provides an example. It had long fuelled an interdependence between Venice and the Mamluk sultanate. The relationship had always been subject to squalls, including for example the extortion and harassment of Venetian traders by Mamluk officials and the policy introduced by Sultan Barsbay in the 1420s that required the Venetians to buy part of the pepper at the heart of the trade from the sultan's warehouses at artificially inflated prices.[8] Despite the difficulties, the trade was so lucrative for both parties that it had continued for centuries.

As the sixteenth century dawned, the trade was however facing unprecedented stress. When Portuguese explorer Vasco da Gama landed in India in 1498, the spice trade would be changed irreparably, as the Portuguese were now able to bring spices and other eastern commodities to Lisbon by sea. Both the Mamluks and Venetians had further problems, including the threat from the Ottomans, against whom the Venetians were at war at the turn of the century. These external stresses challenged the relationship between Venice and the Mamluks. In response to the declining income from the spice trade, the sultan raised both the price and quantity of pepper that the Venetian merchants were required to buy from his warehouses and in 1505 ordered the confiscation of Venetian merchant property in Alexandria after they had in the meantime quit the port without his permission.[9]

Diplomatic missions between the two powers were an attempt both to reach a common response to the external threats and to sort out the bilateral frictions. In 1502, Venice despatched a mission led by Benedetto Sanudo, a former Venetian consul in Damascus, to Sultan Qansuh al-Ghawri. Its objective was to convince the sultan of the seriousness of the Portuguese threat.[10] Sanudo sought to encourage the sultan to lower tariffs on spices and other goods imported from India to make Venetian prices more competitive than Portuguese ones and also to hint that he should take direct action against the Portuguese. The latter request was made in an implicit way, so that Venice should not be seen to be conspiring with a Muslim power against a fellow Catholic one.[11]

The journey to Cairo was challenging because of Venice's ongoing conflict with the Ottomans and, following an enforced stop in Corfu, Sanudo
only reached Cairo in the spring of 1503. The gifts he presented to the
sultan included textiles, furs and cheese, and he had already gifted fine
cloth and more cheese to the emir of Alexandria en route. He returned
with gifts from the sultan for the doge that included porcelain, incense,
civet musk and sugar.[12] The sultan marshalled a fleet, but the Mamluks and
their allies were comprehensively defeated in a naval battle at Diu in 1509
that firmly established Portuguese control of the Indian Ocean.[13]

It was thus against a worsening backdrop that a further Venetian mission,
under Domenico Trevisan, arrived in Cairo in 1512. Trevisan's mandate
included sorting out ongoing disputes over the price of pepper, as well as
securing the release of Pietro Zen, the Venetian consul in Damascus,
detained in Cairo by the sultan over suspicions around his contacts with
the Safavids, and resolving the issue of access to the Holy Land.[14] The mission was a success: Trevisan secured what would be the final Venetian commercial treaty with the Mamluks. And not only was Zen released, but he
even received a parting robe of honour from the sultan.[15]

Both parties were keen to impress throughout the mission. Trevisan
added to his delegation a group of musicians, courtesy of the Venetian
colony in Alexandria, who played fanfares on locally unfamiliar instruments at every village they sailed past on their river voyage to Cairo.[16] The
sultan provided the Venetian party with fine lodgings and sent them on
their arrival in the city a gift of provisions that included twenty geese,
forty-four sugar-loaves and five jugs of Indian honey.[17]

The gifts Trevisan brought for the sultan comprised some 150 gowns of
various types, some velvet, some satin and others threaded with gold, as
well as a large quantity of furs, including sable, ermine and no fewer than
4,500 squirrel furs. The gift also included fifty cheese blocks.[18] A fine gift.
The Mamluk sultanate had only five years left in which to enjoy it, before
it was swept aside by the Ottomans in 1517.

Cheese, then, was an important part of the prestigious Venetian gifts to
Mamluk sultans in the early part of the sixteenth century. What cheeses
were these that they should play such a distinguished role? US historian
Jesse Hysell identified the cheese presented by Sanudo as *piacentinu*, a
Sicilian cheese whose name comes from its pleasing taste.[19] This would
indeed be a worthy gift for an exalted recipient, with its flavouring of saf-
fron. It is tempting to identify the whole peppercorns added to the cheese
as a statement about the importance of the trade in pepper in the relation-

ship between the two powers. Perhaps the cheese in question was however not *piacentinu* but *piacentino*, or cheese from the Piacenza region of Italy. Historian Kenneth Meyer Setton identified the product given by Trevisan nine years later as 'cheeses from Piacenza',[20] and we have seen that these were among the cheeses offered to the visiting Muscovite embassy in 1582. Piacentine cheese was also a preferred Venetian gift to the Ottoman court.[21] This offers the prospect that the cheese gifted by Venice may have been a hard, crumbly, parmesan-like product, akin to the modern Grana Padano.

This is supported by the evident popularity of parmesan-type cheeses as diplomatic gifts from a range of Italian courts. Gifts from Pope Julius II to the young King Henry VIII of England in gratitude for Henry's support for the pope's anti-French 'Holy League' included not only the conferring of a Golden Rose, the prestigious papal token customarily awarded to favoured sovereigns, but also 100 parmesan cheeses.[22] Parmesan was so highly valued in England that when, in 1666, the diarist Samuel Pepys found his property threatened by the Great Fire of London, along with his office papers, wine and other valuables, he placed his parmesan cheese in a pit in a neighbouring garden for its protection.[23]

Cheese could play a role therefore both as a quotidian delicacy offered to diplomatic delegations as part of their provisioning or other hospitality and also as a luxury gift to a ruler.

1514

AN ELEPHANT

A GIFT FROM MANUEL I, KING OF PORTUGAL,
TO POPE LEO X

Four Studies of an Elephant by Giulio Romano,
depicting the animal gifted to Pope Leo X.

The second of our gifted elephants delighted its recipient, secured the objectives of the giver, and inspired artists and writers, yet it was also a gift to those wishing to highlight the excesses of the papacy, helping the path of the Protestant Reformation.

In 1513, a new pope was chosen. Giovanni de' Medici was the second son of Lorenzo the Magnificent, the de facto ruler of the Florentine Republic and a major patron of the Italian Renaissance. As pope, he chose the name Leo X. He followed his father in supporting the arts, providing generous patronage of a wide range of artists, among them Raphael and Michelangelo. He was erudite and enjoyed the company of writers and poets. He was young, crowned pope at the age of just thirty-seven. But he was not youthful. He was so obese that it was said that he needed two servants to lift him out of bed.[1] He suffered from various ailments, including a painful anal fistula, and fretted about his own mortality. Perhaps in response to these ills, he delighted in carnival and buffoonery. He is said to have commented: 'God has given us the Papacy. Let us enjoy it!'[2]

King Manuel I succeeded to the Portuguese throne in 1495. His rule marked a time of great Portuguese maritime expansion. As we have seen in our last story, its navigators were helping Portugal gain control of the spice trade, thereby reshaping the global balance of power. There was a tradition among the rulers of Europe to send a delegation to Rome, a 'mission of obedience', following the election of a new pope, its purpose being formally to recognise the pope as the successor to St Peter.[3] These were grand affairs. Sovereigns attempted to outdo each other in the size of mission and costliness of the gifts brought.

For Manuel, the despatch of a 'mission of obedience' to the Vatican offered the opportunity to present to the new pope the successes of Portuguese expansion[4] and to underline the potential of the new lands to deliver more souls into the Christian family. He had some more specific goals too: the waiver of some of the tithes paid to the clergy, in order to help fund his expeditions; and papal agreement that the Spice Islands fell within the Portuguese rather than Spanish sphere.[5]

Pope Leo X was known to maintain a menagerie of exotic creatures at the Vatican, and Manuel decided that his objective of showcasing Portugal's new conquests in India and elsewhere would be neatly served by selecting creatures from these lands from his own menagerie for the new pope. They included two leopards, a cheetah, parrots and a Persian horse.[6] The star gift was a four-year-old white elephant, recently brought from India. No elephant had been seen in Rome since the time of the empire, and Manuel knew that his gift would cause a stir. Because of the nature of the occasion, gifts of a more directly ecclesiastical character were also chosen, designed to highlight the pope's role as the leader of the church: a gold chalice, an altar frontal, ecclesiastical vestments. Manuel knew however that the elephant would make the most impact.

It is not quite clear which of the four elephants shipped from Cochin to Lisbon between 1510 and 1514 by Afonso de Albuquerque, governor of India, was the one Manuel gifted to the pope, though the likeliest candidate is an elephant specifically purchased for the king by Albuquerque, of which particular care seems to have been taken.[7]

The celebrated navigator Tristão da Cunha was chosen to lead the mission. The journey to Rome proved challenging. The elephant had to be shackled on the deck of the ship, which found itself mobbed at every port of call on the sea journey from Lisbon to Orbetello in Italy by crowds anxious for a glimpse of the creature. On the land journey of some 70 miles from Orbetello to Rome, the ranks of curious onlookers hindered the mission's progress at every turn. When the mission sheltered at the villa of a cardinal just outside Rome, the crowds trampled vineyards and orchards, forcing the Portuguese group to escape to the safety of the pope's cannon factory.[8]

The pope had set 19 March 1514 as the date for the entry of the Portuguese mission into the Eternal City. No longer in their travelling clothes, its members were dressed in great finery. The elephant made a particularly arresting sight. A silver tower-like structure had been placed on its back, containing the ecclesiastical gifts. The elephant's Indian trainer was seated on its neck, with its Saracen custodian leading it.[9] When the procession passed the Castel Sant'Angelo, the elephant stopped in front of the watching pope, knelt to the ground, deferentially bowed its head, trumpeted, filled its trunk from a water trough, and gently sprayed the pope and his companions. The pope was delighted.[10]

The mission's programme included a public consistory at the Apostolic Palace on 20 March at which one of the Portuguese ambassadors delivered a powerful 'oration of obedience'. On the following day, the pope inspected the gifts, with which he was well pleased, especially the elephant. The mission departed Rome in June, its objectives achieved through a range of briefs and bulls that covered most of the Portuguese requests. Pope Leo decided to bestow upon Manuel the award of the Golden Rose for that year, one of the most important favours a pope could offer. Since Manuel had already received a Golden Rose, in 1506, from Pope Julius II, Leo decided additionally to confer the honour of the *Gladius et pileus*, the 'Papal Sword and Ducal Cap', never previously conferred on a Portuguese king.[11] The pope also sent Manuel other gifts, including an illuminated volume and a chimneypiece, some say sculpted by Michelangelo.

The elephant immediately found its way to the pope's heart. Leo was delighted by its tricks of genuflection, trumpeting and showering him with water. It entered the hearts of the Roman people too, acquiring the name Annone (usually rendered in English as Hanno). This may have been derived from *aana*, the word for elephant in the Malayalam language of Kerala, which would have been spoken by the elephant's trainer.[12] Annone was on occasion paraded through the city or brought to one of the piazzas so more Romans could meet it. One of these public displays ended in tragedy: a public viewing of the elephant at the Baths of Diocletian attracted so many people that contemporary sources reported the death of some thirteen souls in the crush.[13]

The most celebrated of the elephant's public outings also ended in unexpected fashion. This took place during one of the festivities beloved by the pope, marking the feast day of Saints Cosmas and Damian. For the amusement of a pope who revelled in carnival mockeries, it was arranged that a court buffoon named Giacomo Baraballo, abbot of Gaeta, would be crowned as arch-poet. The ceremony involved Baraballo mounting the elephant, something he accomplished with great difficulty. He was then paraded around Rome on a throne on the beast's back. Unfortunately, the poor elephant was so spooked by the crowds and noise that it cast off both poet and throne, depositing poor Baraballo on to the riverbank.[14]

By 1516, clouds were gathering over the pope's carnivals. An itinerant preacher named Fra Bonaventura, who claimed to be the Angelic Pope, arrived in the city in May, railing against the excesses of the Vatican and prophesying that the pope, five named cardinals, the elephant and its keeper would all be dead before September of the following year.[15] To an ailing pope, this was troubling indeed, and he ordered the imprisonment of Fra Bonaventura in Castel Sant'Angelo.

Then the elephant fell ill. The pope summoned the finest physicians in Rome to treat the creature. They established that Annone was constipated and prescribed a purgative containing a considerable quantity of gold. This did not prove an effective remedy. The elephant died in June 1516. It seemed a dreadful omen.[16] Even more eerily in line with Bonaventura's prophecy, one of the elephant's keepers also died at this time, the cardinals of Senigaglia and Sanseverino following later that summer.

The disconsolate pope commissioned Raphael to paint a life-size mural of the elephant on the wall at the entrance to the Vatican. Sadly, it no longer survives. The pope himself composed an epitaph to Annone. The elephant was featured in the works of numerous artists and can still be encountered in Rome today. For example, a wooden mosaic depicting the poet Baraballo on the elephant decorates a door between the Stanza della Segnatura and Stanza del Incendio del Borgo in the Apostolic Palace.[17] A fountain designed by Giovanni da Udine for Cardinal Giulio de' Medici in the gardens of Villa Madama features Annone's head in white marble, its trunk serving as the water spout.[18]

A less hagiographic memorial was a satire, the last will and testament of Annone, sometimes attributed to satirist Pietro Aretino, which highlighted the corruption and scandals of Leo X's court through a list of twenty-nine legacies, each one a part of the elephant's anatomy, carefully chosen to highlight weaknesses of the legatee. Thus, the elephant's jawbone was destined for the Cardinal di Santi Quattro, suspected of corruption, to enable him better to 'devour all the money of the entire republic of Christ'.[19]

The embers of the Protestant Reformation were starting to burn: Martin Luther's *Ninety-Five Theses* date from 1517. For Luther, the affair of the pope's elephant was a symbol of the luxury and irresponsibility of the court. Leo X died in 1521. The papal treasury was empty. His successor, Adrian VI, would push back sharply on artistic patronage. The world was changing and, by 1527, the armies of Charles V would sack Rome.

In 1962, workers at the Vatican Library uncovered some bone fragments, which were identified as those of an elephant.[20] Annone's last resting place had been found.

1514

A RHINOCEROS

A GIFT FROM MUZAFFAR SHAH II, SULTAN OF GUJARAT, TO AFONSO DE ALBUQUERQUE, GOVERNOR OF PORTUGUESE INDIA

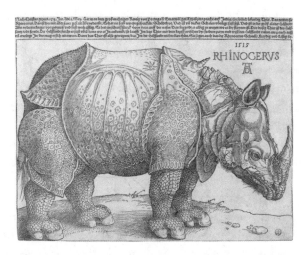

Dürer's *Rhinoceros*, a woodcut based on a sketch of the creature
later gifted by King Manuel I of Portugal to Pope Leo X.

Our next story concerns another pachyderm gifted in the year 1514, in this case not an elephant but a rhinoceros. It was to be gifted, regifted and then regifted again, although (spoiler alert) tragically dying in the course of its transportation to its final intended recipient. Its stuffed carcass then served as a less impressive replacement diplomatic gift. It was the star of one of the most famous representations of an animal in art history, in an illustration that influenced, not entirely accurately, how the rhinoceros was perceived across Europe for several centuries.

The story begins with a great naval commander, Afonso de Albuquerque, conqueror of Goa and governor of Portuguese India. After a period of rapid expansion, Portugal was preoccupied with the retention of its newly established control over the spice trade.[1] Albuquerque determined that the establishment of a fort on the island of Diu off the southern coast of

Gujarat would help to protect the Portuguese shipping lanes. Having secured the authorisation of King Manuel I of Portugal, he prepared a mission to seek the agreement of Sultan Muzaffar Shah II of Gujarat, on whose territory Diu fell, to construct such a fortress.

The mission left Goa in February 1514, armed with a selection of diplomatic gifts for the sultan, including a ruby-handled dagger, rich brocades and a small chandelier.[2] The sultan gave some fine return gifts, including an ivory-encrusted chair for King Manuel and a live rhinoceros from his park for Albuquerque. All most courteous. The only problem was that the negotiations came to nothing. The sultan had no intention of allowing the Portuguese to build a fortress at Diu, fearing quite reasonably that it could be used at some point to attack him.[3]

When the mission returned to Goa, an angry Albuquerque considered launching an attack on the sultan and taking Diu by force, though he eventually decided against such a move. There remained however the problem of his gift from the sultan. Albuquerque does not seem to have been enamoured with the upkeep commitments involved in the retention of a live rhino. He alighted on a solution: he would send the rhinoceros on to Lisbon as a gift for his king, who as we have seen maintained a menagerie of exotic animals, as did other European courts.

The rhinoceros was loaded on to one of the ships of a flotilla leaving Cochin for Lisbon in January 1515. The journey lasted some 120 days, the rhinoceros subsisting, apparently without ill effect, on a diet of cooked rice.[4] The rhinoceros caused a stir on arrival in Lisbon. It was the first live rhino to be seen in Europe since the third century. The rhinoceros had been described by Pliny the Elder and had been part of the menageries of Roman emperors, so the appearance of such a creature in sixteenth-century Portugal seemed to bring the ancient world into the present. The king was reportedly most pleased with his gift.[5]

One of the stories about the rhinoceros recounted by historians of classical times concerned its reported enmity with the elephant. King Manuel decided on a diverting experiment to test this out. The rhinoceros would fight a duel with one of the elephants in the king's collection. The battle was held on 3 June 1515. The youngest elephant in the menagerie was chosen as the rhino's adversary, and the two animals were brought separately into a specially laid out arena. The young elephant went into a blind panic at the first sight of the advancing rhinoceros, charged against a barred grille that formed part of the arena wall, broke it down and headed to safety through the streets of Lisbon. The rhino casually patrolled the enclosure, celebrating its bloodless victory.[6]

The rhino's celebrated place in art history arose through a letter sent from Lisbon to a member of the merchant community of Nuremberg, describing the rhinoceros and enclosing a sketch of the beast. The letter and sketch came into the hands of celebrated Nuremberg artist Albrecht Dürer. The woodcut made by Dürer, based on this sketch and description, was widely reproduced and became the standard image of the rhinoceros across Europe for several centuries.

Dürer was noted for the painstaking detail of his drawings of plants and animals, made from direct observation.[7] His famous watercolours *Young Hare* and *Great Piece of Turf* are striking examples. However, he had of course never actually seen the live rhinoceros. His woodcut of the animal presents the rhinoceros in a surprising degree of detail, given that he was working from a description and sketch.[8] Inevitably, some of this was extrapolated, or guessed at. The rhinoceros of his woodcut has skin like armour plate, and a second, smaller horn at the top of its head, owing something to images of unicorns. The rhinoceros immortalised by Dürer was then at least in part the beast of his imagination.

While Dürer's rhinoceros was immortalised, the actual creature had not long to live. As we saw in our previous story, King Manuel had been well pleased with the outcome of his 'mission of obedience' to Pope Leo X in 1514. Portugal's continuing discoveries in the east required further papal endorsement, and Manuel decided on another mission to Rome to ensure the continuing goodwill of the pope. His gift of an elephant having been such a success, he decided to make the rhinoceros the central gift of his next mission. It was provided with a fringed green velvet collar to look all the smarter. Supporting gifts included large quantities of spices, to underline the wealth of the new territories of the east, and a selection of silver items from the royal treasury.[9] A fine gift indeed, though not of the level of lavishness of the gifts accompanying the king's 'mission of obedience' of the previous year.

The ship bearing the rhinoceros set sail in December 1515. It reached Marseille the following month. By coincidence, the French king, François I, was visiting the city. Learning that there was a Portuguese vessel bearing a rhinoceros in the bay, the French king asked to see the animal. This was arranged, making for a nice diplomatic event, which seems to have fired François' interest in the collection of exotic beasts, for soon afterwards he sent a mission to Lisbon to purchase elephants for his court.[10]

Sailing on, the Portuguese ship ran into a fierce storm off La Spezia. It sank with the loss of all on board. The rhino also drowned: shackled to the deck, it had no chance to attempt to swim to the shore. Indeed, there is speculation that the frightened movements across the deck of the chained rhino may have been a contributory factor to the shipwreck.[11]

The rhino's carcass was recovered on the shore close to Villefranche. Manuel instructed that the beast should be stuffed with straw and mounted. It was placed on another ship and sent to Rome.[12] It seems that a gift of a stuffed rhinoceros was decidedly less exciting for the pope than the living creature, as there is little evidence of what became of this gift. One isolated academic reference from 1892 offers a second-hand report of a preserved sixteenth-century rhinoceros being part of the collection of the Royal Museum of Vertebrates in Florence,[13] but this is a vague and anti-climactic end for the rhinoceros that inspired Dürer, and whose imagined form became the model for how the creature was perceived across Europe.

The story was reimagined at the end of the twentieth century by British novelist Lawrence Norfolk as *The Pope's Rhinoceros*,[14] in which Pope Leo X, delighted with his elephant, now craves a rhino. Portugal and Spain, desiring favourable papal judgements in respect of their claims in the newly explored lands, each endeavour to get him one: Portugal from India, Spain from Africa. This is a story of more than 750 pages, taking in all manner of plot complications, including a group of monks of the island of Usedom, whose monastery is gradually crumbling into the Baltic, and who determine to seek guidance from the pope. A work of fiction, but with a real diplomatic gift at its heart.

1520

A HORSE

A GIFT FROM FRANÇOIS I, KING OF FRANCE, TO HENRY VIII, KING OF ENGLAND

The Field of the Cloth of Gold, a 1545 work of the British school. A venue for competitive gift-giving between King François I of France and King Henry VIII of England.

Among animals presented as diplomatic gifts, horses held a particularly important position in many periods and places. A horse was of use to almost everyone, and therefore a welcome gift, but it was not just a quotidian means of transport. A horse was a symbol of chivalry, a trait shared with gifts of swords and armour, and thus particularly suitable as a gift for a ruler.[1] Horses were an essential part of noble lives, in hunting, tournaments and pageants. An unusual or exotic breed could inspire the wonder achieved by the rarest diplomatic gifts. Gifts of horses could be elaborately packaged, through fine saddles and other trappings. The finest horses represented a lavish gift indeed.[2]

Our equine story unfolds at a spectacular event in the Pas de Calais region of northern France in the summer of 1520, known ever since as the Field of Cloth of Gold. The event involved eighteen days of tournaments, feasts and entertainments during which two young kings representing age-old rival countries attempted to portray themselves to the other as able, athletic and cultivated leaders.

The gathering was an expression of a call for peace between the Christian rulers of Europe. Renaissance humanists such as Erasmus and Thomas More argued that kings could seek glory through peace rather than through war and conquest. The growing threat from the Ottomans was a cause for alarm, and Pope Leo X pushed for peace between the rulers of Europe so they could collectively counter the enemies of Christendom.

Cardinal Thomas Wolsey, Henry VIII's Lord High Chancellor, devised not just a truce to allow European rulers to come together to fight the Ottomans but a more ambitious treaty of universal peace, signed in London in 1518. The treaty required the kings of England and France to meet personally to confirm their commitment to the peace.[3] The stage was set for the Field of Cloth of Gold. It was not itself a place for peace negotiations: the treaty had already been signed. Rather, it was a spectacle allowing the two leaders to be presented in a way that exalted their status as young and powerful rulers, quite capable of leading armies, but who had chosen to forsake war for peace and brotherhood.[4]

Henry VIII of England and François I of France were rivals. Henry VIII greatly admired Henry V, victor of Agincourt, and had already gone to war once with France early in his reign. The two kings also admired each other. This ambivalent relationship was expressed in a display of what historian Glenn Richardson describes as 'demonstrative masculinity'[5] in the sporting competitions and entertainments of the Field of Cloth of Gold.

Diplomatic gifts played an important role at the event, deployed not just to cement the alliance between the two kings but also as instruments of the rivalry between them.[6] This included reciprocated largesse disbursed towards the other royal households. Jewellery and plate were gifted widely, providing an opportunity to showcase the skills of the goldsmiths engaged by the two monarchs. One of the finest exchanges was that of a jewelled collar from Henry to François, reciprocated by a jewelled bracelet.[7]

Some of the most significant gifts were made apparently spontaneously. On 17 June, François rode to Henry's lodgings at the town of Guînes, banged on the door of the chamber of the English king, not long up, and declared himself to be Henry's prisoner. In a sense, he was offering himself as a gift. He helped put on Henry's shirt, and Henry then gave the French king a jewelled collar, which he promptly reciprocated. While helping the English king to dress might appear a show of humility, François' actions feel assertive, not least in claiming the right to behave so familiarly to

Henry. The attention paid by both kings to reciprocity throughout the Field of Cloth of Gold was such that Henry seems to have felt compelled to make a somewhat awkward early morning visit to François' lodgings at Ardres two days later.[8]

Our gift horse was also a spontaneous present. It came early during the Field of Cloth of Gold, when the two kings rode to the tournament. Henry admired the fine horse of the French king, a mount named Dappled Duke, which had come from the Mantuan stud of Federico II Gonzaga. François promptly gave it to him as a gift. Henry reciprocated by giving François his own horse, a Neapolitan courser. According to Soardino, the Mantuan ambassador to the French court, Henry's return gift was by far the inferior of the two animals,[9] but since Soardino's comment was made in a letter back to the Mantuan court that provided the other horse in the first place, it was hardly a neutral judgement.[10] Coursers bred in the Kingdom of Naples, strong and brave horses well suited to the requirements of the tournament and to cavalry warfare, were also highly desirable.[11]

Dappled Duke was but one of many horses gifted during the Field of Cloth of Gold. Henry's habit of openly admiring the horses of French nobles also secured him the gifts of the mounts of Charles, duc de Bourbon, and of Marshal Lescun. François made a gift of a further six horses to Henry later in the event, four of which were from Mantua, a present made to balance the earlier exchange of jewellery in which the French king seems to have worried that his gift to Henry had been inferior in value to the jewelled collar he had received.[12] Queen Catherine of Aragon presented Queen Claude of France with a selection of palfreys, a horse valued for the smoothness of the ride secured by its ambling gait, as well as hobbies, a breed we will encounter later. Queen Claude reciprocated with a cloth of gold, mules and pages.[13]

The gift of Dappled Duke is part of another, wider story, that of the use of diplomatic gifts of horses to and by the Gonzagas of Mantua both in enhancing the quality of their stock and in securing advantage from such a high-quality stock. The Gonzagas had ruled Mantua in northern Italy since 1328, and the family's passion for horses had developed under later marquises, reaching its peak with Francesco II Gonzaga, ruler of the city from 1484 to 1519. While the Gonzagas bred a range of horses at their studs, focused on different activities, their most important goal was to produce horses able to maintain a sustainable speed.[14] The motivation was to secure personal renown through success in the horse races held in many Italian cities on the day of the city's patron saint or another suitably festive occasion. This type of race was known as a *palio*, a term deriving from the ornate and costly banner presented to the winner. The *palio* of Siena, involving three laps of the shell-shaped Piazza del Campo, survives to this day.[15]

To secure the qualities needed for success in these races, the Gonzagas sought out breeds from North Africa and the Ottoman Empire offering both speed and stamina. Their trade with the Ottomans and Islamic Hafsid dynasty in North Africa took place against a backdrop of not just religious differences but also long periods of war between the Ottoman Empire and Christian Europe.[16] Barb or Berber horses were a standard diplomatic gift of the Hafsids of Tunis,[17] and the Gonzagas were dogged in securing the horses they needed, including in overcoming a theoretical prohibition by the Hafsid rulers on the sale of mares.[18]

They used similar persistence in their dealings with the Ottomans, underpinned by a cordial personal relationship between Francesco II Gonzaga and the Ottoman Sultan Bayezid II. This was partly a matter of their shared love of horse breeding[19] but had also been warmed by the assistance given by Francesco to an ambassador of the sultan, robbed in Ancona while en route to deliver money to the sultan's imprisoned brother. Francesco helped the poor envoy complete his mission and return safely to Constantinople. Bayezid offered a thank-you gift of a boatload of Turkish horses, which was reciprocated by Francesco with a gift of Mantuan cheese,[20] offering further evidence of the importance we have already explored of that foodstuff as a diplomatic gift from city-states in Italy. The friendship between the two leaders enabled Francesco to overcome strict Ottoman rules on the selling of horses, for example in securing the purchase of eight mares and a stallion in 1491.[21]

Horses from the Ottoman Empire were also obtained by the Gonzagas in the very different political context of spoils of war. In the early sixteenth century, Gonzagas fought as mercenaries with forces opposing the Ottomans. One of the military captains of Francesco's son, Federico II Gonzaga, wrote to his ruler in 1525 of a horse taken from Turkish prisoners that he intended to send to the marquis, and which he said was the brother of a horse he had sent the year before.[22]

The quality of the Mantuan stud, with the infusion into its bloodstock of the sustainable speed of horses from North Africa and the Ottoman Empire, made Mantuan horses an object of desire of other European courts. The Gonzagas used them as diplomatic gifts to develop their European alliances. The French court were eager recipients. The Mantuan ambassador at the French court wrote in 1504 of Louis XII's impatience to receive two coursers promised by Francesco II Gonzaga.[23] François I's mount at the Field of Cloth of Gold is further evidence of the attachment of the French court to Mantuan horses.

Henry VIII had himself already received Mantuan horses before Dappled Duke. Francesco II Gonzaga appears to have had early misgivings about using his horses as diplomatic gifts for the English king, fearing that Henry lacked the refined knowledge of horsemanship to enable him to appreciate such a gift, but he evidently overcame these, sending four coursers to Henry in 1514. The English king was delighted, reporting that this was the most agreeable present he had ever received.[24] In return, Henry gifted Francesco some hounds as well as an Irish breed of horse known as the hobby, a breed of strong interest to the Gonzagas because of its excellent sprint speed.[25] The Gonzagas had already acquired eight hobbies on a buying trip in 1511.[26] This breed, now extinct, is incidentally an ancestor of the modern term hobby, via the expression 'hobby-horse' and the physical hobby horses ridden round the playrooms of wealthy children of a bygone age.

Henry maintained an interest in Mantuan racehorses. His ambassador at the papal court in Rome attempted to secure Berber horses from Federico II Gonzaga over several years, finally receiving the desired brood mares in 1532. These were housed at the racing stud and stables Henry had established at Greenwich and were clearly aimed at contributing to a breeding programme that would allow the English king to add qualities of sustainable speed to his horses.[27] The Gonzagas' breeding policy and selection of horses, coupled with their use of horses as diplomatic gifts for European courts, would therefore play a role in laying the foundations for the later development of the English thoroughbred and of a horseracing system that would lead the world.[28]

1527

A SUIT OF ARMOUR

A GIFT FROM HENRY VIII, KING OF ENGLAND, TO FRANÇOIS II DE LA TOUR D'AUVERGNE, THE VICOMTE DE TURENNE

The horned helmet given by Holy Roman Emperor Maximilian I
to King Henry VIII.

We explored in our previous story the importance of horses as diplomatic gifts, the associations of these animals with chivalry and with leadership on the battlefield making them particularly suitable presents for kings and princes. For similar reasons, armour was an important medieval and Renaissance gift. It would simultaneously flatter the recipient as a possessor of such attributes and identify them with the giver. A suit of armour had further advantages as a diplomatic gift. It could showcase the technological and manufacturing skill of the gifting country, and it could serve as a canvas for a display of fine artistic work, through engraving and other decoration. Princely armouries across Europe evolved from simple stores of the armour and weapons of the ruler into grand buildings in which the monarch would tell the story of their own dynasty through its arms and armour and display items received as gifts from other rulers.[1]

In exploring the eighth-century gift of an organ from the Byzantine emperor to the king of the Franks, we investigated the role of diplomatic gifts as agents of technological change. Our current story, culminating in the gift of a suit of armour by Henry VIII to the vicomte de Turenne, the head of a French diplomatic mission to London in 1527, involves not only a diplomatic gift spurring the production of comparable armour in the receiving state, but ultimately the triumphant use of the ensuing domestically made armour as fine diplomatic gifts of that state.

Our story starts with Holy Roman Emperor Maximilian I, a ruler who considerably expanded the Habsburg domains, both through war and marriage, his own and that of his son. Maximilian cultivated the image of a military emperor, distinguished by courage and chivalry, using a passion for armour as part of this propagandist endeavour.[2] He developed the armoury at Innsbruck into one of the most notable armour-producing centres in Europe[3] and gave his name to a style of armour featuring elaborate fluting.[4] Armour was a favoured diplomatic gift of Maximilian to the young King Henry VIII, who likewise had ambitions to be seen as a great military ruler. Shared concerns about French ambitions brought the two rulers together in the Holy League.

A diplomatic gift of armour from Maximilian to Henry forms perhaps the most bizarre item in the collection of the Royal Armouries Museum in Leeds, and one that served as the inspiration for the museum's logo. It is an armet, a type of helmet that encloses the entire head. It is however no ordinary armet. It is etched with lifelike, but far from flattering, facial details, including stubble and a dripping nose. It is sporting a pair of spectacles. Oh, and it has a pair of ram's horns, made from sheet iron. It was part of a full suit of armour, the rest now lost, made by Konrad Seusenhofer, a leading armourer in Maximilian's employ, and gifted in 1514.[5] The peculiar countenance is suggestive of a fool, and it seems the armour was intended for court pageants, where Henry may have worn it as a jape. Scholars have though long fretted about the unseemly nature of this strange armet as a gift for a king, particularly the horns, commonly regarded at the time as a symbol of a cuckold. On display at the Tower of London, it was for a long period believed to have been the armour of Will Somers, Henry's jester, though he joined the court more than a decade after the armet was received.[6]

Maximilian made other, more conventional, gifts of armour to Henry. They include a fine horse armour. This has become known as the Burgundian Bard, as its etched surfaces are decorated with symbols representing the Burgundian Order of the Golden Fleece, alongside pomegranates, Maximilian's personal emblem. The bard was probably made for either Maximilian or his son, before being gifted by the Holy Roman Emperor to Henry. It is also now part of the collection of the Royal Armouries Museum in Leeds.

When Henry VIII became king in 1509, England was not a particularly distinguished centre for the production of armour. While the weakness of this industry before Henry arrived on the throne has been overstated,[7] England lacked anything to resemble the great European centres of armour manufacture, such as Milan, Augsburg and Nuremberg, and Henry's predecessors had generally commissioned their armour from overseas.[8] Henry was determined to set up a royal production of armour and established a workshop at Greenwich early in his reign.[9] The diplomatic gifts of armour from Maximilian seem to have been one of the factors stimulating this determination,[10] not least in fuelling a desire on the English king's part to be able to offer fine locally made armour as a diplomatic gift of his own.[11]

The Greenwich armoury was modelled on Maximilian's court workshop at Innsbruck. The king paid the wages of the craftsmen, who worked only for him. He also owned the premises and paid for the raw materials.[12] This was very different from the practice in cities like Milan, whose firms made armour on commission.[13] To develop the manufacture at Greenwich, Henry brought in skilled craftsmen from continental Europe, particularly Italians, Flemings and Germans. The Flemish goldsmith responsible for the decoration of the Burgundian Bard, Paul van Vrelant, was one of those enticed to Greenwich, where he was appointed as Henry's harness gilder.[14]

Our featured diplomatic gift is a richly decorated suit of armour, with accompanying armour for a horse, which bears the date of 1527 and forms part of the collection of the Metropolitan Museum of Art in New York. It was long known as the armour of Galiot de Genouillac, a grand master of artillery and grand equerry of the king of France in the early sixteenth century. It had been handed down through the de Crussol family, ducs d'Uzès, who believed according to family tradition that the armour had belonged to Galiot, whose daughter had married into the family. They sold it to a collector, and the armour later came into the museum's possession.[15]

It is now believed to be the work of the Greenwich armoury, and to have been the suit of armour gifted by Henry VIII to François II de la Tour d'Auvergne, vicomte de Turenne, during a French diplomatic mission to London in 1527. The mission had two central, linked, objectives. To negotiate a marriage between Princess Mary and Henri, duc d'Orléans, the future King Henri II, and to agree an alliance between England and France against the Holy Roman Empire.[16] An account of the mission records that Henry brought Turenne to Greenwich and ordered a suit of armour to be made for him, modelled on his own.[17]

The armour is richly etched and gilded across its entire surface and clearly intended to offer an image of splendour. While some of its decoration hints at strength, notably depictions of the labours of Hercules, much is decidedly unmartial in character. This includes a mermaid and merknight, elephants with castles on their backs, a drunken Bacchus, doves, hares, peacocks, a group including Mars, Venus and Cupid, and loads of putti. The latter play with parrots on leashes and perform what appears to be a Morris dance around a nude girl who is holding a ring and apple as prizes. Much of this decoration hints at love and betrothal, perhaps referencing the central objective of the mission. It is possible too that the castles on the backs of the elephants are intended to suggest the name of the recipient: de la Tour.[18] Hans Holbein the Younger, who was working in England during this period, has been suggested as the artist.[19] The vicomte de Turenne died just five years after his mission to England. It seems likely that the armour was gifted to Genouillac either by Turenne or posthumously by his family.[20]

The suit of armour gifted by Henry VIII was not just richly etched and gilded; it was also technologically innovative. An unusual ventral plate was strapped beneath the breastplate and helped reduce the weight that needed to be supported from the shoulders. Such a plate was also found on a suit of Greenwich armour made for Henry VIII in 1540.

There is however an intriguing indication that the innovation of the ventral plate may have been learned by the armourers of Greenwich through another diplomatic gift. We must travel back to 1520, and to the preparatory meetings ahead of the Field of Cloth of Gold. In March of that year, Sir Richard Wingfield, Henry VIII's ambassador in France, presented François I with a diplomatic gift: a particularly heavy two-handed sword. The French king struggled to wield it and was informed that Henry was able to master the sword with the help of a special type of gauntlet. François clearly wanted to get his hands on one of these gauntlets and offered to swap one for a pair of innovative cuirasses, whose design allowed the weight of those armour pieces that rested on it to be taken off the shoulders.[21] This sounds very much like the ventral plate in the armour Henry gifted to the vicomte de Turenne, suggesting that the exchange mooted by François may indeed have taken place, with the armourers of Greenwich learning the innovation of the ventral plate from the French cuirass.[22]

It seems then that technology contained in a gift from the French king to the English one was studied and improved upon by the armourers of the English king and incorporated in a diplomatic gift that headed back across the English Channel to France. This demonstrates again the role of diplomatic gifts in promoting technological change. The reported behaviour of François suggests too that rulers might request specific items to enable them to understand and develop a technology of interest.

1571

TWENTY-FIVE ROBES OF HONOUR

A GIFT FROM SELIM II, SULTAN OF THE OTTOMAN EMPIRE, TO ISTVÁN BÁTHORY, *VOIVODE* OF TRANSYLVANIA

The Ghaznavid ruler Mahmud of Ghazni receiving a robe of honour from Abbasid
Caliph al-Qadir in 1000.

We have explored the gifting of costly silks by Byzantine emperors, whose
meaning was intended to suggest not reciprocation between equals but the
subservience of the recipient. The use of diplomatic gifts to display a hierarchical rather than equal relationship is also seen in the practice of many
Islamic rulers of gifting robes of honour.

The practice has pre-Islamic origins[1] but also draws from the act of the
Prophet Muhammad of gifting the mantle he was wearing to the poet Ka'b
ibn Zuhayr.[2] It draws too on the aforementioned Byzantine traditions of
the gifting of ceremonial silks. Robes of honour were a central part of the
gifting strategies of the Ottoman sultans, as they had been of the Abbasids,
Fatimids and Mamluks. They were only given from a superior, usually the
sultan, to an inferior. We have seen in an earlier story the anger of the
Mamluk sultan on receiving a robe of honour from another ruler, taking
this as the grave insult it was no doubt intended to be.

The robe was a symbol of the ruler's trust and protection. Accepting it was a mark of the receiver's loyalty to the sultan. Known as *hil'at* in Ottoman Turkish, the robe of honour was used in a wide range of contexts, domestic as well as diplomatic. These included palace celebrations, religious holidays, rewarding a task well executed, marking a promotion or signalling the arrival of the recipient or departure from the presence of the sultan.[3] Their use as diplomatic gifts was linked to the conceptual basis of Ottoman diplomacy, which drew from Islamic principles. The clear division between the abode of Islam and the abode of the infidels[4] could be intermediated through treaties, in which the Ottoman Empire regulated its relations with non-Muslim powers through payment of tribute by the latter.[5]

These relationships were formalised through a charter known as an *ahd-name*, commonly referred to in English as a capitulation. This typically provided commercial privileges and significant rights for citizens under the protection of the ambassador and consuls of the recipient state.[6] There was no attempt on the Ottoman side to negotiate reciprocal rights. This is partly because the commercial imperative was in many cases absent, since the Ottomans were not seeking to establish trading communities across Christian Europe. More fundamentally, its roots lie in the unilateral character of Ottoman diplomacy, which stood apart from participation in the emerging European diplomatic model of reciprocity and equality between states. With the Ottoman Empire strong and expanding, its unilateral diplomacy allowed it to express a contempt for this European model.[7] The Ottoman sultan instead regarded the capitulation itself as a diplomatic gift, whose purpose was to build the friendship that was central to these treaties.[8]

This friendship was expressed through gifts, but gifts of an unequal character. The gifts given by the sultan focused on a set of insignia reflective of the sultan's status and authority, with robes of honour at centre stage. In contrast, the sultan viewed the gifts received as a tribute. Such an explicit recognition of a subordinated relationship was of course uncomfortable for other rulers, who would attempt to frame the gift relationships in a different way. Thus, while the Ottoman Turkish text of the capitulations with Britain of 1641 refers to 'tributary gifts', the English translation speaks of 'presents'.[9] If there was a change of sultan, the *ahd-name* had to be reconfirmed, both reinforcing its character as a personal gift of the sultan and giving the Ottomans a further lever through which to control the relationship.[10]

The insignia gifted by the sultan provided a visual underscoring of Ottoman supremacy. Ambassadors received by the sultan would not only be given a robe of honour but were required to wear it during the reception. While honouring the visiting envoys, this also subjugated them, obliging them to wear the fashion of their hosts.[11] At the Peace of Karlowitz of 1699, following the defeat of the Ottomans at the Battle of Zenta, marking the decline of Ottoman power in Europe after centuries of expansion, no dress code was given to the Habsburg delegation.[12] The gradual acceptance by the Ottomans of the reciprocity-based European state system had begun, though it would not be completed until the mid-nineteenth century.[13]

The requirement for foreign envoys to wear the robe of honour was also a means of bringing lawless infidels into the system: regularising their status within a framework understandable to the Ottomans, and thereby enabling both their presence before the sultan and the conduct of negotiations.[14] The robe obscured the individuality of the wearer.[15]

Every *hil'at* was not, however, identical. They were of markedly different qualities, in terms of the type of textile used and degree of ornamentation. The quality of the *hil'at* received by an envoy would vary according to the Ottoman perception of their rank and the importance of their country. The sultan also used the gifting of different quantities of robes of honour to distinguish between states in and out of favour. Notwithstanding the subjugation implied by the garment, they were marks of prestige, and envoys were concerned if they appeared to receive fewer or poorer quality items than those representing other countries. Thus, the Transylvanian ambassador complained in 1618 that his mission had received few robes, and not particularly good ones at that.[16]

The desirability of the Ottoman *hil'at* was enhanced by an interesting characteristic. They do not appear to have been easily identifiable as robes of honour. Unlike the robes used by Abbasid and Mamluk rulers, they lacked *tiraz* bands – the embroidered inscription bands usually found on the sleeves. They were varied in terms of colour, ornamentation and textile. Art historian Amanda Phillips identifies only one distinguishing characteristic: their particularly long sleeves, which may have hung freely over the back of the shoulders rather than being worn.[17] The varied nature of the robes of honour, and lack of clear identifying characteristics, meant that they could be sold on without risk to either seller or buyer.[18]

The *hil'at* essentially had a dual identity. At the time of gifting, it embodied the sultan, evoking Mauss's concept of the spirit of the gift, serving as a material representation of the sultan's power.[19] When the act of giving and receiving the *hil'at* was completed, and the supremacy of the sultan confirmed, the object itself was transformed into a simple luxury textile. Its symbolic importance disappeared, and the recipient was left with its value as an item of apparel. Arjun Appadurai's work on the changing personality of objects is relevant here. Thus, the robes of honour given to Transylvania were often repurposed into the jacket known as the *dolmány*.[20]

The exchanges between Selim II, Ottoman sultan from 1566 to 1574, and István Báthory, ruler of the principality of Transylvania, a vassal state of the Ottoman Empire, offer a good example of a gift relationship based not on reciprocity but on subservience, in which robes of honour play an important role as symbols of the sultan's authority. Vassal states offered the Ottomans advantages over attempting to rule direct lands distant from Constantinople and provided a buffer zone against powerful enemies such as the Habsburgs.[21] For Transylvania's rulers, vassal status gave them the protection of the sultan, in return for the payment of a yearly tribute and support where necessary for the sultan's armies. István Báthory sought as far as possible to play off his powerful neighbours, Habsburg and Ottoman, to give Transylvania as much autonomy as possible, and it was able to maintain a relatively freer position than vassal states such as Wallachia and Moldavia, closer to the centre of Ottoman power. It was for example not required to send hostages to Constantinople, and paid less tribute.[22]

The relationship between the Ottoman sultan and his Transylvanian vassal was set out in an *ahdname*, the sultan's 'gift' to the Transylvanian ruler.[23] On being informed by the Transylvanian lords of the election of István Báthory as their new ruler in 1571, Sultan Selim sent two imperial orders, known as *fermans*, to the lords and to István himself, confirming the appointment. The confirmation of the hierarchical relationship between the two rulers was also achieved visually through the despatch of gifts representing the sultan's insignia. These were conveyed by an envoy, Mehmed Aga, Selim's falconer, who arrived in Alba Iulia on 15 August with 200 horsemen and not a few camels. He was met by István outside the town, and the first of the insignia was handed over, a banner known as a *sancak*. The same word described an administrative unit within the Ottoman Empire, and the gifting of the banner conveyed that the sultan regarded the ruler of a vassal state in the same way as he would one of his regional governors.[24]

On the third day following Mehmed Aga's arrival, the remaining insignia were handed over at a large ceremony. These included twenty-five robes of honour, one for István himself, the others for his leading lieutenants. István was instructed to allocate these according to the rank of the lords. There was also a hat, a further symbol of loyalty to the sultan, and a mace, which represented the sultan's military authority. Maces gifted by the sultan were, like robes of honour, of different qualities according to the status of the recipient: the heavier and more ornate the better. István also received several horses, which would have been decorated with fine trappings. Horses played a significant role in Ottoman culture, representing both power and military skill.[25] Mehmed's delegation left after a fortnight, and he was given a parting gift of 8,000 gold coins by István, a present that reportedly reduced him to tears, though not in a good way. He had been expecting more.[26]

István's gift to the sultan was similarly determined by the latter. It centred on a yearly tribute of 10,000 gold florins. This however needed to be supplemented by a complex system of gift payments, known as *pişkeş*, to the many Ottoman officials involved in the submission of the tribute. These payments were almost equal to that of the tribute itself. They served an additional purpose for István in helping him to build his network in the Ottoman court, which could help ensure that he remained in favour against the ambitions of rival candidates for his throne. While it is tempting to regard these payments as bribes, they were given to a formula determined by the Ottomans and so were in a sense an unstated part of the tribute. In addition to coin, cups were gifted as part of these payments. Falcons were also involved and were collected separately by Ottoman falconers.[27]

This was therefore a gift exchange based on hierarchy, not reciprocity. The gifts both given to and received by the sultan were determined by the sultan. Those gifted by him were symbols of his authority, underscoring his supremacy. In return, he received gifts of material value, principally gold coins.

The diplomatic gifting of ceremonial robes continues to offer challenges to the recipient. An intricately embroidered cloak known as a *chapan*, together with a matching hat and belt, is for example a favoured gift in Kazakhstan to an honoured guest.[28] During an official visit to that country in 2014, French President François Hollande received from President Nursultan Nazarbayev a particularly fine beige fur-trimmed cloak and fur hat, in which he was dressed for an official photograph.[29] President Hollande gazes uneasily at the camera, as if imagining the online criticism of his attire likely to come. It did.

1613

A TELESCOPE

A GIFT FROM JAMES I AND VI, KING OF ENGLAND, SCOTLAND AND IRELAND, TO TOKUGAWA IEYASU, RETIRED SHŌGUN OF JAPAN

The Japan400 Presentation Telescope, made by I. R. Poyser Telescopes
to mark the 400th anniversary of the telescope gifted by
King James I and VI to Tokugawa Ieyasu.

Our next story is about the use of a diplomatic gift to promote the gifting country as a suitable trading partner over the claims of rival powers. The East India Company would grow to account for half the world's trade, and to control much of the Indian subcontinent, but in 1613 it was still a teenager. In its attempts to secure trading rights with Japan, it came in the wake of the Spanish, Portuguese and Dutch, none of whom wished to see a new competitor on the ground. The first diplomatic gifts presented by the company on behalf of the British king to the Japanese ruler would need to serve as a calling card, to explain what Britain represented and why the Japanese would wish to trade with it in preference to its European rivals.[1] The most unusual of the items chosen for this purpose was a silver-gilt telescope.

The East India Company was born on New Year's Eve 1600, when Queen Elizabeth I of England and Ireland granted a Royal Charter to the Governor and Company of Merchants of London trading into the East

Indies. For an initial period of fifteen years, the company received a monopoly on English trade with all lands to the east of the Cape of Good Hope and west of the Strait of Magellan. Any other English subjects trading with these territories faced forfeiture of their ships and cargos, alongside a jail sentence.[2]

The initial focus of the new company was on the purchase of sought-after spices, setting up a permanent trading post, or 'factory', at Banten on the island of Java in 1603. Aceh on Sumatra was also important from an early stage as a source of pepper. The company however faced a challenge. During the long period of war with Spain, England had a source of silver with which to purchase these valuable products: that looted from Spanish ships. With the signature of the Treaty of London in 1604, concluding the war, that source of silver was lost. Silver could be purchased from the Spanish, but that would impact on the profitability of the enterprise.[3] The company needed to identify a British product that it could sell in exchange for the exotic Asian goods it sought.

The best candidate was woollen cloth, particularly the densely woven broadcloth highly regarded across Europe. There was however a limited demand for woollen cloth in the tropical climes of Java and Sumatra. The company alighted on Japan, a place known to have cold winters and presumably therefore a demand for woollen cloth. It was also a producer of silver that could, it was reasoned, be exchanged for the cloth and used in turn to purchase the spices and pepper.[4] As the company looked to develop its activities across Asia, as well as the engagement with India that would define its place in history, Japan was firmly in its sights.

The company sent out a mission in 1611 comprising three ships under the command of John Saris, an experienced Asia hand who had earlier been chief factor in Banten. Opening up trade with Japan was not the primary objective of the voyage. That honour fell to Surat, the main port of the Mughal Empire in the present-day Indian state of Gujarat. Saris was to follow up another East India Company mission, under Sir Henry Middleton, who had been tasked with securing trading rights at the port. Indeed, if the trade at Surat was sufficiently strong, Saris was instructed to return to England direct from there and not seek to reach Japan at all.[5] Fortunately for our story, the first part of the mission was entirely unsatisfactory and dominated by wrangling with Middleton's expedition. Saris was unable even to visit Surat. Two of his ships returned to London after loading up with spices in Banten, but Saris headed on to Japan with his flagship, the *Clove*, named for one of the most important products traded by the company.

In June 1613, the *Clove* arrived at the island port of Hirado, close to Nagasaki in southern Japan. The Dutch had already established a factory there, and Saris was welcomed by the local feudal lord, or *daimyō*. Hirado was ruled by the Matsura family, and local power was in the hands of Matsura Hōin, although the post of *daimyō* was formally held by his grandson. The *daimyō* reported to the *shōgun*, the military ruler, based in Edo, present-day Tokyo. The Tokugawa shogunate had been born in 1603, after Tokugawa Ieyasu emerged victorious from a period of domestic conflict and succeeded in unifying Japan. Ieyasu too was no longer formally the ruler. He had abdicated in 1605 in favour of his son, Tokugawa Hidetada. Like Hōin in Hirado, Ieyasu remained the real power in the country.

Saris was to receive help in navigating the power structures of Japan from an Englishman already living in the country. Born in Gillingham in Kent, William Adams had seen naval service against the Spanish Armada, before joining a Dutch expedition of five ships that set off from the Netherlands in 1598, seeking to reach Japan via the Strait of Magellan and the Pacific. Following a journey marked by storms, disease and the attacks of native peoples, only one of the ships reached Japan, in April 1600, with just twenty-four members of its crew of more than 100 still alive.[6] Ieyasu seized the ship and initially imprisoned the crew, but Adams's knowledge of maritime matters appealed to the Japanese ruler, for whom he became an adviser in relation to the West. He was accorded the status of a samurai, and his life inspired the character of John Blackthorne in James Clavell's blockbuster novel *Shōgun*.

On the *Clove*'s arrival in Japan, Adams headed to Hirado to meet Saris. The two men did not hit it off. Adams declined Saris's offer of hospitality in favour of Japanese-style accommodation, and Saris clearly felt that the other Englishman had gone bush.[7] Adams was however useful in advising Saris on how best to make a positive impression with the Japanese rulers, including the all-important matter of the selection of gifts.

Together with Adams, Saris headed first to Sunpu, modern-day Shizuoka, and the castle residence of Tokugawa Ieyasu. Adams would have made clear to him that this was the all-important meeting, and the value of the gifts selected for it were accordingly twice that of those earmarked for his son, the *shōgun*. Alongside various cloths and a burning glass was a silver-gilt telescope. Almost certainly the first telescope ever presented as a diplomatic gift, it is interesting to consider what lay behind the choice.

The telescope was a new innovation. It is first recorded in a patent submitted in 1608 in the Netherlands, and the first known mention in England comes from the following year.[8] It would therefore have both served to underline British scientific and technological sophistication and to offer the recipient an object of wonder. Art historian Timon Screech goes further. In his book *The Shogun's Silver Telescope*,[9] he argues that the choice of a telescope as a gift for Ieyasu was a deliberate attempt to undermine the position of Spain and Portugal in Japan, and particularly the Jesuit missionaries active in the country since the 1540s, thereby strengthening the hand of the British.

Screech's argument is that the astronomical observations possible with a telescope, as Galileo had shown in 1610, undermined the Ptolemaic model of the sun revolving around the earth, supporting instead the heliocentric model of the Solar System developed by Copernicus. These findings encountered opposition within the Catholic Church, which saw them as attempting to reinterpret the Bible. Screech argues that, since the Jesuits were valued in Japan in part for their knowledge of astronomy, for example in the prediction of eclipses, a gift that demonstrated the flawed nature of that knowledge would be damaging to their position.[10] In 1614, Ieyasu indeed ordered the expulsion of the missionaries.

It is an interesting hypothesis, though as Screech admits, we do not know the factors leading to the choice of the telescope as a gift for Ieyasu, as surviving documentation is largely silent on the matter.[11] One might question whether the quality of early lenses would make so obvious to the Japanese court the deficiencies of the Ptolemaic model. Galileo's problems with the Catholic hierarchy did not begin in earnest until 1615. Moreover, the telescope was described by Saris in his journal as a 'prospective glass',[12] which is perhaps more suggestive of the terrestrial, including military, uses of a telescope than astronomy. Against this, the second East India Company ship to reach Japan, in 1615, was the *Osiander*,[13] named after the theologian who converted the grand master of the Teutonic Knights to Lutheranism, so the confrontation with Catholicism does seem to have been high on the company's minds. It is not though necessary to invoke a telescope to explain Ieyasu's decision to expel the Catholic missionaries. He had long been concerned with their proselytising activities but had hitherto given priority to the advantages brought by trade with Portugal and Spain. The arrival of the British on the scene in 1613, alongside the Dutch, both of whom had committed not to conduct missionary activities in Japan, meant the importance of the Spanish and Portuguese as trading partners was correspondingly reduced.

From Sunpu, Saris and Adams headed onwards to Edo for their audience with the *shōgun*, Tokugawa Hidetada, presenting him with more cloth, as well as a 'great standing cup and cover'.[14] As a return gift for the king, the *shōgun* offered two suits of armour. One of these, still on display in the Tower of London, features a heraldic design linked to Takeda Katsuyori, leader of the Takeda clan, defeated by Tokugawa Ieyasu at the Battle of Tenmokuzan in 1582. The armour is signed by a Tokugawa armourer named Iwai Yozaemon and thus seems to be a battle trophy, refurbished by Yozaemon and repurposed as a diplomatic gift. If the gift to Ieyasu of a telescope was intended to advertise the technological sophistication of the British, this gifted armour seems similarly to have been intended to make a statement about the Tokugawa rulers, highlighting their unification of Japan through military success. The provenance of the armour was subsequently forgotten, and it suffered for many years a mislabelling as the 'armour of the Great Moghul'.[15]

Saris and Adams headed back to Sunpu, where Saris received an official letter from Ieyasu granting permission for the English to reside in and trade with Japan. Ieyasu's return gift consisted of ten gold-leaf folding screens, known as *byōbu*. Saris and the *Clove* set sail for England in December. Adams declined the offer to return with him, in part perhaps because the relationship between the two men was such that he did not relish being cooped up together in a small vessel, in part because he had made a good life in Japan and had a new family there. Saris's relationship with the East India Company soured on his return, amid concerns at the extent of his private trading activities as well as disgust at his having brought back 'certain lascivious books and pictures'[16] from his stay in Japan. He turned his back on the sea and, enriched from the voyage, lived wealthily in Fulham. The East India Company's trading with Japan was not however to prove fruitful, and they closed the factory at Hirado after just ten years of activity.

While the East India Company's engagement with Tokugawa Japan was a brief one, the Dutch East India Company (VOC) traded with them over a much longer period, for almost two centuries following the establishment of its first factory at Hirado in 1609. This relationship offers an insight into Japanese expectations around diplomatic gifts from its trading partners in the long term. While based at Hirado, until forced by the *shōgun* to relocate to Nagasaki in 1641, the diplomatic gifts presented by the Dutch to the *shōgun* and the *daimyō* were quite different in character. Gifts for the *shōgun* were often exotic or amazing items, from unfamiliar animals to a huge brass chandelier. Those gifted to the Matsura rulers of Hirado were desired quotidian luxuries, like cloth, pepper and cloves. These were items intended to be sold by the recipients for a profit. The *daimyō* gifts essentially served as an alternative to a formal system of taxation of the merchants' goods.[17]

The nature of the gifting relationship between the VOC and the *shōgun* changed over time. In their first exchanges, the VOC representatives invoked a fictional monarch, the 'king of Holland', to provide the *shōgun* with a clearly understandable counterpart with whom to deal, by misrepresenting the role of Prince Maurits, *Stadhouder* of some of the Dutch provinces.[18] This approach was gradually dropped. Instead of attempting to present itself as equal in status to the *shōgun*, the VOC adopted the position of a vassal. Gift-giving was routinised in the *hofreis*, a visit to the Japanese court by the chief merchant of the factory, which took on many of the features of the annual visits of submission to Edo by the *daimyō* across Japan.[19] Gift-giving became a more collaborative process, with Tokugawa officials providing the Dutch with lists of desired gifts. A list of items requested by the *shōgun* in 1652 ranged from an iron device to replace an amputated hand to mermaids' teeth.[20]

The fate of the silver-gilt telescope presented to Ieyasu in 1613 is unknown. The memory of that gift was revived in 2013 in the service of the bilateral relationship between the United Kingdom and Japan, as part of Japan400 celebrations marking the 400th anniversary of that first official encounter.[21] A new telescope was commissioned, crafted by Ian Poyser, a specialist in the construction of traditional brass telescopes. This was unveiled almost 400 years to the day after the presentation to Ieyasu, at a ceremony in Hatfield House, north of London, built by the first earl of Salisbury, who as chief minister to King James I would have been involved in selecting the original gift. The telescope was the subject of an academic seminar at Jesus College Cambridge, highlighting the bilateral partnership in science and technology, and then sent to Japan as a gift to the Japanese people.[22]

1623

GIAMBOLOGNA'S *SAMSON SLAYING A PHILISTINE*

A GIFT FROM FELIPE IV, KING OF SPAIN,
TO CHARLES, PRINCE OF WALES

Giambologna's *Samson Slaying a Philistine*.

The negotiation of marriages between ruling families has been in many historical periods and places one of the most important and fraught of diplomatic tasks, through which wars could be averted, or started, and as a result of which states could flourish, or decline. Diplomatic gifts have often played a central role in such marriage negotiations, as the anguish of poor King Tushratta of Mitanni over his promised two golden statues reminds us from our very first story. This is not just a matter of the agreement of a dowry: gifts are frequently part of different stages of the negotiation.

Our next tale concerns a marriage negotiation that ended in failure, but in which the associated diplomatic gifts helped engender a sea change in the way art was appreciated and collected in the recipient state. It centres on the attempt to broker marriage between the future King Charles I of England and the Infanta Maria Anna, younger sister of King Felipe IV of Spain.

When James Stuart, already king of Scotland, acceded to the English throne in 1603, the country was still at war with Spain. James was determined to pursue a policy of peace and fretted about the devastating impact of religious wars across Europe. He alighted on a policy of promoting the marriage of his children to major Protestant and Catholic ruling families as a means of dampening the flames of war.[1]

His eldest son, Henry, died of typhoid fever at the age of eighteen in 1612, leaving the king with a surviving son, Charles, and a daughter, Elizabeth. The first step in James's matrimonial diplomacy was the wedding of Elizabeth in 1612 to Friedrich V, the Elector Palatine. Friedrich was both ruler of the Palatinate, centred on the Rhineland, and the head of the Protestant Union, an alliance of Protestant princes anxious to prevent the dominance of the Holy Roman Empire by the Catholic Habsburgs.

Since the first wedding of one of James's children was to a Protestant ruler, his policy of seeking religious accord pointed to Charles's marriage into one of the great Catholic royal families. James alighted on the Infanta Maria Anna in Spain, with whom the marriage of his son offered the additional enticing prospect of a significant dowry, which, given his debts and difficulties in securing parliamentary approval for the subsidies to ease them, was an important factor. The Spanish ambassador, Diego Sarmiento de Acuña, count of Gondomar, was a key figure in the negotiations, which proceeded over several years.

As the negotiations continued, events in the Palatinate were clouding the picture and dashing James's vision of European peace. In 1618, largely Protestant Bohemia rebelled against its Catholic king, the future Holy Roman Emperor Ferdinand II, an action initiated by one of Prague's famous defenestrations, when two Catholic governors and a secretary were thrown from a window of the castle. The Thirty Years' War had begun. In 1619, Friedrich V was elected to the vacant Bohemian throne, putting him into the sights of Ferdinand and the House of Habsburg. Neither his father-in-law James nor the princes of the Protestant Union came to his aid, and he quickly lost both his new territories in Bohemia and the old ones in the Palatinate. By 1622, he had set up a Palatinate government-in-exile in The Hague and sought the restoration of his lands.

Charles was enthusiastic at the prospect of the match with the Infanta but frustrated at the slow pace of discussions. Encouraged by Gondomar, he decided to speed matters up. On 7 March 1623, Charles turned up, unannounced, at the residence of the British ambassador in Madrid, accompanied by George Villiers, the duke of Buckingham, a favourite of the king. They had been travelling as John and Tom Smith,[2] sporting false beards. Felipe quickly set up a formal Royal Entry to Madrid to welcome his unexpected guests in suitable style, though the theme chosen for a grand display, the Trojan War, was perhaps a portent of what was to come.[3] For Charles's journey to Spain was based on a misunderstanding of the situation and engendered further misunderstanding. Charles appeared to believe that the negotiations had all but concluded, and his journey to Madrid would simply speed up the process and allow him to collect his bride. He was following a romantic family tradition: James I had himself travelled to Copenhagen to bring back Anne of Denmark. Charles failed to appreciate that the Spanish would interpret his journey as an indication of his willingness to convert to Catholicism.[4] There would be disappointment and confusion when it became clear that he had no such intent. The Spanish role in Friedrich V's loss of the Palatine was a further complicating factor.

A papal dispensation was required to sanction the marriage of a Catholic princess to a Protestant prince, and not all in Madrid were as anxious as Ambassador Gondomar to see the union take place. The count of Olivares, chief minister of Felipe IV, strove to ensure that the pope's conditions for agreeing the dispensation were as burdensome as possible on the British. When it arrived in late April, the dispensation insisted both on freedom of worship for all English Catholics and the repeal of anti-Catholic legislation. These were conditions James would have found it politically extremely difficult to meet.[5] Negotiations stretched on into the summer, with little progress.

Charles had another objective in Madrid. He wanted to acquire art. The English delegation had been strengthened in late March. Among the new arrivals were advisers who would counsel the prince on appropriate purchases, among them Balthazar Gerbier and Tobie Matthew. Gerbier had already carried out an art-buying trip across Italy on behalf of Buckingham two years earlier.[6] Charles and Buckingham spent substantial sums on artworks, notably at the estate sales of deceased collectors. Charles purchased two paintings by Titian: *Young Woman with a Fur Coat* and *The Allegory of Alfonso d'Avalos*. The lure of Titian perhaps owed something to the rarity of the artist's work in English collections at that time, and something to the appeal to the young prince of the naked female flesh on display.[7]

Charles and his representatives made clear their interest in artworks from Felipe's stunning royal collection, but the Spanish king was initially reluctant to offer paintings as a diplomatic gift while the status of the marriage negotiations remained unclear.[8] Following the arrival of the papal dispensation, Felipe did gift a painting to Charles, and a Titian to boot. This was a portrait of Charles V, the Holy Roman Emperor and king of Spain during the first half of the sixteenth century, with a hunting dog. It was a reinterpretation of a slightly earlier painting by Jakob Seisenegger, carried out by Titian at Charles V's request[9] in Bologna following his coronation as Holy Roman Emperor by Pope Clement VII. The choice of painting appears to carry a message from Felipe to the English Prince Charles of invitation to join the Habsburg dynasty – provided he agrees to convert to Catholicism.[10] Felipe gifted another Titian to Charles in June. In *The Pardo Venus,* sometimes described as Jupiter and Antiope, the nudity of a sleeping Antiope, or possibly Venus, is revealed as Jupiter, in the form of a satyr, pulls back her bedsheet. Charles seems to have attempted to claim as his gift not just this mighty canvas but also a whole series of Titian's flesh-filled mythological scenes.[11] These were six paintings produced for Felipe II between 1554 and 1562 and known as the *Poesie.*[12] With the marriage negotiations going badly, Felipe was not playing ball.

Charles's negotiating tactic seemed to consist in large measure of accepting an ever increasing number of the Spanish demands, and by July he had agreed a deal involving the toleration of Catholicism in Britain, agreement to persuade parliament to abrogate anti-Catholic laws and acceptance that the Infanta would control the education of their children to the age of twelve.[13] It is difficult to see how James could have delivered these conditions given the strength of anti-Catholic feeling in parliament and the country. Charles seems to have judged that accepting these demands would allow him to leave Spain with his bride without further ado, but in this he was to be disappointed. The Spanish, with perhaps good reason, did not trust the English to deliver their commitments and would not allow the Infanta to leave Spain until the following year. Charles, increasingly disillusioned with the negotiations in Spain, and needing to return to England, authorised proxies to enable the finalisation of the marriage agreement when the necessary dispensation arrived from the new pope.

In September, Charles and his party left Madrid for Santander, where an English fleet would collect them. There would be one further opportunity to secure artistic diplomatic gifts on the way. The party stopped at Valladolid, visiting the royal residence of the Palacio de la Ribera, built by Francisco Gómez de Sandoval y Rojas, duke of Lerma, chief minister of King Felipe III. In the gardens, Charles was much taken with a fountain centred on a sculptural ensemble nearly 7 feet in height, displaying Samson about to thwack a fallen Philistine with the jawbone of an ass. It was the work of the Florence-based Flemish sculptor Giambologna, made around 1560 for the House of Medici. It had already served once as a diplomatic gift, from Ferdinando I de' Medici, grand duke of Tuscany, to the duke of Lerma, and shipped to Valladolid.

Charles also took a shine to a painting by Paolo Veronese at Valladolid of *Venus, Cupid and Mars*, confirming his predilection for sensually charged classical scenes. He and his party seem to have convinced their Spanish hosts, in the absence of King Felipe who had remained in Madrid, that the two works would make a suitable diplomatic gift to mark the prince's visit. This was behaviour pushing at and beyond the limits of the etiquette around diplomatic gifts. It was typical of the single-mindedness in the pursuit of artworks Charles had demonstrated throughout his Spanish visit.[14]

When Charles returned to England in October, the fact he had done so without a Spanish Catholic bride temporarily made him highly popular in his home country.[15] His humiliating experience in Spain pushed him towards embracing the cause of his brother-in-law Friedrich V in the Palatinate, although some historians argue that his vigour in doing so was an attempt to conceal to his people just how badly he had performed during the marriage negotiations in Madrid. The argument here is that a pretence that the failure of the negotiations was down to a principled stand over the restoration of his sister's place in the Palatinate was more acceptable than the truth that Charles had miscalculated the demands the Spanish would make to allow him to marry.[16] In 1625, the pacifist James I died. The newly enthroned Charles I declared war on Spain the same year. He did though wed a Catholic, Henrietta Maria, the youngest daughter of King Henri IV of France, whom he had first met in Paris in 1623 while heading to Spain to negotiate marriage to the Infanta.

Charles's Spanish trip had fuelled his passion for art. He had clearly been impressed by the Spanish royal collections and on return to England made efforts both to expand and properly inventorise his own collection. These efforts resulted in one of the greatest collections ever assembled by a British monarch. The appointment of Anthony van Dyck as court painter would revolutionise royal portraiture. While his aim may have been to use his art collection as a display of political power, the effect generated however was more that of profligacy, with parliament alarmed at the expense.

Following Charles's execution in 1649, his art collection was sold off and is now scattered throughout Europe. Titian's *Portrait of Charles V with a Dog* is back in Spain, at the Prado Museum. *The Pardo Venus* is in the Louvre. What of Giambologna's *Samson Slaying a Philistine*? Charles seems to have gifted it to his travelling companion, Buckingham, who paid £40 to have it shipped to England. It was installed in the gardens of

Buckingham's York House in London, where it was referred to in contemporary accounts as a statue of Cain and Abel. In the early eighteenth century, it was moved to Buckingham House and thereby came into the possession of King George III when he acquired the house, the future Buckingham Palace. The king then passed the statue on to Thomas Worsley, surveyor general of his majesty's works, who had it moved to his estate at Hovingham in Yorkshire. From there, it was acquired by the Victoria and Albert Museum, where it now resides.[17]

1716

THE AMBER ROOM

A GIFT FROM FRIEDRICH WILHELM I, KING IN PRUSSIA, TO PETER THE GREAT, TSAR OF RUSSIA

The Amber Room, photographed in 1917.

Our next story concerns a gift whose complicated history mirrors the peaks and troughs in the relationship between two European powers, Russia and Germany, over three centuries. It was a fabulous gift, providing enough panels of golden amber to fit out a room that would be acclaimed by visitors as the eighth wonder of the world.[1] The mystery around its current whereabouts has inspired a search stretching from Baltic shipwrecks to abandoned German mine workings in an effort to track down what may be the most valuable missing artwork in the world.[2]

The fossilised tree resin known as amber has been prized since prehistoric times, fashioned into jewellery and other decorative objects of a glorious golden hue. It is also used as an incense, as it burns with a sweet smell. When rubbed with a dry cloth, it produces static electricity, a property that gave us the very word 'electricity' – from *elektron*, the Greek word for amber. It was ascribed various medicinal properties[3] and is still used in teething necklaces, as the succinic acid found in amber is sometimes claimed to have anti-inflammatory qualities.

The southern Baltic enjoys a major reserve of amber, centred on the Samland Peninsula in the present-day Kaliningrad Oblast of the Russian Federation. The amber was traditionally retrieved from the Baltic Sea through a fishing technique, in which hardy souls would walk out into the choppy coastal waters holding large nets when conditions were right, collecting whatever detritus they could in the hope that amber pieces would be among it.[4] Amber, the 'gold of the north', was at the heart of a trade route known as the Amber Road, linking northern Europe and the Mediterranean in ancient times.

When the Hohenzollern dynasty inherited the Duchy of Prussia in 1618, creating the personal union of Brandenburg–Prussia, they took over the proprietary right to the amber within their territory that had been exercised by the rulers of the earlier crusader state, the State of the Teutonic Order.[5] This had been enforced brutally, with those attempting to collect amber privately facing the prospect of being hung from the nearest tree.[6] The direct association of the golden amber with the Hohenzollern rulers provided ideal conditions for its use as a diplomatic gift, as a prized, luxury material that could showcase the artistic talents of those fashioning it into a wide range of decorative objects, and which was closely associated with the Duchy of Prussia.

The Hohenzollern duke of Prussia managed in 1701 to upgrade his position to that of king, though the agreement with the Holy Roman Emperor establishing this monarchy gave him the curious title of 'king in Prussia' rather than king of Prussia. This reflected both the fact that part of the Prussian region fell outside the territory of the Duchy of Prussia and that he remained an elector under the ultimate authority of the Holy Roman Emperor.

The death in 1713 of the first king, Friedrich I, brought to the throne his son, Friedrich Wilhelm I. The latter was as frugal as his father had been lavish. Known as 'the Soldier King', his interests lay not in enhancing the artistic splendours of his court, as his father had done, but in modernising the Prussian army. He focused on sound management of his country's finances and sought to drive down excessive expenditures. This frugality extended to diplomatic gift-giving, where he frequently resorted to repurposing as gifts artworks his predecessors had acquired for their own collections. These made his gifts all the more prized, as they came with a history linked closely with that of the Prussian royal family.[7]

Friedrich Wilhelm I did though continue the family tradition of using amber as a diplomatic gift. One of the finest of these was a large amber cabinet presented in 1728 to Friedrich August I, elector of Saxony and king of Poland, whom we will meet more fully in our next story. The cabinet was not only a delightful piece in itself, but had been filled with further amber objects, including a chess set.[8]

The Amber Room, the greatest of Friedrich Wilhelm I's diplomatic gifts, combined these two traits of his gift-giving: the use of amber, and the repurposing of his predecessors' artworks. The idea of constructing a chamber panelled entirely in amber is usually ascribed to Prussian sculptor Andreas Schlüter, employed at the court of Friedrich I. He enlisted Gottfried Wolfram, craftsman to the Danish court, in producing a room that was intended to be a centrepiece of a dazzling renovation of the Royal Palace in Berlin, as the city was transformed into a suitable capital for the new kingdom. Both Schlüter and Wolfram were however to depart the Prussian court under clouds, and by the time of Friedrich I's death, the Amber Room had not yet been installed.[9]

A visit of the Russian tsar, Peter the Great, in 1716 necessitated a diplomatic gift, and since the two powers were allies in the ongoing Great Northern War against Sweden, a significant gift was called for. The unfinished Amber Room fitted the bill perfectly, since Friedrich Wilhelm I had no great personal interest in his father's project, and Tsar Peter was a known lover of amber and would therefore appreciate such a gift. Friedrich Wilhelm's gift to the Russian tsar also included another repurposed item, a yacht named *Liburnika*.[10] The return gift from Peter the Great conformed to the tsar's habit of offering his fellow rulers items he had crafted himself, both to mark the personal nature of the relationship and to suggest his creative talent. He gave Friedrich Wilhelm an ivory goblet he had made, as well as a lathe to encourage similar creative endeavour in his fellow monarch. Peter's present also included fifty-five giant soldiers, a gift that spoke to a known idiosyncrasy of Friedrich Wilhelm I, who filled a Prussian regiment with so many tall fellows that it became known as the Potsdam Giants. Rulers from across Europe would present to him large soldiers as diplomatic gifts.[11]

The task of fitting together and installing the amber panels was far from straightforward, and the gifted Amber Room was not installed in Russia during Peter the Great's lifetime. When Peter's daughter Elizabeth secured the throne in 1741, she was determined to see this great gift finally assembled in the Winter Palace in St Petersburg. Elizabeth had frequent changes of mind as to the right location for the room within the palace, selecting rooms far larger than the original panels were designed to fill, such that her architects had to beef out the design with such devices as mirrored pillars.

The challenges around the installation of the Amber Room provided Prussia with the occasion for a further diplomatic gift, reinforcing the original present. By this time, Friedrich Wilhelm I's son was king. In 1745, Friedrich II, soon to be known as Frederick the Great, sent to Elizabeth an ornate amber mirror frame to complement the three existing frames and better meet Elizabeth's plans for the room.[12]

Those plans however kept changing. In the 1750s, Elizabeth ordered a sumptuous reconstruction of the Catherine Palace, originally built for the wife of Peter the Great in Tsarskoye Selo, 'the Tsar's Village', south of St Petersburg. The Amber Room was moved there, with additional gilded mirrors and other devices employed to fill out the even larger space. The room was overhauled again by Catherine the Great in the following decade, with the addition of more amber to replace some of the baulked out sections of Elizabeth's room,[13] creating a chamber of stunning golden opulence.

The story of the Amber Room took a new and dark turn in 1941. On 22 June, the Führer of Nazi Germany, Adolf Hitler, launched Operation Barbarossa, the invasion of the Soviet Union. With German forces rapidly threatening St Petersburg and its artistic treasures, a young curator named Anatoly Kuchumov was assigned the task of evacuating the most precious artworks from the palaces of Tsarskoye Selo and taking them by train to the east, away from the advancing Germans.[14] Kuchumov and his colleagues were nervous about dismantling the Amber Room, fearing that the fragile amber would splinter when prized from the wooden backing boards to which it had been attached for centuries.[15] The Soviet authorities agreed that the evacuation of the Amber Room should be abandoned because of these risks, and Kuchumov instead endeavoured to hide the precious amber, covering it with muslin cloth and cotton padding and redecorating the room with hessian strips. On 30 June, Kuchumov accompanied 402 crates of artworks, but minus the Amber Room, to the Soviet interior, where this precious cargo would survive the war intact.[16]

The attempt to conceal the Amber Room did not fool the Germans; nor did they have any qualms about risking damage to the amber panels by dismantling the room. In October 1941, with Tsarskoye Selo now under German control, the panels were taken down by a team led by two German officers with backgrounds in art history and a mission to secure valuable artworks: Ernst-Otto Graf zu Solms-Laubach and Georg Pönsgen. The Amber Room was packed off for display in Königsberg Castle, a symbolic choice as the place of Friedrich I's coronation as 'king in Prussia' in 1701.[17] The venue suggests that the Nazis viewed the Amber Room not simply as a valuable artwork but as a specifically German cultural achievement closely linked with the history of the German state.

With Königsberg the target of allied bombings in 1944, it seems that the director of the Königsberg Castle Museum, Alfred Rohde, himself an amber expert, arranged for the precious amber panels to be dismantled for their protection and stored in crates in the castle. That is the last that is known with any certainty about the fate of the Amber Room. Königsberg was captured by Soviet forces in a bitter three-day assault between 6 and 9 April 1945 that left the city in ruins.

In May, the Soviet authorities sent a Moscow archaeology professor named Alexander Brusov to track down the Amber Room. He concluded that it had been in storage in the Knights' Hall of Königsberg Castle when it had been destroyed by a fire that had broken out at the tail end of the Soviet assault on the city.[18] This downbeat conclusion was not at all palatable to the Soviet authorities in appearing to suggest that Soviet forces might inadvertently have been responsible for the destruction of the great treasure. It was even less palatable for Anatoly Kuchumov, who must have lived in fear of censure for his failure to dismantle and secure the Amber Room in the eight days available to him while the Germans had apparently achieved it in thirty-six hours.[19] In 1946, Kuchumov led another investigation into the fate of the room, concluding that Brusov's findings had been perfunctory and flawed, and that he had been too hasty in determining that the Amber Room had been destroyed.

Kuchumov's conclusion provided the spur for further Soviet efforts to find the missing Amber Room. Over the years, these efforts were joined by East German investigations and by various private treasure-hunting expeditions. Much digging in the city of Königsberg, renamed Kaliningrad in 1946, was undertaken on the basis of the theory that the Nazis might have moved the Amber Room to a bunker under the city for safer storage. A further line of investigation involving castles and old mine workings in Saxony was prompted by indications that Rohde had visited that region in December 1944 when examining options for the evacuation of the panels.[20] Much attention has been paid too to the wreckage of ships sunk while evacuating Germans from Königsberg and neighbouring cities, on the theory that the Amber Room might have formed part of the cargo. The *Wilhelm Gustloff*, whose sinking by a Soviet submarine on 30 January 1945 when packed with refugees and troops resulted in more than 9,000 deaths,[21] was long a favoured candidate, but its wreckage has revealed nothing Amber Room-related. The identification in 2020 of the wreck of a steamer named the *Karlsruhe*, involved in the evacuation of Germans from Königsberg, prompted the latest in a long line of press flurries about whether the Amber Room is about to be found.[22]

The Soviet authorities seem though to have tacitly acknowledged in 1979 that the Amber Room was unlikely ever to be returned to the Catherine Palace, in embarking on the challenging and expensive process of reconstructing it. This long project weathered the fall of the Soviet Union, and having stalled during the economically tough period that followed, was boosted by a gift of 3.5 million US dollars in 1999 from the German energy company Ruhrgas, a major buyer of Russian gas.[23] The Amber Room was thus the subject of a further German gift, albeit one from a private company.

The grant enabled the grand reopening of the glitteringly reconstructed Amber Room in May 2003, the highlight of festivities marking the 300th anniversary of the founding of St Petersburg. Russian President Vladimir Putin and German Chancellor Gerhard Schröder formally opened the room to an audience of world leaders and other dignitaries, demonstrating the continued function of the Amber Room as an object that has both generated controversy in the Russo-German relationship and built connections between the two countries. What the Amber Room represents has however changed fundamentally over its history. The Amber Room of 1716 was a Prussian object, a showcase of the materials and creative talent of that country. The Amber Room of 2003 is a thoroughly Russian one, hence its role in serving as a centrepiece of the commemorations of the tercentenary of Peter the Great's capital.

1745

THE *ST ANDREW SERVICE*

A GIFT FROM FRIEDRICH AUGUST II, ELECTOR OF SAXONY (AND KING AUGUST III OF POLAND), TO ELIZABETH PETROVNA, EMPRESS OF RUSSIA

A salt dish from the *St Andrew Service*.

Porcelain has a special place in the history of diplomatic gifts. This fine, white, translucent material was made in China from around the seventh or eighth centuries, and known in Europe from the fourteenth, where imported Chinese pieces were cherished luxury goods. By the early seventeenth century, the Dutch East India Company was importing 100,000 pieces of Chinese porcelain annually.[1]

Rulers across Europe assembled collections of Chinese porcelain while commissioning attempts to discover the secret of its manufacture, a secret that was worth both a fortune and great prestige. Determination of the combination of materials needed and the high temperatures required to fire it proved, however, elusive for centuries. In their efforts to produce the 'true' or hard-paste porcelain, the Medici were the first to create a similar product, in the late sixteenth century, but this was a weaker ceramic, known as soft-paste porcelain, produced at a lower firing temperature.

It would fall to Saxony, an electorate of the Holy Roman Empire, to uncover the mystery of the manufacture of porcelain. Saxony had many advantages in the search for the elusive 'white gold', including traditions in mining and glassmaking, with artisans used to working with high temperatures.[2] It also had in its elector, Friedrich August I, a ruler obsessed with porcelain, who would gather a collection of more than 20,000 Japanese and Chinese pieces by 1727.[3] Friedrich August had also secured the throne of the Polish–Lithuanian Commonwealth, where he ruled as August II, an act that required his conversion to Roman Catholicism, a disconcerting move for the citizens of Protestant Saxony.

Friedrich August had been impressed by the court at Versailles during a visit there in his youth, and he endeavoured to recreate something of its opulence in his capital of Dresden, through his palaces, his porcelain and his lavish entertaining. Among his favoured entertainments was the alarming sport of fox tossing, in which a poor fox or another wild animal would be catapulted into the air, with the highest throw winning. Friedrich August would demonstrate the truth behind his nickname of Augustus the Strong by holding his end of the sling by one finger, with two strong men pulling on the other end.

The sequence of events that would lead to the uncovering of the secrets to the manufacture of hard-paste porcelain began with a different obsession of Friedrich August: the quest for gold. A young man named Johann Friedrich Böttger, apprentice to an apothecary in Berlin, had devoted himself to the alchemical search for the philosopher's stone, the substance which, it was widely believed, could be combined with ordinary metals to produce gold. Rulers across the Holy Roman Empire were keen to capture the talents of skilled alchemists and secure access to unlimited wealth. Having escaped the clutches of the future King Friedrich I of Prussia, Böttger turned up in Saxony, where Friedrich August had him arrested.[4] It was something of a luxurious imprisonment, and Friedrich August was forced to spend heavily on financing Böttger's experiments, eventually furnishing him with a full laboratory close to his palace in Dresden.

Böttger's search for gold was, predictably, going nowhere, placing the young man in danger from a ruler increasingly agitated about the mounting costs of the enterprise. His future, and place in history, was secured when he was placed under the supervision of a mathematician and scientist named Ehrenfried Walther von Tschirnhaus. The latter had long sought to use science to improve the industries of Saxony and had a particular passion for unlocking the secrets of porcelain making. Tschirnhaus seems to have persuaded Böttger to focus on the quest for white gold rather than, well, *gold* gold, and their partnership finally succeeded in producing hard-paste porcelain in 1708.

Tschirnhaus died suddenly that year. Friedrich August appointed Böttger director of his porcelain manufacturing enterprise, and with the whole venture subject to strict secrecy, the European discovery of the secrets of porcelain making was long accredited to Böttger. The role of Tschirnhaus in the breakthrough has gradually become more strongly appreciated.[5]

The Royal-Polish and Electoral-Saxon Porcelain Factory was opened in 1710 in the largely unused Albrechtsburg Castle in a small town some 25 kilometres outside Dresden, where the secrecy surrounding the manufacture of porcelain could be better maintained than in the Saxon capital itself. The name of that town is now synonymous with its high-quality porcelain: Meissen.

Porcelain from the Meissen factory had obvious attraction for Friedrich August as a diplomatic gift. It was a luxury product, favoured by royal households across Europe, its output firmly of a representational rather than purely functional character.[6] More specifically, the gifting of Meissen ware served as a reminder to the recipient of Saxony's technological achievement as the first European state successfully to manufacture hard-paste porcelain. A further consideration was that the enterprise had been exceedingly costly for Friedrich August. The factory had been poorly managed by Böttger, who was frequently distracted by other schemes and, weakened by alcoholism and the effects of years of working with noxious substances, died in 1719 at the age of just thirty-seven.[7] Friedrich August was keen to bring the factory into profit, which required a broadening of its customer base beyond the Saxon elite, not least as the elector himself, while a major customer, frequently neglected to pay for his purchases. This meant targeting foreign courts, with diplomatic gifts helpfully serving to raise awareness of the product and encourage future purchases.

The earliest known use of Meissen porcelain as a diplomatic gift came in 1711, with a present to King Frederik IV of Denmark and Norway,[8] but it was not used regularly as a diplomatic gift, particularly to recipients not related to the elector, until the 1730s.[9] This delay is explained in part by the fact that raising the quality of the porcelain to the level of the Chinese product took some years. The colourful overglaze painting of Johann Gregorius Höroldt from the early 1720s, and the modelling work of sculptor Johann Joachim Kändler from 1731, elevated the output of the factory and created the look that has defined the Meissen brand ever since.

139

In part, the delay also owes something to the time it would have taken to establish the place of porcelain in the existing, understood, structure of diplomatic gifts offered by the Saxon court. Departing ambassadors might for example receive a gift of a jewel-encrusted miniature portrait.[10] Gifts made of silver were also popular, reflecting the mineral wealth of the country.[11] Gradually however Meissen porcelain emerged as a favoured Saxon diplomatic gift. Tea, coffee and chocolate services were a frequent choice, customarily presented in specially designed green velvet-lined boxes.[12] Snuffboxes, usually painted both outside and inside the lid, were also popular. Garnitures of vases were a grander gift, as was a table service. The gift of the *St Andrew Service* to Empress Elizabeth of Russia in 1745 established a model for grand armorial services for European monarchs.[13]

Saxony had long enjoyed a close relationship with Russia. Some diplomatic gifts from Friedrich August to Peter the Great had a decidedly personal tone, for example a snuffbox decorated with a portrait of his mistress Maria Aurora von Königsmarck in the guise of Leda. The two leaders also exchanged little gifts they had made themselves.[14] Following the death of Friedrich August in 1733, his son Friedrich August II secured the Polish throne against the rival candidacy of the French-backed Stanisław Leszczyński with the help of Russian military support. When Elizabeth Petrovna, daughter of Peter the Great, seized power in Russia in a coup in 1741, Saxony was eager to secure continued Russian support for its interests in the War of Austrian Succession.

The Russian court had moved closer to the practices of the West, through the modernising reforms of Peter the Great and the Western tastes of Empress Anna, whose court was dominated by German advisers. This development of a more European court style included a wider use of porcelain. A Meissen porcelain table service would thus be a highly suitable diplomatic gift for Empress Elizabeth.

A Meissen gift known as the *Elizabeth Service* was sent to the Russian ruler sometime after November 1741 (when archives at Meissen record continuing work on it). The plates are painted in the centre with birds and stylised flowers, with European landscape or harbour scenes around the rim. Since the coup that installed Elizabeth took place at the end of 1741, and work on the service had already begun in April of that year, it was however clearly not originally designed with Elizabeth in mind and may have been intended as a gift for Anna Leopoldovna, the regent of Russia she had overthrown.[15]

The *St Andrew Service* seems in contrast to have been designed with Elizabeth in mind from the outset. The largest service ever produced by Meissen as a diplomatic gift, work began on it in the early summer of 1744.[16] The service honours the Order of St Andrew the Apostle the First-Called, the highest of all the Russian imperial orders, established by Peter the Great in 1698. Its pieces feature the cross of St Andrew, with the letters S, A, P and R at the end of each arm of the cross, denoting St Andrew, patron of Russia. They also bear the Russian double-headed eagle.

The service may have been stimulated by reporting from a Saxon diplomat at the Russian court of the enthusiasm of the empress for Meissen porcelain. In February 1745, the wedding was announced for September that year between the heir to the Russian throne, Karl Peter Ulrich von Schleswig-Holstein-Gottorf, the future Peter III, and Sophia von Anhalt-Zerbst, the future Catherine the Great. It seems that the Saxons decided to use the *St Andrew Service* already in production as a diplomatic gift to the empress to mark the wedding.

The gift arrived in July 1745 and included not just the table service but also a tea, coffee and chocolate service, together with some 190 figurines intended to decorate the dessert table as well as several garnitures of vases.[17] News reached Dresden that the porcelain had arrived safely and been well received by the empress. Evidently a success, it was retained by Elizabeth in her private apartments until November that year. Released at that point to the court pantry, it would have been available for use in the celebration of the order held on St Andrew's Day. The appetite of the empress for Meissen porcelain appears to have been whetted, as she placed an order the same year for three series of custom-made figurines.[18]

Diplomatic gifts of Meissen porcelain services were also made to both the Russian chancellor and vice-chancellor, contributing to maintaining positive relations between the two states as well as to fuelling a taste for Meissen among the Russian aristocracy. Meissen porcelain served as a symbol of the developing European outlook of the Russian court.[19]

The efforts of the Saxon royal court to protect the secrets of the manufacture of 'white gold' were doomed to failure in the face of the determined attempts of sovereigns across the continent to steal them and establish their own factories. The haphazard management style of Böttger in the early years, with craftsmen frequently unpaid, made the task of stealing the secrets much easier, and already by 1719 a Habsburg court official named Claude-Innocent du Paquier had established a porcelain manufactory in Vienna by luring one of Böttger's assistants with a lavish salary.[20]

Other porcelain factories were to follow across the continent and, as the eighteenth century progressed, diplomatic gifts of fine porcelain were to become a staple of a range of European courts.

1759

A DINNER AND DESSERT SERVICE

A GIFT FROM LOUIS XV, KING OF FRANCE, TO MARIA THERESIA, HOLY ROMAN EMPRESS

A plate from the 'green ribbon' service given by King Louis XV of France
to Empress Maria Theresia.

We have seen how the manufacture of hard-paste porcelain at Meissen
provided the rulers of Saxony with a source of highly desired diplomatic
gifts, establishing a practice emulated by other royal courts as the secrets
of porcelain manufacture were disseminated across Europe. The pre-
eminent place of Meissen was to be eclipsed in the mid-eighteenth century
by the porcelain manufactory at Sèvres, just outside Paris, its role and
status closely linked to the French crown.

It had started out life in 1740 as the Vincennes porcelain manufactory,
established in a disused royal palace east of Paris. The arrival on the scene
of Madame de Pompadour as the mistress of King Louis XV in 1745 was to
prove decisive to the fortunes of the manufactory. Madame de Pompadour
became an unfailing champion of Vincennes, using its porcelain both to
establish her own style and as gifts, to cement her position domestically and
internationally.[1] From 1751, she gave a range of diplomatic gifts to the
duke of Newcastle, the longstanding British secretary of state, among them

three Chinese vases, including a potpourri vase filled with Vincennes porcelain flowers.[2] Other gifts included a French chef. She received from Newcastle pineapples from the glasshouses at Claremont, his estate south of London.[3] The exchanges were part of ultimately unsuccessful efforts to maintain peaceful relations between Britain and France against a backdrop of worsening tensions over their North American colonies.[4] Madame de Pompadour was recognised by Newcastle as representing a pacific faction at Versailles,[5] and courting her was an important part of this effort.

Another use by Madame de Pompadour of Vincennes porcelain as a diplomatic gift came in 1754. She sent the duc des Deux-Ponts (Zweibrücken in modern-day Germany) an expensive silver-lined tureen in *bleu céleste*,[6] the turquoise-blue ground colour introduced the previous year to great admiration. It would become one of the signature colours of the manufactory.

In 1756, the manufactory moved to purpose-built accommodation at Sèvres, close to Bellevue, the château built for Madame de Pompadour at the instigation of Louis XV as a meeting place for the two. Madame de Pompadour continued to champion the factory, encouraging her friends to buy pieces from the enterprise and to invest in it. In 1759, with the factory in deep financial trouble, Louis XV was persuaded to buy it out, a striking decision with France embroiled in the Seven Years' War.

The arsenal of diplomatic gifts used by the French king for the most prestigious recipients included products reflecting the best of French artistic and manufacturing skills: Gobelins tapestries, Savonnerie carpets and the miniature portraits of the king encrusted with diamonds known as *boîtes à portrait*.[7] Through the influence of Madame de Pompadour, Louis XV added Sèvres porcelain to that arsenal, particularly grand table services, of which the king was to make ten such gifts.[8] These were at first made of soft-paste porcelain. The kaolin necessary for the manufacture of hard-paste porcelain was not discovered in France until 1768, and the latter was produced at Sèvres only from 1770, initially alongside soft-paste porcelain. However, the high technical standards of the Sèvres manufactory, including in its decoration, colour and gilding, served from the outset as a demonstration of the power and cultural standards of France and its royal court.[9]

The first Sèvres table service presented as a diplomatic gift from Louis XV was offered in 1758 to King Frederick V of Denmark and Norway, a return gift for a stallion of the Danish Frederiksborg breed. The service used a newly developed green ground colour and took around four months to complete. It was commissioned through Lazare Duvaux, the decorative arts dealer who frequently supplied both the king and Madame de Pompadour.

It seems to have been regifted to Catherine the Great of Russia, and much of the service is now to be found in the Hermitage in St Petersburg.

Another Sèvres service was gifted a decade later to Frederick's son and successor, Christian VII. The latter's reign was affected by mental illness, with the king ruling in name only for much of it. In May 1768, Christian embarked on a tour of Europe, returning to Denmark only in January the following year, an unusually long absence for a serving monarch, and one that aimed to establish whether a change of environment could restore the king's mental health. While in Paris, the still teenaged king was showered with gifts by Louis XV, including Gobelins tapestries and Savonnerie carpets, as well as a large Sèvres dinner service. The first part of the service was sent to Christian's hotel following a three-hour visit to the Sèvres manufactory.[10] The balance was sent on to Denmark the following year.

Our featured gift is a large Sèvres dinner and dessert service delivered in 1759 to Maria Theresia, the Holy Roman Empress. The service is decorated with entwined green ribbons, with garlands of flowers suspended from them. Allegorical scenes after paintings of François Boucher occupy the spaces between the ribbons. It was the most expensive of all the Sèvres services given as diplomatic gifts by the king.[11]

The gift celebrates the newfound alliance between France and Austria, after centuries of enmity, in the context of the realignment of forces across Europe as the Seven Years' War dawned. The alliance was established through the First Treaty of Versailles in 1756 and developed through further treaties in the two following years. Madame de Pompadour was an important proponent of the alliance. The strengthening of ties with Austria also owed much to Louise Élisabeth, the eldest daughter of Louis XV, who as duchess of Parma was pursuing the twin objectives of securing the renunciation by Austria of its claims to Parma in favour of Louise Élisabeth's husband, and securing the marriage of her daughter Isabella into the Austrian royal family.[12] Austria, desperate for military and financial support in its efforts to win back Silesia from Prussia, needed the new alliance to continue. As the financial costs of the war mounted, the benefits for France were less obvious, and the extent to which the goals of his daughter in Parma appeared to influence Louis XV's resolve to continue to develop the alliance is striking.[13]

The despatch of the service, which arrived in Vienna in May 1759, came after the confirmation of the agreement to the marriage between Isabella and Maria-Theresia's eldest son, Joseph. A painting by Martin van Meytens the Younger depicts the green ribbon service in use during the festivities in October 1760 to celebrate their wedding. Sadly, Louise Élisabeth, who had worked so hard to engineer the match, was not there to enjoy the celebration: she had died of smallpox at the end of the previous year. The intertwined green ribbons on the service celebrate the alliance of the two countries of France and Austria, but also the entwining of the two royal houses in a more personal sense. Indeed, there is a matrimonial flavour to parts of the decoration, with its putti, Cupid's bow and arrow, doves and the myrtle wreaths associated with weddings.[14]

Gifts of Sèvres dinner services not only served to demonstrate French artistic and technological sophistication. They also promoted a French way of dining. The services were structured around the style of dining known as *service à la française*, in which a range of dishes were served at the same time, with the diners largely serving themselves. This style favoured visually lavish presentations, particularly at the dessert course,[15] where colourful displays of sweet confections would be accompanied by table decorations such as the white unglazed Sèvres biscuit figures, largely supplanting an earlier use of sculpted sugar centrepieces. Such sculptural elements formed part of the diplomatic gifts from Louis XV.

Such exquisite gifts thus placed Sèvres as a standard-setter for European dining. This was true also of individual items of tableware. Take the bowl used to chill wine-glasses, which takes the form of a basin with a notched rim to allow the glasses to hang down, and which in English is known as a monteith. This seems to have appeared in late seventeenth-century England, originally in silver, its name, according to an antiquary of that period named Anthony à Wood, deriving from the notched cloak bottoms of a 'fantastical Scot' of that surname.[16] In its incarnation made by Sèvres, it was oval in form, shallower than its English predecessors, its rim serpentine. The French style of monteith became the European standard, in turn copied by British ceramic factories such as Derby and Wedgewood.[17]

The reputation of Sèvres for the manufacture of the finest dinner services in Europe, in part generated through their use as diplomatic gifts, helped stimulate major commissions for the factory from royal courts across the continent. The largest of these was the *Cameo Service* made for Catherine the Great of Russia, who ordered it as a gift for her favourite, Prince Grigory Potemkin. It was a dinner and dessert service for sixty people and took three years to make. Potemkin is said to have given Catherine an Angora cat in return.[18]

Louis XVI maintained the use of Sèvres porcelain for diplomatic gifts. The factory fell into difficult times during the French Revolution, but Napoléon recognised both the economic potential and propaganda value of Sèvres porcelain, and revived it.[19] The dinner services of this period were however more didactic in their decoration, often featuring Napoléonic triumphs, as we shall see in a later story in the example of the *Egyptian Service* now at Apsley House. Sèvres porcelain has retained an important place among French diplomatic gifts. The gift from the government and people of France for the wedding in London of Princess Elizabeth and Prince Philip in 1947 was a Sèvres dinner service.

As a luxury product, associated with the business of diplomacy through the formal diplomatic dinner, a product designed to be seen and used by elites and a product that lends itself to the demonstration of artistic skill and technological innovation, porcelain continues to prove its worth as a diplomatic gift.

1785

A MINIATURE PORTRAIT OF KING LOUIS XVI OF FRANCE

A GIFT FROM LOUIS XVI, KING OF FRANCE, TO BENJAMIN FRANKLIN, MINISTER OF THE UNITED STATES OF AMERICA TO FRANCE

Porcelain sculpture by Charles-Gabriel Sauvage of US Minister to France Benjamin Franklin in audience with King Louis XVI.

The receipt of a farewell gift from the head of state of the country to which they are accredited has in many times and places been a courtesy of diplomatic life for departing ambassadors. This is the tale of a departing gift that posed a conundrum for its recipient and receiving state, a conundrum that would influence the drafting of a constitution in a way that would have significant implications for the practice of diplomatic gifts. It concerns the man who has been described as the first American diplomat,[1] Benjamin Franklin.

By 1776, Franklin was a celebrity, in Europe as in America. He epitomised the polymath: the inventor of the lightning conductor, bifocals and a musical instrument called the glass armonica; a printer, writer and humourist; a politician and the first postmaster general of the United States. He was the embodiment of the Age of Reason, which was changing the world in the late eighteenth century.

As the bitter fighting of the American War of Independence played out, the Continental Army had great need of military and financial support from France, Britain's old European rival, eager to seek revenge for its losses in the Seven Years' War. In October 1776, the Continental Congress despatched Franklin to France, to secure further support for the colonies and negotiate a formal alliance. He was to join another revolutionary named Silas Deane, sent earlier that year. Together with a third man, Arthur Lee, they formed Congress's diplomatic delegation to France.

Franklin was an immediate hit in France.[2] He was feted as the most famous living American, a symbol of the Enlightenment and of the frontier spirit. He became a familiar figure in French high society, marked out by his unconventional attire, dressing plainly and spurning a wig in favour of the marten fur hat that became a trademark. Despite his patchy command of the language, he was in his element in the salons and dinners of the French aristocracy. He charmed the ladies and created a fashion for the *coiffure à la Franklin* in imitation of his fur headgear.[3] This was all something of a pose – Franklin had been quite willing to sport a wig and local dress during his first visit to France in 1767.[4] It was however a highly successful one.

Franklin's diplomatic skills were less appreciated by his immediate colleagues. Silas Deane had been recalled amid allegations of profiteering from the deals he had been striking, and the future second US president, John Adams, was sent to replace him. Adams regarded Franklin's wining and dining as a distraction from their business in Paris, never properly appreciating its importance. He was envious of Franklin's popularity and regarded him as too pro-French, too extravagant and too prone to indolence. Arthur Lee had no better an opinion of Franklin, describing him in a letter to Samuel Adams, second cousin to John, as 'the most corrupt of all corrupt men'.[5]

The work of Franklin and the American diplomatic delegation to France was bearing fruit. The French, while long supporting the American cause, had been wary of open allegiance until they were more confident that America would emerge victorious. The American victory at the Battle of Saratoga in October 1777 gave the French that confidence. In February 1778, Franklin and his fellow commissioners signed a Treaty of Amity and Commerce and Treaty of Alliance with France, which thereby recognised the United States as an independent nation.

In September of that year, Franklin was appointed as the first minister of the United States to the French court at Versailles. He presented his credentials in March the following year, becoming the first American minister to be received by a foreign court. French support would be crucial to the outcome of the War of Independence, with the French contributing almost as many troops as the Americans at the decisive Battle of Yorktown in 1781.

Franklin was one of five men appointed by the Continental Congress to negotiate the Peace Treaty with Britain. Two took no part in the proceedings: Thomas Jefferson, who declined the role, and Henry Laurens, captured by the British. The others were John Adams and John Jay, a lawyer from New York. An important question arose as to how the peace negotiations were to be conducted. The French had proposed a general peace conference in Paris involving all the combatants. Congress had instructed its negotiators not to do anything without the full knowledge of France.[6] Notwithstanding his close relationship with France, Franklin agreed with Adams and Jay that America's interests were best served through separate peace negotiations with Britain[7] and indeed had laid much of the groundwork for these before Jay and Adams arrived in Paris. They reasoned that France would want an America dependent on its largesse, whereas Britain would see the benefits of a strong United States with whom they could develop a profitable trading relationship, freed from the burdens of administering a troublesome colony. The treaty negotiated with Britain granted the United States territory extending to the Mississippi River in the west: they would hardly have been likely to secure such favourable terms in a treaty negotiated through a general peace conference.

Franklin stayed on pleasurably as United States minister to France until July 1785. On his departure, as was the convention, he was presented with a fine gift by King Louis XVI. It was a miniature portrait of the French king by Louis Marie Sicard, also known as Sicardi, who specialised in such works. The portrait was housed in a gold case and set into two concentric rings of diamonds.[8] A characteristic French diplomatic gift known as a *boîte à portrait*, it is referred to in some sources as a snuffbox.[9] Franklin in his will describes it as 'the King of France's picture set with 408 diamonds'.[10]

There are two notable features of the gift presented by the French king. First, as a portrait of Louis XVI it bore a clear link to the giver. From the French perspective, the gift was inalienable: as a visual representation of the giver, it could not be dissociated from the French king and indeed served to stand in for the absent sovereign.[11] Second, encrusted by diamonds, it was lavish and costly. Indeed, if the gift as a whole was inalienable, individual diamonds could be alienated from it, and sold for profit, a consideration that was far from hypothetical, as we shall see. We will look in more detail at the use of portraits as gifts in our next story. The lavishness of the king's gift to Franklin did however have some far-reaching consequences.

The value of the gift presented Franklin with a dilemma, arising from the different perspectives of French absolute monarchy and Enlightenment America. Franklin could not refuse the gift, for this would insult the French king, yet nor could he accept it, for this would be seen by Congress as an indication that he was beholden to the corrupting influences of the French. Indeed, he was explicitly barred from accepting such a gift by Article VI of the Articles of Confederation, the forerunner to the US Constitution, which prevented any United States office holder from accepting 'any present, emolument, office, or title of any kind whatever, from any king, prince, or foreign state'.[12]

While a clear attempt to part ways with Old World diplomatic practice, this provision drew on an ancient strand of republican thinking. Plato set the penalty for bribery by public officials in his ideal city of Magnesia as death.[13] In 1651, Dutch diplomats were instructed not to accept any gifts, even of food or drink, or face dismissal and public discredit.[14] As we will see in our next story, Britain was by this period fretting too about the risks around the corruption of East India Company officials from lavish gifts from local rulers. For the French court, as with most European courts of the eighteenth century, personal gifts from the sovereign were however a central part of diplomatic ritual, and were not to be refused.

Franklin put his dilemma to Congress, which allowed him to keep the gift. He bequeathed it to his daughter, Sarah Bache. He applied some conditionality of his own, requesting 'that she would not form any of those diamonds into ornaments ... and thereby introduce or countenance the expensive, vain and useless fashion of wearing jewels in this country'.[15] Sarah partly complied: she did not turn any of the diamonds into jewellery, but she did turn some of them into cash, to finance a planned trip to France. Later generations sold off more diamonds, such that when the portrait arrived into the care of the American Philosophical Society in 1959, courtesy of a Franklin descendant named Richard Duane, just one diamond remained, though some others have since made their way back.[16]

Franklin was not the only American diplomat wrestling with the challenge of representing a country that banned the acceptance of gifts while serving in one that expected it. Both Silas Deane and Arthur Lee received jewelled boxes on their departure from France, albeit not as elaborate as the gift received by Franklin. Like Franklin, Lee offered his box up to Congress, which allowed him to keep it.[17] Franklin's successor in Paris, Thomas Jefferson, also received an opulent jewelled box. Rather than report the gift to Congress, he opted to sell the most valuable of the diamonds, using the money to pay for diplomatic presents and to pay off embassy debts.[18]

At the Constitutional Convention of 1787, lavish gifts of the kind bestowed on Franklin by the French king would have been in the minds of delegates as they fretted over the dangers of attempts by the old powers of Europe to corrupt political life in their young state through gifts and favours. Taking their cue from the bar on accepting gifts set out in the Articles of Confederation, they devised the Emoluments Clause. This provision in Article I, Section 9, Clause 8 of the new Constitution sets out that 'no Person holding any Office of Profit or trust under them, shall, without the Consent of the Congress, accept of any present, Emolument, Office or Title, of any kind whatever, from any King, Prince, or foreign State'. The Emoluments Clause was an attempt to guard against corruption by establishing a structure to prevent corruption. In encompassing all gifts, it did not require corrupt intent.[19] Its passage would change the nature of diplomatic gifts from a personal to a regulated transaction.

While an increasing number of countries have followed the United States in introducing regulations to limit what diplomatic gifts may be accepted, in the 1780s US practice still jarred with that of the old European monarchies. This was true of more than diplomatic gifts. While France had helped the United States to independence, the financial costs of doing so were to prove one of the factors igniting the sparks of the French Revolution. The Enlightenment ideas underpinning that independence movement were another. Louis XVI lost his head, and the ensuing decline in the power of European monarchies would herald a world in which approaches to diplomatic gifts would be very different from the one that had preceded it.

1785

STATE PORTRAITS OF KING LOUIS XVI OF FRANCE AND QUEEN MARIE ANTOINETTE

A GIFT FROM LOUIS XVI, KING OF FRANCE, TO THE UNITED STATES CONFEDERATION CONGRESS

Antoine-François Callet's *Portrait of Louis XVI in Coronation Robes.*

The use of portraits of themselves was a favoured diplomatic gift strategy of eighteenth-century European monarchs. If gifts provide a means of establishing and maintaining social relationships, then portraits are particularly helpful in achieving this objective, as they underline the personal relationship by providing a constant visual reminder of the absent donor.[1] Portraits combine this stress on personal connectedness with the recipient with an intent to induce awe at the grandeur and qualities of the gifting monarch. There is a star quality about portrait gifts from powerful or famous rulers that persists today in the popularity of gifts of photographs of US presidents or members of the British royal family.

Portraits have another important quality: they fall into the category of gifts that cannot be easily alienated from the gifting relationship. A nice gift of, say, luxuriant textiles may, once gifted, be sold on or used interchangeably with similar textiles purchased as commodities. It is straightforwardly alienable. If the receiver does not wish to alienate such a product from the

155

gifting relationship, in order to demonstrate their close links with the giver, they have this option, which might be achieved by placing the gifted textiles in a museum, or underlining their provenance as a gifted object whenever they are used. The point though is that the receiver has the choice of retaining the object as a remembered gift or treating it as a commodity.

With the gift of a portrait, no such option is available to the receiver, as the gift carries clear evidence of its source. It is not easily alienated from the context in which it was given. This is not to say that gifted portraits are never sold on, but rather that in any such transaction their provenance as a former gift will be clear, and the transaction is therefore associated with a higher degree of risk.

Art historian Natasha Eaton has explored how their qualities of underlining the personal relationship between giver and receiver and difficulty of alienability made portraits a preferred gift for the British East India Company in its relations with Indian rulers in the late eighteenth century. There were growing concerns in Britain around the corruption of East India Company officials, and especially the emergence of 'nabobs' who returned to Britain with suspiciously large fortunes. The lavish gifting practices of Indian rulers were seen as part of the problem. The Regulating Act of 1773, which sought to overhaul the affairs of the East India Company, included provisions to ban British officials from accepting or soliciting lavish gifts from native rulers.[2]

Eaton demonstrates that the response of Governor-General Warren Hastings was to attempt to replace the traditional gifting practices of Indian rulers, which drew on a Mughal focus on land grants, jewels and money, with the more symbolic gifting of the painted portrait.[3] The latter drew on King George III's practice of sending his own likeness to British colonies around the world, and was a form of gift that would not fall foul of the Regulating Act.

An example predating Hastings's tenure as governor-general was the gifting by George III to Muhammad Ali, nawab of Arcot, of portraits of members of the royal family, including his own likeness painted by Allan Ramsay. The gift was accompanied by a letter from the king, explaining to the nawab that the purpose of the gift was to offer him 'before your eyes a memorial of Our regard and affection'.[4] The nawab reciprocated, sitting for a portrait by English artist Tilly Kettle, and sending this to the king, along with portraits of other members of his family, some textiles and rosewater. He wrote of his hope 'that the picture may have that honor of being affixed in Your Majesty's royal sight'.[5]

Lacking a painting of George III to give to Nizam Ali Khan, ruler of Hyderabad, the East India Company's resident, Richard Johnson, gifted instead a portrait of Hastings. Nizam Ali Khan, unlike Muhammad Ali, showed however little inclination to engage in the new colonial gift practices favoured by Hastings, and did not sit for British artists. Whether he reciprocated with a portrait by an indigenous artist is not known, but he did entrust Hastings with a diamond ring to be gifted to George III. For Nizam Ali Khan, precious gems embodied the spirit of the giver, and indeed of all previous owners, but to a British audience the gift of a diamond ring lacked the inalienable qualities of a portrait, and the task created some difficulties for Hastings, whose detractors accused him of attempting to bribe the king.[6]

While Hastings had little success in independent Hyderabad in imposing a new structure of gifting based around colonial portraiture, this quickly became more firmly embedded at courts where the indirect control of the East India Company was stronger. Here the local rulers sent the governor-general portraits by British artists despatched by the company, and for which they had been required to pay handsomely, yet received no return painting or other gift from the British side. In effect, the portraits had become a form of tribute.[7]

Let us now return to our previous story, the parting gift by King Louis XVI of a bejewelled miniature portrait to the US minister to France, Benjamin Franklin. As we have seen, this gift put its recipient in an awkward spot. He represented a country suspicious of diplomatic gifts as instruments of attempted corruption on the part of Old World regimes intent on exerting their influence on the new. The rise of republics moulded on the thinking of the Enlightenment would have a profound impact on the practice of diplomatic gifting. It would be wrong however to infer that these new republics saw no place for gifts in their international relations armouries. Another gift involving a portrait of the French king, delivered to its recipients in the United States in the same year of 1785, illustrates the point. For this gift was requested by the United States.

We have examined the skilful work of Benjamin Franklin in Paris in securing the French financial and military support that the fledgling United States so badly needed. Franklin and other moderates within the American leadership alighted on the idea of flattering their new French allies with a request that had little to do with the way diplomatic gifts were perceived in their own country and everything to do with the way they were understood in absolute monarchies like France. They decided to ask for portraits of the king and queen.

For monarchies across Europe, large state portraits were considered a sign of special favour, generally given to mark a significant event.[8] Franklin would have understood this when, in November 1778, he wrote to Charles Gravier, comte de Vergennes, Louis XVI's foreign minister, suggesting that 'it would be highly pleasing to our Constituents to have the picture of his Majesty their illustrious ally to be kept in some public place where the Congress sits'.[9] He also requested a portrait of Queen Marie Antoinette. The inalienability of state portraits as diplomatic gifts would have lessened the risks around such a request in American eyes: unlike the diamonds surrounding the miniature portrait Franklin was to receive, a large state portrait could not easily be commodified and sold. Its value would have been perceived as more symbolic than material.

While the risks were lessened, they were not however eliminated. A postscript note to the letter urges that Vergennes treat the request with discretion, as Franklin had not cleared the proposal with his colleague in the Congressional diplomatic delegation to France, Arthur Lee. The implication here is that Franklin was by no means confident that the Congressional leadership as a whole supported the stratagem of soliciting royal state portraits. This is redolent of the wider disagreement between the leaders of the American Revolution about the most appropriate means of securing the support of France and other potential European allies. Franklin, at home in the aristocratic milieux of Paris, favoured an approach that worked with the traditions and style of the French regime. Lee and John Adams were more suspicious of French motives and preferred a more business-like approach.

In December 1778, having been married for more than eight years, Marie Antoinette gave birth to the couple's first child, Marie-Thérèse. It was a difficult birth. Marie Antoinette almost died of suffocation. The birth was nonetheless a cause for celebration. A note penned by the king to Congress, announcing the birth, was delivered by the French minister in Philadelphia in May 1779. Congress set up a committee to draft a reply, consisting of John Jay, Gouverneur Morris and John Witherspoon, a moderate group who shared Franklin's views on the value of soliciting royal portraits. After congratulating the king on the birth of his daughter, they added a request for portraits of himself and his queen, so that 'the representatives of these states may daily have before their eyes the first royal friends and patrons of their cause'.[10] Congress penned another letter to the French at the same time, requesting further military and financial aid, reinforcing the sense that a flattering letter soliciting royal portraits was but part of a wider strategy to secure the concrete support America so badly needed.

Louis responded positively, making clear that he regarded the gift as symbolising the permanence of the ties between the two countries. In selecting portraits for their American allies, it was open to the French to choose a style more in line with the Enlightenment values embodied by the recipients. This they did not do. The selections were traditional in composition, redolent of the authority and grandeur of the French monarchy.

For the portrait of Louis XVI, Vergennes opted for a copy of Antoine-François Callet's *Louis XVI in Coronation Robes*, commissioned in 1778. Some twelve copies of the full-length version were made.[11] Recipients of these diplomatic gifts ranged from the Spanish ambassador to France to King Gustav III of Sweden. One even went in 1783 to America's adversary, to decorate the residence of the French ambassador to London, the comte d'Adhémar, at a time when France was anxious to patch up its relations with Britain following the conclusion of the American War of Independence.[12]

Callet's portrait consciously harks back to Hyacinthe Rigaud's 1701 painting of Louis XIV in coronation robes, which now hangs in the Louvre. Callet's painting emphasises the power and authority of the king, who is raised on a small dais, holds the sceptre of Henri IV, the first monarch of the Bourbon dynasty, and has the *Joyeuse*, the sword of Charlemagne, suspended from his waist.[13]

For the portrait of Marie Antoinette, Vergennes' choice was a copy of a portrait of 1778 by Élisabeth Vigée Le Brun of *Marie Antoinette in Ceremonial Dress*. The original was destined for the queen's mother, Empress Maria Theresia of Austria. The painting was deemed a success, and Le Brun was asked to make a facsimile in order that copies could be produced more straightforwardly. It is another opulent portrait of royal magnificence, with the queen festooned in white satin.

Vergennes timed the despatch of the paintings to America to coincide with the Peace of Paris in September 1783: the signing of the treaties that marked the end of the American War of Independence,[14] a moment of triumph for the two allies. The paintings arrived in Philadelphia in March 1784, by way of Santo Domingo, and were delivered to the residence of the French minister, Anne-César de la Luzerne. The minister prepared a press release for the *Pennsylvania Journal* announcing their arrival, though he only informed Congress of the fact the following month. Congress by then had vacated Philadelphia, following the Pennsylvania Mutiny of 1783 by soldiers demanding payment for their service in the war, and was sitting temporarily in Annapolis, Maryland.

A letter from Louis XVI accompanying the paintings expressed the hope that they would be regarded as 'a perpetual token of the affection that we bear you, as well as of the steadfastness of our friendship for you'.[15] The process of actually handing over the portraits proved to be a protracted one. Luzerne indicated that he would present them once Congress had decided on its long-term location and in the interim installed them in his reception room, where he evidently delighted in the attention they received. The following year, Congress accepted an offer to be housed at New York City Hall. Luzerne had by then departed, and the paintings were handed over by the consul-general, François Barbé de Marbois. There is no record of any grand presentation ceremony.[16]

What accounts for this less than ecstatic welcome for gifts Congress had itself requested? In the first place, the relationship between the United States and France in 1785, when the paintings were finally presented, was very different from that of 1779, when Congress had solicited them. In 1779, America had been desperate for further French support to help secure victory in their war of independence. By 1785, that war won, relations between the two countries were strained. France, burdened by the cost of its support for America, chafed at its ally's failure to repay loans and fulfil promised trade agreements, while the United States had no intention to play the role of a subservient transatlantic partner of France.

The paintings were hung in Congress and played a useful symbolic role for the new state as a demonstration of its international credibility and connections. The real power of the paintings as a diplomatic gift had though lain more in the flattery the request gave to their French ally when the United States was in need of further financial and military support than in the substance of the gift itself. As objects, the paintings were symbols of the absolute power of monarchies: anathema to the new republic. Their eventual fate is uncertain, though they were probably destroyed during the burning of Washington by the British in 1814.[17]

1790

A PORTRAIT OF CATHERINE THE GREAT

A GIFT FROM CATHERINE THE GREAT, EMPRESS OF RUSSIA, TO EMMANUEL DE ROHAN-POLDUC, GRAND MASTER OF THE KNIGHTS OF ST JOHN

The Grand Master's Palace, Valletta.

The title card of John Huston's classic 1941 film *The Maltese Falcon*, with Humphrey Bogart in the role of Sam Spade, announces that

> In 1539, the Knight Templars of Malta, paid tribute to Charles V of Spain, by sending him a Golden Falcon encrusted from beak to claw with rarest jewels – but pirates seized the galley carrying this priceless token and the fate of the Maltese Falcon remains a mystery to this day.[1]

Novelist Dashiell Hammett was drawing on historical fact in setting up the plot of his work of detective fiction. The Maltese Falcon really existed. It was not however a fabulous jewelled statue. It was a falcon.

To understand this tribute, it is necessary to say something about the Knights of St John. The order was established in Jerusalem, initially to care for sick pilgrims to the Holy Land, but quickly developing a military character in providing pilgrims with protection. Caring for the ill has remained an important part of the work of the order – hence the St John Ambulance

Association. The central function of the order at the time of the falcon tribute was however its fight to defend Christian Europe against the Ottoman Turks. With Jerusalem falling under Muslim control, the order had retreated to Rhodes, from which it had harassed Ottoman forces in the eastern Mediterranean, becoming renowned for its skills in naval conflict. The Ottomans, continuing to expand westwards, evicted the knights from Rhodes in 1523, though the order was allowed to leave the island with honour, keeping their ships. The Knights of St John were therefore in search of a new home.

European Christian rulers such as Charles V of Spain were terrified at the rapid westwards expansion of the Ottomans under Suleiman the Magnificent. Charles saw advantage in providing a maritime base for the warrior Knights of St John, whose members were drawn from aristocratic families across Europe, in the hope that they could stop the Turkish advance in the Mediterranean. Thus, in 1530, in his capacity as monarch of Sicily, Charles V granted Tripoli, Malta and Gozo to the knights, for an annual tribute of one falcon. The falcon was duly offered each year until 1798, when the knights were expelled by Napoléon.

Charles's decision was thoroughly unpopular in Malta, whose inhabitants had not been consulted in advance, but it was to prove a wise one. In 1551, a Turkish raid on Gozo took most of the island's population into slavery. Greater danger was to come. In 1565, word reached the grand master of the order, Jean Parisot de la Valette, from spies in Constantinople, that Suleiman was assembling a large force with which to attack Malta. Suleiman aimed to annihilate the troublesome knights and use Malta as a stepping-stone to the western Mediterranean. La Valette summoned the knights of the order from across Europe and petitioned Europe's Christian rulers to send support.

The Ottoman fleet reaching Malta the following year comprised some 200 ships and 40,000 men. The island's defences were fewer than 9,000 strong, only around 600 of whom were knights. Through dogged defence, the Knights of St John hung on through a siege lasting some four months and indeed had already turned the tide of battle against the Ottomans by the time Christian reinforcements arrived from Sicily. The Ottomans would never again threaten the western Mediterranean. At the Battle of Lepanto in 1571, in which the Knights of St John participated as part of the Holy League, the Ottoman navy was decisively defeated and would no longer constitute a major naval threat.

Following their victory over the Ottomans in the Great Siege of Malta, the Knights of St John were showered with diplomatic gifts from grateful European Christian rulers. King Felipe II of Spain sent la Valette an ornamental gold and enamel-decorated sword and dagger: perhaps Dashiell Hammett merged elements of this gift with that of the falcon tribute in creating his fabulous treasure of the Maltese Falcon. Taken off the island during Napoléonic rule, the sword and dagger now rest in the Musée du Louvre in Paris.[2] Pope Pius V gave a practical gift, the loan of military architect Francesco Laparelli, who set about creating a grand new Maltese capital for the order on the Sciberras Peninsula, all thought of returning to Rhodes now having been abandoned. The new grid-patterned city was named Valletta, in honour of the grand master who had saved Europe from the Turks.

The tale of our gift unfolds more than two centuries later, by which time Valletta was a prosperous and elegant Baroque city, the knights now known as much for commerce as conflict. Under Catherine the Great, Russia considered Malta a potential ally, both in helping Russia develop its own naval skills and in supporting Russian ambitions in the Mediterranean. Thus, six Russian officers were sent to Malta in 1766 to learn about maritime matters.[3]

Russia's relationship with Malta underwent certain vicissitudes. In 1775, the Russian plenipotentiary in Malta, Marquis Giorgio Cavalcabo, was briefly arrested and then sent back to Russia following suspicions of his involvement in a failed uprising by Maltese peasants against the governance of the knights of the order.[4] Russian interest in Malta remained. Russia's annexation of Crimea in 1783, and consequent further exacerbation of Russo-Ottoman tensions, strengthened the importance for Russia of good relations with the key Mediterranean ports. A new Russian consul to Malta was appointed in 1784, an ethnic Greek named Antonio Psaro, with an exemplary record as a naval officer in the Russo-Turkish wars. Psaro was tasked with promoting a closer relationship with Malta and seems to have established a good rapport with the grand master. Russian commercial vessels were able to enter Malta for repair and resupply, and Psaro secured an agreement regarding the provision of credit for Russian merchants on advantageous terms.[5]

In 1787, Psaro travelled to Kherson, where Catherine the Great was engaged in a tour of Russia's new lands. He brought a letter from Grand Master Emmanuel de Rohan-Polduc, congratulating the empress on the conquest of Crimea. The grand master had sent diplomatic gifts with the letter. According to one source, these included a display of artificial flowers, probably a reference to the Maltese art of *ganutell*, the fashioning of elaborate artificial flowers using metal wire, thread and beads. The chosen arrangement reportedly incorporated symbols of peace, suggestive of good relations between the two countries.[6] Other sources refer to the gift of a palm branch, as a symbol of the grand master's admiration for the empress.[7] In deciding on a return gift for the grand master, Catherine opted to commission a portrait of herself. As we have seen in our previous story, state portraits were a mark of particular favour across Europe. The portrait would have been intended from a Russian perspective both to convey the qualities and grandeur of the empress and to stress Russian connectedness to Malta. For the grand master of the Knights of St John, the ability to display a portrait of the Russian empress might burnish his image by showing that he possessed powerful friends.

The portrait was chosen carefully. The task was entrusted to Dmitriy Levitskiy, an artist particularly known for allegorical portraits. The empress is depicted as Minerva, the goddess of just war. Her sword is sheathed, possibly in reference to the lack of violence required in the conquest of Crimea.[8] The wrapping of the sword in a laurel branch is a further reference to peaceful conquest. The empress wears the star and sash of the Order of St George, a new award for military service, which Catherine had created in 1769, awarding herself the Order First Class.

It is not clear how the painting reached Malta. Psaro returned in July 1788, but a thank you letter to the empress from Grand Master Rohan-Polduc is dated 20 February 1790, which appears to demonstrate that the portrait only reached Malta that year. There are some indications that it may have been sent with a Neapolitan envoy named Antonino Maresca Donnorso di Serracapriola.[9]

The portrait was given a prominent place in the Ambassador's Hall of the Grand Master's Palace, where it helped to flaunt the grand master's international connections. It continues to support ties between Russia and Malta. Following restoration by Maltese restorer Amy Sciberras, the portrait was lent in 2019 for an exhibition at the Tsaritsyno Museum Reserve in Moscow: a diplomatic gift still performing its diplomatic function.

1793

A PLANETARIUM

A GIFT FROM GEORGE III, KING OF GREAT BRITAIN AND IRELAND, TO THE QIANLONG EMPEROR OF THE QING DYNASTY

The Reception, a caricature by James Gillray, depicting the Qianlong emperor as indifferent to the gifts presented by Lord Macartney during his embassy of 1793.

This is an account of a diplomatic mission, backed by a large number and array of gifts, that failed to meet its objectives. It was beset by problems of communication, in which the two powers involved had very different views of their relationship and of the nature of the exchanges. The failure of the mission was in the end though more to do with the simple calculation that the hosts had no desire to meet its demands. It was the 1793 embassy to China of George Macartney.

In the late eighteenth century, Britain imported many luxury consumer items from China, including porcelain, silk and furniture, reflecting an upper- and middle-class infatuation with Chinese objects.[1] The most important Chinese export to Britain was tea, meeting a tea-drinking habit that had infused British society from the seventeenth century. With the reduction on taxes on tea under the Commutation Act of 1784, imports soared, swelling the profits of the East India Company, which purchased the tea at Canton, now Guangzhou.

A major problem for Britain was however that this trade with China was highly unbalanced. China bought few British products, and the purchase of all that tea, silk and porcelain was draining British reserves of silver.[2] Britain wanted to open the Chinese market to its manufactures and secure a more balanced trading relationship. A major obstruction to its ability to do so was the regulation of all foreign maritime trade with China through the Canton System, which channelled trade through that port in a monopolistic arrangement.

Britain resolved to send an embassy to Beijing to secure more favourable terms. It wanted to put the relationship with China on a treaty basis, a relaxation of the Canton System to allow British traders to operate in ports farther north, a resolution of grievances around arrangements at Canton, and agreement to a permanent legation in Beijing, so British communication with the emperor could avoid the intermediation of the Cantonese merchants.[3]

In 1787, Britain sent an embassy headed by Charles Cathcart, the Member of Parliament for Clackmannanshire, but he unfortunately died on the outward voyage to China in 1788, at the age of just twenty-eight. It tried again in 1792, this time appointing an experienced diplomat and colonial administrator, George Macartney, who had served in Russia, Grenada and India. Macartney was given an Irish peerage for the role. The embassy, whose costs were underwritten by the East India Company, was a considerable undertaking, with ninety-five direct members, transported on three ships, bringing a total complement of almost 700, including sailors.[4] The delegation included Macartney's deputy, Sir George Staunton, the latter's son, a tutor to the young Staunton, a surgeon, watchmaker, botanist, metallurgist and five musicians.[5]

The Chinese conception of its international relations was however quite unlike that of the United Kingdom. China perceived itself as a universal state with a heavenly mandate to rule the world.[6] Its dealings with its neighbours were not relationships of equals. The latter were accorded a tributary status, and the receipt of tribute missions from subordinate powers bearing gifts for the emperor was an important expression of that status.

'Tribute' in the Chinese context had a somewhat different meaning from the way the word was understood in the West, where it had the sense of a, usually swingeing, tax. While subordinates often did have to make large payments to the Qianlong emperor, for example in the form of grain, or of land tax, these were distinguished from the tribute goods brought to the Qing court, which were often less costly than the imperial gifts provided by the emperor in reciprocation.[7] The Chinese court would also bear the costs of accommodating and entertaining the visiting mission. Gifts brought as tribute goods were ideally products local to that country, a stipulation that boosted the emperor's authority by providing an association with desirable products from distant lands. Gifts of food would be served during imperial banquets, while the finest of the artistic objects would be displayed in one of the imperial palaces, so the emperor would live among the gifts.[8]

The gift exchange took place under a set ritual, involving first the inspection of the tributary gifts to establish their suitability. The superiority of the Chinese emperor was established by his seating on an elevated throne as well as by the *kowtow* of the envoy of the subordinate ruler, a form of obeisance involving kneeling three times and, at each of these kneelings, bowing the head three times so that it reached the floor.[9] The occasion was a festive one, involving music, theatrical performances and much food. The Qianlong emperor would reciprocate generously, with gifts such as silk and jade as well as the lavish hospitality offered to the delegation. This exchange of gifts helped reinforce Chinese authority, impressing the subordinate power with the munificence of the gifts.[10]

The British essentially treated the Macartney mission as a diplomatic negotiation between powers of equal status, while the Chinese framed it as a tributary mission and were indeed delighted that the British delegation had undertaken such a long journey for the expressed purpose of paying respects to the Qianlong emperor on his birthday.[11] This difference of perception between Britain and China as to their respective status was to prove challenging to Macartney as he attempted to negotiate the rituals around the mission without placing Britain in a position of subordination.

In accounts of the ultimate failure of the mission, Macartney's refusal to prostrate himself before the emperor in a *kowtow* has often been emphasised.[12] After extensive negotiations on the matter, Macartney instead presented the letter from his king, George III, in a jewelled gold box, while kneeling on one knee. This, he had argued, was how he would present himself before his own sovereign, minus the kissing of the sovereign's hand, an action ruled out by the Chinese as touching the emperor was forbidden.[13]

If Macartney perceived that, by refusing to *kowtow*, he was defending the equality of status of the two powers, this perception in itself illustrated the different understanding of Britain and China. It depended on a view that the acts of an ambassador were those of the sovereign they represented, which was not at all how the Chinese looked at it. For China, the sending of a gift-bearing mission was automatically a confirmation of subordinate status. The only way to avoid this was not to send an embassy in the first place.[14] From the Chinese perspective, a refusal to *kowtow* after having arrived at the helm of such a tributary mission just appeared to be bad mannered.

Macartney accepted, albeit grudgingly, other markers of the tributary nature of the mission. The Chinese hosted the delegation for their entire stay in the country and did so lavishly, providing food in enormous quantities. Macartney's comptroller estimated that the costs of the mission borne by the Chinese far exceeded those to the British, without even counting the cost of the considerable gifts received from the emperor.[15] The hosting of an embassy by the receiving sovereign was not usual in Western European diplomacy at that time, and Macartney attempted to argue that his embassy was willing to pay for its own provisions, but he quickly acquiesced in an arrangement that represented a performance of superiority on the part of the Qianlong emperor.[16] As the embassy travelled upriver towards Beijing, Macartney was informed by his interpreter that the barges provided by the Chinese that carried his gifts were inscribed with a character meaning 'tribute'. Macartney took the decision to let it pass.[17]

The gifts exchanged during the mission were also subject to the failures of communication and understanding that characterised the mission as a whole. The British took a vast quantity of gifts for the emperor, involving 600 packages and requiring 3,000 porters to convey them.[18] Much thought went into their selection. The British were keen to choose gifts that would be appreciated by the emperor. The Chinese interpreters recruited to the mission encouraged the purchase of automata, which they noted were in high demand in Canton. The inclusion of the latest astronomical instruments was made in part because it was widely believed that the Chinese held astronomy in high regard.[19]

There were other motivations at play in the choice of gifts beyond a desire to please. Since the goals of the Macartney mission were focused on opening the Chinese market to British exports, the mission's gifts served as a potential opportunity to showcase the best of British manufactures, which were being exported with increasing success across Europe and beyond, with the aim of stimulating Chinese demand. To this end, manufacturer Matthew Boulton provided an extensive set of recommendations of the finest examples of British manufacture: buttons, buckles, steelware, candlesticks, lamps and cutlery.[20] These were accepted only to a limited degree, as Macartney was concerned to distinguish the gifts to the emperor from King George from the trade goods the East India Company sought to promote.[21]

A stronger theme of the gifts of the Macartney embassy was more about showcasing British achievements in science and technology, a statement of the industrial enlightenment,[22] and presentation of British natural philosophy.[23] One of the members of Macartney's delegation was James Dinwiddie, a natural philosophy lecturer, a scientific populariser of his day, whose role, alongside a Swiss clockmaker named Charles Petitpierre, was to demonstrate to the Chinese the scientific instruments brought as gifts, including astronomical models, burning glasses, air pumps and reflecting telescopes.[24]

The most eye-catching of the scientific gifts was a large glass-cased planetarium, allowing spectators to watch the motions of the planets. It contained three clocks, showing daily time, monthly time and the time between creation and apocalypse, the latter set at 1836.[25] This remarkable instrument was the work of a pastor and clockmaker from Württemberg named Philipp Matthäus Hahn, whose career as planetarium-maker had taken off following a ducal commission in 1769. The *Weltmaschine* taken on the Macartney embassy was his largest project, purchased in London in 1792 at Dinwiddie's recommendation. It cost the East India Company £600. A further £650 was paid to the fashionable London clockmakers Vulliamy to ornately decorate it, including with the addition of ormolu pineapples.[26]

A showcase of British enlightened scientific achievement was thus headed by an object that was not British at all, but German, and whose inspiration was the product of religious concepts such as creation and apocalypse as well as scientific ones. The fact more money was spent on its embellishment than on its purchase suggests too that the presentation of items that would be appealing to the emperor was the strongest overall motive in the choice of gifts.

On the arrival of the Macartney embassy in China, a full list of gifts was requested by Chinese officials. Local etiquette demanded that this contain little description, but that it should include the value of each gift. Macartney both delayed the production of the required list and eventually submitted something that failed to conform to Chinese expectations, being instead a long text offering a detailed commentary on the meaning of the gifts. Much of the technical detail and flattery of the British list was simply cut out in the Chinese translation produced by European missionaries at the emperor's court.[27] Even in the trimmed-down form he received, the emperor seems to have concluded that the style of the list reflected British boastfulness, a verdict reinforced by what the Chinese saw as British exaggeration of the complexity and time required for the assemblage of gifts such as the planetarium.[28]

The emperor received Macartney not in Beijing but in Rehe, a summer palace complex north of the Great Wall, to which Macartney brought the more portable of his gifts. The others, including the planetarium, remained in Beijing to be viewed later by the emperor on his return to that city. In a tour of the palace complex at Rehe, Macartney and his party were shown the full extent of the emperor's collection of European items and realised with evident horror that their gifts were not as special as they had assumed. Macartney wrote that the pavilions contained 'every kind of European toys and sing-songs, with spheres, orreries, clocks and musical automatons of such exquisite workmanship, and in such profusion, that our presents must shrink from the comparison'.[29] Even the planetarium was rivalled by Chinese-made objects of similar function.[30]

The sight of the emperor's collection prompted a rethinking of British plans, and they never even presented some of the less valuable scientific instruments to the Chinese. Some were sold off in Canton by the East India Company, while James Dinwiddie kept a model steam engine and chemical experiments, which he used in his later career as a scientific demonstrator in India.[31] The ambition of using the embassy to present enlightened British achievement in science and technology was lost.

The conclusion has sometimes been drawn that the gifts of the Macartney mission were therefore disappointing to the recipient.[32] The emperor's edict at the end of the mission responding (negatively) to the requests made by the British indeed comments witheringly that 'we have never valued ingenious articles, nor do we have the slightest need of your country's manufactures'.[33] While the public assessment by the emperor was condescending in style, in part perhaps fuelled by what the Chinese viewed as the boastful manner with which Macartney had attempted to present them, the gifts actually seem to have been welcomed. Those not taken to Rehe were placed at the Yuanmingyuan palace complex outside Beijing, for the emperor to inspect on his return from Rehe. While he rejected a few gifts, such as two camera obscura, dismissed as suitable only for children, this action was from a Chinese perspective an appropriate gesture designed to demonstrate an absence of greed on the emperor's part. The military gifts, including cannon, guns, swords and a model warship, particularly engaged the attention of the emperor, who had a strong interest in European military technology. After the mission's departure, some of the most impressive British gifts, including the planetarium, remained on display in the imperial palaces.[34]

In similar fashion, the return gifts presented by the Qianlong emperor for King George III were intended to display Chinese power in a symbolism that was largely lost on Macartney and his delegation. The gifts included a number of jade objects, including goblets and bowls. Jade was a characteristic product of Xinjiang, newly secured from the Dzungars, and thus symbolised Chinese imperial conquest. The British however had no idea of jade's provenance or significance. Similarly, the gifts included boxes of Tibetan sugar, a regifted item the emperor had received from the Gurkhas, who had withdrawn from Tibet in the face of Qing military might. The gift was an assertion of Qing control of an area the emperor would have known lay close to territories of interest to the British. Macartney seems to have been unaware of the messaging here too.[35]

For both the British and Chinese, therefore, attempts to package their gifts with complex meanings were largely lost on their recipients, and the gifts were viewed in a more literal sense, simply as a set of desirable objects. The Macartney embassy did not fail because of any perceived deficiency in the gifts brought by Macartney, or because of any insult occasioned by his failure to *kowtow* or to observe other aspects of Chinese protocol. It failed because the Qianlong emperor had no interest in agreeing to any of the British demands. The negative edict received at the end of the mission was composed before Macartney even arrived in China.[36] Whatever gifts he had brought with him, Macartney's mission was never going to succeed.

1816

THE SPANISH ROYAL COLLECTION

A GIFT FROM FERNANDO VII, KING OF SPAIN, TO THE DUKE OF WELLINGTON

The Duke of Wellington hosting a banquet in the Waterloo Gallery, Apsley House.

Apsley House is a distinguished-looking neo-classical building on London's busy Hyde Park Corner, once boasting the impressive address of 'Number 1 London'.[1] It was originally a more modest brick building, designed by the celebrated architect Robert Adam in the 1770s for Henry Bathurst, the Lord High Chancellor. In 1807, the house was sold by Bathurst's son to Richard, Marquess Wellesley, older brother of the future duke of Wellington. Richard had been governor-general of Bengal and later served as foreign secretary, losing office following the assassination of Prime Minister Spencer Perceval. He found himself heavily in debt, a situation eased by the intervention of his younger brother.

Arthur Wellesley was already a celebrated hero for his successes in the Peninsular War, which saw the French driven out of Spain. He was created duke of Wellington and indeed marquess of Douro following that campaign. The defeat of Napoléon's force at Waterloo raised his standing to something akin to that of the saviour of Europe. The grateful nation of

Britain purchased the estate of Stratfield Saye in Hampshire as the site of 'Waterloo Palace'. The idea harked back to Blenheim Palace, a project based around a reward to John Churchill, the first duke of Marlborough, for his military victories in the War of the Spanish Succession, culminating in the Battle of Blenheim in 1704. Instead of commissioning a grand new palace, Wellington retained the original building at Stratfield Saye.

He instead devoted his attention on a London town house. Through an anonymous bid, he addressed his brother's indebtedness with the generous purchase of Apsley House for £40,000.[2] He engaged architect Benjamin Dean Wyatt, who had earlier served as his private secretary, to extend the building. The work was carried out in two phases. The second, on Wellington's appointment as prime minister in 1828, transformed the house into something more akin to a palace suitable for Wellington's lavish entertaining, in particular his annual Waterloo Banquet.

Apsley House was offered to the nation by the seventh duke of Wellington. The Wellington Museum Act of 1947 retains part of the house as the residence of the dukes, while the grand rooms are open to the public, managed by English Heritage.[3] The house today has the air of a shrine to the first duke of Wellington. His image, and reminders of his illustrious career, are everywhere. This is not simply a function of the remodelling of the place into a Wellington museum. It always had such a feel, even during the lifetime of the first duke. Diplomatic gifts presented to the duke are a key part of the reason.

When Napoléon slipped away from his exile on Elba and regathered an army in France, he was opposed by a coalition encompassing the whole of Europe, from the United Kingdom to Sicily, Portugal to Russia. The army headed by Wellington at Waterloo was a truly international one: little more than a third of his troops were British. Wellington was not just a hero of a grateful Britain, but of a grateful Europe. He received gifts from many European royals. His London residence was a place to show them off. The duke created a museum room with custom-built rosewood cabinets to display the gifts. And while the construction of the grand Waterloo Gallery, more than 28 metres long and 2 storeys in height, was in part necessitated by the desire for a space large enough to host his annual Waterloo Banquet in style, it also provided a suitable home for the grandest of all of his gifts, the paintings of the Spanish Royal Collection.

One impression arising from the diplomatic gifts on display at Apsley House is how alike were the choices of European rulers in the matter of the selection of gifts suitable for the commander who defeated Napoléon.

There is a sense here of a model as to what was appropriate. This is seen in the collection of gifted snuffboxes now on display in the museum room. There are boxes from Maximilian I, king of Bavaria; Friedrich Wilhelm III, king of Prussia; Alexander I, tsar of Russia; and Franz Stefan I, Holy Roman Emperor. All in gold, with an oval portrait of the head of state on top. Guests at Wellington's dinner table were surveyed by European royalty staring down from large, similarly sized, gifted portraits. A portrait of King George IV in Scottish dress joins them over the fireplace.

Several European heads of state concluded that the major gift most appropriate for Wellington was a large dinner service. The sense that this was a special and important gift from the ruler concerned is underlined by the personalised nature of several of these. The dinner service presented to Wellington by Friedrich Wilhelm III, king of Prussia, was made by the Berlin porcelain factory, one of its finest commissions, comprising more than 400 pieces. Its centrepiece is a green porcelain obelisk, listing Wellington's titles and orders. The dessert plates are decorated with scenes of towns and landscapes recalling different episodes of Wellington's life, from Eton to Poonah to the opening ceremony of Waterloo Bridge.

Friedrich August, king of Saxony, deployed the talents of Saxony's Meissen porcelain factory in creating a dinner service fit for the duke. It includes 105 dessert plates, with hand-painted scenes from the Napoléonic Wars. The *Austrian Service*, a gift from Holy Roman Emperor Francis II, takes a different approach. Unlike the Prussian and Saxon services, it does not depict scenes from Wellington's life and career. Instead, its decoration centres on roundels portraying busts of classical heroes, from Socrates to Pythagoras, Hannibal to Cicero. The gift would have been intended to imply that the duke's successes had placed him among the pantheon of classical greats.

The dinner service offered by the grateful restored French monarch, Louis XVIII, is a regifted present, in which the nature of the regifting speaks directly to the duke's achievements. The *Egyptian Service* was an impressive example of the output of the Sèvres porcelain factory. It was a product of the fashion for all things Egyptian in France stimulated by Napoléon's Egyptian campaign. An artist, writer and archaeologist on that campaign, Dominique Vivant Denon, had written the illustrated account *Voyage dans la Basse et la Haute Egypte* and contacted Sèvres to suggest they might use his illustrations for a dinner service.[4] Denon was well connected, serving as Napoléon's arts minister and the first director of the Musée Napoléon, the future Louvre. Sèvres produced a spectacular service, a diplomatic gift to Tsar Alexander I of Russia. It was admired by the

Empress Joséphine, and she commissioned a set, having been given 30,000 francs in credit by Napoléon to purchase Sèvres porcelain as a divorce gift.[5] When Joséphine finally received the service, she felt the result was too severe and sent it back.[6]

It is a remarkable service. The centrepiece, almost 7 metres long, depicts the temples of Karnak, Dendera and Philae. The sixty-six dessert plates offer scenes taken from illustrations in Denon's account. The *Egyptian Service* thus echoed with the vanquished Napoléon. As a diplomatic gift, it celebrated Wellington's success by reminding of the ambitions and excesses of the leader he had defeated.

In gifting the *Egyptian Service* to Wellington, Louis XVIII accompanied it with a handwritten letter in French, though with one underlined phrase in English: 'do little gifts – keep friendship alive'. Wellington had served as ambassador to France following Napoléon's first defeat and exile to Elba. He does not appear to have had a positive opinion of Louis XVIII. The Tory politician Philip Stanhope records a conversation in which Wellington reportedly declared: 'Louis the Eighteenth was a walking sore – a perfect walking sore – not a part of his body was sound – even his head let out a sort of humour.'[7]

The *Portuguese Service* is not porcelain but silver and silver gilt, a gift to the duke from the Portuguese government, designed by the court painter Domingos António de Sequeira, who had not previously undertaken a commission in metal.[8] The neo-classical centrepiece is more than 8 metres long. It features kneeling gryphons with plaques on their heads bearing the names of Wellington's victories in the Peninsular War. Dancing nymphs from the River Tagus parade around. The centrepiece was a star turn in Wellington's annual Waterloo Banquet.

The most lavish and remarkable of all the gifts made to Wellington is not a dinner service. It is an unusual gift, since it was in the possession of the recipient before it was gifted. It is the rich assemblage of paintings known as the Spanish Royal Collection, which today adorn the walls of the Waterloo Gallery in Apsley House, just as they did in Wellington's day.

The origins of the gift lie in the chaotic final days of the Peninsular War. Joseph Bonaparte, older brother of Napoléon, had been made king of Spain by the emperor. Unlike his brother, he was more suited as an art connoisseur than a military commander. As Wellington's forces embarked on their recapture of the Iberian Peninsula, Joseph made a hasty exit from Madrid, taking a large amount of booty with him. More than 150 paintings, largely appropriated from the Spanish Royal Collection, were cut from their frames, rolled in canvases and placed in a large trunk of the type known as an *imperial*, fitted on his personal coach.

In June 1813, the French forces were defeated by Wellington's troops at the Battle of Vitoria, some 85 miles short of the French border. Joseph attempted to flee in his personal coach, but this was stopped by British troops, and Joseph was forced to make good his escape on horseback.

Inspecting the contents of the coach, soldiers of the 14th Light Dragoons were delighted to find a solid silver chamber pot and 'liberated' the item for their regiment. It was duly christened *The Emperor* and is still used as the formidably large receptacle for the quaffing of toasts during mess dinners of the King's Royal Hussars, the successor regiment of the 14th Light Dragoons. The regiment acquired the nickname 'The Emperor's Chambermaids' from the episode.

The paintings were also discovered, and Wellington had these crated up and sent to his brother William in England, to whom he wrote that, from his initial cursory glance, they had not appeared remarkable. Their true value was realised when William had the Keeper of the Royal Pictures look at them. They include four paintings by Diego Velázquez, including an early masterpiece by the Spanish artist, *The Water-Seller of Seville*. Wellington's personal favourite painting in the collection was Correggio's *The Agony in the Garden*. He had a special frame made for it featuring a locking glass window: he kept the key in his pocket and was reportedly wont to lift the window to dust the painting with his handkerchief.[9] The collection has continued to generate surprises. In 2015, an English Heritage conservator uncovered Titian's signature during the cleaning of a painting long known as *Titian's Mistress* but which had been thought a later imitation of the master's style.[10]

Wellington made various attempts to return the paintings. In March 1814, he wrote to another brother, Henry, British ambassador to Spain, asking him to arrange for a Spanish official to come to London to view the paintings and determine which had been expropriated from the Spanish Royal Collection. The Spanish seemed in no hurry to take up the request and, in 1816, Wellington repeated his offer to return the paintings to the Spanish king via Spain's diplomatic representative in England, Count Fernan Nuñez. Having consulted King Fernando VII, the latter replied: 'His Majesty, touched by your delicacy, does not wish to deprive you of that which has come into your possession by means as just as they are honourable.'[11] The paintings were Wellington's, conferred on him by a grateful Spanish king.

Some scholars have argued that Wellington's actions in sending the paintings back to England suggest both that he was well aware of their importance and that he wanted to keep them, making it harder for the Spanish to secure their return. While there is no dispute that he offered to return the paintings, this line of argument suggests that Wellington at least hoped that matters would unfold exactly as they did, culminating in the gifting of the paintings.[12]

What is without doubt is that the paintings of the Spanish Royal Collection serve as a remarkable gift from the Spanish king to the man who helped restore his throne.

1826

A GIRAFFE

A GIFT FROM MUHAMMAD ALI PASHA, GOVERNOR OF EGYPT, TO CHARLES X, KING OF FRANCE

Nicolas Hüet le Jeune, study of the giraffe given to Charles X
by the viceroy of Egypt, 1827.

We have explored the important place of exotic animals among diplomatic gifts. It was a place established through a combination of the ability of strange and remarkable creatures to generate a sense of wonder and excitement and the exclusivity generated by the challenges around gifting exotic animals, from their difficulty to transport to their frequently high cost to maintain, making such creatures the preserve of the powerful and wealthy. As we have seen, while the gifts of some animals, such as beavers, were founded upon the desirability of their meat, fur and even secretions, the value of others lay purely in the wonderment that the creature generated.

Among the creatures of the animal kingdom, none had a greater capacity to instil wonder in lands unfamiliar to it than the giraffe. As tall as a house, with a neck of fantastical length, yet elegant and docile, the giraffe appeared almost magical. Julius Caesar, returning to Rome in 46 BCE from an arduous campaign in the Middle East and Africa, paraded a giraffe

179

through his capital, alongside other beasts such as torch-bearing elephants. This remarkable creature was intended to convey both Caesar's power and the accomplishments of the campaign.[1] The giraffe was torn to pieces by lions in the games that accompanied the celebration of Caesar's return: a gesture that perhaps aimed to imply that Caesar was so powerful he could easily replace such a rare creature if required.[2]

If the value of exotic animals as diplomatic gifts lay in the combination of their ability to generate wonder and the rarity engendered by the difficulties of transporting and maintaining them, the giraffe embodied both these attributes to a high degree. In order to transport the giraffe over the long distances required to present it as a gift in a land where it was unfamiliar, and therefore valuable, it needed to be tamed. This required its capture as an infant, so it could become accustomed to human interaction. Infant giraffes were themselves demanding, consuming up to 25 gallons of milk a day.[3] Giraffes were therefore an exclusive diplomatic gift, reserved for particularly important recipients.

A giraffe was presented to the Yongle emperor in China in 1414 from the ruler of Bengal, who had in turn received it as a gift from Melinde, now Malindi, in East Africa, another example of the frequent regifting of gifts of exotic animals. As we have seen, this reflects the fact that the wonder associated with the first sight of the creature will tend to diminish over time, while the costs and challenges of upkeep do not. The Chinese concluded that the giraffe was a legendary creature known as a *qilin*, something like a unicorn, and definitely a good omen.[4]

The rulers of Egypt were long significant sources of giraffes as diplomatic gifts for their counterparts in Europe and the Middle East. They obtained giraffes from present-day Sudan, as part of a tribute payment stemming from the Baqt Treaty between Egypt and Christian Nubia, the longest-lasting treaty in history, active from the seventh until the fourteenth century. Two giraffes were typically included in the annual tribute.[5] In the thirteenth century, Ayyubid Sultan al-Malik al-Kamil provided Holy Roman Emperor Friedrich II with a giraffe, getting a polar bear in return.[6] Friedrich's son Manfred of Sicily also received a giraffe, this time from the Mamluk Sultan al-Zahir Baybars in 1261.[7]

According to the diary of Florentine apothecary Luca Landucci, a gift package presented to Lorenzo de' Medici in 1487 by the ambassador of the Mamluk Sultan Qaytbay featured a range of animals, including a lion and an exotic breed of sheep, but the star gift was a giraffe.[8] The Mamluk embassy was part of ongoing attempts to negotiate a commercial treaty between the two powers, initiated by an earlier Florentine embassy to Cairo.

Qaytbay may also have been seeking support from Lorenzo on another matter. The Ottoman sultan, Bayezid II, posed a threat to Egypt. It suited Qaytbay to have Bayezid distracted by the rival claim to the Ottoman throne of his half-brother Cem Sultan who, having failed to unseat Bayezid in 1482, had sought the protection of the Knights of St John in Rhodes, who had transferred him to France, where he was a well-treated but politically valuable captive. Qaytbay wanted to persuade the French to give Cem into his care, where he would be a useful asset in dissuading Bayezid from aggressive moves against Egypt.

While historical records are sparse, American author Marina Belozerskaya has argued that the giraffe may have been the central actor in a complex political arrangement aimed at securing Cem's passage to Egypt. She believes Lorenzo may have requested a giraffe from Qaytbay as a means of demonstrating his international influence to the citizens of Florence, all part of his intention to rule in a more direct way than the traditionally behind-the-scenes leadership of the wealthy Medici family. A giraffe would be the perfect gift through which to achieve this objective, both because of its capacity to generate wonder and because it would hark back to Caesar's triumphal procession. Lorenzo's desire for a giraffe was though political rather than zoological in nature. Once the gift had been received, he planned to regift it to Anne of France, in return for her support in getting Cem to Qaytbay.[9]

If this was the plan, it was undone by the unfortunate demise of the giraffe. According to the journal of coppersmith Bartolomeo Masi, the creature died when its head was caught between the projecting supports of the beam above a portal.[10] Anne never received her giraffe, and Cem was sent instead into the custody of Pope Innocent VIII. The receipt of the giraffe nonetheless remained a moment of prestige for Lorenzo. When, long after Lorenzo's death, Giorgio Vasari was commissioned to paint him by Cosimo I de' Medici for the Palazzo Vecchio, he chose to portray Lorenzo receiving gifts from ambassadors. Prominent among these gifts was a giraffe.[11]

The gifting of giraffes to European rulers rather dried up at that point. It was not resurrected until the early nineteenth century. That it recommenced then was primarily down to two people. The first was the governor of Egypt, Muhammad Ali Pasha. He was an ethnic Albanian, born in Kavala, which today lies in Greece but was then, as was Egypt, part of the Ottoman

Empire. He arrived in Egypt in 1801 with Ottoman forces sent to reoccupy the country following the withdrawal of the French. The ruling class in Egypt prior to Napoléon's campaign of 1798 had been the Mamluks, vassals of the Ottomans who dreamt of independence from them.

Muhammad Ali manipulated the power struggle between Ottomans and Mamluks to secure in 1805 the position of governor for himself. He then set about eliminating the Mamluk leadership. He wanted Egypt to be free of Ottoman control, and for that, he had to modernise and strengthen the country. The support of European powers like France and Britain was valuable to Muhammad Ali both strategically and in practical terms, for the assistance they could bring to his modernising agenda. He was also keen to placate these powers, concerned at his support for the Ottomans in their attempts to put down the rebellion in Greece that would lead to its independence.[12] Diplomatic gifts were an important tool for Muhammad Ali since, being technically a simple governor rather than the ruler of an independent country, other diplomatic vehicles such as the right to send ambassadors were not open to him.[13]

The idea of deploying giraffes as diplomatic gifts to achieve these ends appears to have been suggested to Muhammad Ali by our second figure, Bernardino Drovetti, the Turin-born French consul-general in Egypt. In parallel, Drovetti served as an informal adviser to Muhammad Ali as well as a collector of Egyptian antiquities and general opportunist who supplied both the relics of ancient Egypt and exotic animals to European collections.[14] Charles X, the French king, had issued a call to the French diplomatic network to secure exotic flora and fauna, so Drovetti can have been confident that the gift of a giraffe would be highly appreciated, the more so as this would be the first giraffe ever to set foot in France.[15] Muhammad Ali's son Ismail had invaded the Sudan in 1821, facilitating the governor's ability to procure giraffes.[16]

Muhammad Ali was keen to maintain a balance between the rival ambitions of France and Britain and so decided to send a giraffe to each power, a parity of gifting that would extend, as we shall see in a later story, to presents of obelisks. He sent a third giraffe to the emperor of Austria, Francis I. The objectives underpinning these gifts of exotic animals were however different in nature from those surrounding the giraffe gifted to Lorenzo de' Medici. While they were also gifts to rulers, Muhammad Ali would have had in mind generating a positive impact not just on the recipient monarchs but also on the wider publics of the three countries. These were gifts intended not just as suitably regal presents but also as tools of a more public diplomacy. While the giraffes sent to Britain and Austria both generated great interest, neither survived for more than two years. The British giraffe, accommodated in Windsor Park, was though immortalised in a work by the Swiss painter Jacques-Laurent Agasse entitled *The Nubian Giraffe*.[17]

The giraffe sent to France was evidently of a hardier constitution. She was shipped from Alexandria to Marseille in a vessel with a hole cut in its deck through which the giraffe's head protruded. Arriving at the French port in October 1826, the giraffe wintered in the gardens of the prefecture. The prefect evidently grew rather fond of his charge, not least for the giraffe's ability to provide a talking point at dinner parties, in which favoured local nobles would be treated to a viewing.[18]

The French authorities entrusted the naturalist Étienne Geoffroy Saint-Hilaire with the task of collecting the giraffe from Marseille and bringing it safely to the king in Paris. He was a good choice, having participated in Napoléon's invasion of Egypt in 1798 as a scientific adviser, later carving a distinguished career as a professor of zoology.[19] His name lives on in several animal species, including the Geoffroy's cat, a wild cat of South America.

Geoffroy determined that the best way to get the giraffe to Paris, a distance of some 880 kilometres, would be to walk it from Marseille to the French capital. On the morning of 20 May 1827, an unusual convoy duly headed north.[20] The procession was headed by the cows that furnished the giraffe with its milk. There was a cart laden with luggage, solid food for the giraffe, and some further caged exotic animals added by Drovetti, including a roebuck from Tenerife.[21] The giraffe was accompanied by two keepers, Hassan and Atir, who themselves generated considerable attention in their colourful attire.[22] Geoffroy largely travelled by coach, frequently leaving the rest of the procession to sort out accommodation arrangements for the giraffe at the next town, a decision that sometimes required the remodelling of stables.[23]

The giraffe was furnished with a made-to-measure oilskin raincoat, ordered by Geoffroy as protection against the inclement French weather. In a royal blue fabric, decorated on one side with the *fleurs-de-lys* of the French monarchy, on the other with the arms of Muhammad Ali, the raincoat in effect also served as a gift wrapper, advertising its contents as a present for the French king and a symbol of Franco-Egyptian relations.[24] The giraffe attracted huge attention throughout its journey northwards, and the security challenges proved not to be, as Geoffroy had envisaged, around how to control a wild animal, for the giraffe was docile and gentle, but how to protect the giraffe from the crowds.[25] An escort of gendarmes proved invaluable.

Charles X, showing himself a stickler for royal protocol, insisted that the giraffe be brought to him, rather than coming to meet it, so the procession headed to the palace of Saint-Cloud to the west of Paris.[26] The way Muhammad Ali's giraffe was interpreted for its recipient audience was different in nature from the reception accorded to Qaytbay's giraffe, with notable attention given to the scientific aspects of the gift. Thus, Geoffroy gave a scientific presentation to Charles X,[27] and the giraffe was thereafter consigned to the menagerie at the Jardin des Plantes, the largest collection of exotic animals in Europe, under Geoffroy's scientific leadership.

It was also open to the public, unlike the royal menageries of earlier times. Thousands of people came to view the remarkable creature. A giraffe mania took hold in France, with giraffe motifs appearing in textiles, wallpaper and furniture, gingerbread biscuits created in giraffe shapes and even a ladies' hairstyle *à la girafe*. The animal served, in effect, as one of the fads required to fuel the developing mass market in consumer goods.[28] The giraffe's star would though quickly fade. Just three years after its arrival in Paris, the novelist Balzac claimed that its visitors were restricted to retarded provincials, bored nannies and simple and naïve fellows.[29] The giraffe died in 1845 and was disposed of scientifically. Its organs were removed, preserved in alcohol and apparently lost. Its skeleton was displayed in Caen, where it fell victim to allied bombings. Its stuffed skin is still on display in a stairwell of the natural history museum of La Rochelle.[30]

The memory of the gifted giraffe has however not only been retained but embellished. While we do not know what the animal was called by its contemporaries, it has now acquired a name, Zarafa, the word meaning 'giraffe' in Arabic, apparently used by Muhammad Ali's bureaucrats in the paperwork related to the animal's despatch to France.[31] This was the name used by American author Michael Allin in his popular biography of the creature,[32] as well as the title of a Franco-Belgian animated film of 2012, in which the giraffe reaches Paris by hot air balloon accompanied by a Sudanese boy named Maki. Charles X is the villain of that film: his comeuppance involves being smothered by hippopotamus dung. Which shows that diplomatic gifts can have truly unexpected afterlives.

1829

THE *SHAH DIAMOND*

A GIFT FROM FATH-ALI SHAH QAJAR, SHAH OF IRAN, TO NICHOLAS I, TSAR OF RUSSIA

The *Shah Diamond*, depicted on a Soviet stamp of 1971.

This is a diplomatic gift offered as an apology, and to avert the threat of retributions following an act that harmed the recipient. It concerns perhaps the only diplomatic incident prompted by a homesick eunuch.

Our tale centres on the remarkable figure of Alexander Griboedov, Russian playwright and diplomat, whose life was an almost impossibly romantic one, with intrigues in exotic cities, duels over matters of honour and marriage to a beautiful Georgian princess before a tragic early death.[1] As a writer, Griboedov is remembered for one play, *Gore ot uma* (*Woe from Wit*), whose hero, Alexander Andreevich Chatsky, returns from a long foreign tour to find that Moscow has changed, or perhaps he has, and he can no longer communicate with old friends and his old love.[2] It was banned from performance by the Russian censors but widely circulated in manuscript form, and remains one of the most quoted Russian plays.

Our story focuses on Griboedov's diplomatic career rather than his literary one. He joined the Russian Foreign Ministry in 1817 and appears to have been hoping for a relaxed life for a few years in the social and literary circles in St Petersburg. A whiff of scandal around his participation in a duel led though to his being posted to Georgia, starting a career focus on Persia and the Caucasus. Back in St Petersburg, his friendship with some of those involved in the 1825 Decembrist uprising of reform-minded young nobles against the new tsar, Nicholas I, and his own outspokenness, made him the object of suspicion. He was detained in the Russian capital for several months but established his innocence and returned to Georgia for a second stint, working for the Russian commander-in-chief, Ivan Paskevich, to whom he was conveniently related.

Russia had long been pushing south against Persian territories in the Caucasus, and their occupation of Gokcha in present-day Armenia occasioned the Russo-Persian War of 1826.[3] The initial Persian attack led by the crown prince, Abbas Mirza, had delivered some successes, but the tide was quickly turned as the Russians marshalled their superior military strength, and by October 1827, the Russians had reached Tabriz. Persia sued for peace and, in February 1828, Russian and Persian commanders met to sign the Treaty of Turkmenchay, which was substantially the work of Griboedov.[4] The treaty's provisions were tough on Persia, which had to cede large swathes of present-day Armenia and Azerbaijan, bringing its borders to those of present-day Iran. Persia was also forced to make a swingeing payment of 10 *crores* of tomans to Russia. In a provision that would be significant in the events that followed, both sides had the right to claim the repatriation of their subjects.[5]

Griboedov was sent to St Petersburg for the ratification of the treaty, which was greeted with satisfaction by the tsar. For his role in securing it, Griboedov was appointed to the post of minister resident in Persia. According to his friend, the great Russian poet Pushkin, Griboedov had negative premonitions of what lay ahead in Persia.[6] He should have heeded them.

He went first to Georgia, where he married a sixteen-year-old princess named Nina Chavchavadze, daughter of the commander of the new Russian provinces of Nakhichevan and Erevan.[7] With his new bride, he headed to Tabriz, where he presented the ratified treaty to Abbas Mirza. Leaving his wife in the care of the British mission in Tabriz, he left in December 1828 for Tehran, where he would present his credentials to the shah.

All started out cordially enough. A comfortable house in Tehran was put at the disposal of his mission, and his credentials were presented to Fath-

Ali Shah. Griboedov's mission was however never going to be straightforward in a Persia reeling under the terms of the Treaty of Turkmenchay. Things started to go wrong. The diplomatic gifts from the tsar he was supposed to present to the shah had been delayed in transit, and Griboedov had to improvise with the unimpressive gift of twenty-five new Russian coins.[8] The behaviour of some of Griboedov's servants towards local people caused offence, and his own handling of his audiences with the shah was wanting, the Persian ruler bringing the last two of these to an abrupt end in a manner Griboedov found discourteous.[9]

It was however with the eunuch that Griboedov's real problems began. Mirza Yakub Makarian, eunuch to the shah and treasurer of the royal harem, took refuge in the Russian mission, seeking repatriation to his native Armenia under the terms of the treaty Griboedov had negotiated. Rumours circulated that Mirza Yakub had embezzled from the royal coffers and abjured Islam on leaving the harem. Mirza Yakub claimed that two Christian Armenian women were being held involuntarily in the harem of former Grand Vizier Allahyar Khan. Griboedov managed to interview the women, who expressed no desire to leave the city, but he nonetheless ordered them detained in the mission in case they changed their mind, fuelling rumours that the Russians had seized the women with immoral intent.[10] Griboedov was planning to conclude his mission in Tehran and return to his wife in Tabriz and had already had his farewell audience with the shah. It is possible that the arrival of Mirza Yakub may have delayed his departure plans.[11] He was never to leave.

The chief mullah of Tehran, Mirza Messeh, and other religious leaders, incited the people to head to the Russian mission to take Mirza Yakub and the two women by force, arguing that the Russians had insulted both their religion and the shah. On 11 February 1829, a large mob headed to the mission. Mirza Yakub was stabbed to death, and the women carried off by Allahyar Khan's servants. The mob were not satisfied and proceeded to kill all those in the mission, including Griboedov. It is said that his body had been so comprehensively mutilated that it could only be recognised by a deformity of his little finger: the outcome of a duelling injury.[12] Thirty-seven members of the mission perished. The only Russian to survive was the first secretary, a man named Maltsov, who managed to hide in another part of the building.

Pushkin, in an account of his travels through the region, *A Journey to Arzrum during the Campaign of 1829*, recalls a poignant encounter with an ox cart heading towards Tbilisi. He asked the Georgians accompanying the cart where they had come from. 'From Tehran'. What they were carrying? 'Griboed'. It is a famous encounter, but it seems a fictional one: the murdered Griboedov had been conveyed through the area several weeks before Pushkin would have passed by.[13]

The massacre of the Russian mission presented an alarming prospect to the shah, terrified at the likely Russian reaction. In an account of events conveyed via the British envoy, John Macdonald, Crown Prince Abbas Mirza essentially took the line that the Persian authorities had nothing to do with the tragedy. He argued that anger had been generated by the offensive actions of the eunuch, the impropriety of the detention of the two Armenian women, and the bad behaviour of some of the Russian servants.[14] While there was a bellicose faction in Tehran, prominent among the mullahs, who believed that the answer lay in another war with Russia, the shah determined that Russian anger should be soothed. Prince Khosrow Mirza, son of Abbas Mirza, was despatched to St Petersburg to make an official apology to the tsar.

A significant diplomatic gift was clearly called for as part of this apology. The shah alighted on a magnificent diamond. The *Shah Diamond* was discovered in the Golconda region of southern India around 1450. It weighs 88.7 carats and has the shape of a coffin. Three of its faces bear engravings setting out the date and name of the then owner of the diamond, such that the history of the stone is written across the diamond itself. The first name inscribed was that of Burhan Nizam Shah II, ruler of the Ahmadnagar sultanate, in 1591. The stone was then seized by the Mughals, and the second inscription was that of Shah Jahan, the famed Mughal emperor, in 1641. Nader Shah, the shah of Persia, seized the diamond during his attack on the then declining Mughal Empire in the 1730s, and the third name inscribed on the diamond was that of Fath-Ali Shah in 1826. The diamond was accompanied by other gifts, including carpets and ancient manuscripts.

Prince Khosrow Mirza's mission was a success. Tsar Nicholas received him graciously and declared himself content that the shah had nothing to do with Griboedov's murder.[15] He did though insist that those responsible be punished, a matter on which there had been little progress. The shah eventually acted in a manner that satisfied the Russians, imprisoning the chief of police of Tehran and banishing Mirza Messeh. Not only did the tsar not seek to impose further penalties against Persia for the murder of Griboedov, but he also agreed to waive the payment of the tenth *crore* of tomans due under the Treaty of Turkmenchay, and to defer payment of the ninth *crore* for five years.[16] The tsar's evident willingness to settle amicably with Persia and not seek to extract a heavier penalty for Griboedov's murder perhaps had much to do with the fact that Russia and Turkey had been, yet again, at war since 1828. The tsar would have wished to avoid fighting multiple adversaries.

The mission of Prince Khosrow Mirza marked a turning point in Russia's relations with Persia. The relationship improved to such an extent that, by 1856, concerns that further Persian influence in Afghanistan would strengthen the Russian hand in the Anglo-Russian Great Game over Central Asia was one of the underlying factors behind the Anglo-Persian War of that year.

The *Shah Diamond* is today one of the star pieces of the Kremlin Diamond Fund in Moscow, a reminder of an apology for the death of a playwright.

1831

AN OBELISK

A GIFT FROM MUHAMMAD ALI PASHA, GOVERNOR OF EGYPT, TO LOUIS PHILIPPE I, KING OF THE FRENCH

Cleopatra's Needle in London; a gift from the governor of Egypt that took the
recipients decades to collect.

We have seen that, like the child writing to Santa Claus to request a new
bicycle, diplomatic gifts can be solicited. The gift to France of the ancient
obelisks in front of the temple at Luxor provides a good example: a present desired and requested by France, gifted by the governor of Egypt
because it suited his objectives to do so.

The origins of the French desire for an obelisk lie in part in Napoléon's
Egyptian Campaign of 1798. While motivated by geopolitics and trade –
to hinder British access to India and help the cause of Tipu Sultan of
Mysore, and to develop French commercial interests – it also had a strong
scientific and cultural dimension; alongside a 40,000-strong army,
Napoléon took with him 167 scientists.[1] The antiquities uncovered during
the campaign, including the Rosetta Stone, and the account provided by
Dominique Vivant Denon of the *Voyage dans la Basse et la Haute Egypte*,
stimulated both the academic discipline of Egyptology and a surge of

Egyptomania across France and beyond. This enthusiasm for all things Egyptian reinforced a further source of desire for an obelisk, which lay in the reverence in which these slender stone structures were placed by the Roman Empire. The Romans transported some two dozen to their capital,[2] and they were later used by Renaissance popes to emphasise the glories of the Eternal City.

Following Napoléon's defeat and the restoration of the French monarchy, King Louis XVIII, who was among those fascinated by ancient Egypt,[3] directed the French consul-general in Alexandria to approach the governor of Egypt, Muhammad Ali Pasha, about the possibility of being gifted an obelisk.[4] For the French king, an obelisk would serve to both celebrate his restoration and underline the stature of the French capital as an equal to Rome. Why though should the governor agree to part with an obelisk?

In our tale of a giraffe, we have seen the important role of diplomatic gifts in Governor Muhammad Ali Pasha's objectives of securing the acquiescence of the European powers in his adventurism in the eastern Mediterranean and their support for his modernising agenda. As with giraffes, so with obelisks. The surrendering of some of Egypt's antiquities must have seemed a small price to pay for their support, as ancient treasures held little relevance for his agenda of modernisation and the consolidation of power.

The obelisk earmarked for France was one of the two obelisks of Alexandria. These had been installed at Heliopolis during the reign of Thutmose III, but during the period of Roman control over Egypt were moved to Alexandria at the behest of Augustus to adorn the Caesareum, the temple to the deified Julius Caesar.[5] The two obelisks acquired the nickname of Cleopatra's Needles, although Cleopatra herself had died some years before they made the journey to Alexandria.[6] One of these Alexandria obelisks, which had toppled to the ground in an earthquake at the start of the fourteenth century, was set aside as a gift to the British. The French gift would be the standing one.

The celebrated Egyptologist and decipherer of hieroglyphics Jean-François Champollion, undertaking a scientific expedition to Egypt, had other ideas. He considered the Alexandria obelisks to be second rate and urged that France seek to secure the obelisks from the reign of Ramesses II that stood each side of the portal of the Luxor Temple. Which seems to be a distinct case of looking a gift horse in the mouth. The exertions of the expedition weakened Champollion's already poor health, and he was to die in Paris in 1832 at the age of just forty-one.

The French king, by now Charles X, despatched a mission under Baron Isidore Taylor to secure the gift of the Luxor obelisks. The complication that these obelisks had already been promised to the British was overcome with a package deal in which the two Luxor obelisks would go to the French, with the British promised the great obelisk of Hatshepsut at Karnak.[7] The French regarded this as a particularly favourable deal for them, for the Hatshepsut obelisk seemed impossible to move, at least without destroying the temple. The British never tried. The French Revolution of 1830 brought the overthrow of Charles X and the arrival of Louis Philippe I, but the gift was reconfirmed to the new French king.[8]

The French made a half-hearted attempt to collect the Alexandria obelisk also gifted to them, sending a ship called the *Dromadaire*, but this was ill-equipped, and French plans to take down the standing obelisk foundered over a lack of timber.[9] The focus of French efforts was however to secure the western obelisk at Luxor, which Champollion regarded as the most beautiful of the three they had been gifted.[10] Champollion had also cautioned that the eastern obelisk was cracked.[11] On 15 April 1831, a remarkable vessel departed Toulon, bound for Egypt. The *Luxor* was a barge specifically constructed to bring back the western Luxor obelisk, which meant that it had to be able to handle the shallow waters of the Nile and Seine but also the open seas, pass under the bridges of Paris and cope with the size and weight of the obelisk.[12]

The engineer in charge of the operation was Jean-Baptiste Apollinaire Lebas. The dismantling, transportation and re-erection of the obelisk was a huge undertaking. Before he could get going, he met in June with the governor. Lebas was not a tall man, and Muhammad Ali amusingly pretended on introduction not to be able to see him.[13] Oh, how they must have laughed.

Numerous problems confronted Lebas and his team. The western obelisk also proved to be cracked, although fortunately not seriously. Lengthy negotiations were required to compensate the owners of houses abutting the obelisk and blocking its route to the Nile, and which had to be destroyed. There was an outbreak of cholera. They kept to the task and, by December 1831, the obelisk was hauled inside the *Luxor*.[14] Lebas had to wait until the following August and a rise in the level of the Nile until the *Luxor* could depart. The journey back was slow and careful, and the *Luxor* did not reach Paris until December 1833, with a further wait until the following August for a fall in the river waters sufficient to ground the vessel and allow the safe removal of the obelisk.[15] The pedestal had to be prepared. It was decorated with a drawing showing how Lebas had accomplished the lowering of the obelisk in Egypt. A block from the base of the Luxor obelisk, depicting a row of baboons on their hind legs, lifting their front legs in honour of the sun, brought to Paris with the intention of decorating the pedestal, was not however installed and was sent instead to the Louvre. The display of baboon genitalia had evidently proved too much for the puritanical climate of the time.

The chosen location for the obelisk was a central one: the Place de la Concorde. This was an emotive place in recent French history. The square had been laid out in the 1750s to honour King Louis XV, whose statue was placed in the centre. That was torn down in the French Revolution, when the square served as a place of execution. It was here that King Louis XVI met his end. It is possible to see in the choice of an Egyptian obelisk for the square a desire for a monument that had no resonance with the troubled recent history of the country and would therefore be a safe option.[16]

The obelisk was set on its pedestal on 25 October 1836. More than 200,000 people crowded into the square to watch the spectacle. Lebas was feted for his achievements. He died in 1873 and is buried in the Père Lachaise Cemetery in Paris. His tomb, fittingly, features an obelisk.

In 1845, Muhammad Ali received a return gift from Louis Philippe, a large antique clock. This was placed in a tower in the Great Mosque of Muhammad Ali Pasha, commissioned by the governor and lying within the Cairo Citadel. The clock has never worked properly since the time of its installation, despite periodic attempts to repair it. Another was underway at the time of writing.[17] The French made no attempt to take the eastern Luxor obelisk out of Egypt. In 1981, President Mitterrand officially returned it to Egypt.

The two Cleopatra's Needles at Alexandria would also leave Egypt as diplomatic gifts, though not until decades later, and neither to France. The fallen obelisk at Alexandria was a gift from Muhammad Ali to the British for delivering Egypt from Napoléon. The British long showed no great inclination to collect it. The British government fretted about the costs and logistics of transporting the obelisk, and prominent British Egyptologists expressed concerns about its degraded quality.[18] When the governor of Egypt sold the ground on which the obelisk lay to a Greek merchant in 1867, its new owner insisted that the obelisk be removed from the site. The governor pressed the British finally to collect their gift, and with the government still unwilling to meet the transportation costs this was eventually accomplished through the campaigning of soldier and traveller

General Sir James Edward Alexander and the financial support of his friend, Professor Erasmus Wilson, an expert on skin diseases. With Wilson's money, they engaged an engineer named John Dixon to transport the obelisk to London.[19] Dixon arrived in Alexandria in 1877.

The obelisk was encased in a remarkable vessel, a floating iron cylinder with a mast and deckhouse, baptised logically enough the *Cleopatra*. This was to be towed to London by the steam tug *Olga*. Disaster struck in the Bay of Biscay when a storm broke out and the *Cleopatra* became uncontrollable. The six crew members of a rescue boat sent by the *Olga* to retrieve the crew of the *Cleopatra* were drowned when that boat capsized, and the *Cleopatra*, its crew finally rescued, was abandoned. The *Cleopatra* did not sink, was picked up by another ship and collected from a Spanish port after the payment of surely the first ever salvage claim in relation to an obelisk. Cleopatra's Needle was finally erected on the Victoria Embankment in London in 1878, placed at the heart of a somewhat kitsch ensemble featuring two flanking sphinxes, with more little sphinxes decorating adjacent benches.

The second obelisk at Alexandria, never taken by France, attracted the attention of the United States, fired by the press coverage of the transportation of the London obelisk and looking to secure an obelisk of its own to confirm its status as the equal of the European powers. US Consul-General Elbert Farman made repeated efforts to persuade the governor, Isma'il Pasha, to make the United States a gift of the obelisk, finally securing his goal in 1879.[20] As with the London obelisk, a private backer had agreed to underwrite the costs of its removal and transportation: in this case, railroad magnate William H. Vanderbilt. The governor's motivations in agreeing to gift an obelisk paralleled those of Muhammad Ali Pasha decades earlier, including the hope of US support for his efforts to modernise the country. The outcome of the American request had though been less certain, not least because opposition to the loss of Egypt's treasures had built up as the century progressed.

The contract to move the obelisk from Alexandria to New York was won by a naval officer named Henry Honeychurch Gorringe. Arriving in Alexandria in October 1879, Gorringe confronted considerable opposition to the obelisk's removal, particularly from foreign residents of the city. He flew a US flag on the obelisk as a mark of ownership.[21] It was eventually lowered and embarked on the steamer *Dessoug*, purchased from the Egyptian government for the task of transporting it. The obelisk arrived in New York in July 1880 and was erected in Central Park at the beginning of the following year.

The presence of ancient Egyptian obelisks in capitals around the world is not uncontroversial. In 2011, Zahi Hawass, the then minister heading Egypt's Supreme Council of Antiquities, suggested that the New York obelisk was being neglected, and that if the city could not take better care of it, Egypt might seek its return. A restoration programme followed in 2014, though curators at the Metropolitan Museum of Art identified the major source of deterioration of the obelisk as the result, not of the environment in New York, but of the legacy of its having fallen and lain on the desert sands for several centuries while in Heliopolis.[22]

1837

A PEACE MEDAL

A GIFT FROM THE GOVERNMENT OF THE UNITED STATES OF AMERICA TO KEOKUK, CHIEF OF THE SAUK TRIBE

The Thomas Jefferson peace medal of 1801, featuring clasped hands, a crossed tomahawk and peace pipe, and the words 'peace and friendship'.

We have seen, in stories from China and Japan, the array of costly gifts deployed by European powers seeking to develop their trading relationships with the empires of Asia. In North America on the other hand, where Europeans encountered a very different local population, territorial expansion was frequently underpinned by low-value, even trivial, gifts.[1] Peter Minuit, the director of New Netherland, purchased the island of Manhattan in 1626 from the Native Americans for goods valued at a meagre 60 guilders.[2]

Peace medals played an important role in the unequal gift exchange with Native Americans. Such medals, typically featuring a portrait of the monarch, were used by European colonial powers as a gift token of friendship and alliance from the early years of European settlement in the sixteenth century. The practice was adopted by the new government of the United

States during the George Washington administration and continued under every US president until the late nineteenth century.[3]

Medals were characteristically made of silver. Their iconography was intended to suggest equal partnership. Yet this was a partnership set against the backdrop of the progressive westward expansion of the United States, in fulfilment of what would later be couched as its manifest destiny to enter and reshape the new lands in the image of the settled agriculture of the east, underpinned by the institutions of the United States. In short, this could not be an equal partnership, as this 'destiny' involved the progressive dispossession of the Native Americans from their lands.

Thus, the obverse of the 1792 George Washington peace medal displays two standing figures, a Native American and Washington, gazing at each other in friendship. Yet while the foreground of the image offers a balance between the two parties, in the background a team of oxen pulling a plough moves across the picture from the right, offering a pictorial image of the westward spread of settled agriculture.[4] The early George Washington medals were hand engraved and rudimentary. From the Jefferson presidency, they were produced at the US Mint in Philadelphia, becoming more sophisticated.

Imbalance is also created in the 1792 Washington medal by the fact that the Native American is a generic figure, whereas Washington was a real leader. This identification of the medal with the president of the United States became more pronounced from the Jefferson peace medal of 1801, which simply bears a portrait of the president on the obverse, dispensing with the Native American figure. The reverse features clasped hands, one of a Native American, the other of a European, beneath a crossed tomahawk and peace pipe, and the words 'peace and friendship'. The explorers Lewis and Clark carried a considerable supply of these medals in their expedition to the Pacific Ocean from 1804 to 1806.[5] They were typically offered alongside other gifts such as clothing and tobacco. Variations on this design were used in peace medals minted up to the presidency of Zachary Taylor in the late 1840s.[6]

The success of peace medals as gifts owed much to the fact that they were interpretable in the context of an established practice among Native American communities, dating back at least 4,000 years, of the wearing of shell gorgets as a mark of status within the tribal group.[7] The peace medals were worn by tribal chiefs in similar fashion around their necks and were highly desired as a demonstration to members of their tribe of the external esteem in which they were held. From the 1790s, peace medals came in three different sizes, with the larger medals particularly sought after as suggestive of greater importance and respect.[8] Peace medals were valued items and usually handed down to the chief's successor.

The gifting of peace medals typically took place during formal ceremonies either on the frontier or in the US capital, for example to accompany a treaty signing. From the perspective of the United States, the medals were a visual representation of treaties under which the Native Americans had sold their land or pledged to provide military support or raw materials such as furs. While presented in an iconography of friendship and equality, they symbolised the power of the United States over the Native American tribes.[9] Joel Poinsett, secretary for war under President Martin van Buren, is chiefly remembered today because, as an avid amateur botanist, he sent samples of a plant that had grabbed his attention in Mexico to the United States, where it became known as the poinsettia. In 1837, when handing over peace medals to chiefs of the Sauk tribe at a ceremony in Washington, he told them that whenever they looked at the medals they must 'remember your obligations to the whites, and never make them ashamed of your conduct'.[10] The rhetoric here is a mix of imperialism, paternalism and racism. It is certainly not suggestive of partnership.

The understanding by Native American chiefs of the peace medals was more varied. The differing reactions to these medals of two chiefs of the Sauk tribe illustrate this complexity. The Sauk (or Sac) tribe, together with their close associates the Fox (or Meskwaki), had agreed with the United States in 1804 to surrender their lands east of the Mississippi in Wisconsin and Illinois, including their historic villages along the Rock River.

A Sauk leader named Black Hawk, who had earned his position through his leadership of war parties, opposed the settlement of 1804. In the War of 1812, he had allied with the British against the United States, and in 1832 he moved his band back east across the Mississippi into Illinois, precipitating the last Native American war fought on that side of the river, which has passed into history as the Black Hawk War. In his autobiography, dictated towards the end of his period of captivity following that episode, he makes clear his refusal to accept or wear a US peace medal.[11] His was not a rejection of peace medals as a concept; he mentions the wearing of British medals during the War of 1812. Rather, he explains that while the British made few promises, they were reliable, whereas the Americans made fine promises, but never kept them.[12]

Keokuk was a rival Sauk leader who took a different approach to dealings with the United States and to peace medals. Keokuk's approach was one of negotiation, agreeing a series of accommodations with the United States that involved the progressive movement of his tribe westwards. The US authorities were understandably keen to work with him. It is easy to view the treaties he signed, and the peace medals he received, as serving to bolster his position as a leader of his people. From a modern vantage point, the approach of Black Hawk in taking a stance of resistance against unbalanced treaties looks the more noble. Perhaps for this reason, while Black Hawk has given his name to a military helicopter, four US navy vessels and numerous sports teams, Keokuk gets just a town in Iowa, and this received its name during his lifetime.

Keokuk's actions should however be viewed in the context of US military strength and the relentless westwards pressure of white settlers. The selling of territories and relocations to the west were part of an attempt to preserve the traditional economy of the Sauk, based on the seasonal hunt, in a fast-changing landscape. Such an economic system, which involved the seasonal abandonment of the Sauk villages, would not have been possible while remaining close to white settlement. The Sauk did however want to remain close enough to the traders and blacksmiths whose supplies they needed.[13] A gradual westward movement, always slightly beyond the advancing settlers, supported this model.

Keokuk was the central figure in the Sauk delegation that came to Washington in 1837. This was the visit at which he and other tribal leaders received peace medals from Joel Poinsett. The visit came at the behest of Carey Allen Harris, commissioner of Indian affairs, and brought together leaders of the Sauk, Fox, Sioux and Ioway tribes. The US government had two central objectives for the event. To broker peace between the Sauk and Fox on the one hand and the Sioux on the other, and to secure more Native American land.[14] If the first objective was largely unachieved, Keokuk agreed a further land cession of 1.25 million acres west of the land ceded earlier by the Sauk. For this, the Sauk received $100,000, to be paid towards their tribal debts, as well as funding for mills and farming assistance and for annuities.[15] During the negotiations, Keokuk rejected proposed funding support for missionary education and other elements that would have promoted cultural change.

The Ioway delegates in Washington challenged the right of the Sauk to sell this land, claiming it as part of their traditional territories. Keokuk countered that the Sauk had secured the land from the Ioway through right of conquest. That the US government sided with Keokuk is perhaps suggestive of his importance to them as a flexible leader with whom they could negotiate.[16]

Black Hawk, by then released from captivity, was brought by Keokuk to Washington as part of the Sauk group, reportedly because Keokuk was concerned that he would otherwise intrigue against him back at home. A portrait of Black Hawk executed at this time by Charles Bird King, and published in the *History of the Indian Tribes of North America*, depicts him wearing the peace medal of Martin Van Buren around his neck.[17] It feels like the defeat of his approach of resistance to and rejection of the United States' overtures.

If from the perspective of the US authorities the peace medals were a representation of the treaty commitments to which the Native Americans had signed up, for the Native Americans too, the medals embodied the promises made to them. Their engagements with the United States were from this perspective a means of extending their networks of reciprocal social obligations. The ability to call on external assistance had long been crucial for tribes like the Anishinaabeg to the south and west of Lake Superior, whose home was a physically hostile environment where without support winter starvation was a real risk.[18]

Ahead of a meeting in 1832 with Henry Rowe Schoolcraft, the Indian agent, an Anishinaabeg chief named Aishkebugekosh splattered his chiefs' peace medals, as well as flags and wampum, the other symbols of the tribe's alliance with the United States, with red paint. At the meeting, he complained that the United States had failed to fulfil its promises to protect the Anishinaabeg from attacks by the Sioux, neglecting to intervene when members of the community had been killed. The subsequent treatment of the diplomatic gift of the peace medals, daubing them in red, was intended to convey that the United States had similarly defiled the agreement between the two. Aishkebugekosh threw the medals at Schoolcraft's feet, imploring the US authorities to make them bright again. He was hoping, in other words, to negotiate a new agreement. His hopes, it seems, were unrealised, as Schoolcraft departed before nightfall without entering into new talks.[19]

For the Native Americans then, peace medals were not simply a decorative diplomatic gift to accompany the signing of a treaty. The medals themselves defined the agreement just as much as the written document.[20] If the United States failed to respect the undertakings it had made, the peace medal lost its value.

1850

SARAH FORBES BONETTA

A GIFT FROM GHEZO, KING OF DAHOMEY, TO LIEUTENANT COMMANDER FREDERICK E. FORBES, ROYAL NAVY

Palm Cottage, Gillingham, home from 1855 to 1861 of Sarah Forbes Bonetta.

This is the story of a diplomatic gift accepted to save a life. It is a story that highlights the zeal of mid-Victorian Britain to counter the slave trade and the compassion and solicitous care of the British queen for a Yoruba girl from West Africa. It also highlights mid-Victorian attitudes around cultural superiority and women's rights that jar today.

It starts with Frederick Forbes, the youthful captain of HMS *Bonetta*, which in the late 1840s was carrying out anti-slavery duties in West Africa. Forbes recorded in the account of his African adventures the capture of six slavers in the course of just six months in 1848.[1] In 1849, he jumped at the chance to accompany John Duncan, the new vice-consul at Ouidah, the main port of the Kingdom of Dahomey, to meet King Ghezo in his capital, Abomey.

In his account, *Dahomey and the Dahomans*, Forbes describes Ghezo as 'the dreaded oppressor of neighbouring nations',[2] the leader of a military kingdom whose economy was based on the slave trade. Slaves were secured through an annual cycle of wars each November or December.[3] Ghezo had secured power by overthrowing his brother in a coup supported by Brazilian slave trader Francisco Félix de Sousa. Forbes' mission took place shortly after the death of de Sousa, when the British hoped Ghezo would be more open to pressure to end the slave trade.

Forbes found kitting out the expedition to be challenging. The local currency was cowrie shells. He purchased 50 dollars' worth, which proved such a large quantity that he needed to hire five female porters to carry them. Another ten porters were required to convey the 50 gallons of rum purchased for the trip.[4] Forbes' first sight of Ghezo's palace reinforced his views of the king, as its walls were topped with human skulls. The mission nonetheless proceeded cordially, if unproductively in the matter of securing Ghezo's commitment to end the slave trade. The giving and receiving of gifts was a major feature of the mission, and one that Forbes found burdensome, complaining that it was 'a terrible nuisance: the whole system is in donations, expecting more, at least an equivalent, and never satisfied'.[5] Duncan sadly fell ill during the trip and died shortly afterwards.

The following year, Forbes received an invitation from the king to attend the Annual Customs of Dahomey, a series of celebrations lasting several weeks, involving the provision of gifts to the king and their redistribution to the people, military parades and the offering of thanks to the royal ancestors. The latter component of the customs involved human sacrifice: luckless slaves, who were despatched by decapitation. Forbes accompanied John Beecroft, consul to the Bights of Benin and Biafra, already a well-known figure in the region before his appointment as consul the previous year.[6]

Forbes' account of the customs dwells on his attempts to ascertain through the military parades the size of Ghezo's forces, and to derive an estimate of the total cost of the event for the king. The British delegation attempted to persuade Ghezo that the palm oil trade could be more lucrative for Dahomey than the trade in slaves, but the king was not to be moved, maintaining that his people were military, not agricultural, in character. Forbes recounts a small success in the matter of those selected for sacrifice during the customs: he and Beecroft apparently saved the lives of three of the men earmarked for death by offering 100 dollars for each.[7]

Forbes managed to save another slave. This was a young girl, whose age Forbes estimated at around eight years.[8] She had been highborn in the village of Oke-Odan, of the Egbado tribe of the Yoruba people. Oke-Odan was taken by Ghezo's army in 1848, with the aid of a treacherous local who let the army into the walled settlement.[9] The girl's parents had been among the many villagers slaughtered by the Dahomeans. She had no idea of the fate of her brothers or sisters. A biography of this girl contends that Forbes persuaded Ghezo to spare the child from her planned fate as a human sacrifice by encouraging him to offer her to Queen Victoria as a diplomatic gift.[10] His own brief account in *Dahomey and the Dahomans* seems to suggest a more straightforward interpretation: that the child was a diplomatic gift to Forbes himself, and that Forbes decided, given the circumstances of his mission to Abomey, that the girl should be considered crown property.[11] Either way, acceptance of the gift was to save the girl's life. Forbes took her with him on his departure from Abomey and arranged for her baptism at Badagry in Nigeria by the Church Missionary Society.[12] In giving her the name Sarah Forbes Bonetta, he drew on both his own name and that of his ship.

Returning to England in July 1850, Forbes wrote to the secretary of the Admiralty to inform his superiors of King Ghezo's gift, receiving the reply that Her Majesty would be pleased to arrange for the education and subsequent future of the child.[13] Sarah, accompanied by Forbes, was presented to Queen Victoria at Windsor Castle on 9 November 1850. She seems to have charmed the queen, and Forbes writes in his memoirs of her accomplishments: '[S]he is a perfect genius; she now speaks English well and has a great talent for music.'[14] It was arranged that, while Sarah would live with the Forbes family at Winkfield Place near Windsor, the queen would pay for her expenses, a matter entrusted to the Keeper of the Privy Purse, Sir Charles Beaumont Phipps, whose wife Margaret would play an important role in the oversight of Sarah's care.[15]

There were frequent visits to the queen, who referred to the child as Sally and clearly relished her company. Sarah experienced however poor health in England, with frequent winter ailments. The queen appears to have decided in 1851 that she should be educated in Africa, in the hope that the warmer clime would improve her health. The death that year of Lieutenant Commander Forbes, while on another tour in Africa,[16] may also have been a factor in the decision. Sarah was earmarked to be part of the mid-Victorian endeavour of 'Christianising' Africa. She was sent to the Female Institution of the Church Missionary Society in Freetown, Sierra Leone. The queen sent her gifts of books and games, and Sarah was treated with deference at the school, and dressed in fine clothes.[17] For reasons that are unclear, though perhaps relate to Sarah's loneliness in Sierra Leone, Margaret Phipps wrote to the school in 1855 to advise that she be sent back to England.[18]

The widowed Mrs Forbes had moved to Scotland, and a new home was found for Sarah with the Reverend James Frederick Schoen, at Palm Cottage in Gillingham, Kent. The family was considered appropriate for Sarah not least because Reverend Schoen had missionary experience in Africa. Palm Cottage today houses a social club and bears signs announcing that it is also the home of the Medway Deaf Club, Palm Cottage Bowls Club and Slimming World Gillingham. There is also a small plaque, put up by the BBC, recording Sarah Forbes Bonetta's presence in the house from 1855 to 1861.

Her time with the Schoens was a happy one, though her health remained delicate. She resumed her visits to the queen and became friends with Princess Alice. She was a society figure, attending the wedding in 1858 between Princess Victoria and Prince Friedrich Wilhelm of Prussia. The question of Sarah's own matrimonial prospects was however starting to exercise those around her. The queen was keen that Sarah should be well settled, but the possibility of an inter-racial marriage does not appear to have been considered. The queen and Mrs Phipps welcomed a marriage proposal from James Pinson Labulo Davies, who had been born in Sierra Leone to Yoruba parents; victims of the slave trade liberated by the British West Africa Squadron. Davies had studied at the Church Missionary Society school in Freetown, enlisted in the Royal Navy, become a merchant captain and developed business interests in West Africa. He was recently widowed.

Sarah, however, had not fallen in love with Davies, and was resolved to turn down his offer. The queen and Mrs Phipps seem to have decided to focus Sarah's mind on the attractions of the offer by giving her a less satisfactory situation in England. She was moved from the Schoens to stay with two elderly ladies in Brighton, one a relative of Mrs Phipps.[19] Sarah was not enamoured with the suggestion that she act as companion to the two ladies and referred to her accommodation as a 'desolate little pigsty'.[20] The death of Prince Albert in December 1861 may also have decided Sarah not to hold out further against the queen's wishes. She agreed to marry James Davies. The wedding was a society affair, held in a packed St Nicholas' Church in Brighton. Sarah was given away by the brother of the man who had rescued her from the king of Dahomey.

The couple moved to Freetown, where Sarah taught at the Female Institution. Queen Victoria agreed to be godmother to Sarah's first child, suitably named Victoria, provided her with an allowance, and sent her a solid gold christening set. The family moved to Lagos, in Nigeria, and two more children were born. Sarah's health problems however worsened, and she was diagnosed with tuberculosis. She was sent to Madeira to recuperate but died there in 1880. Her daughter Victoria would continue to visit the queen, her godmother, and would marry John Randle, a prominent West African doctor and political figure in Lagos.

Sarah Forbes Bonetta's life was a short but remarkable one. She was rescued from a fate as a human sacrifice by becoming a diplomatic gift, but was moulded by her rescuers in a way that attempted to replace her African culture with a place in Victorian high society, turning her into a symbol of the British moral mission for the continent. Her story has been rediscovered by writers and broadcasters reinterpreting Britain's black history. Broadcaster and historian David Olusoga told Sarah's tale in the BBC's 2016 production *Black and British: a Forgotten History*. This was the source of the plaque decorating Palm Cottage. Her tale also features in Zadie Smith's 2016 novel *Swing Time*, whose narrator meets for trysts outside the church in which Sarah was married.

1880

THE *RESOLUTE* DESK

A GIFT FROM VICTORIA, QUEEN OF THE UNITED KINGDOM, TO RUTHERFORD B. HAYES, PRESIDENT OF THE UNITED STATES OF AMERICA

Caroline and Kerry Kennedy peering from the *Resolute* desk in the Oval Office.

This is a diplomatic gifts success story. A well-chosen gift constructed with materials repurposed from an earlier well-chosen gift, a mark of a warming bilateral relationship. Yet these gifts were born out of a failure following a tragedy.

The story of this gifted desk starts with the longstanding British preoccupation with identifying a Northwest Passage through the Arctic Sea, linking the Atlantic and Pacific Oceans and providing a shorter commercial trading route to China. This had become something of an obsession, with the place names of the Arctic providing a roll call of those who had tried and failed to find such a route: among them Hudson, Frobisher and Baffin.[1]

When the Admiralty were planning their latest expedition in search of the passage in 1845, they alighted on John Franklin to lead it. He had not been their first choice. He was a veteran of Arctic exploration, having led two overland expeditions, but these had been some time in the past, and he was now nearing sixty years of age, and out of shape, having recently served as governor of Van Diemen's Land (today's Tasmania). He was though brave, loyal and popular with his men, and his formidable wife, Lady Jane Franklin, had lobbied skilfully and tirelessly on his behalf.[2] The mission boasted two sturdy ships, the *Erebus* and the *Terror*, well equipped for the voyage. By July 1845, the expedition had reached Baffin Bay, where they encountered two whalers. The Franklin expedition would not be seen again.

With concern mounting in Britain over the fate of Franklin and his team, a three-pronged rescue mission was launched in 1848, involving land and naval expeditions. These uncovered no trace of Franklin. Spearheaded by the campaigning of Lady Franklin, who lobbied the authorities and worked to arouse public sympathy for the cause,[3] finding Franklin became an obsession in Britain. The popular folk ballad 'Lady Franklin's Lament', also known as 'Lord Franklin', captures the mood of the time in describing the mystery surrounding the expedition's disappearance. It has become a folk standard, the subject of fine recordings by Pentangle and by Martin Carthy, and provides the melody and some lyrical references for Bob Dylan's song 'Bob Dylan's Dream'. No fewer than five British expeditions, involving a total of eleven vessels, set out in 1850 to rescue Franklin and his crews, some commissioned by the Admiralty, others private, including one funded by Lady Franklin herself.

The first of the expeditions to set off in 1850 was led by Captain Richard Collinson on the *Enterprise*, supported by Lieutenant Robert McClure on the *Investigator*. They were tasked with approaching the Arctic from the Pacific. Collinson was by nature cautious, McClure reckless, and after the two ships became separated in the Pacific they functioned as two separate expeditions, neither commander waiting for the other at key opportunities to join up. McClure's explorations would lead to him being rewarded by a parliamentary committee as the first to discover a Northwest Passage, though rival candidates for the accolade abound, including Franklin.[4] The passage would turn out to be nothing like as significant as had been hoped. It would eventually transpire that there was not one single Northwest Passage but several, all circuitous, dangerous and seasonal, and none commercially viable.[5]

Another of the expeditions of 1850 was led by Horatio Austin, with four ships headed by HMS *Resolute*, like *Enterprise* and *Investigator* a sailing ship specifically outfitted for Arctic exploration, with strengthened timbers and a furnace-fed internal heating system.

Lady Franklin, anxious to explore every possible route to find her missing husband, had written to the US president, Zachary Taylor, to urge him to launch an American expedition. The president seems both to have been moved by Lady Franklin's pleas and attracted by the possibility of the US discovery of the Northwest Passage and asked Congress to fund a rescue mission. They baulked at the costs, but a shipping merchant named Henry Grinnell stepped in, purchasing the brigs *Advance* and *Rescue* and loaning these to the US Navy to form an expedition under the command of Lieutenant Edwin De Haven.

There were so many expeditions seeking to find Franklin in 1850 that different groups kept encountering each other in the Arctic, and there were three expeditions on Beechey Island when the graves of three members of Franklin's expedition were discovered.[6] This sad discovery offered no clue as to the fate of the expedition as a whole, and the missions of 1850 returned home without success. An additional problem was that not all the ships returned. There was no news of either Collinson and the *Enterprise* or McClure and the *Investigator*.

There was now not only continued pressure to rescue Franklin, but also to rescue those of his rescuers who had not returned. In 1852, a new rescue expedition was mounted under Sir Edward Belcher, a veteran explorer, but lacking experience of or affection for the Arctic and pompous and narrow-minded in outlook.[7] Among the five ships of his expedition was *Resolute*, under the command of the able Captain Henry Kellett. Belcher's fleet split into two groups. He led two ships to the Wellington Channel, while Kellett, with another two ships, headed towards Melville Island. The fifth vessel, *North Star*, remained at Beechey Island as a depot. The ships became frozen in, their crews exploring further with the use of sledge parties. It was *Resolute* that, in 1853, rescued McClure and the crew of the *Investigator*, which had been trapped in the ice for almost three years, its crew in a bad way.

By the spring of 1854, Belcher, who had taken to the bottle and was desperate to leave the Arctic, abandoned his ships, frozen in the ice, and ordered a furious Kellett to do the same. The crews, including those of the rescued McClure, reached the *North Star* by sledge, the only one of the ships not ice-bound. At the ensuing court martial, obligatory in cases of captains who had abandoned their ships, McClure was commended, and Kellett honourably acquitted. While Belcher too was formally acquitted, his sword was handed back to him in silence, and he was never again to command a naval vessel.

In October of that year, John Rae, explorer of the Hudson's Bay Company, arrived in London with news of the fate of Franklin's expedition derived from conversations with Inuit, from whom he had obtained items ranging from a silver teaspoon bearing the initials of the commander of the *Erebus* to a silver plate inscribed 'Sir John Franklin KCB'.[8] Rae's second-hand account suggested that the ships had been crushed by the ice, that their crews had headed south with sledge parties but had gradually died of starvation. Most controversial was the view of the Inuit, based on the mutilated state of the bodies they had seen, that some of the crew had been driven to cannibalism. Victorian Britain, and especially Lady Franklin, were outraged at the suggestion, and while Rae did collect the reward offered for confirming the fate of the expedition, he was the only major nineteenth-century British explorer not to be knighted.[9] Twentieth-century analysis of human bone fragments identified cut marks suggestive of cannibalism. Rae had probably been correct.

The evidence presented by Rae, coupled with the onset of the Crimean War, and the arrival back in England in 1855 of Collinson's *Enterprise* after a tortuous five-year expedition, removed much of the impetus for further attempts to launch rescue missions. An expedition led by Francis McClintock would though find a written communication in 1859 in a message cairn: a note of 25 April 1848 from the Franklin expedition, confirming that Franklin had died in June 1847, and that the *Terror* and *Erebus*, stuck in ice, were abandoned on 22 April 1848.

In the autumn of 1855, the whaler *George Henry*, heading home towards New London, Connecticut, after a disappointing season, encountered the abandoned HMS *Resolute*, drifting some 1,200 miles from where Kellett had left it. The captain of the whaler, James Buddington, resolved to bring the *Resolute* back to port, as a valuable salvage claim, although he only had twenty-six men with whom to crew the two ships.[10] Both vessels made it back, after a difficult, storm-battered voyage. The *Resolute* became a tourist attraction in the whaling town, with special excursion trains laid on for sightseers. What though should be done with the ship?

There were various sources of tension in US relations with Britain in the 1850s, for example over the demarcation of the water boundary in the far west, and over British interests in Central America. Henry Grinnell, bank-roller of the US Franklin expeditions and friend of Lady Franklin, saw an opportunity for the *Resolute* to play a role in improving matters. Grinnell wrote to the US secretary of state to suggest that the US government buy the *Resolute* from the owners of the *George Henry*, restore the vessel, and offer it as a diplomatic gift to Britain.[11] Senator James Murray Mason from Virginia secured a Congressional bill authorising the scheme and allocating some 40,000 dollars for it. Following a refit at the Brooklyn Navy Yard, the *Resolute* was sailed across the Atlantic, arriving in Portsmouth on 12 December 1856. There then followed much celebration and banqueting ahead of the official hand-over. Queen Victoria visited the vessel at Cowes, meeting its US crew. While many hoped the *Resolute* would see further service in the Arctic, it was never again to leave home waters and was retired in 1879.

The use to which some of the salvaged timber from the *Resolute* was put offers an example of inspired diplomatic gifting, helping to cement the bilateral relationship through a gift serving as a reminder of the previous goodwill and generosity of the recipient. A magnificent desk, some 6 feet wide and 4 feet deep, was built at the Chatham dockyard as a gift from Queen Victoria to the US president, Rutherford B. Hayes. Its design incorporates images suggestive of bilateral friendship, such as the flags of the two countries, as well as scenes recalling Arctic exploration. A brass plaque records that the desk is being gifted 'as a memorial of the courtesy and loving kindness which dictated the offer of the gift of the *Resolute*'.[12] Another of the smaller desks made from the timbers of the *Resolute* was gifted to the widow of Henry Grinnell, celebrating his role in supporting the search for Franklin.

The desk was delivered to President Hayes in November 1880. It was installed in the president's office and has been used by most subsequent presidents, though it was out of the White House from 1963 to 1977, when part of a travelling exhibition, then on display at the Smithsonian. It lived in various parts of the White House and was first moved to the Oval Office in 1961 as part of Jacqueline Kennedy's White House restoration project, the first lady having discovered it languishing in a broadcasting room.[13] It has featured in iconic images, such as one from 1963 of the young John F. Kennedy Jr peering out from behind the kneehole panel while his father worked at the desk above him.

The desk has evolved in its role, with presidents making modifications to suit their preferences and circumstances. That panel in the kneehole opening of the desk was ordered by President Roosevelt, in order that his leg braces would not be seen. The panel is decorated with the presidential seal, so its addition gave the overall decoration of the desk a more American feel. A base has been added on various occasions, including under the Reagan administration, when the president found that the top of the kneehole was knocking against his legs. The desk currently stands in the Oval Office: a perfectly positioned diplomatic gift from the perspective of the giver.

The success of the *Resolute* desk as an iconic gift has inspired further diplomatic gifting. Thus in 1965 the then British prime minister, Harold Wilson, presented President Lyndon Johnson with the bell from the *Resolute*. The *Resolute* desk also inspired the choice of gifts selected by Prime Minister Gordon Brown in 2009 for his meeting with US President Obama, as we will see in our last story in this history of diplomatic gifts. All are testament to the way a gift originating in tragedy in the Arctic has become a statement of the strength of the bilateral relationship between Britain and the United States.

1884

THE STATUE OF LIBERTY

A GIFT FROM THE PEOPLE OF FRANCE TO THE PEOPLE OF THE UNITED STATES OF AMERICA

The Statue of Liberty.

Surely the most celebrated and instantly recognisable of all bilateral gifts, the Statue of Liberty, or more properly *Liberty Enlightening the World*, has become a symbol of the United States and of its qualities. This was however a gift whose genesis lay in private, not government, initiative. It was a gift whose meaning changed during the long period from conception to inauguration and was viewed in different ways by the various actors involved in realising it.

While the Statue of Liberty was the work of many hands, the project owes its existence above all to two Frenchmen: Édouard René Lefebvre de Laboulaye and Frédéric Auguste Bartholdi.

Laboulaye was a professor of comparative law at the Collège de France and a passionate admirer of the United States. He saw in that country a model for stable democracy that contrasted with the turbulent French experience of long periods of autocratic rule punctuated by violent revolutions. He followed in a tradition charted by figures such as the marquis de Lafayette, the French general who fought in the American Revolutionary War and later became a tireless supporter of moderate government in France, and Alexis de Tocqueville, the diplomat and scholar whose *Democracy in America* set out the central importance of individual liberty while respecting the rights of others.

Laboulaye used his course at the Collège de France to highlight the strengths of the US Constitution and of its institutions, the lectures forming the basis of his three-volume *Histoire des États-Unis*.[1] His reputation developed as a friend of the United States. The American consul-general in Paris was so impressed by his article on France's historical engagement with the United States that he distributed copies of it, and Laboulaye was awarded an honorary doctorate by Harvard in 1864.[2] He even extolled American virtues through a novel, *Paris en Amérique*, in which the city of Paris finds itself transported to Massachusetts through the power of a spiritualist medium named Jonathan Dream. Laboulaye's fictional self, Dr René Lefebvre, starts out by making fun of the locals but gradually learns to appreciate American virtues, particularly the cohesiveness of the community.[3] For all his passion for the United States, Laboulaye never actually visited the country.

The role of the United States as an exemplary republic founded on liberty was tarnished by the practice of slavery and the divisions that came to a head in the American Civil War. The victory of the Union, and of President Lincoln, was critically important to Laboulaye, in his view serving to demonstrate that its democratic form of government could keep true to its principles while confronting such a grave threat.[4] The leaders of the United States themselves framed their political system in a universal way, consciously providing a model of democratic government that others might follow. Thus, the Declaration of Independence of 4 July 1776 made its case in universal terms, centred on the rights of the people. Lincoln's Gettysburg Address in 1863 similarly sought to make a universal point in framing the Civil War as not just a test for the United States but of whether 'any nation so conceived and so dedicated, can long endure'.[5]

The genesis of the idea that would become the Statue of Liberty is often traced to a dinner hosted by Laboulaye at his home in Glatigny, near Versailles, in 1865. One of his guests was a young sculptor from Colmar in the Alsace region of France named Frédéric Auguste Bartholdi. Laboulaye reportedly suggested over dinner that the commitment shown by the United States to the principle of liberty might be commemorated through a public monument, constructed through a united effort of France and the United States, symbolising the friendship and collaboration between the two peoples that had characterised the American War of Independence.[6]

This account of the statue's origin relies on the recollections of Bartholdi himself, in a promotional pamphlet written in 1885 to support fundraising in the United States for the statue's pedestal. The first written references to the project in both Bartholdi's and Laboulaye's correspondence date from 1871, and even if the statue was indeed proposed by Laboulaye over dinner in 1865, it seems that no action was taken to progress the project for another five or six years.[7]

The years 1870 and 1871 were traumatic for France. The Franco-Prussian War of 1870 led to a humiliating defeat for the French, including the loss to the new German Empire of Bartholdi's home region of Alsace, and the downfall of the Second Empire of Napoléon III. Instability followed the war. The radical revolutionary government of the Paris Commune controlled the French capital until its ouster by the French army during the 'Bloody Week' of May 1871. This was the backdrop against which Laboulaye and Bartholdi developed their plans for the statue. Bartholdi arrived in New York in June 1871 armed with letters of introduction from Laboulaye.[8] During this in-depth visit, Bartholdi alighted on Bedloe's Island in New York Harbor as the ideal site for his statue.

The process of building support for the statue project in both France and the United States and then raising the considerable funds required to realise the colossal statue planned by Bartholdi proved a protracted undertaking. Laboulaye established the Franco-American Union in 1875 as the fundraising organisation for the project, its members drawn from the moderate republican political space.[9] The French side would finance the funding of the statue itself, to be presented as a gift from France, while the costs of the pedestal would fall to the United States. Laboulaye and Bartholdi had hoped that the statue would be ready for the centenary of US independence in 1876, a goal that proved vastly overambitious. In the event, Bartholdi was able to complete just the right arm and torch in time for the final weeks of the Centennial Exhibition in Philadelphia, where it attracted considerable interest, with visitors climbing up to the balcony around the torch. The arm and torch moved on to Madison Square in New York before being brought back across the Atlantic, to be united with the rest of the statue, gradually taking shape.

If the arm and torch were offered as an appetite-whetter for American audiences, those in France had the opportunity to view Liberty's head, presented at the Exposition Universelle in Paris in 1878. Fundraising activities in France ranged from the sale of small terracotta replicas of the statue, signed by Bartholdi, to a musical evening at the Paris Opera featuring a cantata by Charles Gounod specially written for the occasion and entitled *La Liberté éclairant le monde*.

The process of fundraising and of constructing the colossal statue was such a long one that several key figures in the project did not live to see its realisation. The chief engineer, Eugène Viollet-le-Duc, died in 1879 and was replaced by Gustave Eiffel, a civil engineer who had developed a reputation for innovation in bridge building. In 1883, Laboulaye too died. His role as head of the Franco-American Union was taken over by Ferdinand de Lesseps, who had achieved global renown as the developer of the Suez Canal and was president of the company attempting to repeat the feat in Panama.

The statue was initially assembled in France and on the suitably symbolic date of 4 July 1884 was handed over by de Lesseps in the name of the committee of the Franco-American Union to Levi P. Morton, the minister of the United States to France.[10] In his speech at the event, held in the yard of the Gaget, Gauthier and Company workshops in Paris, Morton accepted the statue 'as a work of art and as a monument of the abiding friendship of the people of France'.[11]

Alongside Bartholdi, de Lesseps and committee members of the Franco-American Union, the event was attended by senior representatives of the French government. According to a letter from Morton to US Secretary of State Frederick Frelinghuysen, the French prime minister, Jules Ferry, had confirmed to him before the event that the French government 'did not wish to stand aloof from this great manifestation'.[12] It wished to demonstrate that it shared the views that had inspired Bartholdi, and as a contribution would make available a ship with which to transport the statue to the United States.[13]

There remained, however, the matter of the pedestal. The New York branch of the committee of the Franco-American Union was struggling to raise the required funds to underwrite the US contribution to the project. The allegorical quality of the statue did not resonate with those who would have preferred a more literal depiction of US heroes, and there was some questioning of why the United States should be required to pay towards the realisation of a statue conceived abroad.

The situation was rescued by newspaper publisher Joseph Pulitzer, who ran a fundraising campaign through the *New York World*, capturing the imagination of his public by the inclusive nature of his campaign, promising to publish the names of everyone who contributed, no matter how small their offering. There was a political agenda here, in which the Democrat Pulitzer took the initiative from the predominantly Republican Franco-American Union and cast the gift as one not from the millionaires of France to those of America but from the people of France to the people of America.[14]

The disassembled statue arrived in New York in June 1885, and after the pedestal had finally been completed the following April, Liberty was reassembled. The statue was dedicated on 28 October 1886, at a ceremony presided over by President Grover Cleveland.

Some four major motives underpinned and shaped the project to build the statue, and these varied in importance over the long time period from conception to realisation. The first was to honour the achievement of the United States in providing an enduring model for a stable and democratic form of government. The question of what aspect of US achievement is being celebrated is however not always straightforward.

If the statue was indeed conceived over dinner in 1865, the year of Abraham Lincoln's assassination, the timing is suggestive of a focus on the abolition of slavery. Laboulaye chaired the French Anti-Slavery Society, and the broken shackles at the statue's feet would have been understood as representing liberation from slavery.[15] The first design of the statue shown by Bartholdi to Laboulaye featured broken shackles more prominently, held in the left hand of the female figure as well as at her feet. Laboulaye reportedly suggested that these broken shackles be replaced by a tablet inscribed with 'July 4, 1776', feeling that the shackles were more redolent of the process of liberation than the permanent concept of liberty.[16] Thus while the abolition of slavery was part of the overall message of the statue, it seems to have become more muted with increasing distance from the end of the American Civil War.[17]

The second, linked, motive was to encourage the adoption of such a model of government in France. This is centrally relevant to the question of the form of liberty celebrated by the statue. The character of Liberty depicted by Bartholdi is a world away from that of Eugène Delacroix in his famous 1830 canvas, *Liberty Leading the People*. Delacroix's Liberty is revolutionary in character, bare-breasted, leading the people to fight, sporting the Phrygian cap beloved of French revolutionaries. Bartholdi's Liberty is calm, reassuring, eschewing the Phrygian cap. This is the Liberty of Laboulaye's conservative strand of republicanism, set in opposition not only to monarchism but also to the radical left, and which saw liberty as existing in the space between despotism and revolutionary anarchy.[18] The recent

219

French experience of the autocracy of Napoléon III followed by the revolutionary chaos of the Paris Commune only served to make the US experience an even more enticing example for moderate liberals like Laboulaye.

The third motive was to underscore the strength of Franco-US relations, including to highlight the French role in the American War of Independence. The backdrop was concern that France was losing its influence in the United States, in relation to both Britain and Germany. The United States had favoured the Prussian cause in the war of 1870, and large-scale German immigration to the United States was creating an increasingly strong German lobby. Trade relations were a significant consideration here, and business interests dominated the senior ranks of the Franco-American Union on both sides of the Atlantic. De Lesseps for example saw the statue as a means to secure US support for his Panama Canal project.[19]

The statue, neo-classical in form, was not a great work of art, as Bartholdi himself admitted.[20] It was however a great work of engineering, the thin copper plates that form its surface hanging on Gustave Eiffel's innovatory iron skeleton.[21] It therefore served as a calling card for French entrepreneurial talent and technological ability.[22]

The fourth motive is found in the earlier career of the sculptor, Bartholdi. He had long been interested in colossal sculpture, an interest nurtured through travels in Egypt in the 1850s, when he was entranced by the Colossi of Memnon. Bartholdi was determined to create his own colossus and returned to Egypt in 1869 to put before the khedive, Isma'il Pasha, a proposal for a huge statue at the entrance of the new Suez Canal. His design was based on a *fellaha*, a female Egyptian field-worker. This robed figure, holding a torch aloft as a beacon to light the way for maritime traffic, was to be called *Egypt Bringing Light to the Orient*. The khedive was however in no position to finance the project, and it did not progress.[23]

Bartholdi later did all he could to minimise the connections between his aborted Egyptian project and the Statue of Liberty. This is unsurprising: while fundraising for Lady Liberty, it would hardly have suited Bartholdi to offer any impression that the statue was a repurposing of the failed Egyptian project. Its design however clearly reflects the earlier project.[24] Bartholdi's personal ambition to build a colossal statue thus formed one of the motivations for the Statue of Liberty.

The ability of the statue to respond to so many goals was facilitated by its allegorical character. It was open to a range of interpretations since, aside from the reference to July 4, 1776 on the tablet, it did not directly incorporate any obvious symbols of the United States. It was, of course, itself to *become* a symbol of the United States. What it symbolises does not however precisely correspond to any of the visions its creators had for it.

The message of celebration presented by the statue in respect of the liberty nurtured and protected by the United States provided an obvious and early focus for critique from groups within the country who felt that liberty was precisely what they did not enjoy. Thus for Lillie Devereux Blake, president of the New York State Woman Suffrage Association, 'in erecting a Statue of Liberty embodied as a woman in a land where no woman has political liberty, men have shown a delightful inconsistency which excites the wonder and admiration of the opposite sex'.[25] Many Chinese Americans too felt they had little to celebrate. The Chinese Exclusion Act of 1882 had prohibited the immigration of Chinese labourers, and a Chinese American man named Saum Song Bo wrote to the editor of *The Sun* in 1885 protesting that he was being asked to contribute to the funding of a pedestal for a statue celebrating liberties that were not being offered to all.[26]

The statue's critics were however in the minority. A sonnet written by Emma Lazarus in 1883 as part of the fundraising efforts for the pedestal reinvented the Statue of Liberty as a symbol of the United States as a land of opportunity for immigrants. In *The New Colossus*, Lady Liberty famously calls out to the old world: 'Give me your tired, your poor, your huddled masses yearning to breathe free.'[27] Bartholdi had mentioned the role of the United States in providing refuge for those who had faced persecution in their homelands in setting out the meanings of the statue, for example at a meeting of the New England Society in 1876.[28] However, this interpretation of the statue rapidly overtook its associations with moderate republicanism or Franco-US ties, fuelled by its position on New York Harbor, where it served as a beacon for new arrivals to the country.

In May 2005, Georgian President Mikheil Saakashvili gifted US President George W. Bush a framed photograph taken during the Georgian Rose Revolution of 2003. The photo depicted a demonstrator holding a figurine of the Statue of Liberty in the air.[29] Bartholdi's statue is now able to serve as visual shorthand for the freedoms it symbolises. That is quite a legacy for its creator.

1912

3,020 CHERRY TREES

A GIFT FROM THE CITY OF TOKYO TO THE CITY OF WASHINGTON, DC

Washington, DC cherry blossom: a flowering reminder of a 1912 gift
from Tokyo to the US capital.

The cherry trees around the Tidal Basin in Washington, DC form a signature image of the city, coming into their own during the National Cherry Blossom Festival each springtime, when the blossoms frame countless photographs of the Washington Memorial across the water. The story of the arrival of these trees, like that of the Statue of Liberty, provides a demonstration of how an increasing range of actors, outside government as well as inside it, could now influence the making of a diplomatic gift. In the sending state, a renowned chemist and a city mayor were influential in realising the gift. In the receiving state, three people played a critical role in lobbying for cherry blossoms to come to Washington. One was a private citizen, the second a government official, the third the wife of the president.

The private citizen was Eliza Ruhamah Scidmore, an Iowa-born journalist, who gradually moved into travel writing. Her brother George was a diplomat, whose career was focused on the Far East, culminating in a

223

posting as US consul-general in Yokohama.[1] Eliza, with her mother, made the first of what would be many trips to Japan in 1885. She became enchanted with the country. In 1891, she wrote a travel book, *Jinrikisha Days in Japan*, its pages bursting with admiration for Japan and its people. She became an enthusiastic proponent of Japanese ideas and culture and was reportedly the first to import *tsunami* as an English word.[2] Among the Japanese customs to entrance her was *hanami*, the enjoyment of the fleeting beauty of the cherry blossom trees, a springtime celebration in Japan for many centuries. From 1885, on return from her first trip, she lobbied the Office of Public Buildings and Grounds in Washington to plant cherry blossom trees along the Potomac River.

Like the flowering cherry trees, this lobbying initially bore little fruit, but the idea of bringing cherry blossom trees to Washington was to gain a second key advocate, this time a government official. David Fairchild, the son-in-law of Alexander Graham Bell, was the director of the Seed and Plant Introduction Section at the US Department of Agriculture. The US government was concerned that its agricultural base was founded on a narrow range of crops,[3] and Fairchild's role was to bring in plants from around the world to diversify its production. He brought mangoes from India and soybeans from China and studied cotton growing in Egypt.

Like Scidmore, Fairchild was enraptured by the flowering cherry trees of Japan and collected some thirty types during a visit to that country in 1902.[4] Some American horticulturalists believed that the Washington climate would be too severe for the Japanese trees, but Fairchild was determined to prove that the flowering cherry could thrive in the eastern United States. He planted cherry trees at his Maryland estate, In the Woods, and hired a Japanese gardener to help care for them.[5] On Arbor Day in 1908, he invited children from schools across the city to collect cherry trees to plant in their schoolyards. The Arbor Day programme concluded with a lecture by Fairchild in which he promoted the idea of planting flowering cherries on the reclaimed land of Potomac Park, which he had discussed with Scidmore.

The inauguration of William Howard Taft as US president in 1909 brings into the story our third protagonist, his wife Helen, known as Nellie. There was much criticism of the uninspiring nature of the public spaces of the US capital at the turn of the twentieth century, and the McMillan Commission of 1902 had set out a plan for the development of the monumental core of the city. Nellie Taft identified as a mission for her role as first lady the improvement of the then underdeveloped Potomac Park in support of this beautification scheme. She had lived in the Philippines while her husband served there as governor-general from 1900 to 1903 and had been taken with the pleasant waterside ambiences of Manila's Luneta Park, now Rizal Park.[6]

Scidmore wrote to Nellie Taft, setting out a proposal to plant flowering cherries in Potomac Park funded through public subscription, while Fairchild contacted Spencer Cosby, the new superintendent of public buildings and grounds, with an offer to present fifty flowering cherry trees for the area.[7] These approaches received a positive reception. They fitted the first lady's vision of the park, and Nellie Taft had stayed in Japan en route to join her husband in the Philippines. Although she had not witnessed the cherry blossom season, she was an enthusiast for Japanese culture.[8]

Enter Japan. That country was looking for an opportunity to demonstrate its gratitude to the United States for the latter's role in brokering the Treaty of Portsmouth of 1905, ending the Russo-Japanese War. William Taft himself had played an important role as secretary of war and had visited Japan in both 1905 and 1907. Jokichi Takamine was a US-based Japanese chemist who had become wealthy through the licensing of the production rights of an enzyme he had isolated named takadiastase. His most notable achievement though was the isolation of adrenaline from animal glands. Takamine was focused on building goodwill between Japan and the United States, and on learning when in Washington of the first lady's interest in flowering cherry trees, proposed a gift of 2,000 trees. The mayor of Tokyo, Yukio Ozaki, agreed that the trees would be sent as a gift from that city.

The trees were brought across the Pacific by freighter, and then by railway across the United States, arriving in Washington in January 1910. What happened next highlighted the different objectives within the US Department of Agriculture. While Fairchild was focused on bringing in new plants from around the world, the Bureau of Entomology under Charles Marlatt was concerned by the risks around the introduction of foreign pests.[9] Following an inspection of the trees, Marlatt's report concluded that the consignment was infected with 'practically every pest imaginable',[10] and the flowering cherry trees were consigned to the bonfire. One outcome of this failed diplomatic gift was the passage of the 1912 Plant Quarantine Act, providing a more robust structure for the importation of foreign plants. A new Federal Horticultural Board would enforce the act. Marlatt was chosen to head it.

While there was embarrassment all round about the outcome of the gift, a suitably diplomatic exchange of correspondence smoothed the waters, and the Japanese decided to repeat the gift, donating 3,020 trees in the name of the city of Tokyo. The Japanese had taken care this time to raise the trees under scientific supervision to minimise the risk of disease. The shipment set off from Yokohama on Valentine's Day 1912, accompanied by a similarly sized consignment for Riverside Park in New York.[11] To everyone's relief, this time round the trees passed their inspection with flying colours.

On 27 March 1912, at a modest ceremony, Nellie Taft and Viscountess Chinda, the wife of the Japanese ambassador, planted two trees on the northern bank of the Tidal Basin. From this low-key beginning, the trees have become an increasingly popular part of the Washington fabric. The trees had become so well loved by 1938 that there was public indignation at the prospect of the removal of some of them to accommodate the Thomas Jefferson Memorial. In what became known as 'the Cherry Tree Rebellion', a group of women chained themselves to a tree at the proposed construction site in an attempt to block the work. The rebellion was reportedly brought to a swift conclusion by the offer of numerous cups of coffee, hastening the demonstrators' need for a comfort break. Park officials maintained that the trees would simply be transplanted, not chopped down, though some were to perish in the course of their removal.

The Second World War made a visual display of US–Japanese ties feel inappropriate, and indeed four trees were vandalised in 1941 following the Japanese attack at Pearl Harbor. The US authorities took to describing the trees as 'Oriental'. In the post-war period, the celebration of the cherry blossom has evolved into an increasingly elaborate springtime festival: a major event in the calendar of the US capital, which serves to underscore the warmth of US–Japanese relations.

The success of the gift of flowering cherry trees spawned a series of related diplomatic gifts between the United States and Japan. The Americans offered a more modest reciprocal gift to Tokyo involving dogwood trees and mountain laurel plants. Fairchild was responsible for organising it.[12] The Japanese government made another gift of flowering cherry trees to Washington in 1965, this time involving 3,800 trees, grown in the United States.[13] The then first lady, Lady Bird Johnson, and the wife of the Japanese ambassador, planted trees in what was essentially a re-enactment of the 1912 ceremony. US Department of Agriculture botanist Roland Jefferson developed in 1982 the Friendship in Flowers project in which schoolchildren from each country collected seeds of their native trees, which were then exchanged.[14]

Remarkably, cherry trees have also been sent in the other direction. The *Yoshino* variety that made up the largest component of the 1912 gift had been hit in Tokyo by damage during the Second World War and subsequent redevelopment, and in 1951 US officials sent cuttings from the original trees at Japanese request to restore the stock on the Arakawa River. More cuttings were sent in the 1980s because of the need for additional trees following a change of the river course.[15]

In 2012, on the 100th anniversary of the original gift, the United States announced the 'Friendship Blossoms – Dogwood Tree Initiative', a public–private partnership under which 3,000 dogwood trees would be sent to Japan by the people of the United States in celebration of the original gift of cherry blossom trees.

Offering a stunning display for a few tantalising weeks each spring, the flowering cherry trees in Washington have proved a successful diplomatic gift, weathering the ups and downs in the bilateral relationship across the ensuing century to offer an annual reminder of Japanese culture and generosity in the American capital.

1935

A MAYBACH DS-8 ZEPPELIN

A GIFT FROM ADOLF HITLER, FÜHRER OF GERMANY, TO BHUPINDER SINGH, THE MAHARAJA OF PATIALA

A Maybach DS-8 Zeppelin Cabriolet.

The princely state of Patiala in the Indian Punjab emerged in the eighteenth century in the wake of Mughal decline. It had a reputation as a wealthy place, due both to the fertility of its soils and to its support for the British, including during the 1857 mutiny.

Nine-year-old Bhupinder Singh succeeded as maharaja on the death of his father in 1900. He would become known for his patronage of cricket and polo and was the first captain of an Indian cricket team to tour England, in 1911.[1] He was politically influential, serving from 1926 to 1931 as the chancellor of the Chamber of Princes, the forum through which rulers of the Indian princely states could articulate their needs to the colonial government. He was loyal to the British Empire, promoting Sikh recruitment in the First World War. Most of all, he was known for excess. In 1928, he commissioned the House of Cartier to produce for himself the Patiala Necklace, incorporating an astonishing 2,930 diamonds, including the seventh largest diamond in the world at that time.[2]

He had a particular fondness for expensive cars, owning a fleet of Rolls-Royces.

The maharaja was well known among European royal circles and paid a visit to Germany in 1935. According to an account from his grandson, Raja Malvinder Singh,[3] the maharaja put in a request for a call on the Führer, who grudgingly agreed to a short meeting. They evidently hit it off, because the meeting turned into a lunch, with follow-up meetings over the next two days. At their final encounter, Hitler presented the maharaja with diplomatic gifts, including some German pistols and a Maybach car.

The car was an object of wonder. It was a 1933 Maybach DS-8 Zeppelin. The reference to the legendary German airship is not coincidental. Count Ferdinand von Zeppelin had enlisted the help of renowned German automobile designer Wilhelm Maybach to build the motors for his dirigibles. Maybach set up a facility at Friedrichshafen, the hometown of the Zeppelin Airship Company, and set about producing automobiles using the engines that had powered the Zeppelins. The DS-8, with its 12-litre engine, bore the specific label 'Zeppelin'. It debuted at the Paris Automobile Salon in 1930 and was produced in limited numbers until 1939, when the factory was redirected to the war effort.[4]

The Zeppelin presented by Hitler to the maharaja of Patiala ran to 5 and a half metres in length, with a state limousine body accommodating seven passengers. There were two searchlights mounted one above the other in front of the grille. Which one was lit indicated whether the maharaja or maharani were travelling: both lit meant that they were both in the car.[5]

Hitler's motivation in offering such a generous gift to the maharaja presumably lay in attempting to secure the latter's support for the German cause, or at least neutrality, in the coming hostilities. If so, it was entirely unsuccessful. The maharaja supported the allies, though he did not live to see the Second World War, dying in 1938 at the age of forty-six. For his successor, his son Yadavindra Singh, the provenance of the vehicle was evidently an embarrassment. Having been shipped to India, it lay unused and out of sight in the garages of the Moti Bagh Palace in Patiala. According to Yadavindra Singh's son, Raja Malvinder Singh, the problematic car was gifted away by his father when one Sardar Satyajit Singh asked to buy it. The maharaja replied to the effect that it was not for sale, but that he was welcome to have it as a gift.[6]

The new owner eventually sold it on, and the car has changed hands several times. One of its later owners, a Dr Fassbender, wanted something less unwieldy for a car he usually drove alone, so he had the state body replaced by a two-seater cabriolet. The old body went to the Museum for Historical Maybach Vehicles in Neumarkt in Germany. In its new cabriolet form, the Maybach turned up at an auction in Denmark in 2015, with a guide price of £2.3 to £2.7 million.[7]

From another part of South Asia comes another story with a similar plot: Hitler's gifting of a prestigious car to encourage a pro-British ruler towards a more pro-German or at least neutral position. The story comes from Nepal, but the facts around it are by no means as clear. Decades after the gift was made, press reporting stimulated by the unearthing of a vehicle said to be the gifted car descended into confusion over who exactly had been the recipient of the gift and where the car was now to be found.

It started with a massacre. In 2001, King Birendra and much of the Nepali royal family were gunned down in the Narayanhiti Palace in Kathmandu. The culprit was identified as Birendra's son, Prince Dipendra, who is said to have shot his family in a drunken rage before turning his gun upon himself after he had been forbidden from marrying the bride of his choice. Birendra's unpopular brother Gyanendra acceded to the throne, against a backdrop of both rioting and scepticism about the official account of events. Beset by an increasingly assertive government, backed by public pressure for a return of democracy, and by Maoist rebels, the king was forced to cede power. In 2007, the Nepali parliament announced that the royal palaces would be returned to the public.

The Narayanhiti Palace was duly converted into a museum, although the press reported that a ninety-four-year-old one-time mistress of Gyanendra's grandfather, King Tribhuvan, would be allowed to stay on in the palace complex, as she had nowhere else to go.[8] Nepali officials preparing an inventory of the items in the palace unearthed not just a king's former mistress but also a rusty 1939 Mercedes-Benz, reportedly a gift from Adolf Hitler to King Tribhuvan. Press reports suggested that the car had been used by Tribhuvan until his death in 1955, and later by a local engineering college to train mechanics. It had then been left to rust in a palace garage. The government planned to restore the car and put it on show in the new museum.[9]

The press reporting of the discovery of the Mercedes-Benz gifted to Tribhuvan prompted responses reported in the Indian press from relatives of Juddha Shumsher Rana, prime minister of Nepal before the Second World War, including from his daughter, ninety-two-year-old Janak Rajya Laxmi Shah. These made two claims: firstly, that the car presented by

Hitler was not a gift to Tribhuvan, the head of state, but to Juddha Shumsher Rana, the prime minister; and secondly that it was not currently in Nepal but in India, her father having taken it with him when he left Nepal for Dehradun in 1945.[10] The disagreement over the location of the car typifies that, running across several generations, between the kings of Nepal and the hereditary Rana prime ministers. It is unclear where the truth lies. The press reporting gives no indication that a car was physically tracked down in Dehradun. Yet the 1939 vintage of the car in Narayanhiti Palace makes it an awkward candidate to be a gift from Hitler. The storm clouds of war had already gathered. Would Nepali leaders have really accepted a gift from Hitler at such a late date? If they had done so, how could it have been transported across British India?

The matter of transporting the vehicle presents a further intriguing curiosity. Until 1956, there were no paved roads in Nepal outside the capital city of Kathmandu. The cars destined for the elite of the Nepali capital were hauled by some sixty porters on huge bamboo stretchers along a mountainous trail through the village of Chitlang.[11] It must have been quite a sight.

Did a Mercedes-Benz gifted by Hitler reach the Kathmandu Valley in this way? Hitler's intention in such a gift would presumably have been to encourage Nepal not to declare for the allied side in the coming war. If so, just as with the car gifted to the maharaja of Patiala, he was unsuccessful. Surely, again as with the gift to Patiala, there was no likelihood of any other outcome? Nepal had been a close ally of Britain from the time of the Gurkha Wars of 1814–16. It declared its support to the allies in September 1939, from the outbreak of hostilities.

The Narayanhiti Palace Museum today offers an insight into the courtly life of the Nepali royal family. The self-guided tour proceeds through numerous protocol-oriented rooms with remarkably specific functions, like the room dedicated to banquets of honour on the occasion of the birthdays of the queen mother and crown prince. There are huge ancient television sets, stuffed tigers, photos of visiting dignitaries (including a young Princess Anne) and peeling floral wallpaper. No sign though of a Mercedes-Benz. Indeed, so much about Hitler's gift is shrouded in mystery that it becomes difficult to know whether it was made at all.

1943

THE SWORD OF STALINGRAD

A GIFT FROM GEORGE VI, KING OF THE UNITED KINGDOM, TO THE CITIZENS OF STALINGRAD

Presentation of the Sword of Stalingrad.

The Battle of Stalingrad was among the most brutal in the history of war, its name evoking images of house-to-house fighting amid ruined, snow-covered cityscapes. Around 2 million people died during its long course from August 1942 until the surrender of the last remnants of the encircled German Sixth Army on 2 February 1943. It marked the turning point of the Second World War, with the German position on the Eastern Front transformed from advance to retreat. British gratitude to their Russian allies was immense. A gift was called for to honour the defenders of Stalingrad. It provides an example of a diplomatic gift that aimed to influence feeling in the sending state as well as the receiving one. It is remembered today in large part through a work of literature that uses that gift in a very different way from that intended by the giver.

The chosen gift was a sword of honour, to be presented on behalf of King George VI. A competition to design it was organised by the Worshipful Company of Goldsmiths, with the winning design, selected by the king, that of R. M. Y. Gleadowe, a former Slade Professor of Art at Oxford working at the Admiralty.[1] It was a mighty sword. A two-handed, double-edged longsword, more than 1.2 metres in length, it took inspiration from the weapons of the knights of the Crusades and was thus an interesting choice of gift for the avowedly atheist Soviet Union.

A whole series of artisans was engaged in bringing Gleadowe's design to life. The steelwork was entrusted to the Wilkinson Sword Company, which would later become known for the manufacture of stainless-steel razor blades, but which during the Second World War produced the double-edged Fairbairn–Sykes fighting knife for the British Commandos. Octogenarian swordsmith Tom Beasley, something of a legendary figure in the industry who had made ceremonial swords for five sovereigns and fathered more than twenty children, was reportedly brought from his hospital bed to lead the operation.

The gold and silver features were crafted by Leslie Durbin, a silversmith who learned his craft as an apprentice to Omar Ramsden, the most prominent British silver designer of the interwar period.[2] Durbin, then a corporal in the Royal Air Force, was given an indefinite leave of absence to work on the sword, a commission that would serve as a calling card for a career that advanced rapidly after the war. Durbin carried out the work in what was little more than a garden shed in south London, at the home of Francis Adam, his former tutor at the Central School of Arts and Crafts.[3] The features crafted by Durbin included a large cross-guard, finished at each end with a leopard's head, a grip bound with gold wire, and a pommel (the knob at the end) of rock crystal topped with a gold rose of England. The sword combines features reminding of both Britain and the Soviet Union. Thus, the scabbard includes the Royal Arms, Crown and Cypher, but also three red enamelled stars. The silver point at the end of the scabbard includes flames, symbolising the burning city of Stalingrad.[4]

On the blade, an inscription is etched in English and Russian, reading: 'To the steel-hearted citizens of Stalingrad – the gift of King George VI – in token of the homage of the British people.'[5] The use of the term 'steel-hearted' refers not just to the steel blade of the sword but also to the fact that the Russian word for steel is at the root of the name of the city of Stalingrad, and of the Soviet leader himself, from which the city's name was of course derived. This gift to the people of Stalingrad therefore also aimed to flatter Joseph Stalin personally.

The sword was made at pace, and initially in secrecy. Its existence was announced by the Foreign Office in June, and once public was used to underscore to British domestic audiences the strength of the alliance with the Soviet Union. Newsreel footage of the work of the craftsmen involved in making the sword was broadcast in British cinemas, including interviews with Tom Beasley, sporting a floppy swordsmith's cap and apron. In October, the finished sword, before being presented to the Soviet Union, went on display to the British people, first in London at Goldsmiths Hall and the Victoria and Albert Museum, and then on a tour of the United Kingdom, remaining in each city for one day only. Leslie Durbin accompanied it. There were long queues wherever the sword was exhibited. One estimate suggested that around 30,000 people saw it each day.[6]

Perhaps the most striking of all the venues chosen to exhibit the sword was Westminster Abbey. Its presence in this great church was described by Evelyn Waugh in a key passage in *Unconditional Surrender*, the third volume of his *Sword of Honour* trilogy, which chronicles the wartime exploits of Guy Crouchback, a member of an ancient and aristocratic Catholic family. Waugh describes a large, mostly female, mostly shabby crowd, queuing in a slowly moving column to get a sight of the sword.[7] The crowd falls silent in reverence as they enter the church, with the sword likened to a body lying in state. While some had come to admire the craftsmanship, for most the experience was one of veneration of the sword in gratitude for Britain's Soviet allies.[8] None of which detains Guy Crouchback as he drives past the abbey on his way to lunch.

Guy had enlisted with enthusiasm to fight in the war. For him, the pact between Hitler and Stalin had placed the enemy in clear view, and given him a purpose. The new alignment of forces was problematic for him, and he saw no honour in an alliance with the atheist Soviet Union, bemoaning the way Stalin had been transformed in Britain into the comforting 'Uncle Joe'.[9] The title of the trilogy, *Sword of Honour*, is meant ironically. The loss of the external motivation that led him to sign up is accompanied as the trilogy progresses by what Waugh casts as a deeper and even more problematic trend: the loss of the traditional values of the aristocracy and the unstoppable rise of the meritocracy.[10] Not that Waugh sees much that is meritorious in the character of his upwardly mobile ex-hairdresser, Trimmer.

With evident relish, Waugh introduces into Guy's lunchtime conversation, courtesy of the American Lieutenant Padfield, a small controversy that had exercised the British press over whether the crest on the scabbard might actually be upside down, at least when the sword was worn.[11]

The venue for the presentation of the sword was the Tehran Conference in November 1943, the strategy meeting between the leaders of the United States, United Kingdom and the Soviet Union at which President Roosevelt and Prime Minister Churchill would commit to opening a second front against Nazi Germany. The presentation was made on 29 November in the ballroom of the Soviet embassy in Tehran. In the presence of an honour guard of British and Soviet troops, Churchill offered the sword to Stalin. Roosevelt, seated and ailing, had the chance to inspect it, and it was passed by Stalin at the end of the ceremony to Marshal Voroshilov. While accounts differ as to exactly what happened, and newsreel footage is unclear, the favoured version of events seems to be that Voroshilov was taken somewhat by surprise, grabbed at it, and the sword fell out of its scabbard. Accounts then variously suggest either that the marshal managed to catch the falling sword before it hit the ground, or that he did not.[12]

At a ceremony in the Kremlin in 1944, the sword was in turn passed on to the people of Stalingrad, in the form of the chairman of the city council; the task of delivering the gift to its intended ultimate recipients being entrusted to another senior Soviet military leader, Marshal Budyonny. The sword returned to Britain as part of Cold War-era exhibitions, as a reminder of a warmer period in the Soviet–British relationship. It is now displayed proudly in an exhibition of presents given to the city in honour of its heroism at the Battle of Stalingrad Museum – Panorama Complex. When in 2018 England kicked off their World Cup football campaign against Tunisia in Volgograd, as the city is now known, the Sword of Stalingrad was one of the links between Britain and Russia highlighted in the UK press as evidence that English fans would be given a warm welcome.[13]

Hydraulic organ depicted on a Roman second-century CE mosaic found at Zliten in modern-day Libya.

King Louis IX carrying the Crown of Thorns.

The Pallium of St Lawrence.

Four Studies of an Elephant by Giulio Romano, depicting the animal gifted to Pope Leo X.

The Field of the Cloth of Gold, a 1545 work of the British school. A venue for competitive gift-giving between King François I of France and King Henry VIII of England.

The horned helmet given by Holy Roman Emperor Maximilian I to King Henry VIII.

Giambologna's *Samson Slaying a Philistine*.

The Amber Room, photographed in 1917.

A plate from the 'green ribbon' service given by King Louis XV of France
to Empress Maria Theresia.

The Duke of Wellington hosting a banquet in the Waterloo Gallery, Apsley House.

The *Shah Diamond*, depicted on a Soviet stamp of 1971.

Caroline and Kerry Kennedy peering from the *Resolute* desk in the Oval Office.

The Volgograd Planetarium.

One of the crates used to transport the pandas gifted by China to the United States following President Nixon's visit in 1972.

Windsor Park Stadium, Roseau, Dominica.

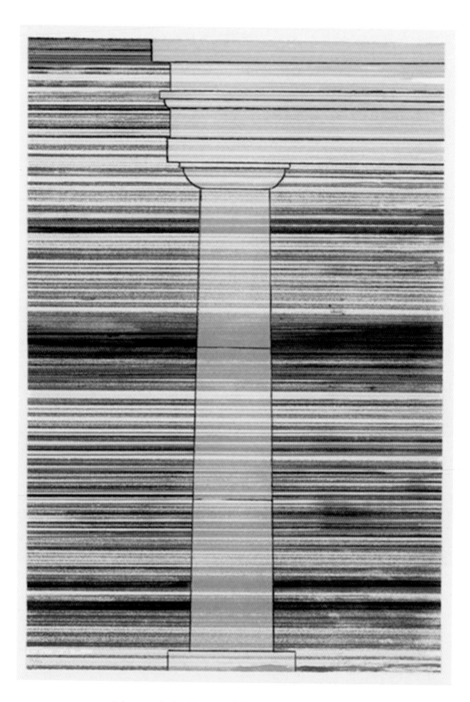

Column with Speed Lines, a lithograph by Ed Ruscha.

1947

A CHRISTMAS TREE

A GIFT FROM THE CITY OF OSLO TO LONDON

The Trafalgar Square Christmas Tree.

The tree given annually since 1947 by the city of Oslo to London, erected in Trafalgar Square in the heart of the British capital, is perhaps the most famous Christmas tree in the world. As a diplomatic gift, it has two distinct qualities. It is a gift of thanks, made without expectation of reciprocity. And it is a gift that has become an established annual tradition. This has given the gift the particular quality of being anticipated with pleasure: a gift that heralds the Christmas season.

Its origins lie in the dark days of the Second World War. On 9 April 1940, Nazi Germany launched Operation Weserübung, its sudden invasion of Denmark and Norway. While Oslo fell that day, King Haakon VII and the Norwegian government were able to escape the capital by special train. They were forced northwards, eventually reaching Tromsø in the far north of the country. Norwegian resistance and the support of British, French and Polish forces were insufficient to withstand the German invasion, and when with the fall of France the allies decided they needed to withdraw from Norway, it was clear that the king and government had to

237

continue their opposition to the German invaders and their puppet government from exile.[1]

The Norwegian king and government were evacuated from Tromsø on 7 June aboard HMS *Devonshire* and would form the Norwegian government-in-exile until 1945, operating from the legation at 10 Palace Gardens in the central London district of Kensington. King Haakon became a rallying point for Norwegians under German occupation, a task he could take on more easily than the government, which was largely composed of members of the Labour Party.[2] The king's monogram, H7, became a symbol of Norwegian resistance.

Haakon was already close to the United Kingdom. He had been married to Princess Maud of Wales, granddaughter of Queen Victoria, who had sadly died in 1938 of heart failure following abdominal surgery. He and Crown Prince Olav were initially guests at Buckingham Palace, moving out to Berkshire at the start of the London Blitz. Through the BBC, his speeches reached the Norwegian people. When the king returned home to rapturous crowds in Oslo aboard HMS *Norfolk* in June 1945, five years after the commencement of his exile, it was with a great feeling of gratitude to the United Kingdom, the ally that had provided him and his government with a home and support during the long years of German occupation.

That gratitude was translated into the gift of a Christmas tree in 1947, erected in Trafalgar Square in the heart of London. Such a tree had obvious attractions as a diplomatic gift. Its association with a time of celebration, and with new birth, resonated in a Britain subjected to post-war austerity. An evergreen conifer was symbolic of Norway. It was a reminder too of Norwegian Christmas trees received by Haakon while in exile in London.[3] The first lighting ceremony was held close to Christmas, on 22 December 1947, presided over by Charles Key, minister of works in the Attlee government, with other dignitaries in attendance including the mayor of Westminster and the Norwegian ambassador.

The gift has been repeated annually ever since. The cutting, transportation, erecting and lighting of the tree now take place to an established timetable and rhythm of ceremonies. The tree is a spruce from the Oslomarka, the forests surrounding Oslo that are an important part of the recreational lives of the city's inhabitants. The Agency for Urban Environment of the City of Oslo is responsible for selecting the tree destined for London. A tree around 21 metres in height, between sixty and 100 years old, is ideal.[4] Prospective candidates are identified years in advance and groomed for their big moment.

The felling of the tree is itself the subject of a ceremony, typically involving the visiting lord mayor of Westminster and the mayor of Oslo. The transportation of the tree has in recent years been carried out by the Danish shipping company DFDS, on their Brevik to Immingham service and thence by road to London. Once in place in Trafalgar Square, it takes a team two days to install it. The major ceremony is the lighting-up of the tree, now held on the first Thursday of December, much earlier in the month than the equivalent event in the first year of 1947. There are speeches from the lord mayor of Westminster, mayor of Oslo and Norwegian ambassador to London. Christmas music is provided by the Regent Hall band of the Salvation Army, with carols sung by the choir of St Martin-in-the-Fields. After a suitable countdown, the tree is illuminated. It is decorated in Norwegian style, rather simply, with strings of white lights running vertically down the tree, which is topped with a white star.

The gift was made on schedule in 2020, despite the challenges of the COVID-19 pandemic, though the lighting-up ceremony was for the first time held virtually. It was conducted by the lord mayor of Westminster and Norwegian ambassador, seated on black leather armchairs. The lord mayor pressed what resembled a large red mushroom atop a green box on the table between them, and the tree was lit.[5]

The Trafalgar Square tree is not the only Christmas tree donated by Norway to Britain. There are a whole series of such gifts, reflecting connections between local authorities in Norway and the United Kingdom, made across the country. Thus, Newcastle upon Tyne receives a tree each year from its twin city of Bergen. Some of these traditions are rather more recent than the Trafalgar tree. Aberdeen first received a Christmas tree from its Norwegian twin city of Stavanger in the 1970s, but this did not become an annual tradition until 2005.[6] The donation of a Christmas tree from the Norwegian Ministry of Foreign Affairs to its British counterpart began in 2016.

While these further donations of trees typically reference British wartime support for Norway, their more recent origins and local contexts are indicative of other motivations behind the gifts. Orkney for example receives two Norwegian Christmas trees each year. A tree that has come since 1983 from Hordaland County is placed outside St Magnus Cathedral in Kirkwall. From the time of the 850th anniversary celebrations of the cathedral in 1987, it has also received a tree from the Fjære Historical Society, placed inside the cathedral building. These gifts celebrate strong local ties. The tree from Fjære recalls not just Norway's links with Orkney in a broad sense but also more specifically the figure of Rögnvald Kali Kolsson, who may have been born in Fjære. Appointed earl of Orkney and Shetland in 1129, Kolsson had to establish himself there against the competing claims of his second cousin. Upon his success, he built the cathedral, in honour of his murdered uncle Magnus. When in 2019 the convener of Orkney Islands Council visited Norway to participate in the tree-cutting ceremony for the Fjære gift, he commented that it was a special moment to be in the forests where Kali Kolsson had walked.[7]

The speeches and other public messaging around the gift of the Trafalgar Square tree have, as the Second World War has become more distant in time, embraced a broader palette. British wartime support for Norway is always mentioned prominently, but this is generally accompanied by an emphasis on the strength of the modern-day partnership between the two countries, highlighting collaborations from the winter training of Royal Marines units in northern Norway to the development of renewable energy.

The repeated annual nature of the gift to London gives it power as an enduring symbol of the warm relationship between the two countries. The arrival of the Trafalgar Square tree has become part of the Christmas tradition for many Britons, awaited with anticipation as one of the moments heralding the festive season. Events linked to the gift have entered the national consciousness, as when in 2008 Andy Akinwolere, presenter of the children's television programme *Blue Peter*, accidentally dropped the star when attempting to place it on top of the tree.

That this is an anticipated gift does though impose particular challenges on the giver. There are advance expectations about what the gift should look like. A 20-metre spruce from the forests of Norway is quite different from the short pyramid-shaped trees found in living rooms across the land. It is more slender, and can appear sparse. The 2019 gift was subject to online criticism of its allegedly disappointing quality. The tree came to its own rescue, courtesy of its Twitter account, @trafalgartree, commenting that 'I thought I'd left the trolls behind in Norway.'[8]

The challenges facing the Trafalgar Square tree are nothing in comparison to the travails of poor Sortland. This small town north of the Arctic Circle sent an annual Christmas tree to the English port town of Grimsby for several years. The 2018 edition however appeared to start to die prematurely, losing needles at an alarming rate, and the local council was obliged to replace it with a locally sourced tree. According to local press reports, the mayor of Sortland wrote apologetically after the event, saying that the town had been pleased to provide trees to Grimsby for the previous fifteen years, a gift that had come at the instigation of the shipping company Eimskip, who had offered to deliver a tree if the town could provide one. However, Sortland had found it increasingly difficult to source a suitable tree, since spruce was not indigenous to the Arctic north, and could no longer maintain the gift.[9] This example also highlights that the public relations interests of transportation companies appear to be a significant factor in at least some of these annual gifts.

If the annual gifting of Christmas trees encounters occasional challenges and controversies, they have overall proved highly successful diplomatic gifts, serving to highlight a long tradition of warm relations. Other countries have followed suit in gifting annual trees. Latvia sends a Christmas tree to the British Foreign, Commonwealth and Development Office each December, where it is placed in the historic Lancaster House. Another annual gift arising from a Second World War context is the annual presentation of tulip bulbs from the royal family of the Netherlands to Canada, reflecting the support of that country in sheltering the Dutch Crown Princess Juliana and her family. The Norwegian Christmas tree in Trafalgar Square is a gift to raise a smile. That is not a bad outcome.

1949

THE MERCI TRAIN

A GIFT FROM THE PEOPLE OF FRANCE TO THE PEOPLE OF THE UNITED STATES OF AMERICA

A boxcar of the Merci Train.

The impact of the Second World War fell like a shadow across Europe, reflected in bomb-damaged cities and industrial facilities, the disruption of trade and millions of people across the continent living in refugee camps. The weather proved a further challenge, with the winter of 1946–7 particularly severe. On 5 June 1947, at a commencement speech at Harvard University, US Secretary of State George Marshall set out a vision of US aid supporting the recovery of the continent of Europe. The vision would be formalised the following year as the Economic Recovery Program, better known as the Marshall Plan, which would eventually provide some $12 billion support. The US authorities were convinced that economic recovery was necessary for political stability in Europe, to avoid further wars and prevent more countries falling prey to Communism.

Food aid was an immediate priority for a starving continent. On 5 October 1947, US President Harry S. Truman broadcast an appeal to the American people, highlighting the food emergency in western Europe and urging sacrifices from Americans in order to help out. They were asked to economise at the meal-table, eating no meat on Tuesdays, no poultry or eggs on Thursdays, and saving a slice of bread every day.[1] A Citizens Food Committee was set up under Charles Luckman to spearhead the conservation efforts.

A newspaper columnist named Drew Pearson felt that the work of the Citizens Food Committee, while laudable, was unlikely to capture the imagination of ordinary Americans. He believed that, rather than simply telling people to eat less, a more emotional initiative was required that could show them the use to which their sacrifice was being put.

Pearson, who had a reputation as something of a showman,[2] used his syndicated column, 'Washington Merry-Go-Round', to set out on 11 October an open letter to Luckman proposing that a 'Friendship Train' be run through the heart of America. The train would collect food donated by ordinary people, demonstrating the generosity of the American people at this time of European need.[3] Pearson made clear that he saw the purpose of the train as part of a propaganda battle against the Soviet Union for the hearts of western Europeans, a battle he feared that the United States was losing. He contrasted the fanfare surrounding the offloading of a consignment of Soviet wheat in Marseille with the lack of any attention paid to the arrival of a much larger consignment of US food aid in Le Havre. The Soviet Union was advertising its support better.

The Friendship Train proposal materialised with astonishing speed. Pearson mobilised influential Americans in support of the scheme, securing the support of Harry M. Warner, one of the eponymous Warner Brothers of film studio fame, as chair of his hastily convened National Friendship Train Committee. Luckman and the Citizens Food Committee bought into the idea and, by late October, the railway companies along the proposed route had committed to offering their support, without charge.[4] The train was ready to leave Los Angeles on 7 November 1947, less than a month after the scheme had first been mooted. It was seen off with a Hollywood parade, with John Wayne, Elizabeth Taylor and Maureen O'Hara among the film stars involved, a sign that publicity was at the heart of the initiative.[5] As the train headed east across the United States, it gathered increasing numbers of boxcars as America got firmly behind the endeavour. The children of Sedgwick County, Kansas, raised the money to buy a carload of wheat through running errands and collecting waste paper.[6] In Pennsylvania, a six-year-old boy wrapped small coins in a note asking for cakes to be purchased for a little boy or girl in Europe.[7]

The train's arrival in Pittsburgh, Pennsylvania, on 15 November, was typical of the welcome it received across the country, although the turnout for the welcoming ceremony, around 500 people, was lower than anticipated: a consequence of the cold and drizzly evening. Five cars were added to the train, each with the logo 'Pittsburgh – Food for Friends'[8] written in French and Italian, reflecting the two countries for which the aid was destined. They were filled with the staple products requested by the committee, from wheat to condensed milk.

The train's arrival in New York was the occasion for a ticker-tape parade on Broadway. On 7 December, the United States Lines' *American Leader* sailed from New York for Le Havre laden with donated food. It was rechristened the *Friend Ship* for the voyage. Further supplies were sent to France and Italy on three more steamships.[9] In France, a Friendship Train Steering Committee bringing together groups such as American Aid to France organised the distribution of the donated goods, with schools, orphanages and old people's homes among the recipients.[10] A ceremonial *Train de l'Amitié* was organised by the French authorities to raise awareness about the initiative in France. Setting out from Paris, it reached Marseille on Christmas Eve.

Not everything went smoothly. A French warehouse fire in January 1948 destroyed large quantities of donated goods and was blamed on Communist sympathisers.[11] Overall, however, the Friendship Train was a welcome and successful initiative, generating much positive publicity on both sides of the Atlantic. As a gift, it is notable for its explicit non-governmental character. Not only was it the product of an idea born outside government, it was based on making a direct connection between the people, not the governments, of the United States and the recipient countries. Its non-governmental character was intended as a contrast with the initiatives of the Soviet Union, to show what was possible through the actions of free people in a democratic society.[12]

A little more than a year later, it generated a response from the people of France. A French war veteran and railway worker named André Picard is credited with the idea of a thank-you gift from France for the food delivered through the Friendship Train. He proposed that a train should similarly be used to deliver the return gift. French officials took up the idea, and the Merci Train, or Gratitude Train, was born.

The concept of the Merci Train was to encourage French citizens to donate gifts of real or sentimental value to recipients across the United States. Personalisation was an important part of the gift. Donations were tagged with the name of the donor, and many included personal messages. The gifts themselves ranged from the valuable to the cute to the poignant. French President Vincent Auriol donated forty-nine Sèvres vases.[13] A young girl offered a painting of a yellow heart, praising American hearts of gold.[14] A couple gave the uniform of their son, killed in the First World War.[15]

The gifts were loaded into forty-nine boxcars, one for each of the forty-eight US States then in existence, with the forty-ninth to be shared between the District of Columbia and Hawaii. In an inspired choice, the boxcars used for the exercise were of the type known as Forty-and-Eights, covered wagons so called because they had originally been designed to hold forty men or eight horses. Inspired not just because of the pleasing identity with the number of US States, but also because these boxcars, already antiques by the late 1940s, had helped move US troops in both world wars and were remembered with affection. The boxcar had given its name to the Société des Quarante Hommes et Huit Chevaux, an organisation of US veterans founded in 1920, whose members are known as Forty-and-Eighters. This meant there was a ready-made US organisation predisposed to supporting the initiative. The boxcars were decorated with coats-of-arms representing the French provinces plus the emblem of the Merci Train, depicting a train accompanied by flowers associated with the battlegrounds of the First World War, emphasising the link between the initiative and veterans of war.[16]

On 2 February 1949, the French freighter *Magellan* was given a rapturous welcome as it steamed into New York Harbor, accompanied by US air force planes overhead, plumes of water from fireboats and a flotilla of small craft.[17] It brought the forty-nine boxcars, each carrying 5 tons of gifts. The boxcars were each transported to their recipient State, though the difference in rail gauge between the two countries meant they had to be conveyed on flatbed railcars or trucks.[18] Handover ceremonies across the United States were attended by French and local officials, and frequently involved parades.

States used different strategies to allocate the gifts. In North Dakota, the Crippled Children's School in Jamestown was given most of the toys, the books went to the University of North Dakota library, and the State Historical Society was given the balance of the gifts, along with the boxcar itself.[19] Others distributed the gifts more widely, in some cases through lotteries. Some prestigious gifts were treated separately. Thus the Brooklyn Museum held an exhibition in September 1949 entitled 'Two Centuries of French Fashion Elegance', based on the gift of forty-nine dolls, each around 60 centimetres tall, dressed immaculately in French fashions of the eighteenth and nineteenth centuries.[20]

There is now little information on the whereabouts of most of the Merci Train gifts, with the exception of those preserved in museum collections. This is not however true of the boxcars themselves. Thanks in many cases to the efforts of the Société des Quarante Hommes et Huit Chevaux in restoring boxcars and ensuring they are displayed prominently in their home State, only six of the forty-nine boxcars have been lost. The others are on display at railway museums and other suitable locations as a permanent reminder of the French gift of friendship. In effect, this is a rare example of an occasion in which what has survived is not the gift but the wrapper.

The Merci Train also demonstrates that gifts can have an impact on third parties, as well as giver and recipient. The United Kingdom did not receive food through the Friendship Train initiative, but it was the largest recipient of Marshall Plan support, and the French decision to send a thank-you gift to the United States put its officials in a quandary. While some British officials were unimpressed with the French initiative, one referring to it as a 'silly ass' idea,[21] others were concerned lest this French gift of gratitude steal a march on the British.

Sir Edmund Hall-Patch at the Foreign Office argued that the UK should come up with a gift that resonated with the American imagination. He proposed the donation of an original copy of the Magna Carta, that great symbol of liberty, which might tour the United States before residing at the Library of Congress.[22] It transpired however that the difficulties around such a gift were considerable: an Act of Parliament would be necessary to secure an original copy, and none of the institutions holding them wanted to part with theirs. Eventually, the British government decided to pursue instead a suggestion first made by Foreign Office official Sir Roger Mellor Makins to establish a prestigious scholarship scheme to bring top US students to the UK.[23] The Marshall Scholarship was born, and continues to thrive.

Other recipients of US support also sent thank-you gifts. Italy cast four bronze statues that had been commissioned for the approaches to the Arlington Memorial Bridge in Washington, while the Netherlands gifted a forty-nine-bell carillon standing adjacent to Arlington National Cemetery. A sentiment of thanks can produce lasting gifts.

1949

A PLANETARIUM

A GIFT FROM THE PEOPLE OF THE GERMAN DEMOCRATIC REPUBLIC TO JOSEPH STALIN, GENERAL SECRETARY OF THE COMMUNIST PARTY OF THE SOVIET UNION

The Volgograd Planetarium.

Like the Sword of Stalingrad, our next story concerns a gift received by the city of Stalingrad. The motivations for the choice of that city as recipient were in both cases linked to Stalingrad's role in changing the fortunes of the Second World War through heroic defence by Soviet forces, and to the derivation of the city's name from that of the Soviet leader, Joseph Stalin. There the similarities end. This story is about a birthday party. It was a birthday like no other; characterised by strong encouragement to the citizens of the Soviet Union, its allies and members of like-minded groups around the world to show their love for the Soviet leader by giving him loads of presents.

The seventieth birthday of Joseph Stalin on 21 December 1949 marked the high point of his personality cult, at a time when internationally he still drew prestige for his role in wartime victory and was still the undisputed leading figure of the socialist world.[1] A special committee was established to oversee birthday preparations, headed by Nikolai Shvernik, who as chairman of the Presidium of the Supreme Soviet of the USSR was titular head of state. Birthday greetings in the official newspaper *Pravda* ran almost daily, at around 200 per day, until well into 1951.[2] This had the curious result that Stalin's seventy-first birthday in 1950 passed almost unnoticed in the paper, as it continued to churn out greetings sent for the previous one.[3]

The birthday programme culminated with a gala event at the Bolshoi Theatre attended by leaders across the socialist bloc and involving numerous speeches to the Soviet leader, who absorbed them impassively. A praise-laden poem was recited by a young girl in Pioneer uniform named Natasha, who then presented Stalin with a bouquet of flowers. Natasha was the daughter of Alexander Poskrebyshev, the head of Stalin's personal chancellery. One wonders at her feelings as she presented the gift, given that Stalin had approved, or at least acquiesced in, the execution of her mother in 1941 over her connections to Trotsky.

Like any birthday, gifts were important. Delegates attending the gala received a gift pack containing a dressing gown, slippers and set of *Moskva* toiletries. The birthday programme as a whole was focused on the 'spontaneous' presentation of gifts by an adoring socialist world. Several institutions in Moscow were selected to host a public exhibition of the birthday gifts received by Stalin, with the primary venue the Pushkin Museum of Fine Arts, whose staff were privately horrified to find that the intention seemed to be that the birthday gifts exhibition was to be permanent.[4] In the event, the exhibition would run until 1953, the year of Stalin's death. From the many thousands of gifts sent from across and beyond the Soviet Union, museum staff were given just ten days to put together the exhibition, showcasing around 8,000 items.[5] The exhibition itself was a birthday gift to Stalin.

The gifts sent to Stalin on his seventieth birthday were portrayed as gifts of gratitude to the Soviet leader. They reciprocated his gift of socialism. The value of the gifts was perceived to lie not in monetary worth, but in uniqueness.[6] Gifts were often handmade items, reflecting the profession of the giver. There were numerous portraits of Stalin, his face captured on canvas, woven into rugs, even depicted on grains of rice.[7] The poem *Gifts*, by Belarusian writer Anton Belevich, describes the gifts to Stalin made by the workers at a collective farm, each appropriate to their occupations. A small boy then resolves that, for his gift, he will grow up more quickly, in order to become a Hero of the Soviet Union.[8] The gifts emphasised the labour involved in their production, contrasting the economic system of the Soviet Union with the capitalist West. The gift from Albanian timber workers was a pledge to overfill their production plan by 210 per cent.[9] Natasha's bouquet of flowers apart, Stalin was rarely filmed personally accepting the gifts. For the most part, they were accepted by officials acting as surrogates of the leader, such as collective farm directors.[10] Nor did Stalin ever visit the exhibition of birthday gifts at the Pushkin Museum. In failing to acknowledge the gifts sent to him on his birthday, Stalin was essentially seeking to ensure that the burden of indebtedness of the Soviet people and satellite countries remained in place.[11] His great gift of socialism had not been reciprocated by these offerings.

There was a strong international dimension to the solicitation of gifts for Stalin's birthday. The exhibition itself was arranged geographically, with the republics of the Soviet Union, the socialist world and the rest of the world each accorded separate galleries.[12] There was an intent to demonstrate the global breadth of the adulation of Stalin. The chairman of the Communist Party of China, Mao Zedong, was in Moscow for the birthday celebrations, his first overseas trip following his proclamation of the establishment of the People's Republic of China less than three months earlier.[13] Mao had come to the Soviet Union to secure a substantial treaty of alliance in a context in which China was economically in ruins while the USSR was a superpower. Stalin was cautious, fearing risks both to post-war Soviet gains in the Far East and of inciting US intervention,[14] and the protracted visit was awkward, with little personal chemistry in evidence between the two leaders. Nonetheless a treaty was signed, the Sino-Soviet Treaty of Friendship, Alliance and Mutual Assistance, which while concluded on Valentine's Day 1950 was perhaps less forward looking than Mao would have wished. Mao's speech at Stalin's birthday gala received a standing ovation, and Mao gave the Soviet leader a birthday gift of imperial vases.[15]

Where Cold War realities had replaced wartime alliances, the organisers of the Stalin birthday gifts exhibition resorted to repackaging earlier gifts to maintain a broad geographical coverage. Thus, a Native American headdress, presented to the Soviet ambassador to Washington on Stalin's behalf in 1942, was pressed into service for the exhibition, an inscription recording that Stalin had been made an 'honorary chief of all Indian tribes'.[16] Coverage across western Europe was secured by gifts from local Communist parties. The French Communists organised their own exhibition of birthday gifts to Stalin, with highlights including the work of socialist realist painter André Fougeron, before sending these eastwards to Moscow.[17]

For the Soviet satellite states of central Europe, participation in the mass gift-giving for Stalin's seventieth birthday was a means of demonstrating their faithfulness and their full integration into the Soviet orbit.[18] This was seen particularly clearly in East Germany, where the immediate post-war experience of Soviet occupation had been traumatic for the local people, with a relationship between Germans and Russians characterised by continuing mistrust.[19] The foundation of the German Democratic Republic in October 1949 gave its new leadership the opportunity to demonstrate their status as a fully committed member of the socialist bloc, with preparations for Stalin's seventieth birthday serving as the first test of that commitment. This would mark its completion of the transition from occupied zone to full membership of the group.[20]

The celebration of Stalin's birthday in East Germany was based around a portrayal of the Soviet leader as not only the bestower of the gift of socialism and liberator from National Socialism, but also more specifically as a friend to the German people, and the only major leader to support German unity. Thus Walter Ulbricht, the deputy chairman of the Council of Ministers, and future East German leader, speaking at the gala event in the Bolshoi Theatre, described Stalin as 'the best friend of the German people'.[21] The contradiction underpinning this approach of simultaneously appealing to nationalism while emphasising Soviet domination was brushed over.[22] The leadership of the new German Democratic Republic attempted to mobilise the population in celebration of Stalin's special day. The birthday celebration also served as a vehicle for teaching the official narrative around the cult of the Soviet leader, including through mass meetings across the country.[23]

Encouragement to offer birthday gifts to Stalin was also an important part of the birthday preparations in the German Democratic Republic. Its leadership announced that one particularly striking gift would be offered from the entire population, paid for through 'voluntary' contributions. This would be a planetarium, to be built in Stalingrad. Wilhelm Pieck, the new president, announced in a telegram congratulating Stalin on his birthday that Stalingrad had been chosen both because the city bore the Soviet leader's name and because the great victory secured there through the genius of the leader had 'put an end to a sad chapter in German history'.[24] The planetarium would therefore serve as a gift marking the beginning of a new friendship between the two peoples.

While the choice of Stalingrad offered a symbolic atonement for the sins of the Second World War, and represented a statement of desire for a new friendship, the specific gift chosen, a planetarium, suggested an additional motive. The optical elements of the planetarium would be the work of the renowned firm of Carl Zeiss, which had become leading makers of scientific instruments in the nineteenth century. A request in 1913 from Oskar von Miller, director of the Deutsches Museum in Munich, for assistance in designing astronomical rooms, had led Zeiss to develop the technology that allowed the portrayal of the night sky not in an abstract way but in a three-dimensional approximation of reality.[25] The firm constructed their first purpose-built planetarium on the roof of their factory in Jena in 1924, thereby chalking up another world first: the geodesic dome. Within a few years, they had built planetariums across Germany, as well as farther afield, including one in Moscow in 1929.[26]

At the end of the Second World War, part of the Zeiss company was moved by allied troops to Oberkochen in Baden-Württemberg, but the rest stayed in Jena in East Germany. The gift of a planetarium by the East German leadership thus allowed it to showcase an example of East German technology superior to that of the Soviet Union. By implication, the gift questioned the Stalinist worldview of Soviet superiority.[27] It also offered a calling card for the construction of its planetariums across the socialist world.

The Stalingrad planetarium was not opened until 1954, thereby violating one of the key rules of birthday gifts: that they should arrive while the recipient is still alive. Stalin had breathed his last the year before. With its neo-classical design, large portico and female statue of *Peace* atop its dome, the architectural style was that of Stalinism, and already becoming outmoded at the time of the building's inauguration.[28] The planetarium though dutifully continues its work to this day of teaching young people about the mysteries of the universe.

1952

A BOX OF SHAMROCKS

A GIFT FROM JOHN HEARNE, AMBASSADOR OF THE REPUBLIC OF IRELAND TO THE UNITED STATES OF AMERICA, TO HARRY S. TRUMAN, PRESIDENT OF THE UNITED STATES OF AMERICA

US President George W. Bush presented with a bowl of shamrocks by Taoiseach Bertie Ahern in 2006.

Like the Christmas tree from the city of Oslo to London, this is the tale of a gift made annually, on a set date. The handing of shamrocks to the president of the United States has developed from modest beginnings as a gift sent to the White House by the local ambassador, to the centrepiece of the annual visit of the taoiseach to Washington around St Patrick's Day. The growth in importance attached to the gift developed, as we shall see, because both giver and receiver perceived this to suit their interests.

There is a bust of diplomat John Hearne, looking dapper in bow tie and jacket, in his hometown of Waterford. The bust was unveiled in 2017, on the eightieth anniversary of the Irish Constitution of 1937, and it is for his contribution to the drafting of that document that Hearne, then a legal expert in the Department of External Affairs, owes his strongest place in history. The driving political force behind the new Constitution, Éamon de Valera, described Hearne as 'Architect in Charge and Draftsman' of the Constitution in a handwritten dedication in the copy of the document he presented to his colleague.[1] As a civil servant, Hearne's role was not strongly emphasised at the time, and it has been left to later historians to bring his contribution centre-stage.[2] John Hearne had a distinguished later career representing the Republic of Ireland overseas, as high commissioner to Ottawa from 1939, and from 1950 as the Republic of Ireland's first ambassador to the United States, his predecessors in the role having held the title of minister plenipotentiary.

It was not a straightforward time to represent the Republic of Ireland in Washington. Hearne had to contend with US resentment at Ireland's war-time neutrality and its refusal to join NATO. Against that backdrop, Hearne recognised the importance of cultural diplomacy, and of the opportunities offered by the political importance of the Irish American community. St Patrick's Day was celebrated enthusiastically by Irish Americans, and the St Patrick's Day parade in New York was a significant event. President Truman attended it in 1948. Hearne recognised the potential gain for the bilateral relationship of bringing this commemoration of Ireland's patron saint out of the ethnic community and into the calendars of the US political leadership.[3] The shamrock, the three-leafed plant reportedly used by St Patrick to teach the concept of the Holy Trinity, provided the perfect calling card.

For St Patrick's Day in 1952, Hearne sent a small box of shamrocks to President Truman, together with a message expressing the hope that relations between the two countries would continue to prosper.[4] This was a low-key diplomatic gift. Truman was out of Washington at the time, and the shamrocks were not delivered to him in person. In many ways, the genius of the gift came the following year, with a new president, Dwight D. Eisenhower, in the White House. Hearne requested permission to call on Eisenhower to deliver shamrock as a St Patrick's Day gift: the request was accepted, the precedent of the gift having already been established.[5] An annual tradition had been born.

The first presentation of shamrock by the taoiseach rather than the local ambassador came in 1956, during a visit of John A. Costello to Washington. In 1959, honours were provided by the Irish president, Seán T. O'Kelly, during his US visit.[6] For the most part though this remained a gift made by the ambassador to Washington. The profile of the presentation rose and fell according to the extent of the Irish connections of the US president, and the extent of their engagement with Irish issues. It was with the arrival in the White House of John F. Kennedy, a president with strong Irish roots, that the ceremony became a prominent media occasion. Its profile became quieter under the presidency of Lyndon Johnson, and Jimmy Carter even delegated the event to his vice-president on one occasion, when preoccupied with the Middle East.[7] It became more prominent again under Ronald Reagan, who, like Kennedy, visited Ireland during his presidency to explore his Irish roots. In Reagan's case, this took him to the village of Ballyporeen in County Tipperary, where his great-grandfather had been baptised in 1829. Both Charles Haughey and Garret FitzGerald presented shamrock to Reagan during his presidency.

It was with Bill Clinton's presidency that the annual presentation of shamrock personally by the taoiseach became established practice. It was in both US and Irish interests to elevate the profile of the event. Clinton aimed to use the St Patrick's Day ceremony to underline his commitment to the peace process in Northern Ireland.[8] For his part, the Irish ambassador, Dermot Gallagher, argued that the shamrock ceremony provided the Republic of Ireland with a unique opportunity for a country of its size to secure annual access to the US president, warranting an annual visit by the taoiseach to make the presentation. The then holder of that office, Albert Reynolds, agreed.[9]

Not only did the seniority of the giver grow, but the event itself also became more elaborate, with the actual gifting of shamrock forming but one component of a series of activities marking Washington's political engagement with St Patrick's Day. One former British ambassador to Washington recalled that in Clinton's time the St Patrick's Day events 'paralysed political Washington for two days'.[10] The shamrock ceremony at the White House was followed by a lunch given by the speaker on Capitol Hill, with both president and taoiseach in attendance, and then an evening reception at the White House to follow.

While not all Clinton's successors have given such strong attention to the event, its main characteristics have largely remained at this elevated level. This is because the event has continued to meet both Irish and US political objectives around it. For the Republic of Ireland, it provides political access to the president of a quality that makes it the envy of the Washington diplomatic corps. For the US president, it provides an opportunity to strengthen their credentials with the politically powerful Irish American lobby.

The gift itself quickly developed too beyond the shamrocks themselves into something rather grander, particularly in respect of the crystal bowl in which the plants are presented. The bowl is now selected from among

Irish craft producers through a tender process.[11] Its design has been used as a piece of cultural diplomacy. Thus the shamrock-filled bowl presented by Taoiseach Enda Kenny to President Obama in 2016, on the 100th anniversary year of the Easter Rebellion, featured etchings of the rebellion; the General Post Office in Dublin, which served as the headquarters of its leaders; and a passage from the Proclamation of the Republic.[12]

The valuations of the shamrock presentation gifts set out in the State Department Office of the Chief of Protocol annual return of gifts to federal employees from foreign government sources have varied considerably over the years. During the sixteen years covered by the presidencies of George W. Bush and Barack Obama, estimated values have ranged from $295, for the Waterford Crystal bowl presented to President Bush by Bertie Ahern in 2001, to $10,566 for the gifts presented to Obama by Enda Kenny in 2015, comprising a crystal bowl inscribed with quotations from W. B. Yeats and a book of Yeats' poetry. There is no entry for a crystal bowl in several returns over this period, suggesting that it was decided that the cost of the bowl did not meet the 'minimal value' criterion for declaration of the gift. While the crystal bowls are destined for the National Archives, it seems they can be kept at the White House during the president's tenure – Ronald Reagan reportedly used one of his bowls to hold jelly beans.[13]

Only once in this sixteen-year period did the State Department provide an estimated value for the shamrocks. That came in 2007, where alongside $350 for the Waterford Crystal bowl presented by Bertie Ahern to George W. Bush, they ascribed $5 for the shamrocks themselves. The revelation that the latter were 'handled pursuant to Secret Service policy' caused a minor stir in the Irish press, with one headline in the *Irish Examiner* announcing a 'White House Furnace Shock for Shamrock'.[14]

The ceremony of the presentation of the shamrock has taken on a familiar quality over the years, with both president and taoiseach sporting green ties for the occasion and much warm language about shared historical and cultural links. One former speechwriter to President George W. Bush, writing in the *New York Times*, complained that this did not make the president's annual speech at the occasion the most exciting of tasks for the speechwriter. 'How many different ways can you accept a bowl of shamrocks, or celebrate the sterling qualities of the noble Irish people?' he wondered.[15] John Hearne's initiative in 1952 has given the Republic of Ireland decades of quality access to the most powerful leader in the world. An impressive outcome for a gift of humble greenery.

1957

TWO SWANS

A GIFT FROM ELIZABETH II, QUEEN OF THE UNITED KINGDOM AND THE OTHER COMMONWEALTH REALMS, TO THE CITY OF LAKELAND, FLORIDA

A mute swan.

Queen Elizabeth II has many titles. She is Head of the Commonwealth, Commander in Chief of the British Armed Forces, Defender of the Faith, and indeed Duke of Lancaster. One of the more unusual is Seigneur of the Swans, a title that speaks to the close relationship over many centuries between this majestic bird and the British royal family. The relationship has underpinned an impressive quantity of swan-related diplomatic gifting over the years. It is associated specifically with the mute swan, the white-plumed orange-beaked waterfowl that fits the textbook image of what a swan should look like, and which is native to the United Kingdom.

From medieval times, swans in Britain were associated with nobility and considered objects of luxury. Their exclusive character may have stemmed from a combination of the creature's grace and beauty, its solitary nature and the fact that keeping them was no straightforward undertaking. Swans were eaten as a particularly lavish dish, especially at Christmas, until the eighteenth century,[1] though they fell rapidly out of fashion thereafter as a gourmet food-stuff, in part perhaps because they are reportedly not particularly tasty.

The Crown has enjoyed the right to claim all unmarked mute swans swimming in open waters since at least the twelfth century. The monarch could however grant others the privilege of owning swans. Concerns seem to have developed by the fifteenth century that swan ownership had spread too far through society, to the detriment of its exclusivity. During the reign of King Edward IV in 1482, the Act concerning Swans endeavoured to ensure that the birds remained in the hands of a very few, stipulating that only those with land worth more than 5 marks a year could own swans. This was a large enough sum to avoid the risk that swans might be in the possession of, as the Act put it, 'yeomen and husbandmen and other persons of little reputation'.[2] Swans' beaks were marked to indicate their ownership, and the right to a swan mark was both expensive and restricted. Legal cases concerning swans were heard at special 'swanmoots'.[3]

The queen today exercises her right to unmarked mute swans mainly in respect of a stretch of the River Thames, which provides the setting for the annual ceremony of Swan Upping. Spread over five days, this involves the passage upriver of traditionally bedecked 'swan uppers' in wooden skiffs. Some represent the monarch, others the City of London Livery Companies of the Dyers and the Vintners, whose rights to own swans were granted in the fifteenth century. The ceremony was the responsibility of the Keeper of the Queen's Swans until 1993, in which year the role was split in two, so the monarch now benefits from the support of both a Warden of the Swans and a Marker of the Swans. As well as being a colourful ceremony, Swan Upping is now focused on conservation, as the birds are counted, weighed and checked for injuries.

Our story takes us across the Atlantic, to Lakeland, a small city of a little over 100,000 people some 35 miles east of Tampa in Florida. As its name implies, the urban geography of the city is dominated by its many lakes, mostly water-filled phosphate mine pits. The swans enlivening those lakes have long been a source of municipal pride. There are records of swans in the city from 1923, and they were traditionally looked after by local residents.[4] The swans were however vulnerable to attacks by dogs and alligators and, by 1953, they had gone. Enter Mr and Mrs Pickhardt, Lakelanders stationed in the United Kingdom, where husband Robert worked at an American air force base. Mrs Pickhardt, distraught at the news that her home city was now without its prized swans, and learning that unmarked mute swans in Britain were the property of the queen, decided to write to

Her Majesty to ask for a couple. Bearing out the adage, 'if you don't ask, you don't get', she received a reply confirming that the queen had agreed to donate a pair of mute swans to the City of Lakeland, provided the city could pay the $300 required to transport the swans to Florida.[5]

The transportation costs almost proved Lakeland's undoing. The city's initial fundraising effort reportedly netted a mighty $7, and press publicity around the challenge resulted in rival offers for the birds from St Petersburg and Orlando. Lakeland's gift was saved by a Mrs Randle Pomeroy, enchanted by the place during a visit the previous year, who stumped up the full $300.[6] The crated swans arrived in Florida on 9 February 1957 and were placed in a caged enclosure on Lake Morton. The next morning, it was discovered that both swans had broken free from their enclosure. The female was swimming close by on Lake Morton. The male had headed off to explore Florida and was caught after a four-day search. He was returned to the female swan, fittingly, on St Valentine's Day.[7]

Lakeland's swan population has since thrived, to the point where the city has in recent years needed to sell off swans to avoid overpopulation. In October 2020, the city announced that thirty-six birds would be sold at $400 each through a swan lottery. Purchasers were required to commit to the provision of a suitable water source and annual veterinary care.[8] Her Majesty's gift to Lakeland appears in one sense an example of royal largesse, in response to a well-argued request. Looked at from the perspective of the United Kingdom's bilateral relationship with the United States, it appears an inspired piece of public diplomacy, with the gifted swans and their descendants serving as a symbol of British friendship with this Florida community.

A better known gift of swans by Queen Elizabeth II came in 1967 when, in commemoration of the centenary of the establishment of the Canadian Confederation, Her Majesty gifted six pairs of mute swans from the River Thames, specially selected by the Keeper of the Queen's Swans. They were given to Ottawa, Canada's capital city, by the queen as Canada's head of state. This was not the first royal gift of mute swans to Canada. Pairs had been donated to different Canadian towns by King George V in 1912 and Edward VIII in 1936.[9] The swans arrived in Ottawa in May 1967 and, after a period of quarantine, eight birds were released into the Rideau River on 28 June, the other two pairs remaining at a 'swan house' at the tree nursery in the suburb of Leitrim. The swans were thus nicely in situ when the queen and Prince Philip arrived in Ottawa on their centennial tour of Canada on 1 July.[10]

The swans proved immediately popular, and thrived, such that there were forty birds by the early 1970s and, concerned about overcapacity, the city had to make discreet enquiries about the etiquette of regifting swans. The answer was reportedly that this was fine, though onward donations could not be described as royal gifts.[11] As the years passed, the city authorities began though to fret about the maintenance costs. Ottawa's harsh climate meant that these were particularly heavy, since the birds had to be physically taken out of the river each year to winter quarters at the tree nursery in Leitrim. The deteriorating state of the swan house there led to press quips about 'Swantanamo Bay',[12] and a new winter quartering arrangement was agreed in 2015 with Parc Safari in Quebec.

While Ottawa's swans retain many admirers, there was a growing critique too that the mute swan is an invasive species. Others have expressed concern about the pinioning of the swans, required to stop them absconding and competing with native wildlife elsewhere, but which involves the surgical removal of the pinion joint of the wing, such that the swans can no longer fly. By 2019, with swan numbers appreciably down, following efforts by the city authorities to reduce their population to cut costs, officials were recommending that the remaining swans be relocated permanently to Parc Safari.[13] At the time of writing, the court, or perhaps swanmoot, was still out on the future of Ottawa's royal swans.

The close connection of the British royal family with the mute swan perhaps helps explain why swans have been chosen as gifts for Queen Elizabeth II as well as from her. The gift in 1952 of five trumpeter swans from the Canadian Federal Department of Resources and Development and the Government of British Columbia is of particular interest in serving as a fine demonstration of the important principle that you should only gift what is already in your possession.

The then Princess Elizabeth, accompanied by her husband, toured Canada in 1951 on behalf of her ailing father. During a visit to Charlottetown, the capital of Prince Edward Island, the minister of resources and development, Robert Winters, announced that she would be given six trumpeter swans. The world's largest waterfowl, deriving its name from its loud call, the trumpeter swan is a Canadian native, and thus a nice example of an animal serving as a signature gift of its country. The only problem was that the minister did not yet have six trumpeter swans to give. The Canadian Wildlife Service was tasked with capturing them to make good the gift.[14]

The official charged with carrying out this operation was Ron Mackay, a naval veteran who had retrained as a wildlife biologist and become dominion wildlife officer for British Columbia.[15] Mackay knew that the best place to trap trumpeter swans was a remote lake, aptly known as Lonesome Lake, some 250 miles north-west of Vancouver.[16] The reason for this trapping opportunity lay in the work of a remarkable man named Ralph Edwards, dubbed by his biographer as 'Crusoe of Lonesome Lake'.[17] Edwards had turned his back on civilisation in 1912 and built himself a cabin at this remote spot, an important and hitherto unknown wintering area for the endangered trumpeter swans. Learning about the swans from a bear hunter named John Holman, who had engaged Edwards as his guide, the Canadian Wildlife Service had recruited Edwards as a bird warden and supplied him with grain as supplementary food for the swans. Over the years, the birds had become quite tame.

In November 1951, Mackay flew to Lonesome Lake with a colleague, David Munro, and there they worked with Ralph Edwards to build a rectangular swan trap, furnished with a door that could be snapped shut through a trip wire.[18] By this time, Edwards had married and brought up a family in this isolated spot, and feeding the swans was entrusted to his adult daughter Trudy. She continued to give the swans food through December and January, so the birds became accustomed to the trap, and in early February, Mackay and Munro returned. On 7 February, Trudy Edwards managed to entice seven cygnets and one adult into the trap, but on dropping the gate, the adult and two cygnets managed to escape.[19] Instead of the promised six trumpeter swans, they had secured just five. The rest of the flock had been alarmed by the frantic escape attempts of the trapped swans and had left the feeding area. With bad weather threatening, Mackay and Munro decided to leave Lonesome Lake with the five birds.[20]

The swans were flown to Britain and took up residence at the Severn Wildfowl Trust reserve at Slimbridge in Gloucestershire. One of the two females died, but the other swans thrived.[21] King George VI having died in February, it was as Queen Elizabeth II that the recipient of the gift viewed the swans on 25 April. Trudy Edwards received a letter of thanks from the queen for her part in securing them,[22] though she reportedly always felt guilty at having betrayed the trust the swans had shown in her.[23]

1965

AN ACRE OF ENGLISH GROUND

A GIFT FROM THE PEOPLE OF BRITAIN TO THE UNITED STATES OF AMERICA

John F. Kennedy Memorial, Runnymede.

It used to be said that everyone could remember where they were when they heard that President Kennedy had been assassinated. It was not just the manner of his death, but the hopes so many around the world had vested in his life that made his murder such a defining moment. As the youngest person elected to the US presidency, taking over from the man who was then the oldest, he symbolised both a new generation and political renewal. He was charming, handsome, a powerful orator, attuned to popular culture, a leader who promised action and dynamism.[1] At the height of the Cold War, he was a president with a vision of peace: '[N]ot merely peace for Americans but peace for all men and women, not merely peace in our time but peace in all time.'[2]

An exchange in the House of Commons on 5 December 1963, two weeks after Kennedy's assassination, revealed cross-party support for a British memorial to the late president. The leader of the opposition, Harold Wilson, suggested that this might take the form either of a physical memorial or a tribute to his achievements, for example in the area of world peace. Norman Pentland, MP for Chester-le-Street in County Durham, suggested that the memorial be located in the town of Washington, given its historic links with the United States. Frank McLeavy, the member for Bradford East, thought it might take the form of scholarships for US students in the UK.[3]

The prime minister, Sir Alec Douglas-Home, announced in January 1964 the establishment of a committee to facilitate discussion on the form a memorial should take and to make recommendations. He appointed as its chair Lord Franks, the former ambassador to Washington whose travails over crystallised fruits we encountered in the introduction to this volume. The prime minister reported back to the House of Commons on 25 March on the outcome of the committee's work. It had concluded that this should be a living memorial, in two parts. The first would be the gift of an acre of ground at Runnymede, west of London, laid out with a plinth and steps. The second, a scholarship fund for young Britons to study at Harvard University, Kennedy's alma mater, at Radcliffe College or at the Massachusetts Institute of Technology, as a tribute to Kennedy's work to promote international understanding.[4]

The prime minister decided that what was needed to give effect to the recommendations of the Franks Committee was another committee, and appointed another former British ambassador to Washington to chair it. This was Sir Roger Makins, who would be ennobled as Lord Sherfield later in the year. The lord mayor of London, Sir James Harman, agreed to make fundraising for the memorial the subject of a lord mayor's appeal.[5]

The Kennedy Scholarships are still going strong. Their alumni list is impressive, encompassing Ed Balls, former shadow chancellor of the Exchequer and *Strictly Come Dancing* contestant; Mervyn King, former governor of the Bank of England; and Lady Justice Arden, Lady Justice of Appeal. Our focus is however on the first part of the memorial, that acre of ground at Runnymede.

An Act of Parliament, the Kennedy Memorial Act of 1964, achieved the transfer of the site to the United States, under the management of the trustees of the Kennedy Memorial Fund. The site was part of the Crown Estate at Runnymede, and the Crown Estate commissioners were normally required to secure the best price obtainable and could only gift land where this would bring a benefit to the Crown Estate. Legislation was therefore required to transfer the land from the Crown to the trustees of the fund.[6] The Act also makes clear that the gift of the land to the United States does not cede UK sovereignty over the land; rather it is a transferral of the land, taking effect under English law, to the trustees.[7]

The choice of Runnymede as the location for the physical memorial, rather than, say, the town of Washington, was a carefully considered one. The meadow of Runnymede alongside the River Thames was famous as the site at which King John sealed the Magna Carta on 15 June 1215: the Great Charter that, across the eight centuries that have followed, has come to be seen as a founding document for the protection of individual rights against tyranny.

The meadow and surrounding hillside are peppered with memorials and sculptures celebrating the ideals found within that document. A sculpture entitled *Writ in Water* arrived in 2018, the work of Mark Wallinger in collaboration with Studio Octopi, and commissioned by the National Trust. An austere-looking windowless circular building on the side of the hill reveals a circular chamber inside centred on a pool around which the text of Clause 39 of the Magna Carta is read through the reflections of its otherwise inverted lettering on the water. 'No free man shall be seized or imprisoned, or stripped of his rights or possessions, or outlawed or exiled, or deprived of his standing in any other way except by the lawful judgement of his equals or by the law of the land.'

There were already memorials at Runnymede in 1964. The meadows themselves had been gifted to the National Trust in 1929 by Cara, Lady Fairhaven, in memory of her husband, a former member of parliament named Urban Broughton. She commissioned Sir Edwin Lutyens to design a pair of steep-roofed lodges. One now houses the estate office, the other the tea room. At the top of Coopers Hill above the site is the poignant quadrangle of the Air Forces Memorial, unveiled in 1953, commemorating more than 20,000 men and women of the Commonwealth air forces who lost their lives during the Second World War and have no known grave.

Runnymede was particularly suitable as the site of the Kennedy Memorial because the principles enshrined in the Magna Carta also underpinned the Constitution and Bill of Rights of the United States. Sir Edward Maufe, the architect of the Air Forces Memorial, was commissioned by the American Bar Association to design a memorial to the Magna Carta on the slopes overlooking the meadow. Dedicated in 1957, it is a Greek-style domed classical temple, with a pillar of granite in the centre inscribed with the words: 'To commemorate Magna Carta, symbol of freedom under law.' Plaques on the floor of the memorial record return visits by the American Bar Association, couched in the language of spiritual pilgrimage: 'On this day the American Bar Association again came here and pledged allegiance to the principles of the Great Charter.' Nearby, an oak tree, planted with soil from Jamestown, Virginia, the first permanent

English settlement in the New World, commemorates the bicentenary of the US Constitution. The plaque here acknowledges 'that the ideals of liberty and justice embodied in the Constitution trace their lineage through institutions of English law to the Magna Carta'.

The Kennedy Memorial lies in woodland on sloping land close to the Magna Carta Memorial. It was designed by landscape architect Geoffrey Jellicoe. Every stone is heavy with symbolism. Echoing the Magna Carta Memorial, the overall motif is one of pilgrimage. The design of the memorial aimed to evoke John Bunyan's *The Pilgrim's Progress*.[8] The visitor enters through a wooden gate and is confronted with a pathway of granite setts representing numerous pilgrims. The pathway climbs the slope through fifty steps, one for each US State. After the trials of this uphill pilgrimage, the visitor reaches an open area in front of the centrepiece of the memorial, a 7-tonne rectangular block of Portland stone. An inscription commemorates the gifting of 'this acre of English ground' to the United States in memory of John F. Kennedy. The inscription concludes with a passage from Kennedy's inaugural address: 'Let every nation know, whether it wishes us well or ill, that we shall pay any price, bear any burden, meet any hardship, support any friend or oppose any foe in order to assure the survival and success of liberty.'[9] To the right, a path leads to two stone seats offering a delightful view to the meadow below: a part of the memorial symbolising spiritual renewal.

The Kennedy Memorial is then a diplomatic gift centred on respect for its subject. In making the gift, the UK government would have had in mind the complementary objective of highlighting the special relationship between the two countries, a cornerstone of post-war British foreign policy.[10] The memorial was inaugurated on 14 May 1965, in the presence of Her Majesty the Queen, British Prime Minister Harold Wilson, US Secretary of State Dean Rusk and President Kennedy's widow and her children. The speeches celebrated President Kennedy's vision and achievements, but celebrated too the shared heritage of the two countries, and the shared values evoked by the liberties enshrined in the Magna Carta. The Kennedy Memorial was a diplomatic gift designed both to honour the life of President Kennedy and to underline the close friendship and worldview of the two countries. The second part of the gift, the Kennedy Scholarships, ensured that it would continue to build ties between the two countries long into the future. The memorial is then an enduring gift, and even though with the passage of time and reassessments of Kennedy's presidency the context in which it is set has changed,[11] it remains a statement of both respect and alliance.

1969

FOUR SPECKS OF MOON ROCK

A GIFT FROM RICHARD NIXON, PRESIDENT OF THE UNITED STATES OF AMERICA, TO THE PEOPLE OF MALTA

The Maltese Apollo 11 moon rock.

The Gozo Nature Museum is housed in an elegant seventeenth-century limestone building within the citadel overlooking Victoria, the diminutive capital of Gozo, the second island of the Maltese archipelago. The museum is a decidedly traditional example of its kind, with display cases bearing labels like 'varieties of quartz', 'coleoptera' and 'bivalves from Gozo'. There is an alligator skin from Venezuela, and numerous stuffed birds.

The vaulted entrance hall hosts a display of stalactites and stalagmites. At the back is a display case containing a small wooden podium, on top of which is laid out a miniature Maltese flag. Above the flag is a half-spherical acrylic dome containing what look like four specks of black grit. There are two inscriptions on the base of the podium. One reads: 'This flag of your nation was carried to the Moon and back by Apollo 11, and this fragment of the Moon's surface was brought to Earth by the crew of that first manned lunar landing.' The second inscription identifies the donor of the gift. 'Presented to the people of Malta by Richard Nixon. President of the United States of America.'

The Apollo 11 moon landing in July 1969, with Commander Neil Armstrong's description of 'one giant leap for mankind' broadcast around the world, was a defining moment of the Sixties. It fulfilled President Kennedy's 1961 vision statement of landing a man on the moon in the decade, still beloved by leadership training programmes everywhere, and ended the Space Race with the USSR. It was hardly a surprise then that President Nixon was keen to crow about it.

In November, he commissioned NASA to put together displays for around 135 nations around the world, along with one for each US State and possession.[1] The format of each was standardised: a flag of the country or State, and four small particles of the moon weighing a total of 0.05 grammes, housed in a magnifying acrylic dome. Each nation received the same wording, with the apparent exception of Venezuela, following the discovery that Apollo 11 had inadvertently headed into space without a Venezuelan flag on board. One was taken on the Apollo 12 mission instead, and the wording on the Venezuelan inscription omitted the specific reference to Apollo 11.[2]

As a diplomatic gift, these tiny souvenirs of the moon offered considerable advantages for Nixon. First, the moon landings had captured the world's imagination, and such gifts would be highly desirable for their recipients. Perhaps however not in Moscow, a consideration that points to the second benefit of the gifts for the US president: that they underlined the US achievement, its technological strength and its victory in the race to the moon.

Such was the power of these gifts that Nixon repeated the exercise. The first diplomatic gifting of lunar material celebrated the first moon landing. The second round of gifts commemorated the last.

This second gift of moon rock was a carefully prepared piece of public relations. As the Apollo 17 moon landing came to its conclusion, and towards the end of his final moonwalk, astronaut Eugene Cernan made a speech. Its subject was a small rock his fellow astronaut and geologist Harrison 'Jack' Schmitt had just picked up from the Taurus–Littrow Valley on the surface of the moon. It was, said Cernan, a 'very significant rock'. It was composed of many fragments of different sizes, shapes and colours, which might have come from all parts of the moon and had grown together to become a cohesive rock, 'sort of living together in a very coherent, very peaceful manner'. Their wish, said Cernan, was to share this rock with countries around the world, as a 'symbol of mankind: that we can live in peace and harmony in the future'.[3] Beyond sounding rather like a hippie manifesto, this is putting a lot of pressure on a rock.

The rock collected by Schmitt, given the prosaic name Sample 70017, was broken into small fragments, and each incorporated into a gift item strongly resembling the Apollo 11 gift, complete with miniature flag that had been flown to the moon, wooden podium, and acrylic dome. These were again sent to foreign heads of state as well as to the US States and possessions. The backdrop was very different. The Apollo 11 gifts had been despatched in a climate of global excitement about the moon landings: those of Apollo 17 went out to waning public interest in the programme, which was curtailed in the face of high costs. The planned Apollo 18, 19 and 20 missions were scrapped. In a letter accompanying the gifts to foreign heads of state dated 21 March 1973, Nixon framed his present as a mark of the successful conclusion of the Apollo lunar landing programme. He described it as an international effort, though making clear that it had been conducted by the United States. He offered a grand wish: 'If people of many nations can act together to achieve the dreams of humanity in space, then surely we can act together to accomplish humanity's dream of peace here on earth.'[4]

The subsequent story of these gifted rocks has not however always placed them in the role of symbols of humanity's dream of peace on earth. Baser considerations have sometimes sadly prevailed. As they were sent out as gifts, the rocks are no longer tracked by NASA, unlike other samples of moon rock collected during the Apollo missions. While many are on display at museums around the world, the whereabouts of others are unknown. Some have been sold for profit. Two very different American citizens have played an important role in efforts to keep track of the gifted rocks, and to return to their intended recipients those that have gone astray: Robert Pearlman, a space historian whose website CollectSPACE. com catalogues all the known gifted moon rocks, and Joseph Gutheinz Jr, a retired NASA special agent and moon rock hunter.

While working at NASA, Gutheinz attempted to address the trade in fake moon rocks, which had been an issue ever since the first moon landing. The first reported sale came in 1969, when a Miami housewife paid $5 to a door-to-door salesman.[5] Seeking to snare fake moon rock peddlers, in 1998 Gutheinz took out an advertisement in USA Today, headed 'Moon Rocks Wanted', and pretended to be a broker for a rich client in search of moon rock. The bait was taken, not by a fake rock peddler but by someone seeking to sell a genuine gifted rock. It was an American named Alan

Rosen, a fruit buyer for a juice company, who was trying to sell the Apollo 17 moon rock gifted to Honduras. This had been sold to him by a retired Honduran colonel named Roberto Agurcia Ugarte, who claimed to have been given it by deposed president López Arellano.

Rosen was reportedly seeking 5 million dollars for the rock, which gives some indication both of the attractiveness of Nixon's diplomatic gift and the temptations around onward sales. He insisted on evidence that the buyer had the funds. Gutheinz was able to proceed with the sting operation thanks to the support of patriotic Texan billionaire and one time US presidential candidate Ross Perot. The meet was arranged at a restaurant in North Miami Beach, where the rock was duly seized by an undercover customs officer, on the basis that it had been imported illegally into the United States. It was presented to Honduran President Ricardo Maduro in 2004 and is now on display in the Honduran capital, Tegucigalpa.[6]

The Apollo 17 moon rock destined for Cyprus was another sample to have had a colourful fate. Cyprus in the early 1970s was a febrile place, with growing tension between the Greek and Turkish Cypriot communities. The US embassy in Nicosia held off presenting the rock to the president of Cyprus, over worries that the use of the official Cyprus flag in the display might anger those favouring union with Greece, and over the difficulties in ensuring a balanced representation of both communities in a presentation ceremony.[7] Events worsened rapidly with the 1974 *coup d'état*, which replaced President Makarios with an irredentist figure close to the Greek junta, and the resultant Turkish invasion and division of the island. The US ambassador, Rodger Davies, was tragically shot by a sniper during a demonstration by Greek Cypriots, angered that the United States had not acted to stop the Turkish invasion. In the ensuing chaos, the goodwill moon rock appears to have been retained by a diplomat at the US embassy and was found after his death by his son, who was eventually persuaded to return it to NASA.[8]

The Apollo 11 gift to Nicaraguan dictator Anastasio Somoza Debayle was apparently pilfered by a Costa Rican mercenary turned rebel, who sold it to a Baptist missionary named Harry Coates. He then sold it on to legendary Las Vegas gambler Bob Stupak, reportedly for $10,000 and 200,000 shares in Stupak's casino, revealing a rather unmissionary-like interest in the world of gambling. Following Stupak's death, the gift has been returned to Nicaragua, by way of NASA.

The fate of the goodwill rocks is most frequently unclear in states whose recent histories have featured revolutions or conflict. The whereabouts of rocks gifted to Afghanistan and Libya are for example unknown. Other gifted rocks have met a range of unfortunate fates. Malta's Apollo 17 gift was stolen from a museum in 2004. Following a fire at Dublin's Dunsink Observatory in 1977, Ireland's Apollo 11 moon rock seems to have simply been disposed of along with other debris; those valuable four tiny specks now lie somewhere within the Finglas landfill. Fortunately, many of these goodwill rocks are, like the Maltese Apollo 11 gift, kept on display in museums around the world, where they continue to enthuse young people with the excitement of space exploration. So, if not quite meeting Eugene Cernan's expectations, the goodwill rocks have overall proved their worth as diplomatic gifts.

1972

TWO PANDAS

A GIFT FROM THE PEOPLE OF CHINA
TO THE PEOPLE OF JAPAN

One of the crates used to transport the pandas gifted by China to the United States
following President Nixon's visit in 1972.

The welcoming party at Ueno Zoo included key members of the Japanese
political elite, including Cabinet Secretary Nikaidō Susumu and the mayor
of Tokyo. An orangutan named Miyo pulled a string on a piñata, bringing
down a banner that announced: 'Welcome to the Giant Pandas, Kang Kang
and Lan Lan.'[1] A curtain was pulled back to reveal the two cuddly
celebrities.

In the days following this official arrival ceremony on 4 November 1972,
the Japanese public were able to view the pandas. Huge queues formed
outside the zoo's new Panda Gate, rather appropriately titled 'Pandamon'
in view of the pandemonium caused by the animals. By mid-morning on
the first day of exhibition, almost 20,000 people had gathered,[2] with a
queue more than a kilometre long. Visitors were able to linger before the
pandas for just a few seconds before they were urged to keep going. The

stress provoked by this mass adulation was such that Lan Lan collapsed on 7 November. Exhibition hours were substantially reduced thereafter.

The delivery of Kang Kang and Lan Lan to Tokyo's Ueno Zoo is part of a long history of Chinese use of giant pandas as diplomatic gifts. Two pandas were presented to Japan during the Tang dynasty more than a millennium earlier.[3] Under Mao Zedong, the People's Republic of China embraced pandas as a favoured prestige diplomatic gift. Three characteristics of pandas made them particularly suited for the role. First, the panda is clearly and exclusively Chinese: it is found nowhere else in the wild. It serves therefore as a readily identifiable calling card for the country. Second, it is utterly cute: it thaws the iciest of hearts. Third, its rarity outside China, combined with that cuteness, made the panda highly sought after; a panda could transform the finances of a zoo. As a diplomatic gift, pandas would thus both be welcomed by the recipient and would serve as an instrument of Chinese soft power wherever they were exhibited.

An early focus of the panda diplomacy of the People's Republic of China was on the two superpowers of the time, the United States and the Soviet Union, into whose ranks China was keen to be admitted. The first of Mao's panda gifts was Ping Ping, sent to Moscow Zoo in 1957, followed by An An two years later.[4] The repeated names characteristic of gifted pandas are apparently a cute Chinese diminutive, as if these gifts needed to be any cuter. North Korea came next, and was to receive five pandas between 1965 and 1980.[5]

The most famous of all the panda gifts came in 1972, with the historic visit to China in February of US President Richard Nixon. Ling-Ling and Hsing-Hsing were despatched to Washington, with first lady Pat Nixon among those present at the dedication of the new Panda House on 20 April.[6] Pat Nixon plays a starring role in accounts of how the gift came about, a tale that involved her seated at dinner in Beijing next to the Chinese premier, Zhou Enlai. Noticing pandas depicted on a cigarette packet on the table, she said something about the cuteness of the animals, prompting her host to offer to give her some.[7] Another, I fear less likely, version of the same tale puts the gift down to an interpreter's error, when the first lady had actually been intent on cadging one of the Chinese premier's panda-branded cigarettes.[8] President Nixon sent a pair of musk oxen to China as a return gift.

While President Nixon did not it seems go to China with any specific intent of persuading his hosts to gift pandas, this is not true of later visitors. For them, the attractiveness of a panda gift was further accentuated by a desire to be treated by the Chinese in the same category as the superpowers of the United States and USSR, and considered worthy of pandas.

Japanese Prime Minister Tanaka Kakuei's visit to China in September 1972 was a historic one. The two countries had been estranged since the Second World War. Japanese policy towards the People's Republic of China had been in step with that of the United States; and Nixon's visit to Beijing had driven a coach and horses through that. The economic measures of the so-called 'Nixon shock' in 1971, including the abandonment of the gold standard and introduction of a 10 per cent import surcharge, had also created huge challenges for Japan's US-focused export-led economy. Tanaka believed that Japan therefore needed to normalise its relations with China. The political heart of the visit lay in a joint statement allowing for the normalisation of ties, in which, inter alia, China agreed to renounce claims for war reparations against Japan, and the latter expressed 'understanding and respect' for the position of the People's Republic of China on the status of Taiwan.

Pandas were also part of Tanaka's wish list. Tokyo's Ueno Zoo played its part in encouraging the Chinese to think about animal-related gifting, by sending Beijing Zoo just ahead of the visit a pair of black swans and another of chimpanzees. The Chinese zoo reciprocated with black cranes and storks.[9] Japan was to get its wish. Cabinet Secretary Nikaidō announced during a live broadcast following the diplomatic talks that the Japanese people were to receive from their Chinese counterparts a gift of a pair of pandas.[10] The Japanese sent to Beijing Zoo as a rather more modest return gift a pair of the antelope-like serows.

There was fierce competition in Japan to be associated with the Chinese gift. Ueno Zoo fought off bids from Kyoto, Osaka and elsewhere for the right to accommodate the pandas. The nation's flag carrier, Japan Airlines, won out against lobbying from All Nippon Airways for the honour of bringing them from China, the latter having argued that their role in conveying Ueno Zoo's animal gifts to Beijing made them more experienced at this kind of task.[11] The pandas were big business. Japanese toy manufacturers would sell more than 10 billion yen worth of panda-themed merchandise in the first three months following the arrival of Kang Kang and Lan Lan in Tokyo.[12] In one key respect, the pandas served better as a symbol of the improved bilateral relationship between Japan and China than did the substance of the joint statement: their simplicity as adorable creatures meant that they evoked no problematic recollections of the conflicts and controversies of the past.

One task assigned to Kang Kang and Lan Lan was however not straight-forward: the production of a baby panda. China's panda diplomatic gifts usually take the form of a pair, one male, one female, mimicking the arrival of animals on to Noah's Ark. There is a clear expectation of repro-duction; important for the survival of the species given its low population numbers in the wild, and enormously lucrative for the zoos concerned, since the only animal cuter than a panda is a baby panda. This has proved however a remarkably difficult task. A female panda has just one oestrous cycle annually, and is only fertile for between one and three days. While in the wild a female panda may mate with several males while in oestrus, in captivity her options are of course more limited. Zoos struggled to imitate the conditions of the pandas' complex mating rituals. The track record of successful births from pandas in captivity is poor.

Lan Lan did eventually become pregnant but sadly died of pregnancy-induced toxaemia.[13] Kang Kang also died young. Replacement pandas were high on the objectives of the visits to China of Japanese prime min-isters in 1979 and 1982, and two new gifted pandas, Fei Fei and Huan Huan, took up residence at Ueno Zoo. It rapidly became clear however that these two pandas could not stand each other. Artificial insemination was the solution alighted on, using semen collected from the sedated Fei Fei, and Huan Huan would give birth to three baby pandas through this process, albeit inadvertently crushing the first soon after birth.[14]

Panda diplomacy remains an important part of China's soft power arse-nal. The way pandas are given has however changed markedly. Since 1984, China has no longer offered pandas as diplomatic gifts, but rather on loan. The change in approach is perhaps down to two main factors. First, con-servation. Pandas are not just a symbol of China, but of the wildlife con-servation movement as a whole. Chi Chi, a panda purchased by London Zoo in 1958 from an animal broker, inspired the original logo of the World Wildlife Fund, now the World Wide Fund for Nature (WWF).[15] The spe-cies was moved in 1984 to Appendix 1, the most highly regulated category, of the Convention on International Trade in Endangered Species (CITES), in part in response to WWF surveys indicating that the wild panda popula-tion was more precarious than had been thought.[16] Simply gifting pandas as a diplomatic offering seemed out of step with the conservation impera-tive. The second factor was the rise to power of Deng Xiaoping in 1978 and the move towards a combination of socialist ideology and free enter-prise which legitimised the use of a capitalist lease model to secure reve-nue from China's pandas.

The model adopted in 1984 was a rent-a-panda scheme involving short-term leases of pandas to major zoos, with North America featuring prominently among the destinations. This scheme quickly attracted controversy on conservation grounds, as it was difficult to reconcile with the CITES requirement that trade in species listed under Appendix 1 was allowable only for scientific reasons.[17]

A revised programme, framed around cooperative breeding, was launched in 1994.[18] This scheme involved much longer loans, typically for ten years at a total cost of 10 million dollars. The lease fees supported the implementation of a giant panda management plan drawn up in collaboration between the WWF and the Chinese authorities.[19] The successful breeding of pandas in captivity is a core part of the programme: cubs born overseas through the programme are the property of China, and under a typical agreement are repatriated at the age of four.[20] The devastating Sichuan earthquake of 2008 prompted an expansion of the scheme, both to provide funds to support the reconstruction of the Wolong nature reserve and breeding centre, damaged in the earthquake, and to help in rehousing pandas from the centre.[21]

Although pandas are now loaned rather than gifted, the Chinese have remained selective in agreeing loan deals, which are signed at the government level.[22] From the perspective of the zoos themselves, the loan of a panda is a commercial proposition, and one not to be taken lightly, given the costs involved, from the loan agreement itself to the construction of appropriate accommodation and sourcing the industrial quantities of bamboo consumed by the animals. The Chinese also consider the loan a diplomatic proposition, and they frequently accompany the negotiation of important trade deals.[23] It is possible to see the panda loans as part of the Chinese system of *guanxi*, the building of productive relationships underpinned by reciprocal commitments and trust.[24] In this sense, the shared care for the precious pandas underscores the joint commitment to the wider commercial relationship.

China's panda diplomacy has evolved then from the use of pandas as iconic diplomatic gifts to something more complex: deals with both commercial and conservation objectives but in which diplomacy is still important. That the deals are able to fulfil these multiple roles is down to one central fact: people like pandas.

1973

DIAMONDS

A GIFT FROM JEAN-BÉDEL BOKASSA, PRESIDENT OF THE CENTRAL AFRICAN REPUBLIC, TO VALÉRY GISCARD D'ESTAING, MINISTER OF THE ECONOMY AND FINANCE OF FRANCE

Valéry Giscard d'Estaing, photographed when president of France in 1975.

In emphasising that diplomatic gifts serve the objectives of the giver, we have explored some of the potential risks for the recipient. The hazy line between gift and bribe has been a perennial minefield, and one that, as we have seen, has been interpreted in different ways in different political cultures.

As a rule, the dangers increase for the recipient as the value of the gift rises and where the giver is not a friend or ally of the receiving state, or is otherwise considered beyond the pale. These dangers were marked when the president of the Central African Republic, Jean-Bédel Bokassa, reportedly made several gifts of diamonds to Valéry Giscard d'Estaing, the French minister of economy and finance, and later president, during the early 1970s. The gifts provoked a political scandal, *l'affaire des diamants*, which contributed to Giscard d'Estaing's defeat in the French presidential election of 1981.

The seeds of the diamond affair lay in part in the structure of French political engagement with Africa in the early decades of the French Fifth Republic, and in part more specifically in Giscard d'Estaing's personal interest in the Central African Republic. As former French colonies in Sub-Saharan Africa gained independence, France developed a distinctive relationship with these newly independent states characterised by strong personal engagement between the French president and their leaders, forming something akin to a family bloc.[1]

The arrangement provided France with a region in which its influence dominated, confirming its global status as a major power, and provided the newly independent states in return with aid, technical assistance and military security.[2] The political model constructed to deliver this relationship under de Gaulle involved the centralisation of African policy within the president's office, linking it firmly with the president himself, who therefore became the focus of attention for African leaders seeking support.[3] Under both de Gaulle and his successor Georges Pompidou, the influential Jacques Foccart, the president's secretary-general for African and Malagasy affairs, was responsible for delivering this policy.

Giscard d'Estaing replaced Foccart with his own adviser, René Journiac, whose position was more junior, reflecting Giscard's determination to strengthen even further the personal involvement of the president in guiding Africa policy.[4] This centralisation of French policy towards Sub-Saharan Africa in the hands of the president brought with it risks, including that of the head of state getting embroiled in personalised dealings with controversial leaders. These risks were increased in relation to the Central African Republic because of Giscard's personal interest in that country, which he visited on several occasions on private big game hunting trips.

The risks for the French president were further magnified by the problematic character of the ruler of the Central African Republic. Jean-Bédel Bokassa was a veteran of the French army, having seen combat in Indochina, receiving both a *Croix de guerre* and membership of the Légion d'honneur, and eventually reaching the rank of captain. Following the independence of the Central African Republic in 1960, Bokassa, a cousin of the new country's president, David Dacko, was entrusted with creating its armed forces, becoming commander-in-chief. On New Year's Eve 1965, against a backdrop of economic stagnation and political mismanagement, Bokassa's *coup d'état* removed Dacko and his government, installing himself at the helm of a new Revolutionary Council. Bokassa ditched the constitution and dissolved the National Assembly, ruling in an increasingly personal manner.[5]

The combination of brutality and eccentricity characterising Bokassa's rule represented a growing embarrassment and challenge for his French allies.[6] In 1976, Bokassa transformed the country into the Central African Empire, designating himself as His Imperial Majesty Bokassa I. The French government reluctantly provided support for his lavish coronation on 4 December 1977, an event modelled on that of Napoléon I as emperor of the French in 1804. The imperial crown, made by Parisian jewellers Arthus-Bertrand, had an 80-carat diamond in the centre, and the total cost of the crown jewels was reported to be $5 million. Eight white horses were sourced from Belgium for the emperor's carriage, sixty new Mercedes cars were acquired to ferry the visiting guests, and 64,000 bottles of wine were purchased to lubricate the celebrations.[7] Not a single foreign head of state attended, not even Giscard d'Estaing, though France did send its minister of cooperation, Robert Galley, who brought with him a diplomatic gift from the French president of a Napoléonic-era sabre,[8] a present in tune with the new emperor's fantasies.

French concerns about Bokassa boiled over in 1979. There were deaths during food riots at the start of the year. The sequence of events precipitating his downfall started with a dispute over school uniforms. In April, students complained about a new requirement to wear expensive uniforms bearing Bokassa's image and produced by a company owned by a relative of His Imperial Majesty.[9] Many students were arrested, and the following month Amnesty International reported that up to 100 had been murdered by Bokassa's imperial guard.[10] When in August a report by a five-nation commission of jurists set up by the Organisation of African Unity substantially supported Amnesty International's claims and concluded that Bokassa had almost certainly been involved in the killings, France resolved to act. On 20 September 1979, taking advantage of Bokassa's absence from the country on a visit to seek support from Libyan leader Muammar Gaddafi, members of two French parachute regiments flew into Bangui in an operation to oust His Imperial Majesty and restore David Dacko. The operation, codenamed Barracuda, proceeded without bloodshed. Bokassa fled to France and was later accommodated in a suburb of Abidjan courtesy of Félix Houphouët-Boigny, president of Côte d'Ivoire.[11] As French troops investigated Bokassa's residences in Bangui, gruesome discoveries were reported, including two human cadavers trussed up in a walk-in freezer, sparking tales of cannibalism, and bone fragments from some thirty people who had apparently been eaten by crocodiles kept in a lake in the grounds.[12]

Bokassa had been deposed, but now the horrors of his regime were clear, the previous closeness of the former leader of the Central African Republic and, indeed, Empire to the French president now had the capacity to do the latter harm, as subsequent events were to prove.

On 10 October 1979, the French satirical weekly *Le Canard enchaîné* published an apparent photostat of an order signed by Bokassa in 1973 for the gifting of diamonds of a total of 30 carats to Giscard d'Estaing, then the French minister of the economy and finance. Journalists speculated that the actions of the French troops during Operation Barracuda in seizing Bokassa's files and transferring them to the French embassy in Bangui had been an attempt to cover up the Central African Republic leader's embarrassing gifts to the French president.[13] The daily *Le Monde* entered the fray, supporting the demands of the opposition Socialist Party for an inquiry into the affair.[14] The next edition of *Le Canard enchaîné* claimed that Giscard had received diamonds from Bokassa on other occasions, during both private and official visits to the Central African Republic, as both minister and president. Relatives of Giscard, as well as Journiac and two ministers of his government, including Galley, were also reported to have received diamonds from Bokassa.

In the face of presidential denials about the claims made in the press, *l'affaire des diamants* was further fuelled by a desire for revenge on the part of Bokassa for having been ousted by the French president. This was a case of the originator of a diplomatic gift deliberately using that gift against the recipient after the relationship between the two had soured. In 1980, from his exile in Côte d'Ivoire, Bokassa managed to pass documents to a journalist and former war correspondent named Roger Delpey. The latter was arrested in Paris on charges of allegedly aiding Libya against France, and Bokassa's documents were seized.[15] Delpey ended up in detention for seven months, although the charges against him were later dropped.

The French presidential election of 1981 was now fast approaching, with the first round of voting scheduled for 26 April. Giscard d'Estaing was seeking re-election and had long been expected to win, not least because of the disunity of the left. His opponents, however, saw the rumbling saga of the diamond affair as an opportunity to attack the president. On 10 March, at a pre-election broadcast on the TF1 television channel, Giscard attempted to put the matter to rest. The value of Bokassa's gift had been vastly exaggerated, he claimed. 'They were not big stones',[16] barely worth the name diamonds at all. In any case, the jewels had been sold, and the money donated to the Red Cross and other charities in the Central African Republic.[17]

This interview failed to achieve its goal of drawing a line under the affair. *Le Canard enchaîné* responded with the publication of a telegram attributed to Jeanne-Marie Ruth-Rolland, president of the Central African Red Cross, claiming that the organisation had received no donation from the president.[18] This resulted in a rather awkward clarification from the presidential administration, specifying that the donation had been made only on 4 February, and that it had gone to the administration of David Dacko for onward transmission. The latter confirmed the receipt of the donation, which had been of $8,000.[19]

Matters went from bad to worse for the French president. Roger Delpey published his book covering the affair, *La manipulation*, which claimed that Giscard had received some 200 diamonds from Bokassa over these years, suggesting if true a value far higher than the $8,000 donated to Central African charities.[20] On 8 May, just two days before the second round of voting in the presidential election, which pitched Giscard in a run-off against the Socialist Party candidate, François Mitterrand, Bokassa gave an interview to *The Washington Post*. Over conversations lasting some six hours, Bokassa was quite open that his motive in speaking to the newspaper was to attempt to scupper Giscard's chances of re-election in revenge for the French president's role in bringing down his regime.[21] Bokassa claimed he had given gifts of diamonds to Giscard d'Estaing on four separate occasions, each time in the presence of witnesses, including some individually large stones, and that he had made a further substantial diamond gift to Giscard's wife, Anne-Aymone. His gifts to Giscard, claimed Bokassa, had also included a large hunting ground.[22]

The French presidential election was won by Mitterrand, with a margin of more than a million votes. Followed by the striking success of the Socialist Party in legislative elections the following month, Mitterrand's victory heralded a profound change in the French political landscape.[23] *L'affaire des diamants* was by no means the only factor behind Giscard's defeat, nor was it probably the most important. It was however a contributory factor. If diamonds are forever, so too, as Giscard d'Estaing was to discover, are the circumstances in which they are given.

2004

A BOX OF COHIBA LANCEROS CIGARS

A GIFT FROM FIDEL CASTRO, PRESIDENT OF CUBA, TO ANDRÉ BAUER, LIEUTENANT GOVERNOR OF SOUTH CAROLINA

A box of Cohiba Lanceros cigars.

The veteran daily newspaper of Charleston, South Carolina, *The Post and Courier*, reported in May 2019 that a diplomatic gift received by a former lieutenant governor of the state, a Republican named André Bauer, was being advertised on the website of Boston auctioneers RR Auction, with an estimated value of some $10,000. It was described as a wooden cigar box containing twenty-five handmade Cuban Cohiba Lanceros cigars, with the signature of Cuban President Fidel Castro scrawled in black felt tip on the box. The gift dated from a 2004 trade mission to Cuba in which Bauer had participated. Bauer, a non-smoker, was quoted as revealing that the cigars had languished in a closet following his trip to Havana.[1]

A range of potential questions arises from this press report. Cigar smokers might lament the probable damage to the quality of these rare cigars from their incarceration for fifteen years in a closet, and the press article indeed quotes Bobby Livingston, executive vice-president of RR Auction, as admitting that the cigars were not considered in good smoking condition.[2] Others might raise eyebrows over the retention and later offer for sale of the gift. We will put such questions to one side and focus instead on the context against which the gift was made, and in particular on the choice of gift.

Bauer visited Cuba in 2004 as the head of a trade delegation from South Carolina put together by Jack Maybank, president of Maybank Shipping. Maybank was one of the businessmen to take advantage of the slight relaxation in 2000 of the US trade embargo on Cuba, permitting cash-paid shipments of certain agricultural and medical products. A Maybank barge named *Helen III*, which arrived in Havana harbour in July 2003, was the first to carry cargo under a US flag and with a US crew since the start of the embargo more than forty years previously.[3] A US flag was flown in greeting from the fort at the harbour entrance.

The delegation were wrapping up a dinner meeting with Cuban trade officials, held in one of the government-owned 'protocol' houses dotted across Havana. They were pleased with the outcome of their mission: an agreement from the Cuban government to purchase $10 million of agricultural produce from the farmers of South Carolina.[4] There had been suggestions during the visit of a possible meeting with the Cuban president, but they had been warned that this could not be guaranteed.

Something was clearly up when Cuban officials started pacing nervously and peering out of the window, while a maid cleared a place in the centre of the table. A convoy of three black Mercedes cars turned up, and Castro entered, attired in his familiar green military-style uniform. A three-hour meeting followed, lasting beyond midnight, with Castro doing most of the talking, on everything from world hunger to education, reportedly resisting all attempts by Bauer to steer the conversation towards more concrete matters of US–Cuban relations. Gifts were exchanged at the end of the meeting. Castro was presented with a crystal candelabra and a pair of cufflinks bearing the seal of South Carolina. He in turn presented the delegation with Cohiba cigars, in personally autographed wooden boxes.[5]

The Cohiba is no ordinary brand of cigar. It was established in the 1960s as a brand produced in small quantities, exclusive to Castro, and used by the Cuban president for diplomatic gifts. It was not available on a commercial basis until 1982. Castro recounted the story of the brand in another late evening discussion with an American, in this case a meeting in Havana in 1994 with Marvin Shanken, the publisher of *Cigar Aficionado* magazine. Castro recalled that he had been introduced to cigar smoking and wine drinking at the age of fifteen by his father. One day, Castro had been taken by the particularly fine aroma of a cigar being smoked by one of his body-guards, and had enquired about it. The bodyguard told him that they were handmade for him by a friend. Castro got in touch with the friend, whose cigar-making secrets formed the basis of production at a factory set up for the task, named El Laguito.[6] The new cigars were named Cohiba, derived from the word for tobacco of the Taíno, the indigenous people of Cuba. Castro both smoked Cohibas himself and gave them as presents. At least he had smoked Cohibas until giving up cigar smoking in 1985, when he felt it would not be right to continue to smoke at the same time as leading a campaign in Cuba drawing attention to the associated health risks.[7]

The use of Cohiba Lanceros cigars as diplomatic gifts had two important advantages for Castro. First, because the brand was so closely identified with the Cuban leader they served to demonstrate the personal nature of the gift; the recipient was presented with cigars perceived as Castro's own. Second, they served as an advertisement for the Cuban cigar industry at a time when it needed to reassert its credentials as the best in the world.

Cigar smoking was practised by the indigenous Taíno and quickly embraced by the Spanish, who brought the habit to the Old World and cultivated tobacco crops in Cuba to meet the burgeoning demand for the product. The discovery that the longevity of cigars was improved by rolling them before they were shipped, rather than in Spanish factories, spawned the growth of cigar factories in Cuba. In 1817, Fernando VII of Spain lifted the century-old tobacco monopoly, which was impeding the growth of the industry,[8] allowing free trade between Cuba and the rest of the world and stimulating a golden age for the Cuban cigar industry. Cigars were both a major export for Cuba and a central part of the brand both of the country and its capital, Havana. The Cuban Revolution posed two challenges for the industry: the exodus of the cigar barons, whose properties were seized, and the imposition of the embargo by the United States, both fac-tors promoting the rise of rival producers of premium cigars in countries such as the Dominican Republic and Honduras. The use as diplomatic gifts of an exclusive brand of cigars was part of an effort to cement the identi-fication of the country with the product and boost the reputation and exports of its premium varieties.

A specific strand of Cuban cigar diplomacy has been that directed towards the United States. In almost every attempt over the decades since the introduction of sanctions to establish some modest unfreezing of rela-tions, the gifting by Cuba of cigars has played a part.[9] It relied on the fact

289

that, while US sanctions prohibited the importation of Cuban cigars into the United States, for American cigar smokers, many in positions of power, Cuban cigars were highly desired as a quality product, the embargo serving to give them an added allure of unattainability. The attraction of Cuban cigars for some American leaders is nicely demonstrated by one widely circulated anecdote dating from February 1962. President Kennedy is said to have summoned his head of press, Pierre Salinger, a fellow cigar smoker, into his office, and asked Pierre to get him 'a lot of cigars' for the next morning. He had in mind 1,000 of his favoured Cuban Petit Upmanns. The enterprising Salinger managed to get hold of 1,200. On informing the president of his success, Kennedy promptly signed the executive order expanding the embargo to include all imports of goods containing Cuban products.[10]

In August 1961, just a few months after the failed Bay of Pigs invasion, a young aide to President Kennedy named Richard Goodwin was a member of the US delegation to a conference in Uruguay of Latin American foreign ministers, to discuss the US Alliance for Progress initiative (which Cuba opposed). Che Guevara, head of the Cuban delegation, spotted that Goodwin was a cigar smoker, and sent round to him a gift of Cuban cigars in a mahogany box, as a gift for Kennedy. Guevara had included a handwritten note, which read: 'To write to the enemy is difficult. I limit myself to extending my hand.'[11] Guevara set up a meeting with Goodwin, where they talked into the night, discussing prospects for peaceful coexistence while recognising that the two countries were not destined to be allies. Goodwin briefed Kennedy on the meeting and handed over the cigars. Kennedy reportedly immediately took one out of the box, bit the end off and lit it up.[12]

A proposal by Secretary of State Henry Kissinger in the summer of 1974 to set up a channel for bilateral discussions was conveyed to Castro by way of an unsigned handwritten note delivered by journalist and political adviser Frank Mankiewicz during a visit to Cuba. Castro's handwritten response, agreeing to secret meetings, was accompanied by a box of Cuban cigars for Kissinger.[13] The initiative came to nought, any prospect of reconciliation dashed by the despatch by Cuba in 1975 of troops to Angola to support the communist MPLA in the civil war.

In 1980, another US envoy was sent to Cuba. Peter Tarnoff, an assistant to the secretary of state, Edmund Muskie, was charged with negotiating a resolution to the mass exodus of Cubans to Florida, an episode known as the Mariel Boatlift. Castro agreed to stem the exodus, perhaps in part to help Jimmy Carter's re-election prospects. Tarnoff returned with a gift of cigars from Castro to Muskie.[14] Carter lost, and the election of Ronald Reagan quashed any early hopes of a restoration of dialogue.

In the charged political atmosphere of Cuban–US relations, the act of receiving gifts of cigars from the Cuban president carried domestic risk for US politicians. At the start of 1996, a New Mexico congressman and future presidential candidate named Bill Richardson, with something of a reputation for humanitarian missions, returned from a visit to Havana in which he had been trying to secure the release of political prisoners. He brought with him a gift from Castro for President Clinton: a box of Cohiba cigars. Richardson passed these to Richard Nuccio, Clinton's Cuban policy adviser, who consulted National Security Adviser Sandy Berger about the gift. The latter was alarmed at the implications of Clinton receiving a gift from Castro of a product banned in the United States and ordered their destruction. They never reached the president.[15]

The moves made under the Obama presidency towards more direct engagement with Cuba also provided an occasion for Cuban cigar diplomacy. The first face-to-face discussions between the leaders of the two countries for more than half a century took place in the margins of the Summit of the Americas in Panama on 11 April 2015, when Obama met with Raúl Castro. The latter gave Obama a whole array of cigar-related gifts. According to the State Department Office of the Chief of Protocol annual returns of gifts to federal employees from foreign government sources, these included in April 2015 some 205 cigars in a wooden humidor with a cigar cutter, and a separate gift of a box of cigars and lighter. Seven more boxes of cigars were gifted by the Cuban president in December. Cigars were not the sole item gifted: presents to the president and first lady included other emblems of Cuba, including a guayabera shirt, rum and CDs of Cuban music. One gift was evidently chosen to flatter its recipient: a wooden bust of Abraham Lincoln. But cigars dominate.[16]

Those twenty-five Cohiba Lanceros gifted to André Bauer are then just one small episode in a long history of Cuban use of cigars as diplomatic gifts in its relationship with the United States.

2007

A STADIUM

A GIFT FROM THE GOVERNMENT AND PEOPLE OF THE PEOPLE'S REPUBLIC OF CHINA TO THE GOVERNMENT AND PEOPLE OF THE COMMONWEALTH OF DOMINICA

Windsor Park Stadium, Roseau, Dominica.

Is overseas aid a gift? The act of a private citizen of a wealthy country in donating to a development charity appears to be not just a gift, but a decidedly pure form of gift. The initial donor and ultimate recipient do not know each other and there is no obligation, or indeed possibility, to reciprocate the gift. No social ties are created between the two.[1] That charitable donation from a private individual will however pass along a complex chain, in which international development charities will be working with non-government organisations in the recipient country, who are in turn supporting smaller grassroots organisations. Anthropologists Roderick Stirrat and Heiko Henkel have argued that what starts as a pure gift is subjected to the pressures of politics and patronage as it passes along this chain.[2]

Development professionals in both the governmental and non-governmental sectors are often reluctant to use the language of gifts to characterise the assistance they are providing. The terminology of the development world has moved away from expressions that imply giving: thus 'aid' has lost favour to 'development cooperation'; 'donor' and 'recipient' to 'development partners'. Assistance is less likely to be characterised by donor or recipient as a gift than, according to their politics and perspective, either a contract, underpinned by a binding agreement, or an entitlement, to which the recipients claim a right through the international human rights framework.[3]

In part, this reticence to use the language of the gift may be linked to an association of gift exchange with pre-modern cultures, thereby appearing to fit awkwardly with the goals of development. The language of the market feels more appropriate to the objectives of modernisation.[4]

The reluctance to define development assistance in the language of the gift also owes much to the consideration at the heart of Marcel Mauss's work, as we have seen in our introduction, of the importance of reciprocation. Development assistance if cast as a pure gift denies the possibility of reciprocation, and thus risks the humiliation of the recipient, placing them in a position of dependence. The response to this is to cast the relationship not in terms of a gift but as a partnership between organisations bringing different aspects of the solution to the development problem.[5]

The avoidance of the language of the gift to characterise overseas aid is not however universal. Geographer Emma Mawdsley draws a distinction between on the one hand the behaviour of the predominantly Western donors who are members of the Development Assistance Committee (DAC) of the Organisation for Economic Co-operation and Development and on the other the donors from the Global South, such as China, India and Brazil.[6] She argues that reluctance to use the language of the gift is more characteristic of the donors of the DAC group, because of the different models of development cooperation adopted by the two groups. It is possible to see the use of the language of partnership rather than gift among the DAC group countries, steeped in a popular tradition of aid as charitable giving, precisely as a means of attempting to avoid the negative social relationships of superiority and inferiority that would follow the casting of the donation as a pure, unreciprocated gift.

In contrast, Mawdsley argues that donors from the Global South frame their cooperation around the assertion of shared experience, and on securing win-win outcomes based on mutual opportunity.[7] Since, unlike Western donors, there is no attempt to deny the desire for a reciprocation of the gift, the casting of these aid transactions in the language of the gift becomes less problematic. Rather than an unreciprocated gift creating a relationship of inferiority and dependence, attention is focused not just on what is given but on what is received in return, whether resources, invest- ment opportunities or markets. The language used highlights mutual ben- efit and solidarity rather than charity.[8]

In October 2007, on the Caribbean 'nature island' of Dominica, a new stadium was opened to much excitement at Windsor Park on the outskirts of the capital, Roseau. With a total capacity of 12,000, the stadium fulfils sporting functions, including as a venue for international cricket matches, as well as cultural and political ones, playing host to the World Creole Music Festival and Dominica's Independence Day celebrations. The stadium was built as development assistance to Dominica from the People's Republic of China, but the language through which it was presented was that of the gift. Vince Henderson, Dominica's minister for education, human resource development, sports and youth affairs, announced proudly that 'this world- class facility was given to the people of Dominica as a gift by our friends: the government and people of the People's Republic of China'.[9]

The gift of Windsor Park Stadium is but one example of a Chinese strat- egy of 'stadium diplomacy' that saw the construction of more than 140 sports facilities across the developing world in the six decades after 1958.[10] In the late 1950s and 1960s, there was much stadium construction in socialist countries in Asia, sometimes supporting China's attempts to build its own international sporting profile during a period in which the conflict within the Olympic movement over the political status of Taiwan meant that the People's Republic of China was absent from the Olympic Games. This included Chinese gifts of stadia in Indonesia and Cambodia to host the Games of the New Emerging Forces (GANEFO) in 1963 and 1966, respectively.[11] China comfortably topped the medals table at both games.

The geographical spread of stadia gifted by China has since fanned out to embrace a wide range of developing countries, with noticeably strong coverage in Africa, the Caribbean and the Pacific. There has been an accel- eration in stadium building, particularly since 1990, with a further accel- eration after 2010, mirroring the growth in overall Chinese overseas aid expenditure.[12] The provision of overseas facilities to showcase Chinese sporting talent has long since fallen away as an objective of these stadium gifts. China has for example little conceivable expectation of requiring the use of a cricket stadium in Dominica.

Two main objectives seem instead to have dominated later projects. The first, underpinning many stadium projects in Africa, is in support of Chinese pursuit of mineral and energy resources needed to maintain its domestic economic growth. The second, at the heart of many of the projects in the Caribbean and Pacific, lies in its One-China policy, with stadia offered following a decision by the recipient country to cease diplomatic recognition of Taiwan.[13] Thus, the construction of Windsor Park stadium in Dominica was one of several projects agreed in March 2004 with the prime minister of Dominica, Roosevelt Skerrit, in return for that country severing links with Taiwan and establishing diplomatic relations with the People's Republic of China.[14]

Another Eastern Caribbean island, Grenada, similarly switched its support from Taiwan to the People's Republic of China in 2005 and was similarly rewarded with a stadium, the 20,000-capacity Queen's Park, opened in time to serve as one of the host stadia for the 2007 Cricket World Cup. The inauguration ceremony proved rather awkward for the donors, as the Royal Grenada Police Band inadvertently struck up the wrong anthem and treated the Chinese ambassador and other dignitaries to that of Taiwan.[15]

The use of stadia as gifts offers China considerable soft power opportunities. Stadia are highly visible buildings, becoming instant landmarks, used both by political elites and by the wider public attending sporting and cultural functions as well as national celebrations.[16] They showcase Chinese skills in designing and building large facilities. And they are cost effective for China. They are typically awarded to Chinese contractors, using imported Chinese labour, materials and equipment.

Stadia are typically offered as an option among a range of possible infrastructure projects, which might also include roads and government buildings.[17] The Chinese have not always gifted the full cost of the stadia, particularly in respect of the projects in Africa. Funding has often come as a mix of grant and concessionary loan, and in some cases, the host government has paid a significant portion of the cost. An example is the National Stadium of Tanzania, opened in 2007.

President Benjamin Mkapa had promised back in 2000 that he would build for Tanzania a modern 60,000-seat stadium before leaving office in 2005. He launched a tender for a strikingly ambitious project, won by a French construction company. But Tanzania was a Highly Indebted Poor Country (HIPC): under the terms of the 1996 HIPC initiative it qualified for debt relief, but only if it stuck to an austere spending programme. The construction of a new stadium did not fit that bill, and Mkapa reluctantly agreed to abandon the French project. He did not want to abandon his promise of building a stadium altogether, however, and turned to China. They provided some 20 million US dollars to construct a much cheaper stadium, delivered by the Beijing Construction Engineering Group. This was less than half of the cost of the project. The Tanzanians had to raise the rest.[18]

For Tanzania, building a new stadium was a symbol of its determination to secure international success in football, an approach accompanied by the recruitment of Brazilian coach Márcio Máximo to manage the national football team,[19] and was more broadly a symbol of national modernisation. During a short visit to Tanzania in June 2006, Chinese Premier Wen Jiabao addressed the Chinese workers at the stadium construction site, underlining their role as the builders of a monument to the friendship between the two countries.[20] For China then, this was not disinterested development assistance but a project for the mutual benefit of the two countries, helping Tanzania secure its goals while pursuing those of China.

The provision of COVID-19 vaccines to countries most in need offers another example of the two approaches at work, one couched in the language of partnership, the other in the language of the gift. The COVID-19 Vaccines Global Access initiative, better known as COVAX, is suffused with the language of partnership. Directed by the World Health Organization, Gavi, the Vaccine Alliance, and the Coalition for Epidemic Preparedness Innovations, COVAX seeks both to accelerate the development and manufacture of COVID-19 vaccines and to guarantee fair and equitable access for every country in the world. China was a rather late adherent to the COVAX initiative, in October 2020,[21] and has remained wedded to the bilateral provision of vaccines through the language of the diplomatic gift. Thus, at the beginning of February 2021, Pakistan took delivery of 500,000 doses of the Sinopharm vaccine, the first tranche of a Chinese gift of 1.2 million doses. The foreign minister of Pakistan, Shah Mahmood Qureshi, described the gift as 'practical proof' of the friendship between the two countries, while the Chinese ambassador to Pakistan called it a 'manifestation of our brotherhood'.[22] China is far from alone in this approach, and indeed the bilateral gifting of vaccines has also been deployed by other contributors to COVAX in parallel to their contributions to COVAX itself. The gift of health is a potent gift indeed.

2008

A PAIR OF R. M. WILLIAMS BOOTS

A GIFT FROM KEVIN RUDD, PRIME MINISTER OF AUSTRALIA, TO SUSILO BAMBANG YUDHOYONO, PRESIDENT OF INDONESIA

A pair of R. M. Williams boots.

Reginald Murray Williams was born in 1908 in a rural community in South Australia. In 1918, the family moved to Adelaide, but young Reginald missed life in the outback and at the age of just fifteen packed a bag and headed for the Australian bush, working at everything from lime burner to camel driver. Having learned leather working from a horseman known as Dollar Mick, and having settled back in Adelaide with a family, he began to produce leather goods, finding particular success with a range of riding boots. The fashioning of the upper of the boots from a single piece of leather has remained his company's hallmark.

Reginald's business expanded across the following decades, until he sold it in 1988. It has had several changes of ownership since then, including that of a consortium involving French luxury products behemoth Louis Vuitton Moët Hennessy, before being acquired by Australian private investment group Tattarang in 2020. Reginald himself died in 2003 at the age of ninety-five, leaving a legacy of a company whose boots have come to symbolise Australia, and particularly its outback.[1]

R. M. Williams boots have been the favoured footwear of many Australian politicians. Their appeal spans the political divide. They were frequently sported by centre-right Liberal Party leaders Tony Abbott and Malcolm Turnbull, but were particularly closely associated with former Labor Party leader Kevin Rudd, who was prime minister of Australia from 2007 to 2010, and again briefly in 2013. The Museum of Australian Democracy even included in a 'Prime Ministers of Australia' exhibition a pair of his black leather R. M. Williams riding boots. Displayed alongside an orange Hugo Boss silk tie, these were worn when he spoke in the Australian parliament in 2008 to make the National Apology to the Stolen Generations to those whose lives were blighted by past government policies of forced child removal and indigenous assimilation.[2] R. M. Williams boots were Kevin Rudd's footwear of choice when he met US President Barack Obama in 2009.[3]

Kevin Rudd also used his favourite boots as a diplomatic gift. In December 2008, he flew to Bali at the invitation of Indonesian President Susilo Bambang Yudhoyono to co-chair the first meeting of the Bali Democracy Forum, a Yudhoyono initiative that sought to advance democracy in the Asia-Pacific region. Rudd announced a 3-million Australian dollar assistance package during his trip, covering support for both the forum and the Indonesian Institute for Peace and Democracy. He also arrived with a personal gift for the Indonesian president – a pair of R. M. Williams boots.[4]

The boots have several attractions as a diplomatic gift. They showcase Australian tradition and craftsmanship and support the export ambitions of an Australian company by associating its product with internationally influential people. The company's website highlights that the boots have been worn by 'millions of people, including some of the most famous on the planet'.[5] That Kevin Rudd was himself so closely identified with the footwear lent the gift a personal touch, suggestive of a friendly relationship in which the Australian prime minister was offering a gift he personally esteemed. The personalised quality of the gift is underlined too by a specific characteristic of boots: they require information about the recipient's shoe size, and thus a diplomatic gift might typically be preceded by a discreet call to the relevant protocol department to obtain the required information.

In some cases, a gift of boots may involve more elaborate fitting procedures. Christopher Meyer, in an account of his time as British ambassador to Washington, recalled the weekend in April 2002 spent by Prime Minister

Tony Blair at President George W. Bush's ranch at Crawford, Texas. While the principals had dinner at the ranch, a bootmaker arrived courtesy of the White House team to the restaurant in nearby Waco at which the accompanying British delegation was dining with their US counterparts. There were reportedly few takers for the custom-made J. B. Hill boots on offer, whose value would have fallen well above the ceiling under which British officials are permitted to keep gifts from foreign counterparts, requiring the officials personally to pay the balance in order to retain their boots. Following a foot measuring in the restaurant's storeroom, the ambassador did though become the proud owner of a pair of high-heeled Texan cowboy boots, decorated with the flags of Britain, America and Texas.[6]

Kevin Rudd is not the only Australian politician to have favoured R. M. Williams boots as diplomatic gifts. Fellow R. M. Williams aficionado Tony Abbott gifted a pair of these black boots, together with a pen made of Australian red gum, on his first overseas visit as prime minister in 2013. This was to Indonesia, the recipient again President Yudhoyono, who one hopes had also become a fan of the footwear.[7] Tony Abbott also gave a pair of these boots in 2014 to visiting Japanese Prime Minister Shinzo Abe, though that gift had an immediate practical application as the two leaders toured the Rio Tinto West Angelas iron ore mine in the Pilbara region of Western Australia. They were photographed showing off their matching boots while adopting a jaunty pose alongside a giant tyre.[8] R. M. Williams boots were also the choice of gift from Prime Minister Malcolm Turnbull when he met US President Donald Trump in February 2018.[9]

In each case, the gift was the choice of a prime minister known personally for his attachment to the footwear. The choice was also made against a set of guidelines governing the offering of diplomatic gifts by Australian ministers. These have been published by the Department of the Prime Minister and Cabinet of the Australian Government and offer an insight into the diplomatic gifting strategy of modern Australia.[10]

What is immediately striking is the degree to which diplomatic gifts are downplayed. Australia, we are told, is 'not traditionally a gift giving country', and diplomatic gifts are only required because of 'other countries' customs, good manners and goodwill'.[11] The Australian government's 'policy of being a non-gift giving country' is to be communicated ahead of official visits, to dissuade hosts from offering lavish gifts. Maximum values for Australian official gifts are suggested, based on the seniority of the recipient. These range from 500 to 750 Australian dollars for heads of state and government, to 25 dollars for host country drivers and security staff supporting the visit.[12]

While the choice of gift is for the Australian minister concerned, their provision has been outsourced to a company named Intandem Holdings, which provides a range of suggested gifts, conforming to the price ranges set out in the policy. The focus is firmly on 'Australian made and crafted items, purchased from sources throughout Australia.'[13] R. M. Williams boots appear neatly to fit this overall framework, as Australian-made items, with a typical cost lying within the suggested maximum range of gifts for heads of state and government.

Australia is by no means the only country to shun the giving of costly gifts. The United States also sets limits on the amount that the president and other senior officials are permitted to spend on individual diplomatic gifts.[14] Concerns that offering expensive gifts sits ill with a country's political culture may be accompanied by budgetary pressures, as well as by public scrutiny of government expenditure, in which lavish gifts to foreign dignitaries are rarely looked upon favourably, in encouraging modest gifting. Thus, the press reported in 2012 that a tough economic picture in the Republic of Ireland had occasioned a crack-down on expensive gifting by that country's Ministry of Foreign Affairs. Typical gifts might now be cufflinks or key rings, though they remained Irish-made products that represented the country.[15]

Governments, including that of the United States, may however seek to maximise bang for buck by negotiating special deals with suppliers in exchange for the publicity value of the association of a prestigious beneficiary with their product, and thereby ensure that the gifts are a little less frugal than the imposed spending limits would otherwise occasion. For their meeting in Cornwall for the G7 Summit in June 2021, US President Joe Biden opted to give British Prime Minister Boris Johnson a bicycle, a gift highlighting their shared love of cycling. The US State Department contacted the Bilenky Cycle Works, a Philadelphia company specialising in the manufacture of high-end handcrafted bikes. According to local journalists, the State Department's budget was just a third of the usual starting price for a Bilenky bike, and this was to be a highly tailored model, in blue with red and white decorations echoing the Union Jack, with a matching helmet with crossed UK and US flags. The company nonetheless agreed to produce the bike, to a particularly challenging timeframe, for the opportunity the commission offered to raise their profile.[16]

The reluctance to offer lavish gifts is mirrored by the attempts many countries make to avoid receiving them. In our discussion of the jewelled portrait of King Louis XVI of France presented to Benjamin Franklin in 1785, we looked at the Emoluments Clause of the US Constitution, under which US officials required the consent of Congress to accept any present, emolument, office or title from a foreign state or monarch. Today, to avoid the requirement for Congress to consider the matter every time a US official is offered a nice present they would like to keep from a foreign state, the Emoluments Clause is put into effect through the 1966 Foreign Gifts and Decorations Act and its subsequent amendments.[17]

US officials are permitted to keep gifts costing less than a 'minimal value', which has risen over time, moving to 415 US dollars from 1 January 2020 from its previous figure of 390.[18] They may also accept gifts of a value higher than this if refusal would cause offence or embarrassment, or otherwise harm the foreign relations of the United States, but such gifts cannot be personally retained by the recipient, unless they choose to pay the US administration their market value. The gift is instead accepted on behalf of the United States of America, and deposited with the National Archives and Records Administration.[19] Gifts to a US president from their international counterparts will often eventually be housed in the Presidential Library and Museum collection.

While by no means all countries have regulations as stringent as those of Australia and the United States governing the offering and acceptance of gifts, the diffusion of rules designed to counter risks around potential corruption by foreign states means that the environment in which diplomatic gifts are offered and accepted is today a regulated one. The rules seek to minimise the risks associated with diplomatic gifts by imposing limits on the value of gifts deemed acceptable. Through such rules, the nature of the diplomatic gift is changed, from an object of material significance to something more akin to a token, an object that serves as a diplomatic signal, underlining or reinforcing the objectives of the giver in their diplomatic encounter, but not in itself shaping the relationship.

R. M. Williams boots serve such a role well. They are desirable objects, but not extravagantly expensive. As an object designed to be worn, they hint at a personal, friendly relationship between the two leaders. Gifted boots help promote the brand, and support exports. And they are identifiably Australian, speaking to the artistic and craft skills of the country, and more deeply to its character and values. These boots are made for talking.

COLUMN WITH SPEED LINES, A LITHOGRAPH BY ED RUSCHA

A GIFT FROM BARACK OBAMA, PRESIDENT OF THE UNITED
STATES OF AMERICA, TO TONY ABBOTT,
PRIME MINISTER OF AUSTRALIA

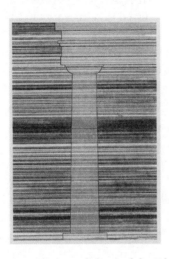

Column with Speed Lines, a lithograph by Ed Ruscha.

The contention of Marcel Mauss that the obligation to repay gifts received is an essential feature of the system of gift exchange[1] has received support from gift reciprocations running through our tales. In our last story, it is time to focus explicitly on the interplay between gift and return gift. Exchanges between US President Barack Obama and prime ministers of the United Kingdom and Australia illustrate the arguments.

We first return to our story from 1880: the inspired gift from Queen Victoria to President Rutherford B. Hayes of a magnificent desk crafted from the salvaged timber of HMS *Resolute*. On his 2009 visit to Washington, British Prime Minister Gordon Brown offered President Barack Obama a thoughtfully prepared collection of gifts, including the framed commissioning papers for *Resolute* and a penholder made from the timbers of HMS *Gannet*. The latter was described in the UK press at the time as a 'sister ship' of the *Resolute*,[2] though this is not accurate, and the choice of the *Gannet* seems instead to have been intended to highlight that ship's role in anti-slavery activities in the late nineteenth century, including in the Red Sea.

The British press, always alert to any suggestion that the special nature of the relationship between the two countries may be under question, also made much of an apparent imbalance in the quality of gifts exchanged by the two leaders. The US State Department Protocol Office estimated the value of the prime minister's gifts to Obama, which also included the multi-volume official biography of Churchill, at $16,510,[3] while the British prime minister received in return a set of DVDs of classic American films.[4] Some commentators fretted about whether the DVDs would even be readable in UK DVD players.[5] The perception was that the gift from the British prime minister had not been fully reciprocated.

Perhaps mindful of this negative reporting, the gift exchange during the visit to Washington the following year of Brown's successor, David Cameron, appears to have been coordinated in advance, with both leaders offering gifts of modern artworks. The British prime minister's choice was *Twenty-First Century City* by Ben Eine, known primarily as a street artist. From numerous brushes with the law over his graffiti tagging,[6] through collaboration with Banksy, Eine emerged as one of Britain's leading street artists through works such as *Alphabet Street* in London's Spitalfields, in which the letters of the alphabet were spray-painted on shop shutters along Middlesex Street.[7]

According to press reporting, the choice of Ben Eine came at the suggestion of David Cameron's wife Samantha, a fan of the artist's work.[8] Identifying an Eine painting suitable as a gift to the US president was not straightforward. The timeframe following the approach from the prime minister's office did not allow a new painting to be created for the occasion, and many of his canvases, mostly featuring words written in colourful fonts, were negative in tone. *Twenty-First Century City*, in which the letters of this phrase are organised over seven rows and five columns, met with approval.[9]

The gift of a canvas from an artist known particularly for street art serves not only to highlight the strength of the British contemporary art scene, but more specifically to offer a nod to the role of US ghetto culture in developing the art form. It also acknowledges the engagement the US president had already had with street art, notably through the use of Shepard Fairey's *Hope*, a stencil portrait of Obama in red, white and blue, in the 2008 presidential election campaign.[10]

The choice of an Eine canvas for such a prestigious gift provided a major fillip to the artist's reputation,[11] as the use of artworks as diplomatic gifts has done for centuries. Eine responded to his surprise at the request from the prime minister's office, and the attendant publicity around the gift, by creating a street work along London's Hackney Road entitled *The Strangest Week*, with that phrase written in large colourful letters made up of little smileys.[12]

Obama's return gift was *Column with Speed Lines*, a lithograph by Ed Ruscha, a Nebraska-born artist linked to the pop art movement. A column at the centre of the canvas evokes the grand portico of a government building, while red, white and blue horizontal lines offer the perfect palette for a gift aiming to underscore the strength of the US–UK relationship. The Obama administration had already shown an interest in Ruscha, having placed in the White House a work entitled *I Think Maybe I'll …*, on loan from the National Gallery of Art in Washington. More directly, *Column with Speed Lines* had been donated by the artist's printers to a non-profit organisation named the Foundation for Art and Preservation in Embassies, which uses artworks to promote the international image of the United States.[13] Obama was therefore drawing on a source of artworks specifically intended to promote the United States abroad.

He was to draw on it again. When Australian Prime Minister Tony Abbott met Obama in Washington in June 2014, he received another copy of the same lithograph. The red, white and blue horizontal lines of *Column with Speed Lines* provided an ideal colour scheme to celebrate the US–Australian relationship as well as the US–UK one. Unlike the exchange four years earlier with the British prime minister, there is no evidence of co-ordination as regards the type of gift. The Australian prime minister's gift to Obama was a surfboard, custom made by Bennett Surfboards of Sydney, its pale blue and white colouring apparently intended to evoke Air Force One.[14] It featured the presidential seal and the flags of the two countries. The package also included that favoured Australian gift item, a pair of black leather boots.[15] A surfboard conforms to the Australian practice of offering gifts that highlight Australian culture and crafts. It also implicitly flatters the recipient by casting him as energetic and sporting, someone who would appreciate a surfboard, as well as hinting at his birth state of Hawaii and its shared love of the sport with Australia.

A second gift exchange between David Cameron and Barack Obama provides further evidence of the strong degree of co-ordination of gifts between these two leaders. If the gifts at their meeting in 2010 were co-ordinated around the contemporary art of their countries, the gifts during the British prime minister's visit to Washington two years later offered a personal, family feel. Cameron presented Obama with a customised Dunlop table tennis table. Obama's return gift was a top of the range barbecue, a Braten 1000 series grill made by Engelbrecht Grills of Paxton, Illinois. Flags of the two countries had been engraved on it. The grill came with two chefs' jackets adorned with the presidential seal and the flags of the two countries.[16] Both gifts in turn referenced Obama's state visit to the UK the previous year during which the two leaders had played table tennis at the Globe Academy school in London and had enjoyed a barbecue in the prime minister's Downing Street garden.

The personal feel of this gift exchange was accentuated by gifts to members of the families of the two leaders. Samantha Cameron received a jar of White House honey, while the prime minister's children were given personalised beanbag chairs. The gift to Michelle Obama was a scarf with a design inspired by Victorian wallpapers, while their children received a set of classic British children's books.[17]

The gift exchanges between David Cameron and Barack Obama thus seem to have involved notably thoughtful collaboration between the two administrations. This is less apparent in the other exchanges examined. There is however a wider point here. All these gift exchanges, in their simultaneity, reflect the short face-to-face meetings between leaders characteristic of modern diplomacy. We might recall the emphasis paid by sociologist Pierre Bourdieu on the time gap between gifts. Where there is no time gap, he argues that the exchange loses the essence of a gift exchange, that is, a means for the giver to secure power over the recipient through the generation of a sense of obligation.[18] The exchange is thereby rendered a safer strategy, but the gift loses its power as a gift. Presents serve as signals of the strength of the bilateral relationship, but without generating the obligations the receipt of a gift would characteristically involve. This is an important consideration as we now look to draw some conclusions from our survey of the history of diplomatic gifts.

CONCLUSION

We have seen that gifts have accompanied diplomacy for as long as groups of people have conducted business with one another. The role of gifts in establishing and maintaining social relationships makes them an invaluable part of the diplomatic trade.

Material versus symbolic value of the diplomatic gift

As our stories have unfolded, from the great king correspondence of the fourteenth century BCE to the packed official visits of twenty-first-century political leaders meeting their far-flung counterparts, it is hard to escape the conclusion that diplomatic gifts have over time both become less central to the diplomatic exchanges and, with some exceptions, less valuable. Diplomatic gifts fuel the exchanges between the great powers of the day described in the Amarna Letters of our first story. These letters are heavy with the desire of their kings for valuable gifts such as Egyptian gold and show little hesitation in spelling out exactly what gifts would be most appreciated, or when proffered gifts have failed to come up to expectations. The gifts described in these letters are gifts of considerable material value.

Compare these exchanges with the objects gifted by prominent leaders in our century: the lithograph gifted by President Barack Obama of the United States to Australian Prime Minister Tony Abbott in 2014, for example, or the R. M. Williams boots given in the same year by Tony Abbott to his Japanese counterpart Shinzo Abe. In both cases thoughtfully chosen items, presumably received with pleasure. In neither case though were these gifts central to the exchange. Over the course of some thirty-five centuries, the gifts used in diplomacy seem to have moved from items of high material value, powering exchanges between polities, to items of largely symbolic value, regarded as a diplomatic nicety.

This is not to say that the diplomatic gifts of earlier periods lacked symbolic meaning. The tale of the whip, ball and chest of gold supposedly offered by Darius III to Alexander in the fourth century BCE combines a gift of high material value, enough gold for Alexander to get his army home, with symbolic items, albeit in this context expressed as a taunt. The use by the Mamluks as diplomatic gifts of items of clothing personally worn by the sultan, the habit of Peter the Great of Russia to gift craft items he had personally made in his workshop, and the use of portraits of themselves by European monarchs all show the continuing importance of symbolic value in the choice of gift. Our history of diplomatic gifts appears though to suggest that, where diplomatic gifts long possessed both a material and a symbolic value, the material value has declined over time, leaving the gifts as primarily a symbol of the diplomatic relationship.

One possible explanation for this decline in the material value of diplomatic gifts is to suggest that it mirrors a decline in the importance of gift exchange as societies develop. Mauss saw the systems of gift exchange and market-based commodity exchange as characteristic of different kinds of societies, with those based around the latter tending to replace the former.[1] Some later scholars have argued that gift exchange and commodity exchange can coexist within the same societies, although not always easily.[2] A gradual reduction in the scope of diplomatic gifts from significant material exchanges to more symbolic ones would chime with an increasing dominance of market-based exchange over gift exchange in the wider society.

This line of reasoning suggests that gifts of high material value were more characteristic of certain, mostly earlier, periods because they were expected, and indeed served to confirm the role and status of the giver. Consider the visit of the future King Henri III of France to Venice in 1574. In May of that year, King Charles IX of France died of tuberculosis at the age of just twenty-three. His brother Henri was heir, but he was already king of Poland. The Poles not wishing him to depart the country to take up the French throne, Henri was forced to flee Kraków under cover of night. Once out of Poland, Henri's journey to France took the form of a staged triumphal procession, the rulers of Europe offering lavish hospitality to the new French king. For Venice, the visit of the future King Henri III offered a timely opportunity to reassert itself following decades of decline as the spice trade had shifted to the Atlantic, and the recent peace signed with the Ottomans in 1573 that had dented its image as a defender of European Christianity.[3]

CONCLUSION

Henri spent close to a month in Venetian territories in the summer of 1574, with Venice underwriting the entire cost of his stay. It did so in exuberant style, particularly in respect of his week-long visit to the city of Venice itself, an extravaganza of processions, feasts, theatrical performances and regattas.[4] While formal gifts were presented to Henri, notably a manuscript containing the original statutes of the Ordre du Saint-Esprit, which he would re-establish in 1578, the focus of Venetian gifting was mostly practical in nature, ensuring a successful programme befitting one of the most important rulers of Europe. The Venetian government covered the costs of everything, including board, lodging, entertainment and even fresh horses. This was a massive outlay, estimated at around 100,000 ducats.[5]

The return gifts offered by Henri were different in character. They included gold chains or gifts of money to numerous individuals who supported the visit, from the four Venetian ambassadors extraordinary designated to his mission to cooks, orators and members of the military detail. These acts of giving presented Henri as a generous king, exactly the behaviour expected of the ruler of such an important country as France.[6] The competitive gift-giving of King Henry VIII of England and François I of France at the Field of Cloth of Gold in 1520 similarly reinforced the status of the givers as important and munificent monarchs.

Where diplomatic gifts of high material value are encountered today, they are often associated with a group of wealthy, mainly Islamic, countries in which a similar cultural tradition is still encountered with lavish gifting considered the mark of an enlightened and powerful ruler, a tradition nourished by the value placed by Islam on generous giving. The commissioning for use as diplomatic gifts by rulers in several Middle Eastern countries of luxury watches, particularly Rolex, often featuring details such as the national emblem of the gifting country on the dial, is a well-known example.[7] The use of exclusive Swiss-made watches rather than products made in the gifting country serves to emphasise the material rather than symbolic value of the gift.

Sherard Cowper-Coles, a former British ambassador to Saudi Arabia, recalled a desert expedition with a well-connected host in which falcons were used to hunt bustard. In conversation with the host, his wife had expressed admiration for the beauty of the falcons, a comment that resulted in a gift of a Siberian Gyrfalcon worth perhaps £150,000. The bird was housed in the ambassadorial residence in Riyadh, where it posed with visiting British government ministers and dined on a diet of live quail.[8]

A different explanation for the decline in the material value of diplomatic gifts is based around the argument that, while gift exchange as a mechanism of exchange has continued, the nature of the exchanged gifts has changed over time. It is found in the work of Norwegian political scientist Iver Neumann, who ventures a broad classification of diplomatic gifts according to their value to both giver and receiver.[9] He refers to 'unique gifts' as those of high value to both parties. The organ gifted by Byzantine Emperor Constantine V to Pépin III, king of the Franks, would fall into that category. So too would the 'gifting' of humans of royal birth, through marriage or through such arrangements as that seen in the fostering out of his son Haakon in the 920s by Harald Fairhair, king of Norway, to Æthelstan, king of England.[10] Gifts that are low value to the giver but high to the receiver are characterised as 'personalised gifts', where good results can be achieved at relatively low outlay by appealing to the specific interests of the recipient. Those that are high value to the giver but low to the receiver are called 'culturally irrelevant gifts' – these are gifts that miss their mark, presented to a recipient lacking the cultural or ritual context to appreciate them. Neumann dismisses gifts of low value to both parties as 'fluff'.

Neumann argues that the 'unique gifts', of high value to both giver and receiver, will be characteristic of polities that are not well acquainted, where one is seeking to build a relationship with the other. A high-value gift will, in Maussian terms, generate the expectation of a reciprocal gift of equivalent value. He argues that the emerging state system of early modern Europe provides an environment propitious for such valuable gifts. In the modern period, in contrast, characterised by an international order whose members are in frequent contact with each other, and in which reciprocation of gifts is well established, the focus will instead be on maintaining a series of gift exchanges of equal value. In this framework of balanced exchange, high-value unique gifts will be much rarer.[11]

A further explanation suggested by our stories is that the use of valuable items as diplomatic gifts was seen as increasingly problematic because of the risks associated with gifts, in particular that they may place the receiver in a position of subordination to the giver, opening up concerns around corruption. The blurriness of the line between gift and bribe has long been a concern. Such fears have been a longstanding strand of republican thinking: note the death penalty for bribery of public officials set by Plato in his model city of Magnesia.[12] In sixteenth-century Venice, individuals were not allowed to accept valuable diplomatic gifts from foreign powers, a consideration at the root of much awkwardness in the face of the largesse displayed by the future Henri III of France during his visit in 1574. The gift of a diamond ring from Henri to the doge occasioned a senate debate about what to do with it. The decision was to mount it in a gold lily, commemorating Henri's goodwill towards Venice, and place it in the treasury of St Mark's.[13] Concerns around the risks of bribery led the founding fathers of the United States to devise the Emoluments Clause in their new constitution, requiring the approval of Congress for the acceptance of any sort of diplomatic gift, emolument, office or title.

A growing number of countries have instituted limits on the value of a gift that may be accepted by public officials, including in many cases by heads of state and government. Such stipulations characteristically do not prevent the receipt of diplomatic gifts of a higher value. Rather, the latter can normally be accepted on behalf of the receiving state, but not retained as personal gifts. Such rules act however to dissuade lavish gifts. As we have seen in our story of the diplomatic gifting practices of twenty-first-century Australia, some states have instituted rules to limit the value of gifts that can be offered as diplomatic gifts, as well as on the value of gifts that may be received.

Reciprocation and time lags

A Maussian analysis would focus on the importance of reciprocation of the gift in avoiding the generation of risks around bribery, as well as avoiding the humiliation of the recipient or the creation of a culture of dependency. Indeed, reciprocation was for Mauss at the heart of the role of the gift in developing a social relationship. Our stories have demonstrated that reciprocation has indeed been a central concern in diplomatic gift exchange in many contexts and periods.

What is being reciprocated is not always a like gift. 'Thank you' gifts are a case in point. The Christmas tree donated annually by Oslo to London acknowledges British support to Norway during the Second World War. Such a gift may be seen as a means of replacing a status of indebtedness with an ongoing positive social relationship, in this case reinforced each year by a gift recalling the wartime support. The planetarium given by the German Democratic Republic to mark the seventieth birthday of Soviet leader Joseph Stalin was seen from the Soviet perspective as reciprocating Stalin's gift of socialism; from an East German one, it sought to bring that country towards a position of partnership rather than subordination in respect of the USSR.

Where a gift is not reciprocated, it may be something else entirely. For example, a bribe, or a tribute payment. As we have seen, development assistance appears to offer the prospect of a 'pure' form of gift in which reciprocation is not expected. Yet both aid donors and recipients are reluctant to describe such assistance in the language of the gift as, without the possibility of reciprocation, the recipient is placed in a position of humiliation and dependency. As we saw in the example of stadia gifted by China, development assistance is more likely to be cast as a gift where it is placed in a framework of a win-win outcome based on mutual opportunity;[14] in other words, where reciprocation is made explicit.

The time lag between gift and return gift is an important consideration here. The work of sociologist Pierre Bourdieu suggests that in order to maintain the social relationship at the heart of a system of gift exchange, a time lag is essential. Immediate reciprocation may suggest ingratitude, while a long delay before reciprocation suggests indifference.[15]

The evolution of diplomatic practice through innovation in transport and communications has been highly significant in loosening the constraints around the ability of leaders to shorten the time lag between gift and reciprocation. Isaac the Jew, the sole surviving senior member of the diplomatic delegation sent by Charlemagne to Abbasid Caliph Harun al-Rashid in 797, arrived back in Aachen only some five years later with Harun's wondrous gift, the elephant named Abu'l Abbas. As we have seen, the emergence of permanent ambassadors in Renaissance Italy altered the way states engaged with each other. Much more recently, the ability, through a revolution in transportation, for heads of state and government to meet directly with each other on a regular basis rather than rely on communication through a diplomatic agent has underpinned a further major change in the way diplomatic gifts are given.

The arrival of a non-resident diplomatic mission involved a complex pattern of diplomatic gifting. The mission would bring the principal gifts from its ruler to that of the receiving state. The head of the mission might also offer gifts to the receiving ruler in their own name, as well as gifts to a range of people in the receiving country involved in supporting the mission. Some might essentially be bribes, for example to reward gatekeepers involved in securing access to the local ruler. The receiving ruler would offer in return principal gifts to the sending ruler, as well as gifts to the head and possibly other members of the mission. The mission might be accommodated, fed and entertained by the host state. In a sense, the mission itself was a gift, a mark of the willingness of the sending ruler to engage with the receiving one, providing the opportunity for festivity in the host country. While there would be immediate reciprocation of some of these gifts, the ruler of the sending country would not receive the principal gifts for some time, brought back either by the returning mission or by a return diplomatic mission of the receiving state. This time lag in reciprocation helped ensure the continuation of the social relationship, since receipt would in turn initiate consideration of a suitable follow-up gift.

Today's diplomatic gift exchanges between political leaders are more characteristically simultaneous, or nearly so. Thanks to the speed of travel, heads meet each other face-to-face. The visiting leader presents a suitable gift brought from the capital, and this is immediately reciprocated by the host with a prepared gift. Protocol officials and members of staff of the embassies of the two countries will often have been engaged in discreet enquiries ahead of the visit to ascertain whether diplomatic gifts will be presented and their likely approximate value or nature, to ensure their principal is duly armed with gifts of an equivalent value effectively to reciprocate the gifts received.

There are exceptions. Modern-day diplomatic gifts can occasionally involve considerable logistical feats. In a speech to the Australia–Britain Society in Melbourne in October 1999, the British high commissioner, Sir Alex Allan, a former private secretary to Prime Minister John Major, recounted the tale of Maksat, the Turkmen stallion.[16] On a visit to Britain in 1992, the then president of the newly independent state of Turkmenistan, Saparmurat Niyazov, had handed the prime minister a leather-bound book featuring photographs of a fine Turkmen Akhal-Teke stallion. The prime minister leafed through the book with polite interest. It transpired however that the Turkmen president's gift was not the book, but the horse itself, and that it was in Turkmenistan, awaiting collection.

An enterprising third secretary at the British embassy in Moscow named Laura Brady was tasked with making arrangements, hooking up with her French counterpart, as President Mitterrand had also been gifted a horse. The two horses were sent by train from Turkmenistan to Moscow the following year in the charge of local grooms. The years immediately following the break-up of the USSR were challenging ones, and the grooms had brought with them a large consignment of the celebrated Turkmen melons, along with various vegetables, with which to purchase their return ticket to Ashgabat, Turkmenistan lacking the required post-1992 banknotes. Plans had nearly come unstuck when the train had been held up by armed bandits en route, but fortunately the robbers had been unable to make off with the skittish horses and had instead contented themselves with as many melons as they could carry.

On the arrival of the horses in Moscow, which happened to coincide with the highly charged and dangerous Russian constitutional crisis of October 1993, the two diplomats navigated the considerable challenges of veterinary and customs clearance, their fretting over the time required to secure the release of the poor horses eliciting the sad tale of the Finnish ambassador's parrot from an animal-loving receptionist at the customs post. The final hurdle proved to be the task of removing enough of the accumulated horse manure from the railway carriage to pass the threshold of required cleanliness, a task resolved through the gifting of several Turkmen melons.[17] On arrival in Britain, Maksat was destined for life in the Household Cavalry, but he proved too temperamental for their needs and was sent to the Defence Animal Centre in Melton Mowbray. No happier there, Maksat was eventually stabled in Wales, where he went on to win show jumping awards.[18]

The tale of the Turkmen stallion stands out however precisely because of the rarity of such sagas in the world of modern-day diplomatic gifting. More typically, the combination of the placing of limits on the value of the gifts that may be given or received and the tendency immediately to reciprocate gifts provides a safety mechanism to avoid the obligations typically generated by a gift.[19] By negating such obligations, however, the ability of such offerings to maintain the social relationships at the heart of gift exchange is weakened. They appear to fulfil a different, lesser, function as artefacts of non-verbal diplomatic signalling: minor supporting actors to the overall business of the meeting.[20]

Actors in the gift

Our stories have demonstrated too that the changing nature of diplomatic practice and revolutions in transportation have altered the cast list of actors involved in the making of diplomatic gifts. Most obviously, the fact that gifts between heads of state and government are now characteristically made during face-to-face encounters has largely removed the requirement for the intermediary envoys, like Liudprand of Cremona, who have so enlivened our tales, except in the sense of the backstage work of the protocol departments of the giving and receiving states.

Of course, not all diplomatic gifts are made between rulers. Gifts can involve more junior figures: from the farewell present offered to a departing ambassador on the completion of their mandate, to gifts given and received during a foreign visit of a modern-day government minister. A question that arises here is the extent to which such gifts are different in nature from those offered in an exchange between heads of state. In some contexts, the difference appears to be simply a matter of cost. Thus the guidelines issued by the Australian government relating to the offering of diplomatic gifts by Australian ministers set higher maximum values the more senior the recipient.[21] In other contexts, gifts given by or to other actors are also qualitatively different to those made between rulers. We have explored the gifting of robes of honour by Mamluk and Ottoman sultans: always to an inferior, and certainly not an appropriate gift to a ruler of equal standing. Historian Sarah Bercusson, in an account of three Austrian archduchesses who married into sixteenth-century Italian courts, found that her subjects used diplomatic gifts of a quite different nature to those employed by their husbands. Food gifts, informal in character, frequently offering a home-made quality and of a low cost, were, for example, deployed widely to develop and maintain their social relationships. Thus Giovanna d'Austria, the wife of Francesco I de' Medici, sent home-made pastes and jams to both the pope and the Holy Roman Emperor.[22]

A change in the relationship between ruler and ruled, heralding a proliferation of actors involved in the making of foreign policy and the increasing importance of 'public diplomacy', coupled with the advent of mass-circulation media, have accompanied a change too in the cast involved in making decisions around the highest profile gifts. As we have seen, the gifting of cherry trees to Washington in 1912 followed the enthusiastic campaigning of several individuals with different levels of proximity to power. The Merci Train of 1949 was an idea credited to a French railway worker named André Picard, taken up with enthusiasm by the French government. The Statue of Liberty project was a private initiative, later embraced by the governments concerned.

The advent of social media has brought a new level of openness to debates around some proposed diplomatic gifts. A retired employee of the Norwegian Mapping Authority named Bjørn Geirr Harsson proposed that Norway offer a special gift to Finland for its centenary celebrations in 2017: a mountain peak.[23] The highest point of Finland falls on a spur of the Halti fell that straddles the two countries, known as Háldiťsohkka. However, not only is the peak of Mount Halti itself, at 1,365 metres, on Norwegian territory, so too is the subordinate peak of Háldiťsohkka, at

1,331 metres. So the highest point of Finland is currently a nondescript piece of mountainside. Moving the border just 40 metres would give Finland the actual summit of Hálditšohkka as its highest point.[24]

A Facebook group, 'Halti as an Anniversary Gift' (*Halti som jubileumsgave*), took up Bjørn's idea. The mayor of the local community of Kåfjord, Svein Oddvar Leiros, joined the campaign and wrote to the Norwegian prime minister in support. The reply however regretted that such a gift would fall foul of the Norwegian constitution, which stipulated that the country was an 'indivisible and inalienable realm'.[25] The gift was never made.

Social media is bringing changes not just to participation in decision-making around diplomatic gifts, but also in the use of such gifts to fulfil certain objectives, for example around the promotion of awareness of the culture and achievements of the gifting polity. In September 2020, the British newspaper the *Evening Standard* commented on a particularly splendid tie sported by Minister for Africa James Duddridge in the House of Commons. The minister told journalists that the tie had been a gift from the Ethiopian minister of finance. The tie took its design from a colourful stained-glass window by Afewerk Tekle, depicting *The Struggle and Aspiration of the African People*. Mr Duddridge had promised the Ethiopian minister that he would send him a photo of himself wearing the tie at the despatch box.[26] The minister duly tweeted a photo on 10 September, confirming that 'diplomatic "ties" are strong with Ethiopia'.[27]

Our stories have offered many examples of the attention given in the chronicles of the lives of rulers and in more contemporary media presentations to the use of diplomatic gifts to convey specific narratives in a way that suits the objectives of the teller. The qualities of social media enhance the scope and possibilities around such time-honoured ruses as depictions of the recipient sporting, consuming or otherwise using diplomatic gifts. It is to the strategies underlying different types of gifted objects that we will now turn.

The gifted object and the strategy of the gift

Our stories have illustrated the huge range of objects offered as diplomatic gifts, from beavers to boots, cheese to cherry trees, desks to diamonds. In attempting to understand what lies behind the choice of modern-era gifts between heads of state and government, the annual publication in the US Federal Register of gifts received from foreign government sources by US government employees, including the president, falling above the defined 'minimal value', forms a useful quarry. Thus, over the sixteen years of the George W. Bush and Barack Obama administrations, 1,099 gift packages were recorded as received by the president, either alone or jointly with the first lady, averaging at close to sixty-nine per year.[28]

While dividing lines are decidedly blurred, and the briefness of the descriptions in the Federal Register means that the nature of the gift and what it represents is not always completely clear, it is possible to identify seven broad types of gifting strategy in the choice of these presents. Three of these treat the gifts essentially as formal exchanges between the two states.

The first highlights the culture of the gifting country: for example, the framed copy of W. B. Yeats' poem *The Lake Isle of Innisfree* given by Enda Kenny, taoiseach of the Republic of Ireland, to Barack Obama in 2013.[29]

The second highlights the strength of the bilateral relationship, exemplified by gifts recalling specific positive links between the gifting country and the United States. As we have discussed, the framed commissioning papers for HMS *Resolute* and a penholder from the timbers of HMS *Gannet* offered to Obama in 2009 by British Prime Minister Gordon Brown referenced the highly successful gift of the *Resolute* desk from Queen Victoria to President Rutherford B. Hayes, and through that bilateral cooperation in the exploration of the Arctic. The use of diplomatic gifts to reference earlier gifts, thereby generating a feeling of a continuing warm relationship, is seen also in Chinese gifts to US presidents linked to the painting *Five Oxen*, a 1,300-year-old work attributed to Tang dynasty official Han Huang. Chinese President Hu Jintao gifted a porcelain sculpture based on the painting to President Obama in 2009,[30] and then Vice-President Xi Jinping followed up with a replica of the painting three years later, along with an autographed basketball.[31] These gifts in turn hint at the musk oxen presented by President Nixon in return for the two Chinese pandas he received in 1972.[32]

The third strategy seeks to praise US culture and values: for example, the woollen rug in the pattern of the US flag gifted by Mexican President Enrique Peña Nieto to Obama in 2014.[33]

A further three gifting strategies highlight the personal nature of the gifts, despite the fact that in these regulated transactions there are considerable constraints on the ability of the US president to retain the gift or to use it in a personal way. Thus, the fourth gifting strategy seeks specifically to appeal to the personal interests of the US president. For example, gifts offered by Israeli Prime Minister Ehud Olmert to President Bush in 2008 included a mountain bike, cycling jerseys, shorts and a backpack, all speaking to the president's love of mountain biking.[34] A fifth strategy involves offering generic nice presents, which can serve to imply a familial feel to the relationship between the two leaders. Thus, the sultan of Brunei gave President Obama in 2014 a selection of gifts including a walnut cheese tray and penguin-shaped tea infuser.[35] A sixth strategy involves the offering of particularly lavish and costly gifts, and is characteristic, as we have noted, of a small group of countries, mainly in the Middle East, in which expensive giving underlines the status and munificence of the giver. In 2015, Saudi Arabian King Salman bin Abdulaziz al Saud gave President Obama presents valued at 522,972 US dollars, including two bronze horse sculptures decorated with precious stones.[36]

The gifting of luxury brands of the sending country is a seventh strategy that appears to combine elements of both these clusters, in maintaining the pretence of a personal gift while highlighting the goods and image of the gifting country. Those three Battistoni ties gifted by Italian Prime Minister Silvio Berlusconi to President Bush we encountered in the introduction fall into this category, as do the cigars gifted by Raúl Castro to President Obama in 2015.

Some gifts to US presidents seem to have been chosen as symbolic instruments of the business of the visit. The gifting of pens during visits associated with the signature of diplomatic agreements, or those focused around working summit meetings, is one example. Thus in May 2003 the prime minister of Singapore, Goh Chok Tong, visited Washington to sign the United States–Singapore Free Trade Agreement. His gift to President Bush on the occasion included a black Namiki pen.[37] Summit meetings often involve intense discussions in windowless conference venues. A sense of place is lost. The gift packages offered to the visiting heads of delegation can serve to underline the business nature of the meeting, through items such as pens, briefcases and USB sticks, but also to serve as a geographical marker, helping to restore that sense of place. Thus gifts to President Obama from British Prime Minister David Cameron on the occasion of the 2013 G8 summit at the Lough Erne Resort in Northern Ireland included local Co Couture chocolates, a bottle of whiskey, books about Northern Ireland and porcelain cups decorated with shamrocks.[38]

A distinction between gifting strategies treating diplomatic gifts as objects of formal exchange between two states and those treating them as personal gifts also finds support in the work of Eline Ceulemans, who has examined the diplomatic gifts made by Chinese Presidents Hu Jintao and Xi Jinping between 2003 and 2019.[39] She records two quite distinct forms of gift-giving. Ceremonial gift-giving is typical of situations in which the People's Republic of China views itself as the senior partner, such as its relationship with North Korea. It is characterised by lavish state dinners and expensive gifts often based around traditional crafts demonstrating Chinese technical skills, such as silks, lacquer objects and cloisonné vases. This is contrasted with the convivial gift-giving characteristic of encounters with senior world leaders that take a tone of studied informality, with gifts more personal and emotional in character, speaking to the recipient's image or tastes.[40] The more personal gifts seem to involve a greater investment of time and effort, in determining what will best resonate with the recipient, though they may be more modest in financial terms than the ceremonial gifts.

These gifting strategies are not new, but echo through our stories and through history. The selection of gifts highlighting the technological achievements and cultural sophistication of the gifting country is a common thread, and one that gives rise to the identification of iconic gifts with specific polities: the silks of Byzantium, for example, or the Meissen porcelain gifted by the rulers of Saxony. The latter presents underscored the success of that country in uncovering the secrets of the manufacture of 'white gold'.

Our stories also suggest though that the use of gifts as a means of showcasing the gifting country is constrained by an overarching requirement to conform to the expectations of the time around the sort of gift that might be appropriate. Where polities are already in frequent contact, sharing an agreed 'language' on what constitutes an acceptable gift, the use of gifts to present the culture and identity of the gifting country will be made through objects conforming to that language. Take the array of dinner services presented by grateful European rulers to the duke of Wellington. All sought to portray the culture and artistic skills of the gifting country, as well as to highlight its relationship with the duke, but all did so through the medium of a large dinner service; clearly understood by European rulers of the time as the right gift for such an occasion. A tension appears in diplomatic gift-giving with distinct parallels with the challenge of selecting an outfit for a prestigious social occasion. It is the tension between the desire to stand out, to be remarked upon, and to be remembered, against the desire to fit in, to be part of the group, to avoid a *faux pas*.

Rulers in some contexts favoured the use of gifts that served to underline not the culture of their own country but the breadth of their international connections, size of their empire or importance of their military conquests. Such signposting might be achieved through gifts manifestly not characteristic of the gifting country, including regifted items that brought with them their own histories, or as Mauss might put it, their own spirit. The use of Chinese porcelain as gifts by Mamluk sultans, demonstrating the strength of their trading connections with the east, fell into that category. The elephant gifted by King Manuel I of Portugal to Leo X similarly served to remind the pope of the recent Portuguese conquests in India.

A macabre diplomatic gift that served vividly to demonstrate territorial conquest was the severed head of a defeated ruler. Thus in 1468 the Turkmen Aq Qoyunlus (White Sheep) ruler Uzun Hasan sent the Mamluk Sultan Qaytbay the severed head of his Qara Qoyunlus (Black Sheep) rival, Jahan Shah, confirming both his allegiance and military prowess. The use of severed heads of neighbouring rulers could however be overdone: when Uzun Hasan sent Qaytbay the head of the Timurid sultan the following year, it was interpreted more as a sign of menace than fidelity.[41]

Gifts might be chosen not to represent the gifting polity in a general sense, but its ruler in a specific one. Underscoring the role of gifts in establishing social relationships, the choice of gift might aim to build a direct personal connection with the ruler of the recipient polity. A portrait of the gifting ruler offers one example. A gift of a portrait to a subordinate polity might however be less a matter of emphasising the personal connection between the two rulers and more about the provision of a constant visual reminder of the authority of the gifting ruler. The gift might also speak of the qualities of both gifting and recipient rulers. For example, suits of armour, weaponry and horses might suggest military leadership and battlefield success. The gifting of exotic animals to enrich the collections of royal menageries served to set apart the diplomatic gift from the kind of object that might be traded between the two countries, emphasising the status of the gift as the purview of royalty.

Diplomatic gifts were not always qualitatively different from commercially traded goods. Indeed, in our stories we have seen several examples, from porcelain to cigars, of the use of diplomatic gifts to stimulate export markets for luxury products. Diplomatic gifts could take on the role of signalling devices, with the aim of advertising commercial goods.[42] Thus, sales of Russian ice cream in China reportedly rocketed after President Putin gifted his Chinese counterpart Xi Jinping a box of the stuff at a meeting in the margins of the G20 summit at Hangzhou in 2016.[43]

Objects that cannot easily be alienated however have the advantage of offering a lasting symbol of the social relationship, whether through portraits or pandas. Such objects, because onward sale or regifting tends to be riskier for the recipient, may also be perceived as less open to accusations of bribery, which was a factor behind the use of portraits as gifts in late eighteenth-century India. In some situations, the gifter specifically wanted to offer a present that was both personal and materially valuable to the recipient. Thus the Ottoman *hil'at*, while serving as a material representation of the sultan's power at the time of gifting, was as a textile not clearly identifiable as a robe of honour when divorced from the presentation ceremony, allowing it to be sold on without risk.[44]

There is a sense running through our history of the diplomatic gift that such presents should be special. The concept of *tuhaf*, or 'marvels', in the gifting strategy of the Mamluks expresses this clearly: gifts should have the capacity to generate wonder.[45] While, as noted above, it was not invariably observed, a qualitative differentiation between diplomatic gifts and other objects recalls Mauss's observations of the *kula* gift exchange in Melanesia. Highly specific items were gifted, and these were quite unlike the useful goods exchanged in the same societies through other systems such as bargaining.[46]

Exotic animals have proved potent diplomatic gifts for their ability to create such wonder. So too have gifts of materials and technologies unknown in the recipient land. The organ gifted by the Byzantine emperor to Pépin III, and the telescope offered by King James I and VI of England, Scotland and Ireland to the retired Japanese Shōgun Tokugawa Ieyasu, provide examples. Such gifts serve the dual objective of generating wonder and highlighting the power and sophistication of the gifting country, though they may be accompanied too by some risk around the loss of technological advantage. Our story of the suit of armour gifted by Henry VIII of England to the vicomte de Turenne offers an example of the recipient of a gift that embodies a technological advance first learning from that advance, then bettering it, and finally incorporating it in a return gift. The use of technologically advanced items as diplomatic gifts, for their ability to generate awe and wonder, has given such gifts a role in the diffusion of innovations.

The creation for use as a diplomatic gift of a particularly fine, complex or innovative item to ensure that the recipient will be impressed by its wondrous nature has served as a motor of technological change, for example in late Renaissance Venice. That republic's trading links with the Ottoman Empire were underpinned by a system of diplomatic gift-giving to the Ottomans that included large quantities of silks and other cloths, as well as 'extraordinary gifts', given to appease the sultan at a tense moment, or for specific goals such as securing the freedom of Christian slaves.[47] These extraordinary gifts often involved clear and challenging demands from the Ottoman court, requesting silk fabrics in entirely new patterns, complex items of glassware or jewelled caskets of elaborate design. Such requests essentially generated a system of cross-cultural commissioning that served as a driver of innovation in Venice's artisanal sectors.[48]

A related important feature of diplomatic gifts is their role in cross-cultural exchange. We have explored the purpose of diplomacy as the conduct of business between geographically separated communities. Sometimes, that geographical distance has been very great indeed, as highlighted by our stories from the European Age of Exploration. With increased geographical and cultural distance comes both an enhanced ability of diplomatic gifts to embody the unknown or unimagined and also an enhanced likelihood of misunderstandings and misreadings. An example lies around objects viewed by one party as the embodiment of a hierarchical relationship, for example as a form of tribute, and by the other as marking a relationship between equals. As we have seen, such different understandings underlay some of the difficulties encountered in George Macartney's embassy to China in 1793.

First encounters between polities offer a uniquely challenging environment for the giving of diplomatic gifts, since they take place in the absence of an agreed common understanding of what is appropriate. We have already noted Neumann's argument that, in such circumstances, where one polity is seeking to establish a relationship with the other, high-value gifts are particularly likely.[49] But much depends on how the gifting polity perceives the receiving one. Note the contrast between the deployment by European powers of valuable gifts in their first dealings with the empires of Asia, but often small, almost trivial, ones offered in encounters with tribal leaders in North America. Gifts made during first encounters seek to establish rather than simply to maintain a social relationship. They are about trust. The stakes for both giver and receiver are high. Mistakes may even prove fatal.

The afterlife, and the spirit, of the gift

Diplomatic gifts decorate many of the buildings associated with international diplomacy, providing a truly international space for diplomats to conduct their craft.[50] More than 140 member states have for example donated at least one gift to furnish the headquarters of the United Nations.[51]

Conversely, we do not always now know whether items adorning the world's royal palaces were once received as gifts or not. As their histories have been lost, so too has evaporated the spirit of the gift, leaving us with valuable works of art, bereft of a story. The gift has become commodified.

The spirit of the diplomatic gift can though prove resilient. Leaving the main body of the Gothic cathedral of Seville, the modern visitor enters a cloister surrounding the picturesque Court of the Oranges. Suspended from the ceiling at this point are three rather unexpected objects: a horse's bit, an elephant's tusk and, most eye-catchingly, a painted wooden crocodile. The latter is popularly known as 'the cathedral lizard'. The visitor is told that these objects recall a diplomatic gift from the sultan of Egypt that included an elephant, a giraffe, or possibly zebra, and a crocodile. The tusk is all that remains of the elephant. The bit was used to lead the giraffe, or possibly zebra. The crocodile was stuffed upon its demise and placed in the cathedral. When the stuffed animal fell to pieces, a wooden replica replaced it.

The *Chronicle of Alfonso X*, recording the exploits of the king of Castile– Léon remembered by history as 'the Wise', carries an account of a visit to Alfonso's court in Seville of envoys of the ruler of Egypt, identified as 'Alvandexáver'.[52] They brought presents of precious cloth, rare jewels and an assortment of exotic animals, including an elephant, giraffe and zebra. A crocodile is not mentioned. The *Chronicle* appears to suggest that the mission arrived in 1260, which would identify the sultan as either the Mamluk ruler Sultan Qutuz, assassinated towards the end of that year, or his successor, and probable nemesis, Sultan Baybars. Historians have theorised that 'Alvandexáver' may either have been a distortion of Qutuz's honorific title al-Muẓaffar[53] or that of Baybars, al-Bunduqdārī.[54] There seems to be no record in Islamic sources of this mission.[55]

The objects in the cathedral may recollect the diplomatic mission described in the *Chronicle*. In the intervening centuries, the stories told about these artefacts have taken new directions. The visitor is likely to be informed confidently that the animals were offered as gifts in an unsuccessful attempt to secure the hand of a Spanish princess. A tour guide might add a jocular anecdote that the crocodile converted to Christianity. Here, far from being commodified, the gifts have been invested with a new spirit.

The legend of a diplomatic gift may even take concrete form when all trace of the original gift is lost, in some cases leading to doubts as to whether there was a gift in the first place. To illustrate this, we will leave the story of a crocodile and turn to an alligator, supposedly gifted by the French military officer the marquis de Lafayette to US President John

Quincy Adams. According to this tale, the president kept the alligator as a pet in a bathroom in the East Room of the White House and enjoyed giving his guests a fright during tours of the building.[56] The alligator gets star billing in the illustrated children's book *President Adams' Alligator and Other White House Pets*,[57] a canter through the history of presidential pets, in which the reader is invited to spot the alligator hidden in every illustration. The dedicated fan of the creature can even buy a John Quincy Adams' alligator soft toy, part of the Presidential Pets Collection.

Researchers have however encountered difficulties in verifying the historical accuracy of this tale. Some historians have concluded that, rather than a gift from the marquis to the president, the alligator was one of the many gifts received by de Lafayette during his long and triumphal tour of the United States in 1824 and 1825, at which he was feted as a hero of the American War of Independence. The marquis stayed with President John Quincy Adams at the White House in 1825, and it has been surmised that the alligator was among the gifts temporarily stored in the East Room, still under repair following the damage sustained by the burning of Washington by the British in 1814. The gifts were then taken to France along with the returning marquis aboard the USS *Brandywine*.[58]

Even this more muted account of the alligator's sojourn at the White House seems though to have eluded clear verification. The earliest identified written account of de Lafayette's alligator postdates the events it refers to by more than sixty years.[59] It appears in an article written for children by political activist Harriet Taylor Upton, who mentions briefly that the East Room of the White House was allotted to de Lafayette during his visit for the storage of the curiosities he had received, including 'some live alligators'.[60] It seems that the spirit of the gift does not always need a gift.

Solidarity versus authority

Our stories have shown that the purpose of diplomatic gifting is complex. Following the work of Mauss, much sociological research has focused on the role of gifts in building and maintaining social relationships,[61] and our tales of diplomatic gifting have provided examples of their use in the creation and reinforcement of ties of solidarity. Our stories have also amply demonstrated though that the building of social relationships is far from a complete answer to the question of the motivation behind the diplomatic gift.

Jorg Kustermans, Associate Professor of International Politics at the University of Antwerp, in an analysis of the Achaemenid, Qing and

Byzantine empires, argues that diplomatic gift-giving is better defined not in terms of solidarity but as a means of consolidating international authority.[62] We have explored the use of diplomatic gifts by Byzantium as a statement of its vision of the emperor as God's regent on earth, placing all other Christian rulers in a subordinated position. Kustermans argues that the use of gifts to claim and justify authority was however also characteristic of its gift exchanges with the caliphs, with whom there was no such hierarchical relationship. Here, he contends, exchanges of luxury goods generated a shared culture of privilege allowing both Byzantine emperor and caliph to project authority in respect both of lesser rulers and their own subjects.[63]

Diplomatic gifts do seek to build and maintain social relationships, but this is not a full statement of their purpose. They may claim the authority of the giving polity or showcase its attractiveness, serving, in other words, as an instrument of both hard power and soft. They may do both. They may be offered from positions of dominance or desperation. They may be the product of intense preparation, planning and consultation, or they may be an afterthought. They may seek to ingratiate or insult. They may be remembered for centuries, or forgotten instantly. They have been a part of the story of our planet, and of the interactions between the different political entities that populate it, since the dawn of recorded time.

Chairman Mao's mangoes

We started our journey with the story of the baby camel gifted to French President François Hollande, a diplomatic gift whose fate was to be treated over-casually. It was a gift not intended to be consumed, but which was eaten by its custodians. We will end with a gift that reverses this tale: a diplomatic gift that was intended to be consumed, but was not. It was instead treated with far more reverence than was intended by the giver, becoming the object of veneration.

It was the gift of a case of mangoes on 4 August 1968 by Mian Arshad Hussain, foreign minister of Pakistan, to Mao Zedong, chairman of the Communist Party of China, during an official visit to that country.[64] It was a pleasant diplomatic gift, but not a particularly remarkable one, mangoes having long been a staple of the gift-giving repertoire of South Asian leaders, except in respect of the novelty of the fruit in China. Having offered his gift, Mian Arshad Hussain rather fades from the story, the mangoes being generally referred to in the Chinese press as a gift from unspecified 'foreign friends'.[65] The gift arrived though at a particularly turbulent moment in the Chinese Cultural Revolution. The student-led Red Guards that had carried through the first phase of the Cultural Revolution through 1966 and 1967 had become beset by factionalism, and in the face of an increasingly anarchic domestic situation the Red Guards were suppressed, with many students sent into the countryside for harsh programmes of re-education.

In late July 1968, workers from factories personally directed by Mao were sent to Qinghua University in Beijing to sort out a particularly difficult situation there: an ongoing campus skirmish between two militant Red Guard factions. In a decision that was to transform Mian Arshad Hussain's quotidian gift into something quite remarkable, Mao opted not to consume the mangoes he had received himself, but rather to gift them on to the workers occupying Qinghua University.[66] This was seen as sending a clear message that official approval now lay with the Worker–Peasant Thought Propaganda Teams and not with the Red Guards. The action that was decisive in changing the gift from ordinary to extraordinary was however made not by Chairman Mao, but by the factory workers receiving the regifted mangoes. They chose not to eat the gift. They venerated it.

A single mango was sent to each of the factories whose workers had been involved in the restoration of order at the university.[67] According to the memoirs of Mao's personal physician, Li Zhisui, workers at the Beijing Textile Factory sealed the mango in wax in an attempt to preserve it, placing it on an altar in the factory auditorium. The mango soon however began to show evidence of rot. The rotting mango was boiled in a huge pot of water, with each worker at the factory drinking a spoonful of the sacred water. At another factory, an attempt was made to preserve the fruit by bottling it in formaldehyde. Li Zhisui recalled in his memoirs that when he informed Mao about the veneration of the mango gift, he laughed,[68] an action that suggests that Mao was not the deliberate orchestrator of the mango fever unleashed by his action in regifting the fruit.

Li Zhisui recorded that the workers of the Beijing Textile Factory solved the problem of the now absent mango by ordering a wax model of the fruit, which was duly placed on the altar and revered as a continuing mark of the gift from Chairman Mao establishing the leadership role of the workers.[69] Wax replica mangoes were produced in large quantities, presented in small glass containers. These were given to factory workers and presented as gifts to activists volunteering to move to far-flung regions of China to advance Maoist thought.[70] Replica mangoes were sent out across China: recipient cities in turn manufactured their own replicas to cater for the demand for a mango from smaller settlements.[71] Failure to embrace the cult of the mango could have appalling consequences. In Sichuan Province, locals waited expectantly for a sight of a travelling mango, which eventually arrived, the worse for wear, carried on a tray by the head of the counter-revolutionary committee. A dentist named Dr Han remarked on seeing the mango that it didn't appear to be anything special, and rather resembled a sweet potato, a frankness that earned the poor dentist a trial and subsequent execution.[72] Mango fever descended on China, with the production of household enamelware and cotton quilt covers employing mango designs, as well as more than seventy different badges featuring mangoes, distributed free within factories.[73] Mango-brand cigarettes were produced by a factory in Xinzheng.[74]

Two characteristics of the gifted mangoes facilitated this transformation from humble fruit to objects of veneration. First, their propitious golden colour, which in China has associations with both authority and wealth.[75] Second, their novelty. Mangoes were unknown in northern China in the late 1960s. They had the ability to generate wonder, which, as we have seen, has long been a central consideration in the most important diplomatic gifts. Since this was an unknown fruit, no symbolic meaning had yet been assigned to it. Such a meaning was quickly appropriated from the tale of the magical peach, the 'longevity fruit' that assured a long and healthy life.[76] This cultural assignation had the effect of making Chairman Mao's gift all the more remarkable and self-sacrificing: the gift of a leader who had turned down the prospect of long life and instead gifted it to humble workers engaged in an important mission.

The cult of the mango quickly waned, particularly following Mao's death in 1976. By the early 1980s, it became prudent to dispose of wax replica mangoes along with other Mao memorabilia. The fate of many a wax mango was to be converted to a candle to illuminate the home during power outages.[77] The replica of the gift now projected the spirit of the giver in a way that became dangerous once that giver was out of favour. Chairman Mao's mangoes have made a journey from quotidian courtesy gift, to a means of signalling political favour to a particular group, to object of veneration, to object with potentially risky associations with a former leadership, to curio. They exemplify the complexity and fascination of the history of diplomatic gifts.

NOTES

INTRODUCTION

1. Reuters 2013.
2. See, for example, Hogan 2015, Gramer 2017.
3. Hogan 2015.
4. Gramer 2017.
5. See, for example, Parris and Bryson 2012, pp. 9–10, and Renwick 2016.
6. Mauss 1966.
7. Malinowski 1922.
8. Ibid., p. 81.
9. Mauss 1966, p. 22.
10. Ibid., p. 20.
11. Ibid., p. 72.
12. Ibid., p. 73.
13. Ibid., p. 41.
14. Mawdsley 2012, p. 258.
15. Carrier 1991, p. 121.
16. Ceulemans 2021, p. 134.
17. Fiske 1993, p. 3.
18. Komter 2007, p. 99.
19. Ibid., p. 100.
20. Quoted in Tremml-Werner, Hellman and van Meersbergen 2020, p. 194.
21. Windler 2001, p. 79.
22. Carrier 1991, pp. 125–7.
23. Mauss 1966, p. 9.
24. Office of the Chief of Protocol 2002.
25. Brummell 2021, p. 146.
26. Appadurai 1988, p. 3.
27. Appadurai 2006, p. 15.
28. Weiner 1992.
29. Weiner 1985, p. 210.
30. Ibid., p. 211.
31. Mosko 2000, p. 379.

32. Weiner 1985, p. 223.

33. Mauss 1966, p. 10.

34. Carrier 1991, p. 123.

35. Mauss 1966, p. 9.

36. Clarke 1981, p. 42.

37. Ibid., p. 44.

38. Mauss 1966, p. 57.

39. Parry 1986, p. 459.

40. Ibid., p 461.

41. Ibid., p. 468.

42. Biedermann, Gerritsen and Riello 2019, p. 1.

43. Lane 2000, p. 104.

44. Ssorin-Chaikov 2006, p. 362.

45. Jönsson and Hall 2005, p. 51.

46. Leira 2016, p. 28.

47. Nicolson 1942, p. 17.

48. Fletcher 2016, p. 25.

49. Numelin 1950.

50. Jönsson and Hall 2005, p. 10.

51. 2 Kings 18:15–16, Holy Bible: King James Version.

52. Ibid., 18:21.

53. Ibid., 18:27.

54. Nicolson 1942, p. 19.

55. Ibid., p. 20.

56. Jönsson and Hall 2005, p. 88.

57. Nicolson 1942, p. 22.

58. Jönsson and Hall 2005, p. 11.

59. McClanahan 1989, p. 22.

60. Nicolson 1942, p. 24.

61. Jönsson and Hall 2005, p. 11.

62. Ibid., p. 74.

63. McClanahan 1989, p. 24.

64. Mattingly 1937, p. 427.

65. Ibid., p. 431.

66. Ibid., p. 432.

67. Jönsson and Hall 2005, p. 40.

68. Croxton 1999, p. 582.

69. Osiander 2001, p. 266.

70. Croxton 1999, p. 575.

71. Ibid., p. 574.

72. Ibid., p. 575.

73. Jönsson and Hall 2005, p. 36.

74. Rienow 1961, p. 207.

75. Jönsson and Hall 2005, p. 11.

76. Ibid., p. 41.

77. Nicolson 1942, p. 26.

78. Leira 2016, p. 31.

79. Ibid.

80. Frey and Frey 2011, p. 3.

81. Leira 2016, p. 34.

82. Jönsson and Hall 2005, p. 90.

83. Nicolson 1942, pp. 31–2.

84. Quoted in Eban 1985, p. 11. Jönsson and Hall 2005, p. 91, give the figure as two years.

85. Quoted in Jönsson and Hall 2005, p. 91.

86. Tremml-Werner, Hellman and van Meersbergen 2020, p. 188.

87. Jönsson and Hall 2005, p. 132.

88. Nix 2018.

89. Jönsson and Hall 2005, p. 124.

90. Ibid.

91. Tremml-Werner, Hellman and van Meersbergen 2020, p. 188.

92. Müderrisoğlu 2014, p. 270.

93. Ocak 2016, p. 29.

94. Jonsson and Hall 2005, p. 127.

*c.*1353 BCE: TWO GOLD-PLATED WOODEN STATUES

1. Reeves 2019, p. 57.

2. Campbell 1960, p. 4.

3. See Reeves 2019.

4. Holmes 1975, p. 376.

5. Amarna Letter EA 21 (the number refers to the standard classification), quoted in Holmes 1975, p. 377.

6. Holmes 1975, p. 380.

7. EA 10, cited in Holmes 1975, p. 379.

8. EA 19, quoted in Scoville 2018, p. 72.

9. EA 44, quoted in Hoffner 2009, p. 280.

10. Ibid., p. 281.

11. Podany 2010, p. 240.

12. EA27, quoted in Scoville 2018, p. 75.

13. Scoville 2018, p. 76.

14. Podany 2010, p. 241.

15. Ibid., p. 242.

*c.*1250 BCE: A WOODEN HORSE

1. Nagy 1981, p. 191.

2. Quoted in Bogdanor 2020, p. 43.
3. Alexander 2009, p. 2.
4. Franko 2005/6, p. 123.
5. Murphy 2017, p. 19.
6. Bryce 2002, p. 188.
7. Murphy 2017, pp. 22–5.
8. The Epitome of Apollodorus. Quoted in Murphy 2017, p. 25.
9. Bryce 2002, p. 185.
10. Ibid., p. 190.
11. Ibid., p. 192.
12. Alexander 2009, p. 5.
13. Murphy 2017, p. 25.
14. Ibid., p. 21.
15. Rouman and Held 1972, p. 328.
16. Murphy 2017, p. 21.
17. Ibid., p. 31.
18. Ibid., p. 21.
19. Finglass 2020.
20. Harford 2019.
21. Ibid.

332 BCE: A WHIP, A BALL AND A CHEST OF GOLD

1. Wolohojian 1969, p. 1.
2. Perkins and Woolsey 1854, p. 360.
3. Wolohojian 1969, p. 2.
4. Ibid., pp. 58–9.
5. Ibid., p. 61.
6. Konstantakos 2015, p. 137.
7. Perkins and Woolsey 1854, pp. 375–6.
8. Ibid., p. 376.
9. Konstantakos 2015, p. 134.
10. Ibid., p. 138.
11. Shakespeare, *Henry V* Act 1, Scene 2.
12. Ibid.
13. Jackson 2016.
14. Hilton 2015.
15. Ibid.
16. Taylor 1932, p. 146.
17. Behrens-Abouseif 2016, p. 25.

*c.*4 BCE: GOLD, FRANKINCENSE AND MYRRH

1. Matthew 2:9, Holy Bible: King James Version.

2. Ibid., 2:1.
3. Ibid., 2:2.
4. Mobbs 2006, p. 601.
5. Boyce 2001, p. 48.
6. Hegedus 2003, pp. 82–3.
7. Ibid., p. 82.
8. Matthew 2:2, Holy Bible: King James Version.
9. Numbers 23:7, Holy Bible: King James Version.
10. Ibid., 24:17.
11. Hannah 2015, p. 434.
12. Quoted in ibid., p. 438.
13. Mobbs 2006, p. 601.
14. Quoted in Hone 1890, p. 40.
15. Hannah 2015, p. 450.
16. Landau 2016, p.20.
17. Hannah 2015, p. 446.
18. Landau 2016, pp. 30–8.
19. Psalm 72:11, Holy Bible: King James Version.
20. Garstad 2011, p. 3.
21. Duchesne-Guillemin 1973, p. 97.
22. Jones 2020.
23. Duchesne-Guillemin 1973, p. 96.
24. Polo 1871, p. 73.
25. Ibid., pp. 74–5.
26. Roberts 2007, pp. 31–43.
27. Behrens-Abouseif 2016, p. 122.
28. Isaiah 60:6, Holy Bible: King James Version.
29. Polo 1871, pp. 74–5.

757: AN ORGAN

1. Williams 2005, p. 137.
2. This is the argument of Apel 1948, p. 212.
3. Williams 2005, p. 137.
4. Ibid.
5. Ibid., p. 140.
6. Emerick 2017, p. 144.
7. Ibid., p. 146.
8. Ibid.
9. Apel 1948, p. 204.
10. Williams 2005, p. 142.
11. Apel 1948, p. 192.
12. Hyde 1938, p. 394.

13. Ibid., p. 405.
14. Leverett 1996, p. 776.
15. Hyde 1938, p. 407.
16. Ibid., p. 409.
17. Williams 2005, p. 140.
18. Leverett 1996, p. 777.
19. Williams 2005, p. 144.
20. Apel 1948, p. 210.

802: AN ELEPHANT

1. Runciman 1935, pp. 618–19.
2. Ibid., p. 609.
3. Gil 1997, p. 286.
4. Runciman 1935, p. 610.
5. Gil 1997, p. 285.
6. Khadduri 2006, p. 247.
7. Gil 1997, p. 285.
8. Ibid., p. 286.
9. Ibid.
10. Subramaniam 2018, p. 208.
11. Ibid.
12. Latowsky 2005, p. 25.
13. Ibid.
14. See Brubaker 2004, p. 176.
15. Quoted in Runciman 1935, p. 611.
16. Runciman 1935, p. 613.
17. Butt 2002, p. 146.
18. Latowsky 2005, p. 27.
19. Khadduri 2006, p. 249.
20. See Runciman 1935, p. 612.
21. Latowsky 2005, p. 51.
22. Ibid.
23. Neis 2018.

950: A SILK CLOAK AND A BAG OF GOLD COINS

1. Muthesius 1992, p. 99.
2. Muthesius 2015, p. 352.
3. Ibid., p. 353.
4. Muthesius 1992, p. 99.
5. Brubaker 2004, p. 193.
6. Ibid., p. 190.

7.   Ibid., p. 193.
8.   Woodfin 2008, p. 33.
9.   Ibid., p. 44.
10. Brubaker 2004, p. 194.
11. Woodfin 2008, p. 45.
12. Wright 1930, p. 1.
13. Liudprand 1930, p. 206.
14. Ibid., p. 207.
15. Ibid., p. 209.
16. Ibid.
17. Quoted in Liudprand 1930, p. 212.
18. Ibid.
19. Ibid., p.263.
20. Ibid., p. 264.
21. Ibid., p. 236.
22. Ibid., p. 267.
23. Ibid., p. 268.

*c.*1028: A FRAGMENT OF THE TRUE CROSS

1.   Wycherley 2019, p. 48.
2.   Twain 1869, p. 165.
3.   Klein 2004, p. 284.
4.   Majeska 2002, pp. 93–4.
5.   Messenger 1947, p. 208.
6.   Wolfram 2006, p. 197.
7.   Ibid., p. 199.
8.   Ibid., p. 201.
9.   Klein 2004, p. 296.
10. Ibid., p. 297.
11. Ibid., p. 298.
12. Ibid., pp. 301–2.
13. Nicol 1992, p. 168.
14. Ibid., p. 169.
15. Ibid., p. 170.
16. Wycherley 2019, p. 49.
17. Wolff 1954, p. 45.
18. Klein 2004, pp. 310–11.
19. Toth 2011, p. 107.

1261: AN EMBROIDERED SILK

1.   Woodfin 2008, p. 33.

2. Toth 2011, p. 92.
3. Hilsdale 2010, p. 155.
4. Ibid., p. 158.
5. Ibid., p. 160.
6. Ibid.
7. Toth 2011, pp. 95–6.
8. Ibid., p. 105.
9. Ibid., pp. 106–7.
10. Ibid., p. 106.
11. Ibid., p. 107.
12. Hilsdale 2010, p. 199.

1353: SIXTY SLAVES

1. Behrens-Abouseif 2008, p. 295.
2. Quoted in AlSayyad 2011, p. 93.
3. Behrens-Abouseif 2016.
4. Ibid., p. 30.
5. Ibid., p. 169.
6. Ibid., p. 17.
7. Ibid., p. 113.
8. Ibid., p. 31.
9. Mauss 1966, p. 8.
10. Behrens-Abouseif 2016, p. 176.
11. Ibid., p. 24.
12. Ibid., p. 150.
13. Sadek 2006, p. 668.
14. Ibid., p. 669.
15. Vallet 2019, pp. 582–3.
16. Behrens-Abouseif 2016, p. 37.
17. Ibid., p. 41.
18. Vallet 2019, p. 592.
19. Behrens-Abouseif 2016, p. 38.
20. Ibid., p. 43.
21. Ibid., p. 32.

1489: SEVEN BEAVERS

1. Kivimäe 1996, p. 10.
2. Ibid., p. 11.
3. Mänd 2016, p. 9.
4. Ibid., p.10
5. Ketcham Wheaton 1983, p. 12.

6. Albala 2017, p. 39.
7. Albala 2003, p. 71.
8. Mänd 2016, p. 13.
9. Ibid.
10. Bingen 1998, p. 219.
11. Acheson 2009, p. 34.
12. Mänd 2016, p. 10.
13. Ibid.
14. Acheson 2009, p. 38.
15. HBC Heritage n.d.

1512: FIFTY BLOCKS OF CHEESE

1. Brummell 2020, p. 68.
2. Ibid., p. 67.
3. Quoted, for example, in Office of the Chief of Protocol 2018.
4. Mesotten 2017, p. 143.
5. Ibid., pp. 136–7.
6. Ibid., p. 141.
7. Ibid., p. 142.
8. Arbel 2004, pp. 37–8.
9. Wansbrough 1963, p. 514.
10. Ciocîltan 2012, p. 17.
11. Diffie and Winius 1977, p. 231.
12. Hysell 2016.
13. Diffie and Winius 1977, p. 240.
14. Howard 2007 B, p. 84.
15. Setton 1984, p. 33.
16. Howard 2007 B, p. 84.
17. Setton 1984, p. 30.
18. Behrens-Abouseif 2016, p. 110.
19. Hysell 2016.
20. Setton 1984, p. 31.
21. Dursteler 2013, p. 169.
22. Wills 2003, p. 170.
23. Moote and Moote 2004, p. 264.

1514: AN ELEPHANT

1. Bedini 2000, p. 23.
2. Quoted in ibid., p. 20.
3. Bedini 1981, p. 75.
4. Ibid., p. 76.

5.   Bedini 2000, pp. 25–6.
6.   Ibid., p. 28.
7.   Ibid., p. 31.
8.   Bedini 1981, p. 77.
9.   Ibid.
10. Bedini 2000, pp. 51–2.
11. Ibid., p. 72.
12. This is the view of Bedini 2000, p. 80.
13. Ibid., p. 109.
14. Ibid., p. 98.
15. Ibid., p. 139.
16. Pimentel 2017.
17. Farrar 2020.
18. Bedini 2000, p. 170.
19. Quoted in ibid., p. 159.
20. Ibid., p. 233.

1514: A RHINOCEROS

1.   Bedini 2000, p. 111.
2.   Ibid., p. 112.
3.   Ibid., p. 112.
4.   Ibid., p. 114.
5.   Bedini 1981, p. 80.
6.   Bedini 2000, p. 119.
7.   Feiman 2012, p. 23.
8.   Ibid., pp. 22–3.
9.   Bedini 2000, p. 126.
10. Ibid., p. 128.
11. Ibid., p. 129.
12. Ibid., p. 129.
13. Ibid., p. 133.
14. Norfolk 1998.

1520: A HORSE

1.   Syndram and von Bloh 2007, p. 53.
2.   Mänd 2016, p. 4.
3.   Richardson 2013, p. 6.
4.   Ibid., p. 9.
5.   Ibid., p. 8.
6.   Richardson 2016.
7.   Ibid.

8. Ibid.
9. Tonni 2012, p. 270.
10. Bolland 2011, p. 95.
11. Richardson 2016.
12. Bolland 2011, p. 95.
13. Ibid.
14. Tonni 2012, p. 276.
15. Tobey 2005, pp. 64–5.
16. Ibid., p. 71.
17. Behrens-Abouseif 2016, p. 53.
18. Tobey 2005, pp. 71–2.
19. Tonni 2012, p. 268.
20. Tobey 2005, p. 72.
21. Ibid., p. 73.
22. Ibid.
23. Tonni 2012, p. 270.
24. Ibid., p. 271.
25. Tobey 2005, p. 70.
26. Tonni 2012, p. 274.
27. Ibid., pp. 275–6.
28. Ibid., p. 276.

1527: A SUIT OF ARMOUR

1. Syndram and von Bloh 2007, p. 51.
2. Farago 2019.
3. Grancsay 1928, pp. 100–1.
4. Ibid., p. 100.
5. Kendall 2020, p. 61.
6. Ibid.
7. Mercer 2014, p. 2.
8. Mann 1951, p. 380.
9. Mercer 2014, p. 1.
10. Mann 1951, p. 380.
11. Bolland 2011, p. 94
12. Terjanian 2009.
13. Mann 1951, p. 380.
14. Terjanian 2009.
15. Nickel 1972, pp. 75–9.
16. Ibid., pp. 115–20.
17. Ibid., p. 80.
18. Ibid., p. 115.
19. Ibid., p. 110.

20. Ibid., p. 124.
21. Richardson 2016.
22. Ibid.

1571: TWENTY-FIVE ROBES OF HONOUR

1. Phillips 2015, p. 113.
2. Sanders 2001, p. 225.
3. Phillips 2015, p. 120.
4. Müderrisoğlu 2014, p. 270.
5. Ocak 2016, p. 29.
6. Talbot 2016, p. 358.
7. Hurewitz 1961, p. 145.
8. Talbot 2016, p. 367.
9. Ibid., p. 372.
10. Ocak 2016, p. 33.
11. Howard 2007 A, p. 143.
12. Ocak 2016, p. 39.
13. Hurewitz 1961, p. 146.
14. Ocak 2016, p. 39.
15. Phillips 2015, p. 129.
16. Ibid., p. 123.
17. Ibid., pp. 124–5.
18. Ibid., p. 128.
19. Ocak 2016, p. 40.
20. Ibid., p. 42.
21. Ibid., p. 14.
22. Ibid., pp. 19–20.
23. Ibid., p. 30.
24. Ibid., p. 36.
25. Ibid., pp. 39–47.
26. Ibid., p. 50.
27. Ibid., pp. 56–79.
28. Brummell 2018, p. 54.
29. Caron 2014.

1613: A TELESCOPE

1. Screech 2020, pp. 7–8.
2. Kerr 1824, p. 102.
3. Screech 2020, pp. 32–3.
4. Ibid., p. 34.
5. Satow 1900, p. xv.

6. Ibid., p. xlvii.
7. Ibid., p. lii.
8. Screech 2020, p. 10.
9. Screech 2020.
10. Ibid., pp. 72–4.
11. Ibid., pp. 68–9.
12. Saris 1900, p. 113.
13. Screech 2020, p. 79.
14. Saris 1900, p. 113.
15. Royal Armouries Collections n.d.
16. Satow 1900, p. lxvii.
17. Clulow 2010, p. 8.
18. Clulow 2019, p. 202.
19. Ibid., p. 205.
20. Ibid., p. 214.
21. Curtin 2014, p. 7.
22. Ibid., pp. 7–8.

1623: GIAMBOLOGNA'S *SAMSON SLAYING A PHILISTINE*

1. Redworth 2003, p. 1.
2. Ibid.
3. Samson 2016, p. 4.
4. Ibid., p. 2.
5. Brotton 2016, pp. 18–19.
6. Ibid., p. 11.
7. Ibid., p.17.
8. Ibid., p. 16.
9. Matthews 2001, p. 86.
10. Brotton 2016, p. 19.
11. Ibid., p. 20.
12. Rosand 1972, p. 533.
13. Pursell 2002, p. 714.
14. Brotton 2016, p. 24.
15. Pursell 2002, p. 720.
16. See Redworth 2003, p. 5.
17. Avery 1978.

1716: THE AMBER ROOM

1. Scott-Clark and Levy 2004, p. 4.
2. Ibid., p. 6.
3. Czajkowski 2009, p. 86.
4. King 2014, p. 1.

5. Wittwer 2007, p. 89.
6. Scott-Clark and Levy 2004, pp. 72–3.
7. Wittwer 2007, pp. 88–9.
8. Syndram and von Bloh 2007, p. 50.
9. Scott-Clark and Levy 2004, pp. 22–6.
10. Ibid., pp. 27–8.
11. Wittwer 2007, p. 89.
12. Scott-Clark and Levy 2004, p. 54.
13. Ibid, p. 55.
14. Ibid., p. 17.
15. Ibid., p. 22.
16. Ibid., p. 31–3.
17. Ibid., p. 75.
18. Ibid., p. 329.
19. Ibid., p. 199.
20. Ibid., p. 103.
21. Moorhouse 2013.
22. Gershon 2020.
23. Eggleston 1999.

1745: THE *ST ANDREW SERVICE*

1. Marchand 2020, p. 14.
2. Ibid., p. 30.
3. Cassidy-Geiger 2007, p. 3.
4. Marchand 2020, p. 32.
5. Queiroz and Agathopoulos 2005, p. 214.
6. Cassidy-Geiger 2007, p. 4.
7. Marchand 2020, p. 39.
8. Cassidy-Geiger 2007, p. 14.
9. Ibid., p. 18.
10. Syndram and von Bloh 2007, p. 44.
11. Cassidy-Geiger 2007, p. 11.
12. Ibid., p. 16.
13. Ibid.
14. Liackhova 2007, p. 65.
15. Ibid., p. 73.
16. Ibid., p. 72.
17. Ibid., p. 74.
18. Ibid., p. 79.
19. Ibid., p. 80.
20. Marchand 2020, p. 41.

1759: A DINNER AND DESSERT SERVICE

1. Savill 2018.
2. Ibid.
3. Simms 2007.
4. Yagi 2017, pp. 9–10.
5. Clayton 1981, p. 585.
6. Savill 2018.
7. Rochebrune 2018.
8. Schroeder 2018.
9. Adams 2007, p. 184.
10. Schroeder 2018.
11. Schwartz 2015, p. 84.
12. Ibid., p. 90.
13. Ibid.
14. Ibid., p. 88.
15. Schroeder 2018.
16. McNab 1961, p. 173.
17. Ibid., p. 180.
18. Prodger 2012.
19. Adams 2007, p. 185.

1785: A MINIATURE PORTRAIT OF KING LOUIS XVI OF FRANCE

1. Office of the Historian n.d.
2. Fleming 2014.
3. Isaacson 2003, p. 325.
4. Ibid., p. 328.
5. Quoted in McCullough 2002, p. 196.
6. Isaacson 2003, p. 406.
7. Ibid., p. 411.
8. American Philosophical Society 2006.
9. For example Teachout 2014, McDuffee 2017.
10. Quoted in McDuffee 2017.
11. Eaton 2004, p. 820.
12. Ibid.
13. O'Regan 2020, p. 69.
14. Kozmanová 2019, p. 240.
15. Quoted in American Philosophical Society 2006.
16. Ibid.
17. Teachout 2014, p. 25.
18. Ibid., p. 29.
19. Ibid., p. 4.

1785: STATE PORTRAITS OF KING LOUIS XVI OF FRANCE AND QUEEN MARIE ANTOINETTE

1. Eaton 2004, p. 820.
2. Eaton 2019, p. 272.
3. Ibid., p. 273.
4. Quoted in ibid., p. 274.
5. Ibid., p. 277.
6. Ibid., pp. 282–3.
7. Eaton 2004, p. 831.
8. Larkin 2010, p. 41.
9. Quoted in ibid., p. 39.
10. Ibid., p. 44.
11. Medlam 2007, p. 146.
12. Ibid., p. 143.
13. Carey 2008.
14. Larkin 2010, p. 68.
15. Quoted in ibid., p. 70.
16. Ibid., p. 73.
17. Ibid., p. 32.

1790: A PORTRAIT OF CATHERINE THE GREAT

1. Quoted in Sobchack 2007, p. 220.
2. Drury 2019.
3. Markina 2019, p. 21.
4. Ibid.
5. Ibid., p. 25.
6. Sciberras and Grech 2019.
7. Markina 2019, p. 28.
8. Sciberras and Grech 2019.
9. Markina 2019, pp. 36–8.

1793: A PLANETARIUM

1. Berg 2006, p. 271.
2. Meyer 2009, pp. 104–5.
3. Pritchard 1943, p. 163.
4. Berg 2006, pp. 275–6.
5. Lindorff 2012, p. 441.
6. Hurewitz 1961, p. 143.
7. Kustermans 2019, p. 422.
8. Ibid., p. 423.
9. Pritchard 1943, p. 165.

10. Kustermans 2019, p. 425.
11. Lindorff 2012, p. 446.
12. For example Meyer 2009, pp. 115–21.
13. Ibid.
14. Pritchard 1943, p. 199.
15. Harrison 2018, pp. 79–80.
16. Ibid.
17. Ibid., p. 76.
18. Turton 2016, p. 117.
19. Berg 2006, p. 278.
20. Ibid., p. 283.
21. Ibid., p. 281.
22. Ibid., p. 272.
23. Harrison 2018, p. 84.
24. Schaffer 2006, p. 221.
25. Ibid., pp. 233–4.
26. Ibid., pp. 233–6.
27. Harrison 2018, pp. 81–2.
28. Turton 2016, p. 118.
29. Quoted in Schaffer 2006, p. 227.
30. Harrison 2018, p. 83.
31. Ibid., p. 84.
32. See for example Turton 2016, pp. 117–18.
33. Quoted in Meyer 2009, pp. 121–2.
34. Harrison 2018, pp. 87–92.
35. Ibid., pp. 85–7.
36. Meyer 2009, p. 122.

1816: THE SPANISH ROYAL COLLECTION

1. Reynolds 2017 notes that the address arose from its position as the first house encountered after the main turnpike into central London.
2. Bryant 2005, p. 42.
3. Ibid., p. 48.
4. Brier 2013, p. 65.
5. Ibid., p. 66.
6. Hoskin 2015.
7. Stanhope 1888, p. 32.
8. Heath 1995.
9. Bryant 2005, p. 19.
10. Kennedy 2015.
11. Quoted in McNay 2015, p. 209.
12. This is the argument presented by Lindsay 2014.

1826: A GIRAFFE

1. Joost-Gaugier 1987, pp. 94–5.
2. Belozerskaya 2006.
3. Sharkey 2015.
4. Ringmar 2006, pp. 390–1.
5. Sharkey 2015.
6. Behrens-Abouseif 2016, p. 141.
7. Cuttler 1991, p. 165.
8. Joost-Gaugier 1987, p. 94.
9. Belozerskaya 2006.
10. Joost-Gaugier 1987, p. 94.
11. Ibid., p. 91.
12. Ringmar 2006, p. 383.
13. Gordon 2016.
14. Sharkey 2015.
15. Lagueux 2003, p. 225.
16. Sharkey 2015.
17. Lagueux 2003, p. 231.
18. Ibid., p. 233.
19. Ibid., pp. 229–30.
20. Ibid., p. 233.
21. Ibid., p. 234.
22. Sharkey 2015.
23. Lagueux 2003, p. 235.
24. Sharkey 2015.
25. Ringmar 2006, p. 384.
26. Sharkey 2015.
27. Ringmar 2006, p. 384.
28. Ibid., p. 385.
29. Lagueux 2003, p. 242.
30. Sharkey 2015.
31. Ibid.
32. Allin 1998.

1829: THE *SHAH DIAMOND*

1. Brintlinger 2003, p. 372.
2. Brintlinger 2020.
3. Lang 1948, p. 319.
4. Ibid., p. 321.
5. Ibid., p. 321.
6. Brintlinger 2003, p. 391.
7. Ibid., p. 379.

8. Lang 1948, p. 326.
9. Ibid., p. 326.
10. Ibid., p. 327.
11. Harden 1971, p. 78.
12. Binyon 2003, p. 295.
13. Ibid., p. 300.
14. Lang 1948, p. 329.
15. Ibid., p. 337.
16. Piper 1990, p. 172.

1831: AN OBELISK

1. Gordon 2016.
2. Brier 2018, p. 76.
3. Hassan 2016, p. 61.
4. Gordon 2016.
5. D'Alton 1993, p. 7.
6. Ibid.
7. Thompson 2015, p. 171.
8. Wilkinson 2014, p. 97.
9. Brier 2018, p. 81.
10. Thompson 2015, p. 171.
11. Brier 2018, p. 81.
12. Wilkinson 2014, pp. 97–8.
13. Gordon 2016.
14. Wilkinson 2014, p. 98.
15. Brier 2018, p. 88.
16. See Hollier 1994, p. 673.
17. Salama 2020.
18. King 1883, p. 42.
19. Ibid., p. 43.
20. D'Alton 1993, p. 15.
21. Ibid., p. 21.
22. Foderaro 2014.

1837: A PEACE MEDAL

1. Clulow 2019, p. 198.
2. Francis 1986, p. 11.
3. Depkat 2016, p. 83.
4. Ibid., p. 86.
5. Nash 2017.
6. Bentley 1958, p. 154.
7. Depkat 2016, p. 83.

8. Ibid., p. 84.
9. Ibid., p. 93.
10. Quoted in ibid., p. 94.
11. Johnson 2007, p. 771.
12. Ibid., p. 773.
13. Kelderman 2019, p. 104.
14. Ibid., p. 105.
15. Ibid., p. 111.
16. Ibid., p. 109.
17. Johnson 2007, p. 777.
18. Miller 2002, p. 222.
19. Ibid., pp. 237–40.
20. Depkat 2016, p. 96.

1850: SARAH FORBES BONETTA

1. Forbes 1851, Vol. 1, p. vi.
2. Ibid., p. 7.
3. Ibid., p. 15.
4. Ibid., p. 51.
5. Ibid., p. 87.
6. Dike 1956, p. 13.
7. Forbes 1851, Vol. 2, p. 50.
8. Ibid., p. 208.
9. Ibid., p. 10.
10. Myers 1999, p. 14.
11. Forbes 1851, Vol. 2, p. 207.
12. Myers 1999, p. 17.
13. Forbes 1851, Vol. 2, p. 207.
14. Ibid., p. 208.
15. Myers 1999, p. 29.
16. Ibid., p. 43.
17. Ibid., pp. 57–9.
18. Ibid., p. 62.
19. Ibid., p. 102.
20. Quoted in Myers 1999, p. 110.

1880: THE *RESOLUTE* DESK

1. Sandler 2006, p. 6.
2. Ibid., p. 69.
3. Russell 2005, p. 51.
4. Cavell 2018, p. 292.
5. Sandler 2006, p. 227.

6. Ibid., p. 106.
7. Ibid., p. 115.
8. Ibid., p. 138.
9. Finnis 2014.
10. Sandler 2006, p. 150.
11. Ibid., p. 155.
12. Quoted in Sandler 2006, p. 216.
13. Grundhauser 2016.

1884: THE STATUE OF LIBERTY

1. Khan 2010, p. 25.
2. Ibid., p. 10.
3. Harrison 2011, pp. 149–50.
4. Khan 2010, p. 3.
5. Quoted in ibid., p. 8.
6. Ibid., pp. 14–15.
7. Joseph, Rosenblatt and Kinebrew 2000, pp. 25–7.
8. Berenson 2012.
9. Ibid.
10. US House of Representatives 1885, p. 162.
11. Quoted in ibid., p. 161.
12. Ibid., p. 158.
13. Ibid.
14. Boime 1986, p. 13.
15. Joseph, Rosenblatt and Kinebrew 2000, p. 59.
16. Ibid., p. 55.
17. Berenson 2012.
18. Boime 1986, p. 12.
19. Ibid., p. 13.
20. Berenson 2012.
21. Ibid.
22. Boime 1986, p. 13.
23. Oren 2008.
24. Viano 2018, p. 8.
25. Quoted in Boime 1986, p. 13.
26. Serratore 2019.
27. Quoted in Khan 2010, p. 6.
28. Ibid., p. 5.
29. Office of the Chief of Protocol 2006.

1912: 3,020 CHERRY TREES

1. Butler 2017, p. 83.

2. Ibid., p. 82.
3. Stone 2018.
4. USDA Foreign Agricultural Service 2010, p. 2.
5. Ibid.
6. McClellan 2012, p. 24.
7. Ibid.
8. Ibid.
9. USDA Foreign Agricultural Service 2010, p. 4.
10. Quoted in ibid., p. 5.
11. McClellan 2012, p. 25.
12. USDA Foreign Agricultural Service 2010, p. 7.
13. Ibid., p. 8.
14. Ibid., p. 9.
15. Ibid., p. 8.

1935: A MAYBACH DS-8 ZEPPELIN

1. Kidambi 2019.
2. Choudhary 2020.
3. Raja Malvinder Singh's account is found in Dwivedi 2003, quoted in Chavan 2019.
4. Bonhams 2015.
5. Ibid.
6. Quoted in Chavan 2019.
7. Bonhams 2015.
8. See Buncombe 2008.
9. Ibid.
10. PTI 2008.
11. AFP 2015.

1943: THE SWORD OF STALINGRAD

1. Andrew and Styles 2014, p. 190.
2. Ibid., p. 186.
3. Ibid., p. 189.
4. Ibid., p. 191.
5. Quoted in Andrew and Styles 2014, p. 190.
6. MacCarthy 2005.
7. Waugh 1964, p. 22.
8. Ibid.
9. Ibid., p. 23.
10. Lively 2001.
11. Waugh 1964, p. 26.
12. Gallagher and Villar Flor 2014, p. 100.
13. Brady 2018.

1947: A CHRISTMAS TREE

1. Friis 1965, p. 423.
2. Grimnes 2013, p. 384.
3. Rowston 2009/10, p. 8.
4. Westminster City Council 2020.
5. Ibid.
6. Keane 2014.
7. Larsen 2019.
8. Quoted in Magra 2019.
9. Lynch 2019.

1949: THE MERCI TRAIN

1. Ball 1999.
2. Sweetland 2019.
3. Kelly 2019.
4. Sweetland 2019.
5. Ibid.
6. Kelly 2019.
7. Scheele 2002, p. 36.
8. Quoted in ibid., p. 37.
9. Kelly 2019.
10. Griswold 2011.
11. Ibid.
12. Sweetland 2019.
13. Scheele 2002, p. 40.
14. Mukharji 2016, p. 16.
15. Scheele 2002, p. 40.
16. Ibid., p. 35.
17. Ibid., p. 39.
18. Ibid., p. 40.
19. State Historical Society of North Dakota 2007.
20. Brooklyn Museum 1949.
21. HM Treasury official Edward Wilder Playfair, quoted in Mukharji 2016, p. 16.
22. Mukharji 2016, p. 16.
23. Ibid., p. 18.

1949: A PLANETARIUM

1. Ssorin-Chaikov 2006, p. 365.
2. McNeal 1988, p. 291.
3. Ssorin-Chaikov 2006, p. 366.
4. Ibid., p. 359.

5. Ibid.
6. Knight 2012.
7. Ssorin-Chaikov 2006, p. 360.
8. McNeal 1988, p. 292.
9. Ibid.
10. Ssorin-Chaikov 2006, p. 364.
11. Knight 2012.
12. Ssorin-Chaikov 2006, p. 368.
13. Radchenko 2013.
14. Ibid.
15. Ssorin-Chaikov 2006, p. 369.
16. Quoted in ibid., p. 367.
17. Wilson 1998.
18. Behrends 2004, p. 162.
19. Ibid., p. 167.
20. Tikhomirov 2010, p. 309.
21. Ibid.
22. Behrends 2004, p. 169.
23. Ibid.
24. Quoted in Tikhomirov 2010, p. 310.
25. Firebrace 2013, pp. 134–5.
26. Ibid., p. 136.
27. Behrends 2004, p. 169.
28. Firebrace 2017.

1952: A BOX OF SHAMROCKS

1. Quoted in Broderick 2017.
2. Ibid.
3. Wunner 2010.
4. Driscoll 2016.
5. Kelly 2017.
6. Collins 2017.
7. Wunner 2010.
8. Ibid.
9. Collins 2017.
10. Meyer 2005, p. 111.
11. Kelly 2017.
12. Office of the Chief of Protocol 2018.
13. Kelly 2017.
14. Baker 2010.
15. Scully 2005.

1957:TWO SWANS

1. Cleaver 2017.
2. Quoted in Tomlins 1819, p. 1012.
3. Cleaver 2017.
4. Crosby 2016.
5. Ibid.
6. Ibid.
7. Ibid.
8. Diaz 2020.
9. Powell 2018.
10. Ibid.
11. Ibid.
12. Ibid.
13. Kupfer 2019.
14. Harrison Lewis, Chief of the Canadian Wildlife Service, quoted in Burnett 2003, p. 229.
15. Burnett 2003, p. 227.
16. Lewis 1951/2, p. 71.
17. Stowe 1957.
18. Lewis 1951/2, p. 71.
19. Mackay 1953, p. 49.
20. Lewis 1951/2, p. 71.
21. Connelly 1970, p. 56.
22. Houston 2012, p. 272.
23. Connelly 1970, p. 56.

1965: AN ACRE OF ENGLISH GROUND

1. Brinkley 2013.
2. Kennedy 1963.
3. House of Commons 1963.
4. House of Commons 1964, c.471.
5. Ibid.
6. Evans 1965, p. 704.
7. Ibid.
8. Turner 2017.
9. Kennedy 1961.
10. Cook and Webb 2015.
11. Entwistle 2019, p. 53.

1969: FOUR SPECKS OF MOON ROCK

1. Pearlman n.d. A.

2. Ibid.
3. Pearlman n.d. B.
4. Ibid.
5. Kloc 2012.
6. The sting operation was gloriously named Operation Lunar Eclipse. There is a detailed account in ibid.
7. Ibid.
8. Ibid.

1972: TWO PANDAS

1. Quoted in Miller 2013, p. 209.
2. Ibid., p. 212.
3. Buckingham, David and Jepson 2013, p. 2.
4. Miller 2013, p. 203.
5. Ibid.
6. Byron 2011.
7. Ibid.
8. Miller 2013, p. 203.
9. Ibid., p. 207.
10. Ibid.
11. Ibid., p. 209.
12. Ibid., p. 212.
13. Ibid., p. 226.
14. Ibid., pp. 226–7.
15. Buckingham, David and Jepson 2013, p. 2.
16. Miller 2013, pp. 203–4.
17. Buckingham, David and Jepson 2013, p. 2.
18. Qianhui 2016.
19. Buckingham, David and Jepson 2013, p. 3.
20. Qianhui 2016.
21. Buckingham, David and Jepson 2013, p. 3.
22. Ibid., p. 4.
23. Ibid.
24. Ibid.

1973: DIAMONDS

1. Greer 2000, p. 7.
2. Ibid., p. 13.
3. Ibid., p. 18.
4. Ibid., pp. 21–2.
5. O'Toole 1982, p. 140.

6. Greer 2000, p. 24.
7. Kłosowicz 2018, p. 10.
8. Ibid.
9. Ubaku, Emeh and Okoro 2015, p. 6; Kenyon 2018, p. 365.
10. O'Toole 1982, p. 142.
11. Titley 1997, p. 135.
12. Ibid., p. 137.
13. Lewis 1979.
14. Ibid.
15. Dowell 1980.
16. Quoted by Reuters 1981.
17. Reuters 1981.
18. AP 1981.
19. Hoyle 1981.
20. Ibid.
21. Koven 1981.
22. Ibid.
23. Wright 1981, p. 414.

2004: A BOX OF COHIBA LANCEROS CIGARS

1. Kropf 2019.
2. Ibid.
3. Rice 2003.
4. Menchaca 2004.
5. Ibid.
6. Shanken 1994.
7. Ibid.
8. Cosner 2015, p. 133.
9. Kornbluh and LeoGrande 2014.
10. Salinger 1992.
11. Quoted in Kornbluh and LeoGrande 2014.
12. Ibid.
13. Ibid., p. 119.
14. Kornbluh and LeoGrande 2014.
15. LeoGrande and Kornbluh 2015, p. 310.
16. Office of the Chief of Protocol 2018.

2007: A STADIUM

1. Stirrat and Henkel 1997, p. 72.
2. Ibid., p. 74.
3. Eyben 2006, p. 88.

4.   Kowalski 2011, p. 196.
5.   Stirrat and Henkel 1997, p. 75.
6.   Mawdsley 2012, pp. 256–8.
7.   Ibid., p. 263.
8.   Ibid., pp. 264–5.
9.   Quoted in Douglas 2007.
10. Vondracek 2019, p. 62.
11. Xue, Ding, Chang and Wan 2019, p. 3.
12. Vondracek 2019, p. 68
13. Ibid., p. 66.
14. Douglas 2007.
15. AP 2007.
16. Xue, Ding, Chang and Wan 2019, p. 1.
17. Vondracek 2019, pp. 62–3.
18. Brautigam 2009, pp. 72–3.
19. Sortijas 2007, p. 30.
20. Ibid.
21. Adlakha 2020.
22. Quoted in Albert 2021.

2008: A PAIR OF R. M. WILLIAMS BOOTS

1.   Williams n.d.
2.   Jolliffe 2012.
3.   Nicholls and Dunn 2009.
4.   Laidlaw 2008.
5.   Quoted in Williams n.d.
6.   Meyer 2005, pp. 265–6.
7.   Wright 2013.
8.   AFP 2014.
9.   Office of the Chief of Protocol 2020.
10. Australian Government Department of the Prime Minister and Cabinet n.d.
11. Ibid.
12. Ibid.
13. Ibid.
14. Wright 2016.
15. Counihan 2012.
16. Brubaker 2021.
17. Brummell 2021, p. 146.
18. General Services Administration 2020.
19. Maskell 2012, p. 5.

2014: *COLUMN WITH SPEED LINES*, A LITHOGRAPH BY ED RUSCHA

1. Mauss 1966, p. 10.
2. See Lester 2009.
3. Office of the Chief of Protocol 2011.
4. Lester 2009.
5. Spiering 2012.
6. Henley 2010.
7. Battersby 2014.
8. Henley 2010.
9. Briggs 2010.
10. Ibid.
11. Battersby 2014.
12. *Hackney Citizen* 2010.
13. Howorth 2010.
14. Heber 2014.
15. Office of the Chief of Protocol 2015.
16. Watt 2012.
17. Ibid.
18. Lane 2000, p. 104.

CONCLUSION

1. Mauss 1966, p. 45.
2. Carrier 1991, p. 121.
3. Korsch 2007/8, p. 100.
4. Krondl 2020, p. 167.
5. Korsch 2007/8, p. 87.
6. Ibid., p. 100.
7. Youde 2016.
8. Cowper-Coles 2012, pp. 280–1.
9. Neumann 2021.
10. Ibid., p 188.
11. Ibid., p. 191.
12. O'Regan 2020, p. 69.
13. Korsch 2007/8, pp. 93–5.
14. Mawdsley 2012, p. 263.
15. Ssorin-Chaikov 2006, p. 362.
16. Allan 1999.
17. Ibid.
18. Wightwick 2012.
19. Brummell 2021, p. 152.
20. Ibid.
21. Australian Government Department of the Prime Minister and Cabinet n.d.

22. Bercusson 2009, p. 217.
23. Taylor 2016.
24. Henley 2016.
25. Quoted in Taylor 2016.
26. *Evening Standard* 2020.
27. Duddridge 2020.
28. Brummell 2021, pp. 146–7.
29. Office of the Chief of Protocol 2014.
30. Office of the Chief of Protocol 2011.
31. Office of the Chief of Protocol 2013.
32. Ceulemans 2021, p. 139.
33. Office of the Chief of Protocol 2015.
34. Office of the Chief of Protocol 2009.
35. Office of the Chief of Protocol 2015.
36. Office of the Chief of Protocol 2016.
37. Office of the Chief of Protocol 2004.
38. Office of the Chief of Protocol 2014.
39. Ceulemans 2021.
40. Ibid., pp. 136–40.
41. Behrens-Abouseif 2016, p. 79.
42. Tremml-Werner, Hellman and van Meersbergen 2020, p. 196.
43. Wishnick 2019.
44. Phillips 2015, pp. 124–8.
45. Behrens-Abouseif 2016, p. 17.
46. Mauss 1966, p. 20.
47. Molà 2019, p. 65.
48. Ibid., pp. 86–7.
49. Neumann 2021, p. 191.
50. Kustermans 2021 A, p. 107.
51. Sievers 2021, p. 117.
52. Thacker and Escobar 2002, p. 47.
53. Ibid., p. 48.
54. Buquet 2013, p. 381.
55. Ibid.
56. Dorre 2018.
57. Barnes and Barnes 2013.
58. Whitcomb and Whitcomb 2002, p. 52.
59. See Dorre 2018, Emery 2018.
60. Upton 1888, p. 368.
61. Kustermans 2021 B, p. 156.
62. Kustermans 2019, p. 395; 2021 B, p. 155.
63. Kustermans 2021 B, p. 162.
64. Murck 2007, p. 2.

65. Quoted in ibid., p. 4.

66. Ibid., p. 2.

67. Ibid., p. 4.

68. Quoted in Chau 2010, pp. 258–61.

69. Murck 2007, p. 4.

70. Ibid., pp. 4–5.

71. Chau 2010, p. 269.

72. Murck 2007, pp. 15–16.

73. Ibid., pp. 10–14.

74. Chau 2010, p. 259.

75. Ibid., pp. 261–2.

76. Murck 2007, p. 8.

77. Ibid., pp. 19–20.

BIBLIOGRAPHY

Acheson, Katherine, 'The Picture of Nature: Seventeenth-Century English *Aesop's Fables*', *Journal for Early Modern Cultural Studies*, Fall/Winter 2009, Vol. 9, No. 2, pp. 25–50.

Adams, Steven, 'Sèvres Porcelain and the Articulation of Imperial Identity in Napoleonic France', *Journal of Design History*, Autumn 2007, Vol. 20, No. 3, pp. 183–204.

Adlakha, Hemant, 'Did China Join COVAX to Counter or Promote Vaccine Nationalism?', *The Diplomat*, 23 October 2020.

AFP, 'Australian PM Ribbed Over "Cringe-Worthy" Abe Photo', 10 July 2014.

—— 'The Man Who Carried a Mercedes up a Mountain', 10 April 2015.

Albala, Ken, *Food in Early Modern Europe* (Westport, CT: Greenwood Press, 2003).

—— *Beans: A History* (London: Bloomsbury, 2017).

Albert, Eleanor, 'China Gifts Pakistan 1.2 Million COVID-19 Vaccine Doses', *The Diplomat*, 4 February 2021.

Alexander, Caroline, *The War That Killed Achilles: The True Story of Homer's Iliad and the Trojan War* (New York: Viking Penguin, 2009).

Allan, Alex, 'The Tale of the Turkmen Stallion', Speech to the Australia–Britain Society, Melbourne, 26 October 1999, https://whitegum.com/~acsa/journal/turkmen.htm, accessed 7 August 2021.

Allin, Michael, *Zarafa: A Giraffe's True Story, from Deep in Africa to the Heart of Paris* (New York: Walker & Company, 1998).

AlSayyad, Nezar, *Cairo: Histories of a City* (Cambridge, MA: Harvard University Press, 2011).

American Philosophical Society, 'Treasures of the APS: A Miniature Portrait of King Louis XVI', 2006, https://www.amphilsoc.org/exhibits/treasures/louis.htm, accessed 22 September 2021.

BIBLIOGRAPHY

Andrew, John, and Derek Styles, *Designer British Silver: From Studios Established 1930–1985* (Woodbridge, Suffolk: Antique Collectors' Club, 2014).

AP, 'Giscard Accused Anew on African Diamonds', 18 March 1981.

—— 'Grenada "Thanks" China by Playing Wrong Anthem', 3 February 2007.

Apel, Willi, 'Early History of the Organ', *Speculum*, April 1948, Vol. 23, No. 2, pp. 191–216.

Appadurai, Arjun, 'Introduction: Commodities and the Politics of Value', in *The Social Life of Things: Commodities in Cultural Perspective*, ed. Arjun Appadurai (Cambridge: Cambridge University Press, 1988), pp. 3–63.

—— 'The Thing Itself', *Public Culture*, 2006, Vol. 18, No. 1, pp. 15–21.

Arbel, Benjamin, 'The Last Decades of Venice's Trade with the Mamluks: Importations into Egypt and Syria', *Mamlūk Studies Review*, 2004, Vol. 8, No. 2, pp. 37–86.

Australian Government Department of the Prime Minister and Cabinet, 'Guidelines Relating to Official Gifts for Presentation by Ministers', n.d., https://www.pmc.gov.au/government/official-gifts/guidelines-relating-official-gifts-presentation-ministers, accessed 3 April 2021.

Avery, Charles, '*Samson Slaying a Philistine*, by Giambologna, 1560–2', Victoria and Albert Museum, 1978, http://www.vam.ac.uk/content/articles/s/giambolognas-samson-and-a-philistine, accessed 23 August 2020.

Baker, Noel, 'White House Furnace Shock for Shamrock', *The Irish Examiner*, 18 March 2010.

Ball, John W., 'Marshalling America', *The Washington Post*, 6 October 1999.

Barnes, Peter W., and Cheryl Shaw Barnes, *President Adams' Alligator: And Other White House Pets* (Washington: Little Patriot Press, 2013).

Battersby, Matilda, 'Ben Eine: Street Art is a Luxury Product', *The Independent*, 3 December 2014.

Bedini, Silvio A., 'The Papal Pachyderms', *Proceedings of the American Philosophical Society*, 30 April 1981, Vol. 125, No. 2, pp. 75–90.

—— *The Pope's Elephant* (Harmondsworth: Penguin, 2000).

Behrends, Jan C., 'Exporting the Leader: The Stalin Cult in Poland and East Germany (1944/5–1956)', in *The Leader Cult in Communist Dictatorships: Stalin and the Eastern Bloc,* eds. Balázs Apor. Jan C. Behrends, Polly Jones and E. A. Rees. (Basingstoke: Palgrave Macmillan, 2004), pp. 161–78.

Behrens-Abouseif, Doris, 'The Mamluk City', in *The City in the Islamic World*, eds. Salma Khadra Jayyusi, Renata Holod, Atillio Petruccioli and André Raymond (Leiden: Brill, 2008), pp. 295–316.

—— *Practising Diplomacy in the Mamluk Sultanate: Gifts and Material Culture in the Medieval Islamic World* (London: I. B. Tauris, 2016).

Belozerskaya, Marina, *The Medici Giraffe: And Other Tales of Exotic Animals and Power* (New York: Little, Brown and Co., 2006).

Bentley, Esther Felt, 'The Madison Medal and Chief Keokuk', *The Princeton University Library Chronicle*, Spring and Summer 1958, Vol. 19, No. 3/4, pp. 153–8.

Bercusson, Sarah Jemima, 'Gift-Giving, Consumption and the Female Court in Sixteenth-Century Italy' (Unpublished PhD Thesis: Queen Mary, University of London, 2009).

Berenson, Edward, *The Statue of Liberty: A Transatlantic Story* (New Haven: Yale University Press, 2012).

Berg, Maxine, 'Britain, Industry and Perceptions of China: Matthew Boulton, "Useful Knowledge" and the Macartney Embassy to China 1792–94', *Journal of Global History*, 2006, Vol. 1, pp. 269–88.

Biedermann, Zoltán, Anne Gerritsen and Giorgio Riello, 'Introduction', in *Global Gifts: The Material Culture of Diplomacy in Early Modern Eurasia*, eds. Zoltán Biedermann, Anne Gerritsen and Giorgio Riello (Cambridge: Cambridge University Press, 2019), pp. 1–33.

Bingen, Hildegard von, *Hildegard von Bingen's Physica: The Complete English Translation of Her Classic Work on Health and Healing*, trans. Priscilla Throop (Rochester, VT: Healing Arts Press, 1998).

Binyon, T. J., *Pushkin: A Biography* (London: HarperCollins, 2003).

Bogdanor, Vernon, *Britain and Europe in a Troubled World* (New Haven, CT: Yale University Press, 2020).

Boime, Albert, 'Liberty: Inside Story of a Hollow Symbol', *In These Times*, 11–24 June 1986, Vol. 10, No. 27, pp. 12–13.

Bolland, Charlotte, 'Italian Material Culture at the Tudor Court' (Unpublished PhD Thesis: Department of History, Queen Mary, University of London, 2011).

365

BIBLIOGRAPHY

Bonhams, 'The Frederiksen Auction, Lot 48: The Ex-Maharaja of Patiala 1933 Maybach DS-8 Zeppelin Cabriolet', Bonhams, 26 September 2015, https://www.bonhams.com/auctions/23234/lot/48, accessed 22 September 2021.

Boyce, Mary, *Zoroastrians: Their Religious Beliefs and Practices* (London: Routledge, 2001).

Brady, Enda, 'World Cup: Volgograd Will Offer Warm Welcome to England Fans', Sky News, 17 June 2018, https://news.sky.com/story/world-cup-volgograd-will-offer-warm-welcome-to-england-fans-11407409, accessed 22 September 2021.

Brautigam, Deborah, *The Dragon's Gift: The Real Story of China in Africa* (Oxford: Oxford University Press, 2009).

Brier, Bob, *Egyptomania: Our Three Thousand Year Obsession with the Land of the Pharaohs* (New York: Palgrave Macmillan, 2013).

—— 'The Secret Life of the Paris Obelisk', *Aegyptiaca: Journal of the History of Reception of Ancient Egypt*, 2018, No. 2, pp. 75–91.

Briggs, Caroline, 'A Painting for the President', BBC, 21 July 2010, https://www.bbc.co.uk/news/entertainment-arts-10712170, accessed 22 September 2021.

Brinkley, Alan, 'The Legacy of John F. Kennedy', *The Atlantic*, Fall 2013.

Brintlinger, Angela, 'The Persian Frontier: Griboedov as Orientalist and Literary Hero', *Canadian Slavonic Papers*, September–December 2003, Vol. 45, No. 3/4, pp. 371–93.

—— 'Introduction', in *Woe from Wit: A Verse Comedy in Four Acts*, by Alexander Griboedov, trans. Betsy Hulick (New York: Columbia University Press, 2020).

Broderick, Eugene, *John Hearne: Architect of the 1937 Constitution of Ireland* (Newbridge, Co. Kildare: Irish Academic Press, 2017).

Brooklyn Museum, '"Merci Train" Dolls Given to Brooklyn Museum', Press Release, 1 September 1949.

Brotton, Jerry, 'Buying the Renaissance: Prince Charles's Art Purchases in Madrid, 1623', in *The Spanish Match: Prince Charles's Journey to Madrid, 1623*, ed. Alexander Samson (Abingdon: Routledge, 2016), pp. 9–26.

Brubaker, Harold, 'How a Philly Shop Built a Bike – Quickly and at a Discount – for British Prime Minister Boris Johnson; The Buyer: Joe Biden', *The Philadelphia Inquirer*, 11 June 2021.

BIBLIOGRAPHY

Brubaker, Leslie, 'The Elephant and the Ark: Cultural and Material Interchange across the Mediterranean in the Eighth and Ninth Centuries', *Dumbarton Oaks Papers*, 2004, Vol. 58, pp. 175–95.

Brummell, Paul, *Kazakhstan: The Bradt Travel Guide* (Chalfont St Peter: Bradt Travel Guides, 2018).

—— 'Gastrodiplomacy and the UK Diplomatic Network', in *Food and Power: Proceedings of the Oxford Symposium on Food and Cookery 2019*, ed. Mark McWilliams (London: Prospect, 2020), pp. 67–72.

—— 'A Gift for a President', *The Hague Journal of Diplomacy*, 2021, Vol. 16, Issue 1, pp. 145–54.

Bryant, Julius, *Apsley House: The Wellington Collection* (London: English Heritage, 2005).

Bryce, Trevor R., 'The Trojan War: Is There Truth behind the Legend?', *Near Eastern Archaeology*, September 2002, Vol. 65, No. 3, pp. 182–95.

Buckingham, Kathleen, Jonathan Neil William David and Paul Jepson, 'Diplomats and Refugees: Panda Diplomacy, Soft "Cuddly" Power, and the New Trajectory in Panda Conservation', *Environmental Practice*, January 2013, pp. 1–9.

Buncombe, Andrew, 'Nepal Puts Hitler's Mercedes Gift on Show', *The Independent*, 16 June 2008.

Buquet, Thierry, 'Nommer les animaux exotiques de Baybars, d'orient en occident', in *Les non-dits du nom: Onomastique et documents en terres d'islam; Mélanges offerts à Jacqueline Sublet,* eds. Christian Müller and Muriel Roiland-Rouabah (Beirut: Presses de l'Ifpo, 2013), pp. 375–402.

Burnett, J. Alexander, *A Passion for Wildlife: The History of the Canadian Wildlife Service* (Vancouver: UBC Press, 2003).

Butler, John, *Essays on Unfamiliar Travel-Writing: Off the Beaten Track* (Newcastle upon Tyne: Cambridge Scholars Publishing, 2017).

Butt, John J., *Daily Life in the Age of Charlemagne* (Westport, CT: Greenwood Press, 2002).

Byron, Jim, 'Pat Nixon and Panda Diplomacy', Nixon Foundation, 1 February 2011, https://www.nixonfoundation.org/2011/02/pat-nixon-and-panda-diplomacy, accessed 22 September 2021.

Campbell Jr, Edward F., 'The Amarna Letters and the Amarna Period', *The Biblical Archaeologist*, February 1960, Vol. 23, No. 1, pp. 1–22.

BIBLIOGRAPHY

Carey, Juliet, 'King Louis XVI (1754–1793)', Waddesdon Manor, 2008, https://waddesdon.org.uk/the-collection/item/?id=15772, accessed 22 September 2021.

Caron, Julie, 'François Hollande en fourrure et chapka: La photo qui inspire le web', *Grazia*, 7 December 2014, https://www.grazia.fr/news-et-societe/news/francois-hollande-en-fourrure-et-chapka-la-photo-qui-inspire-le-web-716758, accessed 22 September 2021.

Carrier, James, 'Gifts, Commodities, and Social Relations: A Maussian View of Exchange', *Sociological Forum*, March 1991, Vol. 6, No. 1, pp. 119–36.

Cassidy-Geiger, Maureen, 'Porcelain and Prestige: Princely Gifts and "White Gold" from Meissen', in *Fragile Diplomacy: Meissen Porcelain for European Courts ca. 1710–63*, ed. Maureen Cassidy-Geiger (New Haven: Yale University Press, 2007), pp. 3–24.

Cavell, Janice, 'Who Discovered the Northwest Passage?', *Arctic*, September 2018, Vol. 71, No. 3, pp. 292–308.

Ceulemans, Eline, 'Ceremonial or Convivial Gifts: Two Forms of Gift-Giving in Contemporary Chinese Diplomacy', *The Hague Journal of Diplomacy*, 2021, Vol. 16, Issue 1, pp. 133–44.

Chau, Adam Yuet, 'Mao's Travelling Mangoes: Food as Relic in Revolutionary China', *Past and Present*, 2010, Vol. 206, Supplement 5, pp. 256–75.

Chavan, Akshay, 'Hitler's Gift to the Maharaja of Patiala', Live History India, 15 February 2019, https://www.livehistoryindia.com/story/living-history/hitlers-gift-to-the-maharaja-of-patiala, accessed 22 September 2021.

Choudhary, Renu, 'Made for Maharajas', The Diamond Talk, 7 February 2020, https://thediamondtalk.in/made-for-maharajas, accessed 22 September 2021.

Ciocîltan, Virgil, *The Mongols and the Black Sea Trade in the Thirteenth and Fourteenth Centuries*, trans. Samuel Willcocks (Leiden: Brill, 2012).

Clarke, Simon, *The Foundations of Structuralism: A Critique of Lévi-Strauss and the Structuralist Movement* (Brighton: The Harvester Press, 1981).

Clayton, T. R., 'The Duke of Newcastle, the Earl of Halifax, and the American Origins of the Seven Years' War', *The Historical Journal*, September 1981, Vol. 24, No. 3, pp. 571–603.

Cleaver, Emily, 'The Fascinating, Regal History behind Britain's Swans', *Smithsonian*, 31 July 2017, https://www.smithsonianmag.com/history/fascinating-history-british-thrones-swans-180964249, accessed 22 September 2021.

BIBLIOGRAPHY

Clulow, Adam, 'From Global Entrepôt to Early Modern Domain: Hirado, 1609–1641', *Monumenta Nipponica*, Spring 2010, Vol. 65, No. 1, pp. 1–35.

—— 'Gifts for the Shogun: The Dutch East India Company, Global Networks and Tokugawa Japan', in *Global Gifts: The Material Culture of Diplomacy in Early Modern Eurasia*, eds. Zoltán Biedermann, Anne Gerritsen and Giorgio Riello (Cambridge: Cambridge University Press, 2019), pp. 198–216.

Collins, Stephen, 'A Short History of Taoisigh Visiting the White House on St Patrick's Day', *The Irish Times*, 11 March 2017.

Connelly, Dolly, 'The Wilderness Family That Helped Save the Swans', *Life*, 10 April 1970.

Cook, Robert, and Clive Webb, 'Unraveling the Special Relationship: British Responses to the Assassination of President John F. Kennedy', *The Sixties: A Journal of History, Politics and Culture*, 2015, Vol. 8, Issue 2, pp. 179–94.

Cosner, Charlotte, *The Golden Leaf: How Tobacco Shaped Cuba and the Atlantic World* (Nashville: Vanderbilt University Press, 2015).

Counihan, Patrick, 'Ireland's Diplomatic Service Forced to Shop for Bargain Basement Gifts', IrishCentral, 7 October 2012, https://www.irishcentral.com/news/irelands-diplomatic-service-forced-to-shop-for-bargain-basement-gifts-173020281-237532331, accessed 22 September 2021.

Cowper-Coles, Sherard, *Ever the Diplomat: Confessions of a Foreign Office Mandarin* (London: HarperPress, 2012).

Crosby, Kristin, 'Swan City: An Untold Tale of Lakeland's Iconic Birds', Lakelander, 30 August 2016, https://thelakelander.com/swan-city, accessed 29 September 2021.

Croxton, Derek, 'The Peace of Westphalia of 1648 and the Origins of Sovereignty', *The International History Review*, September 1999, Vol. 21, No. 3, pp. 569–91.

Curtin, Sean, 'The Return of Japan's Long Lost Telescope', *The Japan Society Review*, April 2014, Issue 50, Vol. 9, No. 2, pp. 7–8.

Cuttler, Charles D., 'Exotics in Post-Medieval European Art: Giraffes and Centaurs', *Artibus et historiae*, 1991, Vol. 12, No. 23, pp. 161–79.

Czajkowski, Michael J., 'Amber from the Baltic', *Mercian Geologist*, 2009, Vol. 17, No. 2, pp. 86–92.

D'Alton, Martina, *The New York Obelisk: Or How Cleopatra's Needle Came to New York and What Happened When It Got Here* (New York: Metropolitan Museum of Art, 1993).

369

BIBLIOGRAPHY

Depkat, Volker, 'Peace Medal Diplomacy in Indian–White Relations in Nineteenth-Century North America', in *European History Yearbook: Material Culture in Modern Diplomacy from the 15th to the 20th Century*, eds. Harriet Rudolph and Gregor M. Metzig (Berlin: Walter de Gruyter GmbH, 2016), pp. 80–99.

Diaz, Johnny, 'A Florida City Is Selling Some of Its Beloved Swans', *The New York Times*, 15 October 2020.

Diffie, Bailey W., and George D. Winius, *Foundations of the Portuguese Empire, 1415–1580* (Minneapolis: University of Minnesota Press, 1977).

Dike, K. O., 'John Beecroft, 1790–1854: Her Britannic Majesty's Consul to the Bights of Benin and Biafra 1849–1854', *Journal of the Historical Society of Nigeria*, December 1956, Vol. 1, No. 1, pp. 5–14.

Dorre, Howard, 'John Quincy Adams's Pet Alligator Was a Crock', Plodding through the Presidents, 19 February 2018, https://www.ploddingthroughthepresidents.com/2018/02/john-quincy-adams-pet-alligator-is-crock.html, accessed 29 September 2021.

Douglas, Sean, 'Thousands Join in the Opening of the Windsor Park Stadium', 29 October 2007, https://www.thedominican.net/articles/stadiumthree.htm, accessed 29 September 2021.

Dowell, William, '*Le Monde* Raises Government Hackles with Diamond Scandal Questions', *The Christian Science Monitor*, 18 November 1980.

Driscoll, Amanda, 'History of the White House Shamrock St Patrick's Day Ceremony', IrishCentral, 16 March 2016, https://www.irishcentral.com/culture/entertainment/history-shamrocks-white-house-patricks-day, accessed 29 September 2021.

Drury, Melanie, 'Lost (and Found) Maltese Treasures: The Sword and Dagger of Grandmaster de la Valette', Guide Me Malta, 30 May 2019, https://www.guidememalta.com/en/lost-found-maltese-treasures-the-sword-dagger-of-grandmaster-de-la-valette, accessed 29 September 2021.

Duchesne-Guillemin, J., 'Jesus' Trimorphism and the Differentiation of the Magi', in *Man and His Salvation: Studies in Memory of S. G. F. Brandon*, eds. Eric J. Sharpe and John R. Hinnells (Manchester: Manchester University Press, 1973), pp. 91–8.

Duddridge, James, 'Diplomatic "Ties" are Strong with Ethiopia ...', Twitter @ JamesDuddridge, https://mobile.twitter.com/jamesduddridge/status/1304143989801717760?lang=ar-x-fm, 10 September 2020, accessed 29 September 2021.

Dursteler, Eric R., '"A Continual Tavern in My House": Food and Diplomacy in Early Modern Constantinople', in *Renaissance Studies in Honor of Joseph Connors*, eds. Machtelt Israëls and Louis A. Waldman (Cambridge, MA: Harvard University Press, 2013), pp. 166–71.

Dwivedi, Sharada, *The Automobiles of the Maharajas* (Mumbai: Eminence Designs Pvt. Ltd., 2003).

Eaton, Natasha, 'Between Mimesis and Alterity: Art, Gift, and Diplomacy in Colonial India, 1770–1800', *Comparative Studies in Society and History*, October 2004, Vol. 46, No. 4, pp. 816–44.

—— 'Coercion and the Gift: Art, Jewels and the Body in British Diplomacy in Colonial India', in *Global Gifts: The Material Culture of Diplomacy in Early Modern Eurasia*, eds. Zoltán Biedermann, Anne Gerritsen and Giorgio Riello (Cambridge: Cambridge University Press, 2019), pp. 266–90.

Eban, Abba, *Interest and Conscience in Modern Diplomacy* (New York: Council on Religion and International Affairs, 1985).

Eggleston, Roland, 'Russia: German Firm Gives Millions to Restore Amber Room', Radio Free Europe/Radio Free Liberty, 9 August 1999, https://www.rferl.org/a/1091985.html, accessed 29 September 2021.

Emerick, Judson, 'Charlemagne: A New Constantine?', in *The Life and Legacy of Constantine: Traditions through the Ages*, ed. M. Shane Bjornlie (Abingdon: Routledge, 2017), pp. 133–61.

Emery, David, 'Were Alligators Ever Kept as White House Pets?', Snopes, 19 February 2018, https://www.snopes.com/fact-check/alligators-white-house-pets, accessed 29 September 2021.

Entwistle, George, 'From Consensus to Dissensus – History and Meaning in Flux at Sir Geoffrey Jellicoe's Kennedy Memorial Landscape', *Studies in the History of Gardens and Designed Landscapes*, 2019, Vol. 39, Issue 1, pp. 53–76.

Evans, D. M. Emrys, 'John F. Kennedy Memorial Act, 1964', *The Modern Law Review*, November 1965, Vol. 28, No. 6, pp. 703–6.

Evening Standard, 'SW1A', 9 September 2020.

Eyben, Rosalind, 'The Power of the Gift and the New Aid Modalities', *IDS Bulletin*, November 2006, Vol. 37, No. 6, pp. 88–98.

Farago, Jason, 'At the Met, Heavy Metal on a Continental Scale', *The New York Times*, 24 October 2019.

BIBLIOGRAPHY

Farrar, Katie, 'The Pope's Elephant', Eyes of Rome, 28 May 2020, https://eyesofrome. com/blog/eyes-on-storytelling/the-pope-s-elephant, accessed 29 September 2021.

Feiman, Jesse, 'The Matrix and the Meaning in Dürer's *Rhinoceros*', *Art in Print*, November–December 2012, Vol. 2, No. 4, pp. 22–6.

Finglass, Patrick, 'Did the Trojan Horse Really Exist?', British Museum lecture, 1 February 2020.

Finnis, Alex, 'Great Arctic Explorer to Be Finally Honoured after Having Career Discredited for Telling Truth about British Voyagers' Cannibalism', *Daily Mail*, 27 September 2014, https://www.dailymail.co.uk/news/article-2772090/Great-Arctic-explorer-finally-honoured-having-career-discredited-reporting-British-voyagers-cannibalism.html, accessed 29 September 2021.

Firebrace, William, 'The Missing Planet', *AA Files*, 2013, No. 66, pp. 126–44.

—— *Star Theatre: The Story of the Planetarium* (London: Reaktion Books, 2017).

Fiske, Alan Page, *Structures of Social Life: The Four Elementary Forms of Human Relations* (New York: The Free Press, 1993).

Fleming, Thomas, 'Taking Paris by Storm: Benjamin Franklin, American Founding Father and First Ambassador to France', *Medicographia*, 2014, Issue 36, pp. 112–22.

Fletcher, Tom, *Naked Diplomacy: Power and Statecraft in the Digital Age* (London: William Collins, 2016).

Foderaro, Lisa W., 'For "Cleopatra's Needle", a Cleaning to Last 500 Years', *The New York Times*, 7 May 2014.

Forbes, Frederick E., *Dahomey and the Dahomans* (London: Longman, Brown, Green and Longmans, 1851).

Francis Jr, Peter, 'The Beads That Did *Not* Buy Manhattan Island', *New York History*, January 1986, Vol. 67, No. 1, pp. 4–22.

Franko, George Frederic, 'The Trojan Horse at the Close of the *Iliad*', *The Classical Journal*, December 2005–January 2006, Vol. 101, No. 2, pp. 121–3.

Frey, Linda S., and Marsha L. Frey, *Proven Patriots: The French Diplomatic Corps 1789–1799* (St Andrews: University of St Andrews, 2011).

Friis, Erik J., 'The Norwegian Government-in-Exile, 1940–45', in *Scandinavian Studies: Essays Presented to Dr Henry Goddard Leach on the Occasion of His Eighty-Fifth Birthday*, eds. Carl Frank Bayerschmidt and Erik J. Friis (Seattle: University of Washington Press, 1965), pp. 422–44.

BIBLIOGRAPHY

Gallagher, Donat, and Carlos Villar Flor, *In the Picture: The Facts behind the Fiction in Evelyn Waugh's Sword of Honour* (Amsterdam: Rodopi, 2014).

Garstad, Benjamin, 'Barbarian Interest in *Excerpta Latina Barbari*', *Early Medieval Europe*, 2011, Vol. 19, No. 1, pp. 3–42.

General Services Administration, 'Revision to Foreign Gift Minimal Value', Federal Register, 17 March 2020.

Gershon, Livia, 'Shipwrecked Nazi Steamer May Hold Clues to the Amber Room's Fate', *Smithsonian*, 23 October 2020, https://www.smithsonianmag.com/smart-news/shipwrecked-nazi-steamer-found-180976119, accessed 29 September 2021.

Gil, Moshe, *A History of Palestine 634–1099* (Cambridge: Cambridge University Press, 1997).

Gordon, John Steele, *Washington's Monument: And the Fascinating History of the Obelisk* (New York: Bloomsbury, 2016).

Gramer, Robbie, 'Eight of the Weirdest Gifts Foreign Dignitaries Gave the President', *Foreign Policy*, 27 April 2017, https://foreignpolicy.com/2017/04/27/eight-of-the-weirdest-gifts-foreign-dignitaries-gave-the-president, accessed 29 September 2021.

Grancsay, Stephen V., 'Maximilian Armor', *The Metropolitan Museum of Art Bulletin*, April 1928, Vol. 23, No. 4, pp. 100–3.

Greer, Scott, 'Chacun pour soi: Africa and the French State 1958-1998', PAS Working Papers, No. 6 (Evanston: Northwestern University Program of African Studies, 2000).

Grimnes, Ole Kristian, 'The Two Norways, 1940–41', in *Northern European Overture to War, 1939–1941: From Memel to Barbarossa*, eds. Michael H. Clemmesen and Marcus S. Faulkner (Leiden: Brill, 2013), pp. 383–402.

Griswold, Gabrielle, 'Memories of the Friendship Train in France', The Friendship Train of 1947, 2011, http://www.thefriendshiptrain1947.org/friendship-train-history-france-memories.htm, accessed 29 September 2021.

Grundhauser, Eric, 'From Roosevelt to *Resolute*, the Secrets of All 6 Oval Office Desks', Atlas Obscura, 7 April 2016, https://www.atlasobscura.com/articles/from-roosevelt-to-resolute-the-secrets-of-all-6-oval-office-desks, accessed 29 September 2021.

Hackney Citizen, 'Ben Eine: The Art of the States', 3 August 2010, http://www.hackneycitizen.co.uk/2010/08/03/ben-eine-the-art-of-the-states, accessed 29 September 2021.

BIBLIOGRAPHY

Hannah, Darrell D., 'The Star of the Magi and the Prophecy of Balaam in Earliest Christianity, with Special Attention to the Lost *Books of Balaam*', in *The Star of Bethlehem and the Magi*, eds. Peter Barthel and George van Kooten (Leiden: Brill, 2015), pp. 433–62.

Harden, Evelyn Jasiulko, 'Griboedov and the Willock Affair', *Slavic Review*, March 1971, Vol. 30, No. 1, pp. 74–92.

Harford, Tim, 'The Cold War Spy Technology Which We All Use', BBC, 21 August 2019, https://www.bbc.co.uk/news/business-48859331, accessed 6 September 2021.

Harrison, Carol E., 'Edouard Laboulaye, Liberal and Romantic Catholic', in *French History and Civilization, Vol. 4: Papers from the George Rudé Seminar*, eds. Briony Neilson and Robert Aldrich (Charleston: H-France, 2011), pp. 149–58.

Harrison, Henrietta, 'Chinese and British Diplomatic Gifts in the Macartney Embassy of 1793', *English Historical Review*, 2018, Vol. 133, No. 560, pp. 65–97.

Hassan, Fekri A., 'Imperialist Appropriations of Egyptian Obelisks', in *Views of Ancient Egypt since Napoleon Bonaparte: Imperialism, Colonialism and Modern Appropriations*, ed. David Jeffreys (London: Routledge, 2016), pp. 19–68.

HBC Heritage, 'The Rent Ceremony', n.d., https://www.hbcheritage.ca/history/fur-trade/the-rent-ceremony, accessed 8 December 2020.

Heath, Diana, 'Conservation of the Portuguese Centrepiece', *Victoria and Albert Museum Conservation Journal*, Autumn 1995, Issue 17.

Heber, Alex, 'Tony Abbott Gave Barack Obama This Ridiculous Surfboard', *Business Insider Australia*, 13 June 2014.

Hegedus, Tim, 'The Magi and the Star in the Gospel of Matthew and Early Christian Tradition', *Laval théologique et philosophique*, February 2003, Vol. 59, No. 1, pp. 81–95.

Henley, Jon, 'Ben Eine: The Street Artist Who's Made It to the White House', *The Guardian*, 21 July 2010.

—— 'Norway Considers Giving Mountain to Finland as 100th Birthday Present', *The Guardian*, 28 July 2016.

Hilsdale, Cecily J., 'The Imperial Image at the End of Exile: The Byzantine Embroidered Silk in Genoa and the Treaty of Nymphaion (1261)', *Dumbarton Oaks Papers*, 2010, Vol. 64, pp. 151–99.

Hilton, Geoff, 'Kenilworth Castle: The King, the Castle and the Canon', Agincourt 600, 23 January 2015, http://www.agincourt600.com/2015/01/23/kenilworth-castle-the-king-the-castle-and-the-canon, accessed 29 September 2021.

BIBLIOGRAPHY

Hoffner, Harry A., *Letters from the Hittite Kingdom* (Atlanta: Society of Biblical Literature, 2009).

Hogan, Michael, 'From Camels to Tinned Fruit: The Strangest Diplomatic Gifts', *The Guardian*, 25 October 2015.

Hollier, Denis, 'Egypt in Paris', in *A New History of French Literature*, ed. Denis Hollier (Cambridge, MA: Harvard University Press, 1994), pp. 672–5.

Holmes, Y. Lynn, 'The Messengers of the Amarna Letters', *Journal of the American Oriental Society*, July–September 1975, Vol. 95, No. 3, pp. 376–81.

Hone, William, ed., *The Apocryphal Books of the New Testament* (Philadelphia: Gebbie and Co., 1890).

Hoskin, Dawn, 'The Rejected Divorce Gift and the Egyptian Pharaoh', V&A Blog, 1 April 2015, https://www.vam.ac.uk/blog/creating-new-europe-1600-1800-galleries/the-rejected-divorce-gift-the-egyptian-pharaoh, accessed 29 September 2021.

House of Commons, 'President Kennedy (National Monument)', Hansard, 5 December 1963, Vol. 685, cc. 1363–4.

——— 'Memorial to President Kennedy', Hansard, 25 March 1964, Vol. 692, cc. 471–4.

Houston, C. Stuart, 'Regina's Mute Swan Mystery', *Blue Jay*, December 2012, Vol. 70, No. 4, pp. 270–3.

Howard, Deborah, 'Cultural Transfer between Venice and the Ottomans in the Fifteenth and Sixteenth Centuries', in *Cultural Exchange in Early Modern Europe Volume IV: Forging European Identities, 1400–1700*, ed. Herman Roodenburg (Cambridge: Cambridge University Press, 2007 A), pp. 138–77.

——— 'Venice and the Mamluks', in *Venice and the Islamic World 828–1797*, Institut du Monde Arabe/Metropolitan Museum of Art (New Haven: Yale University Press, 2007 B), pp. 72–89.

Howorth, Claire, 'Obama and Cameron Exchange Gifts, an Ed Ruscha for a Ben Eine', The Daily Beast, 21 July 2010, https://www.thedailybeast.com/obama-and-cameron-exchange-gifts-an-ed-ruscha-for-a-ben-eine, accessed 29 September 2021.

Hoyle, Russ, 'A Campaign Catches Fire', *Time*, 30 March 1981.

Hurewitz, J. C., 'Ottoman Diplomacy and the European State System', *Middle East Journal*, Spring 1961, Vol. 15, No. 2, pp. 141–52.

BIBLIOGRAPHY

Hyde, Walter Woodburn, 'The Recent Discovery of an Inscribed Water-Organ at Budapest', *Transactions and Proceedings of the American Philological Association*, 1938, Vol. 69, pp. 392–410.

Hysell, Jesse, 'The Politics of Pepper: Deciphering a Venetian–Mamluk Gift Exchange', AHA Today, 6 July 2016, https://www.historians.org/publications-and-directories/perspectives-on-history/summer-2016/the-politics-of-pepper-deciphering-a-venetian-mamluk-gift-exchange, accessed 29 September 2021.

Isaacson, Walter, *Benjamin Franklin: An American Life* (New York: Simon & Schuster, 2003).

Jackson, Brian, 'From the Archives: Anyone for Tennis?', Kenilworth History and Archaeology Society, 6 February 2016, https://www.khas.co.uk/from-the-archives-anyone-for-tennis, accessed 29 September 2021.

Johnson, Kendall, 'Peace, Friendship, and Financial Panic: Reading the Mark of Black Hawk in *Life of Ma-Ka-Tai-Me-She-Kia-Kiak*', *American Literary History*, Winter 2007, Vol. 19, No. 4, pp. 771–99.

Jolliffe, David, 'Kevin Rudd's Riding Boots', Museum of Australian Diplomacy, 14 November 2012, https://www.moadoph.gov.au/blog/kevin-rudd-s-riding-boots/#, accessed 29 September 2021.

Jones, Jonathan, 'Myrrh Mystery: How Did Balthasar, One of the Three Kings, Become Black?', *The Guardian*, 21 December 2020.

Jönsson, Christer, and Martin Hall, *Essence of Diplomacy* (Basingstoke: Palgrave Macmillan, 2005).

Joost-Gaugier, Christiane L., 'Lorenzo the Magnificent and the Giraffe as a Symbol of Power', *Artibus et historiae*, 1987, Vol. 8, No. 16, pp. 91–9.

Joseph, Rebecca M, with Brooke Rosenblatt and Carolyn Kinebrew, *The Black Statue of Liberty Rumor: An Inquiry into the History and Meaning of Bartholdi's Liberté éclairant le Monde* (Boston: National Park Service, 2000).

Keane, Kevin, 'Last Stavanger Christmas Tree to Shine in Aberdeen', BBC, 27 November 2014, https://www.bbc.co.uk/news/uk-scotland-north-east-orkney-shetland-30214800, accessed 29 September 2021.

Kelderman, Frank, *Authorized Agents: Publication and Diplomacy in the Era of Indian Removal* (Albany, NY: State University of New York Press, 2019).

BIBLIOGRAPHY

Kelly, John, 'How Ireland Uses Shamrocks to Gain Access to the US President', Atlas Obscura, 17 March 2017, https://www.atlasobscura.com/articles/shamrock-ceremony-st-patricks-day, accessed 29 September 2021.

—— 'In 1947, Friendship Train Crossed U.S. Gathering Food for Hungry Europe', *The Washington Post*, 18 May 2019.

Kendall, Paul, *Henry VIII in 100 Objects: The Tyrant King Who Had Six Wives* (Barnsley: Frontline Books, 2020).

Kennedy, John F., Inaugural Address, 20 January 1961.

—— American University Commencement Address, 10 June 1963.

Kennedy, Maev, 'The Restoration Game: Painting Revealed as Genuine Titian', *The Guardian*, 8 May 2015.

Kenyon, Paul, *Dictatorland: The Men Who Stole Africa* (London: Head of Zeus, 2018).

Kerr, Robert, *A General History and Collection of Voyages and Travels, Arranged in Systematic Order: Forming a Complete History of the Origin and Progress of Navigation, Discovery and Commerce, by Sea and Land, from the Earliest Ages to the Present Time, Vol. 8* (Edinburgh: William Blackwood, 1824).

Ketcham Wheaton, Barbara, *Savoring the Past: The French Kitchen and Table from 1300 to 1789* (New York: Touchstone, 1983).

Khadduri, Majid, *War and Peace in the Law of Islam* (Clark, NJ: The Lawbook Exchange, 2006).

Khan, Yasmin Sabina, *Enlightening the World: The Creation of the Statue of Liberty* (Ithaca, NY: Cornell University Press, 2010).

Kidambi, Prashant, 'How the British Forged the First Indian Cricket Team', BBC, 30 June 2019, https://www.bbc.co.uk/news/world-asia-india-48659324, accessed 29 September 2021.

King, James, *Cleopatra's Needle: A History of the London Obelisk, with an Exposition of the Hieroglyphics* (London: The Religious Tract Society, 1883).

King, Rachel, 'Whose Amber? Changing Notions of Amber's Geographical Origin', kunsttexte.de/ostblick, *Gemeine Artefakte*, 2014, No. 2, pp. 1–22.

Kivimäe, Jüri, 'Medieval Estonia, an Introduction', in *Quotidianum Estonicum: Aspects of Daily Life in Medieval Estonia*, eds. Jüri Kivimäe and Juhan Kreem (Krems: Medium Aevum Quotidianum, 1996).

BIBLIOGRAPHY

Klein, Holger A., 'Eastern Objects and Western Desires: Relics and Reliquaries between Byzantium and the West', *Dumbarton Oaks Papers*, 2004, Vol. 58, pp. 283–314.

Kloc, Joe, 'The Case of the Missing Moon Rocks', *The Atavist*, February 2012, Issue 12.

Kłosowicz, Robert, 'The Problem of Bad Governance as a Determinant of State Dysfunctionality in Sub-Saharan Africa', *Politeja*, 2018, Vol. 5, No. 56, pp. 9–22.

Knight, Claire, 'Mrs Churchill Goes to Russia: The Wartime Gift Exchange between Britain and the Soviet Union', in *A People Passing Rude: British Responses to Russian Culture*, ed. Anthony Cross (Cambridge: Open Book Publishers, 2012), pp. 253–67.

Komter, Aafke, 'Gifts and Social Relations: The Mechanisms of Reciprocity', *International Sociology*, January 2007, Vol. 22, No. 1, pp. 93–107.

Konstantakos, Ioannis M., 'Alexander and Darius in a Contest of Wit (*Alexander Romance* 1.36–38): Sources, Formation, and Storytelling Traditions', *Annuali della Facoltà di Studi Umanistici dell'Università degli Studi di Milano*, 2015, Vol. 68, No. 1, pp. 129–56.

Kornbluh, Peter, and William M. LeoGrande, 'Cigar Diplomacy', *Cigar Aficionado*, November/December 2014.

Korsch, Evelyn, 'Diplomatic Gifts on Henri III's Visit to Venice in 1574', trans. Nicola Imrie, *Studies in the Decorative Arts*, Fall–Winter 2007–8, Vol. 15, pp. 83–113.

Koven, Ronald, 'Angry Ex-Emperor Bokassa Seeks to Thwart Giscard's Reelection', *The Washington Post*, 8 May 1981.

Kowalski, R., 'The Gift – Marcel Mauss and International Aid', *Journal of Comparative Social Welfare*, October 2011, Vol. 27, No. 3, pp. 189–205.

Kozmanová, Irena, 'Corruption as an External Threat? Anti-Corruption Legislation during the Dutch "Great Assembly" (1651)', in *The Representation of External Threats: From the Middle Ages to the Modern World*, eds. Eberhard Crailsheim and María Dolores Elizalde (Leiden: Brill, 2019), pp. 240–62.

Krondl, Michael, 'Sugar and Show: Power, Conspicuous Display, and Sweet Banquets during Henri III's 1574 Visit to Venice', in *Food and Power: Proceedings of the Oxford Symposium on Food and Cookery 2019*, ed. Mark McWilliams (London: Prospect, 2020), pp. 167–76.

Kropf, Schuyler, 'Former SC Lt. Gov. André Bauer Selling Cuban Cigars Gifted by Castro in 2004 Trade Visit', *The Post and Courier*, 6 May 2019.

BIBLIOGRAPHY

Kupfer, Matthew, 'City Staff Recommend Saying So Long to Ottawa's Royal Swans', CBC, 11 June 2019, https://www.cbc.ca/news/canada/ottawa/royal-swan-ottawa-parc-safari-1.5171614, accessed 29 September 2021.

Kustermans, Jorg, 'Gift-Giving as a Source of International Authority', *The Chinese Journal of International Politics*, 2019, Vol. 12, No. 3, pp. 395–426.

—— 'Diplomatic Gifts: An Introduction to the Forum', *The Hague Journal of Diplomacy*, 2021 A, Vol. 16, Issue 1, pp. 105–9.

—— 'Gift-Giving in Byzantine Diplomacy', *The Hague Journal of Diplomacy*, 2021 B, Vol. 16, Issue 1, pp. 155–65.

Lagueux, Olivier, 'Geoffroy's Giraffe: The Hagiography of a Charismatic Mammal', *Journal of the History of Biology*, Summer 2003, Vol. 36, No. 2, pp. 225–47.

Laidlaw, Richard, 'New Boots, But Still the Same Old Walk', *The Bali Times*, 19 December 2008.

Landau, Brent, 'The *Revelation of the Magi*: A Summary and Introduction', in *New Testament Apocrypha: More Noncanonical Scriptures, Volume 1*, eds. Tony Burke and Brent Landau (Grand Rapids, MI: William B. Eerdmans, 2016), pp. 19–38.

Lane, Jeremy F., *Pierre Bourdieu: A Critical Introduction* (London: Pluto Press, 2000).

Lang, David M., 'Griboedov's Last Years in Persia', *The American Slavic and East European Review*, December 1948, Vol. 7, No. 4, pp. 317–39.

Larkin, T. Lawrence, 'A "Gift" Strategically Solicited and Magnanimously Conferred: The American Congress, the French Monarchy and the State Portraits of Louis XVI and Marie-Antoinette', *Winterthur Portfolio*, Spring 2010, Vol. 44, No. 1, pp. 31–76.

Larsen, Baard, 'Orkney Norway Friendship Marked with 2019 Christmas Tree Cutting in Bringsværd Forest', *The Orkney News*, 12 November 2019.

Latowsky, Anne, 'Foreign Embassies and Roman Universality in Einhard's *Life of Charlemagne*', *Florilegium*, 2005, Vol. 22, pp. 25–57.

Leira, Halvard, 'A Conceptual History of Diplomacy', in *The Sage Handbook of Diplomacy*, eds. Costas M. Constantinou, Pauline Kerr and Paul Sharp (London: Sage Publications, 2016), pp. 28–38.

LeoGrande, William M., and Peter Kornbluh, *Back Channel to Cuba: The Hidden History of Negotiations between Washington and Havana* (Chapel Hill, NC: The University of North Carolina Press, 2015).

Lester, Paul, 'Obama's "Special Gift" to Brown? 25 DVDs', *The Guardian*, 6 March 2009.

BIBLIOGRAPHY

Leverett, Adelyn Peck, 'Review: Peter Williams, *The Organ in Western Culture, 750–1250*', *Speculum*, July 1996, Vol. 71, No. 3, pp. 776–8.

Lewis, Flora, 'Bokassa Order Sending Diamonds to Giscard Reported', *The New York Times*, 11 October 1979.

Lewis, Harrison F., 'Capture of Trumpeter Swans in British Columbia for H. M. Queen Elizabeth II', *Severn Wildfowl Trust Annual Report*, 1951–2, p. 71.

Liackhova, Lydia, 'In a Porcelain Mirror: Reflections of Russia from Peter I to Empress Elizabeth', in *Fragile Diplomacy: Meissen Porcelain for European Courts ca. 1710–63*, ed. Maureen Cassidy-Geiger (New Haven: Yale University Press, 2007), pp. 63–86.

Lindorff, Joyce, 'Burney, Macartney and the Qianlong Emperor: The Role of Music in the British Embassy to China, 1792–1794', *Early Music*, August 2012, Vol. 40, No. 3, pp. 441–53.

Lindsay, Ivan, *The History of Loot and Stolen Art: From Antiquity until the Present Day* (London: Unicorn Press, 2014).

Liudprand of Cremona, *The Works of Liudprand of Cremona*, trans. F. A. Wright (New York: E. P. Dutton and Co., 1930).

Lively, Penelope, 'A Maverick Historian', *The Atlantic*, February 2001.

Lynch, Connor, 'Norway Cancels 15-Year Christmas Gift to Grimsby Tradition Admitting "Our Trees are Not Good Enough for You"', *Grimsby Telegraph*, 16 March 2019, https://www.grimsbytelegraph.co.uk/news/grimsby-news/sortland-cancel-christmas-tree-tradition-2649891, accessed 29 September 2021.

MacCarthy, Fiona, 'Leslie Durbin', *The Guardian*, 1 March 2005.

Mackay, R. H., 'Trapping of the Queen's Trumpeter Swans in British Columbia', *Severn Wildfowl Trust Annual Report*, 1952–3, pp. 47–50.

Magra, Iliana, '"A Present from Norway and It's Dead": Christmas Tree Unites London in Dismay', *The New York Times*, 5 December 2019.

Majeska, George, 'Russian Pilgrims in Constantinople', *Dumbarton Oaks Papers*, 2002, Vol. 56, pp. 93–108.

Malinowski, Bronisław, *Argonauts of the Western Pacific: An Account of Native Enterprise and Adventure in the Archipelagoes of Melanesian New Guinea* (London: George Routledge and Sons, 1922).

Mänd, Anu, 'Horses, Stags and Beavers: Animals as Presents in Late-Medieval Livonia', *Acta Historica Tallinnensia*, 2016, Vol. 22, pp. 3–17.

BIBLIOGRAPHY

Mann, James, 'The Exhibition of Greenwich Armour at the Tower of London', *The Burlington Magazine*, December 1951, Vol. 93, No. 585, pp. 378–83.

Marchand, Suzanne L., *Porcelain: A History from the Heart of Europe* (Princeton: Princeton University Press, 2020).

Markina, Ludmila, *Malta's Portrait of Catherine the Great* (Tsaritsyno State Museum Reserve, 2019).

Maskell, Jack, 'Gifts to the President of the United States', Congressional Research Service, 16 August 2012, pp. 1–6.

Matthews, P. G., 'Jakob Seisenegger's Portraits of Charles V, 1530–32', *The Burlington Magazine*, February 2001, Vol. 143, No. 1175, pp. 86–90.

Mattingly, Garrett, 'The First Resident Embassies: Medieval Italian Origins of Modern Diplomacy', *Speculum*, October 1937, Vol. 12, No. 4, pp. 423–39.

Mauss, Marcel, *The Gift: Forms and Functions of Exchange in Archaic Societies*, trans. Ian Cunnison (London: Cohen and West, 1966).

Mawdsley, Emma, 'The Changing Geographies of Foreign Aid and Development Cooperation: Contributions from Gift Theory', *Transactions of the Institute of British Geographers*, New Series, 2012, Vol. 37, No. 12, pp. 256–72.

McClanahan, Grant V., *Diplomatic Immunity: Principles, Practices, Problems* (London: Hurst, 1989).

McClellan, Ann, *Cherry Blossoms: The Official Book of the National Cherry Blossom Festival* (Washington, DC: National Geographic, 2012).

McCullough, David, *John Adams* (New York: Simon & Schuster, 2002).

McDuffee, Allen, 'This Diamond Gift to Benjamin Franklin Is the Reason Donald Trump Can't Profit from the Presidency', Timeline, 22 September 2017, https://timeline.com/benjamin-franklin-emoluments-constitution-40339b04c159, accessed 29 September 2021.

McNab, Jessie, 'The Legacy of a Fantastical Scot', *The Metropolitan Museum of Art Bulletin*, February 1961, pp. 172–80.

McNay, Michael, *Hidden Treasures of London: A Guide to the Capital's Best-Kept Secrets* (London: Random House, 2015).

McNeal, Robert H., *Stalin: Man and Ruler* (Basingstoke: Macmillan Press, 1988).

Medlam, Sarah, 'Callet's Portrait of Louis XVI: A Picture Frame as a Diplomatic Tool', *Furniture History*, 2007, Vol. 43, pp. 143–54.

Menchaca, Ron, 'Up Close with Castro', *The Post and Courier*, 12 January 2004.

Mercer, Malcolm, 'King's Armourers and the Growth of the Armourer's Craft in Early Fourteenth-Century London', in *Fourteenth Century England VIII*, ed. J. S. Hamilton (Woodbridge: The Boydell Press, 2014), pp. 1–20.

Mesotten, Laura, 'A Taste of Diplomacy: Food Gifts for the Muscovite Embassy in Venice (1582)', *Legatio*, 2017, No. 1, pp. 131–62.

Messenger, Ruth Ellis, 'Salve Festa Dies', *Transactions and Proceedings of the American Philological Association*, 1947, Vol. 78, pp. 208–22.

Meyer, Christopher, *DC Confidential* (London: Weidenfeld & Nicolson, 2005).

—— *Getting Our Way: 500 Years of Adventure and Intrigue; The Inside Story of British Diplomacy* (London: Weidenfeld & Nicolson, 2009).

Miller, Cary, 'Gifts as Treaties: The Political Use of Received Gifts in Anishinaabeg Communities, 1820–1832', *American Indian Quarterly*, Spring 2002, Vol. 26, No. 2, pp. 221–45.

Miller, Ian Jared, *The Nature of the Beasts: Empire and Exhibition at the Tokyo Imperial Zoo* (Berkeley: University of California Press, 2013).

Mobbs, Frank, 'The Meaning of the Visit of the Magi', *New Blackfriars*, November 2006, Vol. 87, No. 1012, pp. 593–604.

Molà, Luca, 'Material Diplomacy: Venetian Luxury Gifts for the Ottoman Empire in the Late Renaissance', in *Global Gifts: The Material Culture of Diplomacy in Early Modern Eurasia*, eds. Zoltán Biedermann, Anne Gerritsen and Giorgio Riello (Cambridge: Cambridge University Press, 2019), pp. 56–87.

Moorhouse, Roger, 'Death in the Baltic', *History Today*, 7 July 2013, Vol. 63, Issue 7.

Moote, A. Lloyd, and Dorothy C. Moote, *The Great Plague: The Story of London's Most Deadly Year* (Baltimore: The Johns Hopkins University Press, 2004).

Mosko, Mark S, 'Inalienable Ethnography: Keeping-While-Giving and the Trobriand Case', *Journal of the Royal Anthropological Institute*, New Series, September 2000, Vol. 6, No. 3, pp. 377–96.

Müderrisoğlu, Ayşen, 'Ottoman Gifts in the Eighteenth Century through the East–West Perspective', *Uluslararasi Sosyal Araştirmalar Dergisi*, 2014, Vol. 7, Issue 34, pp. 269–76.

Mukharji, Aroop, *Diplomas and Diplomacy: The History of the Marshall Scholarship* (New York: Palgrave Macmillan, 2016).

Murck, Alfreda, 'Golden Mangoes – The Life Cycle of a Cultural Revolution Symbol', *Archives of Asian Art*, 2007, Vol. 57, No. 1, pp. 1–21.

Murphy, Lauren, 'Horses, Ships and Earthquakes: The Trojan Horse in Myth and Art', *Journal of the Classical Association of Victoria,* 2017, New Series, Vol. 30, pp. 18-36.

Muthesius, Anna Maria, 'Silk, Power and Diplomacy in Byzantium', *Textile Society of America Symposium Proceedings*, 1992, pp. 99–110.

—— 'Silk, Culture and Being in Byzantium: How Far did Precious Cloth Enrich "Memory" and Shape "Culture" across the Empire (4th–15th Centuries)?', *Deltion Tes Christianikes Archaiologikes Hetaireias*, 2015, Vol. 36, pp. 345–62.

Myers, Walter Dean, *At Her Majesty's Request: An African Princess in Victorian England* (New York: Scholastic, 1999).

Nagy, Joseph Falaky, 'The Deceptive Gift in Greek Mythology', *Arethusa*, Fall 1981, Vol. 14, No. 2, pp. 191–204.

Nash, Stephen E., 'Were Peace Medals the Price of Loyalty?', Sapiens, 5 October 2017, https://www.sapiens.org/column/curiosities/peace-medals, accessed 29 September 2021.

Neis, Karen, *Abul-Abbas, the Elephant* (El Dorado Hills, CA: MacLaren-Cochrane Publishing, 2018).

Neumann, Iver B., 'Diplomatic Gifts as Ordering Devices', *The Hague Journal of Diplomacy*, 2021, Vol. 16, Issue 1, pp. 186–94.

Nicholls, Sean, and Emily Dunn, 'Politicians a Little Elastic', *The Sydney Morning Herald*, 28 September 2009.

Nickel, Helmut, '"A Harnes all Gilte": A Study of the Armor of Galiot de Genouilhac and the Iconography of Its Decoration', *Metropolitan Museum Journal*, 1972, Vol. 5, pp. 75–124.

Nicol, Donald M., *Byzantium and Venice: A Study in Diplomatic and Cultural Relations* (Cambridge: Cambridge University Press, 1992).

Nicolson, Harold, *Diplomacy* (London: Oxford University Press, 1942).

Nix, Elizabeth, 'Who was the First U.S. President to Travel Abroad while in Office?', Sky History, 22 August 2018, https://www.history.com/news/who-was-the-first-u-s-president-to-travel-abroad-while-in-office, accessed 29 September 2021.

BIBLIOGRAPHY

Norfolk, Lawrence, *The Pope's Rhinoceros* (London: Vintage, 1998).

Numelin, Ragnar, *The Beginnings of Diplomacy: A Sociological Study of Intertribal and International Relations* (New York: The Philosophical Library, 1950).

Ocak, Derya, 'Gifts and Purpose: Diplomatic Gift Exchange between the Ottomans and Transylvania during the Reign of István Báthory (1571–1576)' (Unpublished MA Thesis: Central European University, Budapest, 2016).

Office of the Chief of Protocol, US State Department, 'Gifts to Federal Employees from Foreign Government Sources Reported to Employing Agencies in Calendar Year 2001', Federal Register, 22 July 2002.

—— 'Gifts to Federal Employees from Foreign Government Sources Reported to Employing Agencies in Calendar Year 2003', Federal Register, 2 August 2004.

—— 'Gifts to Federal Employees from Foreign Government Sources Reported to Employing Agencies in Calendar Year 2005', Federal Register, 9 August 2006.

—— 'Gifts to Federal Employees from Foreign Government Sources Reported to Employing Agencies in Calendar Year 2008', Federal Register, 25 June 2009.

—— 'Gifts to Federal Employees from Foreign Government Sources Reported to Employing Agencies in Calendar Year 2009', Federal Register, 18 January 2011.

—— 'Gifts to Federal Employees from Foreign Government Sources Reported to Employing Agencies in Calendar Year 2012', Federal Register, 30 August 2013.

—— 'Gifts to Federal Employees from Foreign Government Sources Reported to Employing Agencies in Calendar Year 2013', Federal Register, 12 November 2014.

—— 'Gifts to Federal Employees from Foreign Government Sources Reported to Employing Agencies in Calendar Year 2014', Federal Register, 25 November 2015.

—— 'Gifts to Federal Employees from Foreign Government Sources Reported to Employing Agencies in Calendar Year 2015', Federal Register, 12 October 2016.

—— 'Gifts to Federal Employees from Foreign Government Sources Reported to Employing Agencies in Calendar Year 2016', Federal Register, 11 January 2018.

—— 'Gifts to Federal Employees from Foreign Government Sources Reported to Employing Agencies in Calendar Year 2018', Federal Register, 25 February 2020.

Office of the Historian, US State Department, 'Benjamin Franklin: First American Diplomat, 1776–1785', n.d., https://history.state.gov/milestones/1776-1783/b-franklin, accessed 4 April 2020.

O'Regan, David J., *The Paradox of the Good Bribe: A Discussion Defining and Protecting the Public Interest* (Irvine: Universal Publishers, 2020).

Oren, Michael B., *Power, Faith, and Fantasy: America in the Middle East; 1776 to the Present* (New York: W. W. Norton and Company, 2008).

Osiander, Andreas, 'Sovereignty, International Relations, and the Westphalian Myth', *International Organization*, Spring 2001, Vol. 55, No. 2, pp. 251–87.

O'Toole, Thomas, '"Made in France": The Second Central African Republic', *Proceedings of the Meeting of the French Colonial Historical Society*, 1982, Vol. 6/7, pp. 136–46.

Parris, Matthew, and Andrew Bryson, *The Spanish Ambassador's Suitcase: Stories from the Diplomatic Bag* (London: Penguin Viking, 2012).

Parry, Jonathan, '*The Gift,* the Indian Gift and the "Indian Gift"', *Man*, September 1986, New Series, Vol. 21, No. 3, pp. 453–73.

Pearlman, Robert, 'Where Today are the Apollo 11 Lunar Sample Displays?', CollectSPACE, n.d. A, http://www.collectspace.com/resources/moonrocks_apollo11.html, accessed 29 September 2021.

—— 'Where Today are the Apollo 17 Goodwill Moon Rocks?', CollectSPACE, n.d. B, http://www.collectspace.com/resources/moonrocks_goodwill.html, accessed 29 September 2021.

Perkins, Justin, and Theodore D. Woolsey, 'Notice of a Life of Alexander the Great', *Journal of the American Oriental Society*, 1854, Vol. 4, pp. 357–440.

Phillips, Amanda, 'Ottoman *Hil'at*: Between Commodity and Charisma', in *Frontiers of the Ottoman Imagination: Studies in Honour of Rhoads Murphey*, ed. Marios Hadjianastasis (Leiden: Brill, 2015), pp. 111–38.

Pimentel, Juan, *The Rhinoceros and the Megatherium: An Essay in Natural History* (Cambridge, MA: Harvard University Press, 2017).

Piper, Don, 'Tynianov's *Smert' Vazir-Mukhtara*', in *From Pushkin to Palisandriia: Essays in the Russian Novel in Honor of Richard Freeborn*, ed. Arnold McMillin (New York: Palgrave Macmillan, 1990), pp. 168–80.

Podany, Amanda H., *Brotherhood of Kings: How International Relations Shaped the Ancient Near East* (New York: Oxford University Press, 2010).

Polo, Marco, *The Book of Ser Marco Polo, the Venetian, concerning the Kingdoms and Marvels of the East, Volume 1*, ed. and trans. Col. Sir Henry Yule (London: John Murray, 1871).

BIBLIOGRAPHY

Powell, James, 'Remember This? Ottawa's Royal Swans', Ottawa City News, 25 June 2018, https://ottawa.citynews.ca/remember-this/remember-this-ottawas-royal-swans-3912295, accessed 29 September 2021.

Pritchard, Earl H., 'The Kotow in the Macartney Embassy to China in 1793', The Far Eastern Quarterly, February 1943, Vol. 2. No. 2, pp. 163–203.

Prodger, Michael, 'Making Russia Great', The Spectator, 25 August 2012.

PTI, 'Hitler's Car Was Taken to India, Not in Palace: Report', 20 June 2008.

Pursell, Brendan C., 'The End of the Spanish Match', The Historical Journal, December 2002, Vol. 45, No. 4, pp. 699–726.

Qianhui, Zhan, 'A Short History of Panda Fever Worldwide', China Daily / Asia News Network, 4 November 2016.

Queiroz, C. M., and S. Agathopoulos, 'The Discovery of European Porcelain Technology', in Understanding People through their Pottery, eds. M. Isabel Prudêncio, M. Isabel Dias and J. C. Waerenborgh (Lisbon: Instituto Português de Arqueologia, 2005), pp. 211–15.

Radchenko, Sergey, '"Face" and Something "Delicious"', Foreign Policy, 27 March 2013, https://foreignpolicy.com/2013/03/27/face-and-something-delicious, accessed 29 September 2021.

Redworth, Glyn, The Prince and the Infanta: The Cultural Politics of the Spanish Match (New Haven, CT: Yale University Press, 2003).

Reeves, Nicholas, Akhenaten: Egypt's False Prophet (London: Thames & Hudson, 2019).

Renwick, Robin, Fighting with Allies: America and Britain in Peace and War (Hull: Biteback Publishing, 2016).

Reuters, 'France's President Says He Sold Bokassa Jewels', 11 March 1981.

—— 'Mali to Give France New Camel after First One Is Eaten', reuters.com, 9 April 2013.

Reynolds, Laura, 'Why Does Apsley House Have the Address Number 1 London?', Londonist, 7 December 2017.

Rice, John, 'Historic Arrival in Havana Harbour', The Miami Herald, 12 July 2003.

Richardson, Glenn, The Field of Cloth of Gold (New Haven: Yale University Press, 2013).

—— '"As Presence Did Present Them": Personal Gift-Giving at the Field of Cloth of Gold', in Henry VIII and the Court: Art, Politics and Performance, eds. Thomas Betteridge and Suzannah Lipscomb (Abingdon: Routledge, 2016), pp. 47–64.

Rienow, Robert, Contemporary International Politics (New York: Thomas Y. Crowell, 1961).

BIBLIOGRAPHY

Ringmar, Erik, 'Audience for a Giraffe: European Expansionism and the Quest for the Exotic', *Journal of World History*, December 2006, Vol. 17, No. 4, pp. 375–97.

Roberts, Paul William, *Journey of the Magi: Travels in Search of the Birth of Jesus* (London: Tauris Parke, 2007).

Rochebrune, Marie-Laure de, 'Sèvres Porcelain Given as Diplomatic Gifts to the Chinese Emperor by Louis XV and Louis XVI', Haughton International Ceramics Seminar, Christie's, 28 June 2018, https://www.haughton.com/articles/2018/10/15/svres-porcelain-given-as-diplomatic-gifts-to-the-chinese-emperor-by-louis-xv-and-louis-xvi, accessed 29 September 2021.

Rosand, David, '*Ut Pictor Poeta*: Meaning in Titian's *Poesie*', *New Literary History*, Spring 1972, Vol. 3, No. 3, pp. 527–46.

Rouman, John C., and Warren H. Held, 'More Still on the Trojan Horse', *The Classical Journal*, April–May 1972, Vol. 67, No. 4, pp. 327–30.

Rowston, Guy, 'Scandinavia in Rotherhithe', *The Bridge*, December 2009–January 2010, p. 8.

Royal Armouries Collections, 'Armour (Domaru) – Domaru (1570)', n.d., https://collections.royalarmouries.org/object/rac-object-30423.html, accessed 14 February 2021.

Runciman, Steven, 'Charlemagne and Palestine', *The English Historical Review*, October 1935, Vol. 50, No. 200, pp. 606–19.

Russell, Penny, 'Wife Stories: Narrating Marriage and Self in the Life of Jane Franklin', *Victorian Studies*, Autumn 2005, Vol. 48, No. 1, pp. 35–57.

Sadek, Noha, 'Rasulids', in *Medieval Islamic Civilization: An Encyclopedia; Volume 2, L–Z, Index*, ed. Josef W. Meri (New York: Routledge, 2006), pp. 668–9.

Salama, Samir, 'Antique Clock at Egypt's Citadel of Saladin to Tick Again', Gulf News, 26 June 2020, https://gulfnews.com/world/gulf/saudi/antique-clock-at-egypts-cita-del-of-saladin-to-tick-again-1.72265642, accessed 29 September 2021.

Salinger, Pierre, 'Great Moments: Kennedy, Cuba and Cigars', *Cigar Aficionado*, Autumn 1992.

Samson, Alexander, 'The Spanish Match', in *The Spanish Match: Prince Charles's Journey to Madrid, 1623*, ed. Alexander Samson (Abingdon: Routledge, 2016), pp. 1–8.

Sanders, Paula, 'Robes of Honor in Fatimid Egypt', in *Robes and Honor: The New Middle Ages*, ed. S. Gordon (New York: Palgrave Macmillan, 2001), pp. 225–39.

BIBLIOGRAPHY

Sandler, Martin W., *Resolute: The Epic Search for the Northwest Passage and John Franklin, and the Discovery of the Queen's Ghost Ship* (New York: Sterling, 2006).

Saris, John, *The Voyage of Captain John Saris to Japan, 1613*, ed. Sir Ernest M. Satow (London: The Hakluyt Society, 1900).

Satow, Sir Ernest M., 'Introduction', in *The Voyage of Captain John Saris to Japan, 1613*, ed. Sir Ernest M. Satow (London: The Hakluyt Society, 1900), pp. i–lxxxvii.

Savill, Rosalind, 'Madame de Pompadour and the Porcelain Power of the Mistress', Haughton International Ceramics Seminar, Christie's, 28 June 2018, https://www.haughton.com/articles/2018/10/15/madame-de-pompadour-and-the-porcelain-power-of-the-mistress, accessed 29 September 2021.

Schaffer, Simon, 'Instruments as Cargo in the China Trade', *History of Science*, 2006, Vol. 44, pp. 217–46.

Scheele, Dorothy, 'The Friendship and Merci Trains Visit Western Pennsylvania', *Western Pennsylvania History*, Fall 2002, pp. 34–42.

Schroeder, Avery, 'Porcelain, Prestige and Power: Louis XV's Sèvres in Diplomacy', Paper Delivered to the QP Symposium at the Bard Graduate Centre, 24 May 2018.

Schwartz, Selma, 'A Family Affair: Maria Theresa's Green Ribbon Sèvres Porcelain Service', *Journal of the French Porcelain Society*, 2015, Vol. 5, pp. 84–96.

Sciberras, Amy, and Christopher Grech, 'Catherine the Great to Head from Valletta to Moscow and Then Back', *Times of Malta*, 18 August 2019.

Scott-Clark, Catherine, and Adrian Levy, *The Amber Room* (London: Atlantic Books, 2004).

Scoville, Priscila, 'The Ancient Near East in Contact: An Introduction to the Egypt–Mitanni Affairs in the Amarna Letters', *Estudos Internacionais*, 2018, Vol. 6, No. 2, pp. 65–78.

Screech, Timon, *The Shogun's Silver Telescope: God, Art, and Money in the English Quest for Japan, 1600–25* (Oxford: Oxford University Press, 2020).

Scully, Matthew, 'Building a Better State of the Union Address', *The New York Times*, 2 February 2005.

Serratore, Angela, 'The Americans Who Saw Lady Liberty as a False Idol of Broken Promises', *Smithsonian*, 28 May 2019, https://www.smithsonianmag.com/history/americans-who-saw-lady-liberty-false-idol-broken-promises-180972285, accessed 29 September 2021.

Setton, Kenneth M., *The Papacy and the Levant (1204–1571), Vol. III, The Sixteenth Century* (Philadelphia: The American Philosophical Society, 1984).

BIBLIOGRAPHY

Shanken, Marvin R., 'A Conversation with Fidel', *Cigar Aficionado*, Summer 1994.

Sharkey, Heather J., '*La Belle Africaine*: The Sudanese Giraffe Who Went to France', *Canadian Journal of African Studies*, 2015, Vol. 49, No. 1, pp. 39–65.

Sievers, Loraine, 'Purposes, Politicisation and Pitfalls of Diplomatic Gift-Giving to the United Nations', *The Hague Journal of Diplomacy*, 2021, Vol. 16, Issue 1, pp. 110–19.

Simms, Brendan, *Three Victories and a Defeat: The Rise and Fall of the First British Empire, 1714–1783* (London: Penguin, 2007).

Sobchack, Vivian, 'Chasing the Maltese Falcon: On the Fabrications of a Film Prop', *Journal of Visual Culture*, 2007, Vol. 6, No. 2, pp. 219–46.

Sortijas, Steve, 'Tanzania's New National Stadium and the Rhetoric of Development', *Ufahamu: A Journal of African Studies*, Winter and Spring 2007, Vol. 33, Issue 2–3, pp. 24–35.

Spiering, Charlie, 'President Obama's Biggest British Gaffes', *The Washington Examiner*, 27 July 2012.

Ssorin-Chaikov, Nikolai, 'On Heterochrony: Birthday Gifts to Stalin, 1949', *Journal of the Royal Anthropological Institute*, New Series, 2006, Vol. 12, pp. 355–75.

Stanhope, Philip Henry, 5th Earl, *Notes of Conversations with the Duke of Wellington 1831–1851* (New York: Longmans, Green and Co, 1888).

State Historical Society of North Dakota, 'French Gratitude Train', State Historical Society of North Dakota, 2007, https://www.history.nd.gov/fgt/index.html, accessed 29 September 2021.

Stirrat, R. L., and Heiko Henkel, 'The Development Gift: The Problem of Reciprocity in the NGO World', *The Annals of the American Academy of Political and Social Science*, November 1997, Vol. 554, pp. 66–80.

Stone, Daniel, 'How the Man Who Brought the Cherry Blossoms to Washington Narrowly Avoided a Diplomatic Crisis', *Time*, 20 March 2018, https://time.com/5207183/cherry-blossom-trees-history-fairchild, accessed 29 September 2021.

Stowe, Leland, *Crusoe of Lonesome Lake* (New York: Random House, 1957).

Subramaniam, Radhika, 'The Elephant's I: Looking for Abu'l Abbas', in *Animal Biography: Re-Framing Animal Lives,* eds. André Krebber and Mieke Roscher (Cham, Switzerland: Palgrave Macmillan, 2018), pp. 207–26.

Sweetland, Jane, *Boxcar Diplomacy: Two Trains That Crossed an Ocean* (Pennsauken, NJ: BookBaby, 2019).

Syndram, Dirk, and Charlotte Jutta von Bloh, 'Artistry and Chivalry: Diplomatic Gifts from the *Kunstkammer* and *Rüstkammer*', in *Fragile Diplomacy: Meissen Porcelain for European Courts ca. 1710–63*, ed. Maureen Cassidy-Geiger (New Haven: Yale University Press, 2007), pp. 43–62.

Talbot, Michael, 'A Treaty of Narratives: Friendship, Gifts, and Diplomatic History in the British Capitulations of 1641', *The Journal of Ottoman Studies*, 2016, Vol. 48, pp. 357–98.

Taylor, Adam, 'Norway's Prime Minister Says It Might Give Finland a Mountain', *The Washington Post*, 29 July 2016.

Taylor, Frank, 'The Chronicle of John Strecche for the Reign of Henry V (1414–1422)', *Bulletin of the John Rylands Library*, 1932, Vol. 16, Issue 1, pp. 137–87.

Teachout, Zephyr, *Corruption in America: From Benjamin Franklin's Snuff Box to Citizens United* (Cambridge, MA: Harvard University Press, 2014).

Terjanian, Pierre, 'The King and the Armourers of Flanders', in *Henry VIII: Arms and the Man*, eds. Graeme Rimer, Thom Richardson and J. P. D. Cooper (Leeds: Royal Armouries, 2009), pp. 155–9.

Thacker, Shelby, and José Escobar, trans., *Chronicle of Alfonso X* (Lexington: The University Press of Kentucky, 2002).

Thompson, Jason, *Wonderful Things: A History of Egyptology* (Cairo: The American University in Cairo Press, 2015).

Tikhomirov, Alexey, 'The Stalin Cult between Center and Periphery: The Structures of the Cult Community in the Empire of Socialism, 1949–1956; The Case of GDR', in *Der Führer im Europa des 20. Jahrhunderts*, eds. Benno Ennker and Heidi Hein-Kircher (Marburg: Herder-Institut, 2010), pp. 297–321.

Titley, Brian, *Dark Age: The Political Odyssey of Emperor Bokassa* (Montreal and Kingston: McGill-Queen's University Press, 1997).

Tobey, Elizabeth, 'The *Palio* Horse in Renaissance and Early Modern Italy', in *The Culture of the Horse: Status, Discipline and Identity in the Early Modern World*, eds. Karen Raber and Treva J. Tucker (New York: Palgrave Macmillan, 2005), pp. 63–90.

Tomlins, Harold Nuttall, *A Digest of the Criminal Statute Law of England, Part the Second* (London: Henry Butterworth, 1819).

Tonni, Andrea, 'The Renaissance Studs of the Gonzagas of Mantua', in *The Horse as Cultural Icon: The Real and the Symbolic Horse in the Early Modern World*, eds. Peter Edwards, Karl A. E. Enenkel and Elspeth Graham (Leiden: Brill, 2012), pp. 261–78.

BIBLIOGRAPHY

Toth, Ida, 'The Narrative Fabric of the Genoese *Pallio* and the Silken Diplomacy of Michael VIII Palaiologos', in *Objects in Motion: The Circulation of Religion and Sacred Objects in the Late Antique and Byzantine World*, ed. Hallie G. Meredith (Oxford: Archaeopress, 2011), pp. 91–109.

Tremml-Werner, Birgit, Lisa Hellman and Guido van Meersbergen, 'Introduction: Gift and Tribute in Early Modern Diplomacy; Afro-Eurasian Perspectives', *Diplomatica*, December 2020, Vol. 2, Issue 2, pp. 185–200.

Turner, Tom, 'Geoffrey Jellicoe's Landscape Design Methods and Methodology', Landscape Institute, 19 January 2017, https://www.landscapeinstitute.org/blog/jellicoe-method-methodology, accessed 29 September 2021.

Turton, Andrew, 'Disappointing Gifts: Dialectics of Gift Exchange in Early Modern European–East Asian Diplomatic Practice', *Journal of the Siam Society*, 2016, Vol. 104, pp. 111–27.

Twain, Mark, *The Innocents Abroad, or the New Pilgrims' Progress* (Hartford, CT: American Publishing Company, 1869).

Ubaku, Kelechi Chika, Chikezie Anyalewachi Emeh and Kelechi Collins Okoro, 'Imperialism and Underdevelopment in Post-Independence Africa: Focus on Central African Republic', *International Journal of Humanities, Social Science and Education*, June 2015, Vol. 2, Issue 6, pp. 1–9.

Upton, Harriet Taylor, 'The Household of John Quincy Adams (Children of the White House)', in *Wide Awake: Volume AA* (Boston: D Lothrop Company, 1888), pp. 363–77.

USDA Foreign Agricultural Service, 'Flowering Cherry Trees: A Gift from Japan', GAIN Report No. JA0507, 30 March 2010.

US House of Representatives, *Executive Documents of the House of Representatives for the Second Session of the Forty-Eighth Congress, 1884–'85* (Washington, DC: Government Printing Office, 1885).

Vallet, Éric, 'Diplomatic Networks of Rasulid Yemen in Egypt (Seventh/Thirteenth to Early Ninth/Fifteenth Centuries)', in *Mamluk Cairo, a Crossroads for Embassies: Studies on Diplomacy and Diplomatics*, eds. Frédéric Bauden and Malika Dekkiche (Leiden: Brill, 2019), pp. 581–603.

Viano, Francesca Lidia, *Sentinel: The Unlikely Origins of the Statue of Liberty* (Cambridge, MA: Harvard University Press, 2018).

BIBLIOGRAPHY

Vondracek, Hugh, 'China's Stadium Diplomacy and Its Determinants: A Typological Investigation of Soft Power', *Journal of China and International Relations*, 2019, Vol. 7, No. 1, pp. 62–86.

Wansbrough, John, 'A Mamluk Ambassador to Venice in 913/1507', *Bulletin of the School of Oriental and African Studies, University of London*, 1963, Vol. 26, No. 3, pp. 503–30.

Watt, Nicholas, 'Cameron Gives Obama Table Tennis Table and Gets Barbecue in Return', *The Guardian*, 14 March 2012.

Waugh, Evelyn, *Unconditional Surrender* (London: Penguin, 1964, Reprinted 2001).

Weiner, Annette B., 'Inalienable Wealth', *American Ethnologist*, May 1985, Vol. 12, No. 2, pp. 210–27.

—— *Inalienable Possessions: The Paradox of Keeping-While-Giving* (Berkeley: University of California Press, 1992).

Westminster City Council, 'Trafalgar Square Christmas Tree: Virtual Lighting-Up Ceremony', YouTube, 3 December 2020, https://www.youtube.com/watch?v=jLTVSJoV87k, accessed 29 September 2021.

Whitcomb, John, and Claire Whitcomb, *Real Life at the White House: 200 Years of Daily Life at America's Most Famous Residence* (New York: Routledge, 2002).

Wightwick, Abbie, 'How John Major's Horse Was Given a New Home in Wales', Wales Online, 29 September 2012, https://www.walesonline.co.uk/news/local-news/how-john-majors-horse-given-2024854, accessed 29 September 2021.

Wilkinson, Toby A. H., *The Nile: Downriver through Egypt's Past and Present* (London: Bloomsbury, 2014).

Williams, Peter, *The Organ in Western Culture 750–1250* (Cambridge: Cambridge University Press, 2005).

Williams, R. M., 'R. M. Williams History', n.d., https://www.rmwilliams.com/uk/our-history/RMWhistory.html?lang=en_GB, accessed 3 April 2021.

Wills, Garry, *Why I Am a Catholic* (Boston: Mariner, 2003).

Wilson, Sarah, 'Obituary: André Fougeron', *The Independent*, 18 September 1998.

Windler, Christian, 'Diplomatic History as a Field for Cultural Analysis: Muslim–Christian Relations in Tunis, 1700–1840', *The Historical Journal*, March 2001, Vol. 44, No. 1, pp. 79–106.

BIBLIOGRAPHY

Wishnick, Elizabeth, 'Putin and Xi: Ice Cream Buddies and Tandem Strongmen', PONARS Eurasia, 25 October 2019, https://www.ponarseurasia.org/putin-and-xi-ice-cream-buddies-and-tandem-strongmen, accessed 29 September 2021.

Wittwer, Samuel, 'Liaisons Fragiles: Exchanges of Gifts between Saxony and Prussia in the Early Eighteenth Century', in *Fragile Diplomacy: Meissen Porcelain for European Courts ca. 1710–63*, ed. Maureen Cassidy-Geiger (New Haven: Yale University Press, 2007), pp. 87–109.

Wolff, Robert Lee, 'Mortgage and Redemption of an Emperor's Son: Castile and the Latin Empire of Constantinople', *Speculum*, January 1954, Vol. 29, No. 1, pp. 45–84.

Wolfram, Herwig, *Conrad II, 990–1039: Emperor of Three Kingdoms*, trans. Denise A. Kaiser (University Park, PA: The Pennsylvania State University Press, 2006).

Wolohojian, Albert Mugrdich, *The Romance of Alexander the Great by Pseudo-Callisthenes* (New York: Columbia University Press, 1969).

Woodfin, Warren T., 'Presents Given and Presence Subverted: The Cunegunda Chormantel in Bamberg and the Ideology of Byzantine Textiles', *Gesta*, 2008, Vol. 47, No. 1, pp. 33–50.

Wright, F. A., 'Introduction', in *The Works of Liudprand of Cremona*, trans. F. A. Wright (New York: E. P. Dutton and Co., 1930), pp. 1–24.

Wright, Robin, 'Presidential Swag and the Gift Horse', *The New Yorker*, 20 May 2016.

Wright, Tony, 'Trying Not to Tread on Diplomatic Toes, PM Offers Boots', *The Sydney Morning Herald*, 1 October 2013.

Wright, Vincent, 'The Change in France', *Government and Opposition*, Autumn 1981, Vol. 16, No. 4, pp. 414–31.

Wunner, Bill, 'Presidential Shamrock Ceremony Had Inauspicious Beginning', CNN, 17 March 2010, http://edition.cnn.com/2010/POLITICS/03/17/shamrock.ceremony/index.html, accessed 29 September 2021.

Wycherley, Niamh, 'The Notre Dame Fire and the Cult of Relics', *History Ireland*, July/August 2019, Vol. 27, No. 4, pp. 48–50.

Xue, Charlie Q. L., Guanghui Ding, Wei Chang and Yan Wan, 'Architecture of "Stadium Diplomacy": China-Aid Sport Buildings in Africa', *Habitat International*, June 2019, Vol. 90, pp. 1–11.

Yagi, George, *The Struggle for North America, 1754–1758: Britannia's Tarnished Laurels* (London: Bloomsbury, 2017).

Youde, Kate, 'Watches as Diplomatic Gifts Find Their Time has Come Again', *The Financial Times*, 3 September 2016.

INDEX

INDEX

INDEX

INDEX

INDEX

INDEX

INDEX

INDEX

Russia, Soviet Republic (1917–91), *see under* Soviet Union

Russia, Federation (1991–), 136, 322

Ruth-Rolland, Jeanne-Marie, 285

Saakashvili, Mikheil, 221

Safavid Empire (1501–1736), 88

Sainte Chapelle, Paris, 67

al-Salih Salih, Mamluk Sultan, 76–7

Salinger, Pierre, 290

Salisbury, Robert Cecil, 1st Earl, 124

Salman, King of Saudi Arabia, 320

Salvation Army, 239

Samaria, 11

Samland Peninsula, Kaliningrad, 132

Samson Slaying a Philistine (Giambologna), 125, 128–30

sancak, 116

Santo Domingo, 159

Sanudo, Benedetto, 87

Saris, John, 120–22

Sarmiento de Acuña, Diego, 126, 127

Satyajit Singh, Sardar, 230

Saudi Arabia, 311, 320

Sauk tribe, 199–201

Sauvage, Charles-Gabriel, 149

Savonnerie carpets, 144, 145

Saxony
    Electorate of (1356–1806), 132–3, 138–42, 321
    Kingdom of (1806–1918), 175

Schliemann, Heinrich, 28

Schlüter, Andreas, 133

Schmitt, Harrison 'Jack', 270–71

Schoen, James Frederick, 206

Schoolcraft, Henry Rowe, 201

Schröder, Gerhard, 136

Sciberras, Amy, 164

Scidmore, Eliza Ruhamah, 223–4, 225

Screech, Timon, 122

Scythians, 33

Seisenegger, Jakob, 128

Selim II, Ottoman Sultan, 116–17

Sennacherib, King of Assyria, 12

de Sequeira, Domingos António, 176

Setton, Kenneth Meyer, 89

Seusenhofer, Konrad, 108

Seven Years' War (1756–63), 145, 150

Seventh Crusade (1248–1254), 73

severed heads, 322

Severn Wildfowl Trust, 263

Seville, Spain, 324

Sèvres porcelain, 143–7, 175–6, 246

Sforza, Francesco, 14

Shah Jahan, Mughal Emperor, 188

Shah Rukh, Timurid Emperor, 75

Shah, Janak Rajya Laxmi, 231–2

Shakespeare, William, 33–5

shamrocks, 255–8

Shanken, Marvin, 288

Sherfield, Roger Makins, 1st Baron, 247, 266

Shōgun (Clavell), 121

Shogun's Silver Telescope, The (Screech), 122

Shvernik, Nikolai, 250

Sicard, Louis Marie, 151

Sichuan earthquake (2008), 279

Sicily, Kingdom of (1130–1816), 162, 174, 180

Siena, 104

Sierra Leone, 205, 206

Sigimund, 53

Sikhs, 229

Silesia, 145

silk, 7–8, 57–62, 69–72, 113, 165, 166, 167, 321, 323–4

silver, 120, 124, 140, 144, 146, 166, 176, 198

Singapore, 320

Sinopharm vaccine, 297

Sioux tribe, 200, 201

Sixtus, Saint, 69

417

INDEX

INDEX